KNIGHTS AND ESQUIRES:

The Gloucestershire Gentry in the Fourteenth Century

BY

NIGEL SAUL

CLARENDON PRESS · OXFORD
1981

Oxford University Press, Walton Street, Oxford OX2 6DP

OXFORD LONDON GLASGOW
NEW YORK TORONTO MELBOURNE WELLINGTON
KUALA LUMPUR SINGAPORE JAKARTA HONG KONG TOKYO
DELHI BOMBAY CALCUTTA MADRAS KARACHI
NAIROBI DAR ES SALAAM CAPE TOWN

Published in the United States
by Oxford University Press, New York

British Library Cataloguing in Publication Data

Saul, Nigel
  Knights and esquires. – (Oxford historical
  monographs).
  1. Gloucestershire, Eng. – Gentry
  I. Title   II. Series
  301.44′1   HT657   80–41149

  ISBN 0–19–821883–4

Typeset in India by Macmillan India Ltd, Bangalore
Printed and bound in Great Britain
by Billing and Sons Limited
Guildford, London, Oxford, Worcester

PREFACE

The attitude of the medievalist to those whom we know as the gentry is founded on a combination of good intentions and missed opportunities. On the one hand the dependence of medieval monarchy in England on the goodwill and co-operation of the gentry in the shires has long been recognized by all who have studied the workings of government and the network of connections that bound King, magnates, and gentry together. On the other hand the importance with which historians agree the subject is to be regarded has hardly been matched by a wealth of detailed study.

This imbalance becomes all the more noticeable when we come to look at the contrasting approach to this problem of the early modernists. For the late Middle Ages we have nothing like the numerous studies of county society in the sixteenth and seventeenth centuries which have told us so much about the attitudes and organization of the provincial governing class in a later period. Medievalists have been more concerned with the workings of the central government than with the way in which its orders were obeyed in the shires. To a large extent this imbalance in the direction of historical research is a reflection of the uneven nature of the surviving sources. The workings of the King's government can be reconstructed in detail from the ample archives of the Public Record Office, but until the sixteenth century we have very little to illuminate the lives of those whose importance was confined to the shires in which they lived.

The sources which we have at our disposal, therefore, are mainly administrative rather than economic, and derive more often from the centre than from the localities. The strictly economic history of the late medieval gentry is the most neglected territory of all, perhaps surprisingly so in view of the arguments that have raged about the fortunes of their descendants in the sixteenth century and more recently about their ancestors in the thirteenth. Nevertheless, the sources are few and scattered not just for the Middle Ages but for the sixteenth century too. There has been insufficient continuity in the ownership of the smaller estates to permit the survival of account rolls in any number.

For these reasons the reluctance of historians to tackle the questions that need to be asked about the gentry in the Middle Ages can certainly be understood, if not excused. The gentry are elusive; but they are not altogether beyond recall. What little work has been done in this field we owe largely to Noel Denholm-Young, whose books, though of a very impressionistic nature, have at least rescued parts of the subject from neglect.

The present work started life as an examination in detail of the gentry families of just one county—Gloucestershire—in the hope that the conclusions drawn would not be too unrepresentative of the English gentry as a whole in the fourteenth century. Because of the scattered nature of some of the evidence, particularly the sources for economic history, it proved necessary to depart somewhat from the original plan to the extent of drawing on evidence from elsewhere to substantiate the argument. Certainly, the more that the book draws on evidence from a wider geographical area, the greater may be the value of its conclusions. But there are difficulties. For example, the treatment may appear to be somewhat uneven when social status is discussed in very general terms and 'bastard feudalism', on the other hand, so much more narrowly. And if the character and structure of the book stand in need of some justification, so too do the omissions. Since my theme is mainly social and economic, I have decided in the interests of both brevity and unity to leave the religious sympathies of the gentry for discussion in my forthcoming article in the *Transactions of the Bristol and Gloucestershire Archaeological Society*. I can only plead in mitigation that these irregularities of approach were largely unavoidable.

Along the way I have incurred many debts. First of all I must acknowledge the inspiration given by my tutor at Hertford, Mr C. A. J. Armstrong, who in his inimitable way first guided me in the direction of medieval history. Miss B. F. Harvey, Mr M. H. Keen, Dr P. Chaplais and Mr J. Campbell have all given generously of their knowledge. To Mr Brian Smith and Mr Baldwin, Major Berkeley's agent, I am grateful for co-operation in arranging visits to the Muniment Room at Berkeley Castle. Last but not least my thanks are due to Dr J. R. Maddicott who supervised the thesis on which the

present study is based. Whatever merit this book may claim owes much to the guidance which he has given to my labours.

Nigel Saul,
Royal Holloway College, London
September 1980

The text of this book was completed before the publication of Dr P. R. Coss's edition of *The Langley Cartulary* (Dugdale Society, xxxii, 1980), which (p. 1) confirms that Richard de Foxcote (sheriff of Gloucester, 1332–8, 1351–2) did in fact hold an estate at Turkdean, as suggested below, p. 118n, on the evidence of the parliamentary subsidy returns of 1327. D. A. Carpenter, 'Was there a crisis of the knightly class in the thirteenth century? The Oxfordshire evidence', *English Historical Review*, xcv (1980), 721–52, also appeared too late to be taken into account when discussing the economic fortunes of the knights (below, ch. vi). Suffice it to say that, despite the arguments to the contrary put forward by Dr Carpenter, I am still inclined to think that most demesnes on manors held by the knights at the end of the thirteenth century were smaller than those on manors held by the magnates.

January 1981

CONTENTS

TABLES AND GENEALOGIES

Tables

Genealogies

ABBREVIATIONS

Bod. Lib.	Bodleian Library.
Brit. Lib.	British Library.
Bull. Inst. Hist. Res.	*Bulletin of the Institute of Historical Research.*
Cal. Close Rolls	*Calendar of Close Rolls.*
Cal. Fine Rolls	*Calendar of Fine Rolls.*
Cal. Inqs. Misc.	*Calendar of Inquisitions Miscellaneous.*
Cal. Mem. Rolls.	*Calendar of Memoranda Rolls 1326–7.*
Cal. Pat. Rolls.	*Calendar of Patent Rolls.*
C.I.P.M.	*Calendar of Inquisitions Post Mortem.*
Econ. Hist. Rev.	*Economic History Review*
Eng. Hist. Rev.	*English Historical Review.*
Feud. Aids	*Feudal Aids, 1284–1431.*
G.E.C.	*The Complete Peerage*, ed. G. E. Cokayne, revised by Vicary Gibbs, H. A. Doubleday and Lord Howard de Walden, 12 vols. in 13 (London, 1910–57).
Gloucs. Inqs. post Mortem	*Abstracts of Inquisitiones post Mortem for Gloucestershire*, iv, ed. S. J. Madge (Index Lib., 1903); v, ed. E. A. Fry (Index Lib., 1910); vi, ed. E. Stokes (Index Lib., 1914).
Gloucs. Subsidy Roll	*Gloucestershire Subsidy Roll, I Edward III, 1327.* (Middle Hill Press, n.d.).
Jeayes	I. H. Jeayes, *Catalogue of the Charters and Muniments . . . at Berkeley Castle (Bristol, 1892).*
List of Escheators	*List of Escheators for England and Wales* (Public Record Office, Lists and Indexes, 72, 1932).
List of Sheriffs	*List of Sheriffs for England and Wales* (Public Record Office, Lists and Indexes, ix, 1898).
Moor	C. Moor, *Knights of Edward I*, i–v (Harleian Soc. 80–84, 1929–1932).
Parl. Writs	*Parliamentary Writs*, ed. F. Palgrave, 2 vols. in 4 (London, 1827–34).
Rot. Parl.	*Rotuli Parliamentorum.*
Smyth	J. Smyth, *The Berkeley MSS. I and II, Lives of the Berkeleys; III, The Hundred of Berkeley*, ed. J. Maclean (Gloucester, 1883–5).
Trans. Roy. Hist. Soc.	*Transactions of the Royal Historical Society.*
Trans. Bristol & Gloucs. Arch. Soc.	*Transactions of the Bristol and Gloucestershire Archaeological Society.*

V.C.H.Gloucs.	*Victoria History of the County of Gloucester.*
V.C.H.Worcs.	*Victoria History of the County of Worcester.*
Visitation of the County of	*Visitation of the County of Gloucester*, ed. J. Maclean and
Gloucester	W. C. Heane (Harleian Soc., xxi, 1885).

All unpublished documents to which reference is made are preserved in the Public Record Office unless otherwise stated.

I

INTRODUCTION

i

Though not pre-eminent in either size or population Gloucestershire is distinguished for the variety of its terrain and topography;
it is the three-fold division of the county into wold, vale and forest
which has shaped its economic and social history.

In terms of recorded population Domesday Gloucestershire
ranked eleventh among the English counties. East of the River
Severn there were between five and ten people per square mile,
but in large parts of East Anglia, by contrast, density reached
more than fifteen per square mile.[1] Domesday Book, however, is
not always a reliable guide, for when we come to consider urban
population, we have some surveys, compiled perhaps within a
decade of Domesday, which emphasize how the size of towns was
underestimated in 1086. The survey of Winchcombe shows that
141 burgesses resided in that borough, where Domesday Book
gives only twenty-nine; and the survey of Gloucester records the
residence of 614 burgesses, where Domesday noted only eighty-
one.[2] About the other two boroughs in Domesday, Tewkesbury
and Bristol, we know much less, though we would not be far
wrong in supposing that Bristol was the largest single town in the
county. Trading took place of course at other centres, but none
was very large. Domesday tells us that there were markets at
Berkeley, Cirencester, Thornbury, and Tewkesbury, of which
only the last was a borough.[3]

The returns for the lay subsidy of 1334, another useful source
for historical geography, show how far this picture had changed
by the fourteenth century. Gloucestershire was now among the

[1] H. C. Darby, *Domesday England* (Cambridge, 1977), pp. 90, 336.
[2] S. P. J. Harvey, 'Evidence for Settlement Study: Domesday Book', in
Medieval Settlement, ed. P. H. Sawyer (London, 1976), pp. 196–7; cf. Darby, op.
cit., pp. 306–7, 365.
[3] *Gloucestershire Studies*, ed. H. P. R. Finberg (Leicester, 1957), p. 64.

richest counties of England, ranking seventh in total assessed
wealth. In terms of moveable wealth per square mile the picture
was not dissimilar. Parts of East Anglia and the Thames Valley
had moveable property worth more than £30 per square mile
while most of Gloucestershire had assessed wealth of £10–£19
per square mile, rising to £20–£29 in the north and east of the
shire.⁴ Of the towns Gloucester was reckoned to have moveable
wealth worth £540, Cirencester £250 and Winchcombe £105.
Yet by the early fourteenth century these old-established centres
were coming to be rivalled in wealth by the Cotswold vills that
were thriving on the wool trade. In 1334 moveable wealth at
Chipping Campden totalled £255, at Painswick £180, at
Fairford £165 and at the south Cotswold town of Marshfield
£270. But the equally evident prosperity of vills in the Vale of
Berkeley is hardly likely to be explained by wool; for example
Cam paid £11 19s. 11d., Slimbridge £11 8s. 5d. and Kingsweston
£10 13s. 4d., representing assessed moveable wealth in each of the
order of £170.⁵ The account rolls of these manors, which were
held by the Berkeleys, and the returns to the lay subsidy of 1327
reveal that the social structure of the Vale was radically different
from that represented by the nucleated vill. Settlements were
dispersed and the land was cultivated by wealthy free tenants
who paid money rents.⁶ The other part of the county which was
imperfectly manorialized was of course the Forest of Dean, where
coal and iron had been mined at least from Roman times.

The economic landscape of Gloucestershire was moulded in
the Anglo-Saxon period by the large ecclesiastical estates, the
earliest of which were those of the Benedictine abbeys of
Gloucester, Tewkesbury and Winchcombe, founded in the
seventh and eighth centuries. The next wave of monastic
enthusiasm, under the Norman kings, resulted in the foundation
of three Augustinian communities in Gloucestershire at St.
Augustine's, Bristol, Cirencester and Llanthony-by-Gloucester.
The Cistercians were not as important in this county as they were
in the north but their order was represented by the abbeys of
Flaxley, Hailes and Kingswood. And in addition to minor houses
like Leonard Stanley, Horsley and St. Oswald's, Gloucester,

⁴ R. E. Glasscock, *The Lay Subsidy of 1334* (London, 1975), p. xxvii.
⁵ Ibid., pp. 90–6.
⁶ Berkeley Castle, S(elect) R(olls), 43–8; *Gloucs. Subsidy Roll*, pp. 25–7.

there were the alien priories of Beckford, Brimpsfield, Deerhurst and Newent. By the mid thirteenth century, when the age of monastic foundations was reaching its close,[7] there were more religious houses in Gloucestershire than in any other of the western or midland counties. Moreover, the area of land in Gloucestershire held in mortmain was augmented still more by the estates of communities which lay outside the shire. Perhaps the largest belonged to Westminster Abbey, endowed with lands which Edward the Confessor had taken from Pershore Abbey and Deerhurst Priory, but Osney Abbey and the Bishop of Worcester each held several manors in the county too.[8] Hardly any real property passed into the hands of the Religious after the thirteenth century; the continued devotions of patrons now found expression instead in ambitious programmes of rebuilding such as that which the Despensers undertook at the abbey church of Tewkesbury, where they were laid to rest.[9]

Manors held by the Religious were held by absentee lords; most of the houses were situated in the Severn Valley, their manors on the Cotswold plateau. For the tenants, then, lordship was represented only by the abbot's steward who toured the estates perhaps twice each year to preside over the manorial court. The monastic estates had played a more important part in shaping the economic life of the county than those of the secular lords because of their antiquity, their number and sheer extent. But the influence of the abbots in the affairs of the shire is more difficult to estimate. Power was shared with the local baronage, the gentry and the richer freeholders. The greatest of the lay magnates with estates in Gloucestershire did not reside in the county. The de Clare earls of Gloucester, for example, though taking their title from the shire and holding the manors of Tewkesbury, Fairford, Chipping Sodbury, Thornbury and Rendcombe, spent most of their time at court or on their estates

[7] The last abbey to be called into being in Gloucestershire was Hailes, founded by Richard, earl of Cornwall in 1246. For the chronology of monastic foundations in the county see R. Graham, 'The Religious Houses of Gloucestershire', in *V.C.H. Gloucs.*, ii, 52.

[8] For the monastic landowners of the West Midlands see R. H. Hilton, *A Medieval Society* (London, 1966) pp. 26–41.

[9] R. Morris, 'Tewkesbury Abbey, the Despenser Mausoleum', *Trans. Bristol & Gloucs. Arch. Soc.*, xciii (1974), 142–55.

in Kent, Essex and Glamorgan. Nor perhaps did the Despensers, who succeeded to most of the Clare estates in Gloucestershire, often reside in the county.[10] Political leadership in the shire therefore fell by default to magnates of the second rank, of whom the Berkeleys of Berkeley Castle were foremost. Of sufficient standing to act on the stage of national politics, their principal interests were nevertheless in Gloucestershire and northern Somerset, where they were territorially dominant.[11] Two other families deserve mention. In the first two decades of the fourteenth century John Giffard (d. 1299) and his son John were substantial landowners in the Welsh Marches, Wiltshire and Gloucestershire, where they resided at Brimpsfield Castle. But with the execution of the younger John in 1322 for his part in the rebellion against Edward II the family became extinct in the male line, and their estates passed to Sir John Maltravers and then to the Berkeleys of Uley.[12] In the middle of the century a new star rose on the local horizon: Sir Thomas de Bradeston, whose immediate ancestors had been in the service of the Berkeleys, made a reputation for himself as a captain in Edward III's wars. The King heaped on him rewards in money and in land which entitled him to be summoned to parliament between 1347 and 1360.[13] None of his descendants received a summons, however, and at the end of the century the main challenge to Berkeley dominance in the county came, as it had in the reign of Edward II, from the Despenser family.

But such a survey of the greater lords, lay and ecclesiastical, can easily exaggerate their territorial importance in the shire, to the exclusion of the many estates of the smaller landowners. A fairly clear picture of the distribution of landed wealth in Gloucestershire is given in the *Nomina Villarum*, a survey occasioned by the grant of a foot soldier from each vill in the Lincoln Parliament of 1316. It lists the holders of manors in the

[10] The Despensers were lords of Glamorgan, where they resided at Cardiff Castle (see, for example, S.C.1/39/194). Of the fourteenth-century representatives of the family only Sir Edward Despenser (d.1375) was regularly appointed to commissions in Gloucestershire, though his son Thomas rose briefly to prominence in the closing years of Richard II's reign. See below, pp. 112–3.

[11] See below, p. 62.   [12] *G.E.C.*, viii, 584 and n.

[13] Smyth, i, 282–6; and see below, p. 76.

English counties.[14] Although it is not exhaustive, it gives as complete a cross-section of county society as can be obtained for the early fourteenth century. The vills in the shire are listed hundred by hundred. Manor and vill are coincident in Gloucestershire more often than in the eastern counties, but in the Cotswolds each vill was frequently divided into two or three manors. Thus in 1316 235 vills in the shire contained 312 manors. Of these, 111 manors, or just over a third, were held by the Religious. Another thirty-five were held by the lay magnates, but as some of the lords—Thomas de Berkeley, for example— were able to practise successful evasion, their manors may well have been more numerous than that. The remaining manors, 166 in all, numbering just over half of all the manors in the county, were held by the gentry.

The *Nomina Villarum* also tell a little about the geography of lordship in Gloucestershire in the middle ages. Most of the gentry were settled in the Severn Valley and on the western flanks of the Cotswolds.[15] This striking concentration is no coincidence in a country of great geographical contrasts. In the triangle between the Severn and the Wye lies the Forest of Dean where the manorial system typical of arable England was practically unknown. In 1086 the three villages on the eastern side of the Forest, Ruardean, Abenhall and Littledean, were not separate manors but were gelded under the great manor of Dean;[16] in the fourteenth century the parish of Newland embraced most of the Forest, its very name suggestive of newly assarted land cut out of the virgin scrub. For different reasons not many gentry families were to be found on the Cotswolds in the east of the county. Abbeys like Gloucester, Winchcombe, Hailes, Evesham and Osney held most of the lands: six of the ten manors in Britwell's Barrow Hundred, seven of the nineteen in Salmonsbury and seven of the fifteen in Holford and Gretton were held by the Religious. On these windswept uplands, where the topsoil was thin, sheepruns would have been a characteristic of the rural economy. Lordship was represented by the monastic grange rather than the local knight. Hence most of the gentry were concentrated on the western slopes of the Cotswolds and in the

[14] *Feud. Aids*, ii, 263–76.   [15] See below, Appendix II.
[16] Sir J. Maclean, 'The History of the Manors of Dene Magna and Abenhall', *Trans. Bristol & Gloucs. Arch. Soc.*, vi (1881–2), 124.

Severn valley, where settlement was most intense. In a county where fewer than a third of all vills had a resident lord of the manor the contrast between the Severn valley and the areas to its east and west must have been all the greater.

ii

The emergence of those whom we know as the 'gentry' as a separate social order was, as McFarlane showed, a legacy of the process by which in the late middle ages the nobility became identified solely with the parliamentary peerage.[17] But within the ranks of the gentry themselves another process of evolution was taking place at the same time: the undifferentiated group of lesser landowners below the rank of knight was yielding to an ordered hierarchy, a transition which was reflected in changes in the vocabulary of social status.

The task of tracing these changes is hardly facilitated by the employment in the fourteenth century of three languages— Latin, French and later on of the vernacular too. The French *chivaler* could obviously be identified with the Latin *miles*. But not always was there an accepted translation. In 1319 the phrase *pour gentil homme* in a letter under the privy seal was rendered in letters patent as *pro uno valletto*.[18] *Vallettus* could be expressed in French by *vadlet*; but for the French *gentil homme* there was no widely accepted equivalent in Latin until *generosus* found favour in the fifteenth century. In 1300 *vallettus* was probably the nearest approximation. In middle English the word *gentil* served as both noun and adjective to describe the landed classes, including the knights. 'Alle ye gentiles that had be with ye Erl Symond were desheritede', records the Brut of the defeated supporters of Simon de Montfort.[19] That men who were not knights could be of gentle blood is clearly indicated by the sumptuary laws of 1363 which speak of 'esquiers et toutes maneres des Gentils desouth lestat de Chivaler, qe nont terre ou rent a la value de Cent livres par an'.[20]

---

[17] K. B. McFarlane, *The Nobility of Later Medieval England* (Oxford, 1973), pp. 268–78.

[18] *Cal. Pat. Rolls 1317–21*, p. 320.

[19] *Middle English Dictionary*, 4, ed. S. H. Kuhn & J. Reidy (Ann Arbor, 1963), 76.

[20] *Stat. Realm*, i. 380–1.

But if a *vallettus* could be a *gentil homme* in 1319 it is doubtful
whether he could still be so described in 1400. By then *vallettus* or
vadlet was rendered in the vernacular by the word *yoman*, and it is
at least open to question whether a man as lowly as a *yoman* of
1400 could still be considered a *gentil homme*. Thus the words
themselves change in meaning over the course of the century.

The difficulty of rendering a description of status in one
language accurately in another is just the first problem we
encounter. A second is the lack of a clear vocabulary of nobility in
medieval England. Since the words 'noble' and 'gentle' were
synonymous, we are strictly speaking more correct if we refer not
to nobility and gentry but to the higher and lower nobility. To
adopt a vocabulary that would have been more intelligible to
contemporaries nevertheless has the effect only of stating the
problem in a different way. For where do we draw the line that
divides the lesser nobility from their superiors? This absence of
definition makes it particularly difficult to determine the place of
the bannerets, an enigmatic group who bestrode the borderland
between the higher nobility and the knights until their eventual
disappearance at the end of the middle ages. Such want of
precision has to be recognized, but we are probably justified in
discarding the term gentry in favour of banneret, knight and
esquire, the ranks which we find in fourteenth-century society.
To whom could these words be applied, and what changes in the
relative importance of those so described can we discern over the
course of the century? It is when we come to tackle these
questions that we enter the realm of uncertainty, and any answers
that are offered are bound to be speculative and suggestive rather
than conclusive and definitive.

That the assumptions of medieval aristocratic society were
chivalric in origin is clearly illustrated by the terminology which
it employed. Banneret, knight and esquire were words whose
application was extended from the battlefield to civilian society,
though the extent to which we may take the orders of military
command to represent the hierarchy of society is something of
which we can never be entirely certain. Of no group is this truer
than of the bannerets, with whom it is convenient to begin our
analysis. The superiority of the banneret was marked by his
entitlement to the use of a rectangular banner on the field,
instead of the bachelor's pennon, and by his payment at the rate

of 4s. a day instead of the bachelor's 2s. A banneret, moreover, was a man of wealth and experience enough to lead a substantial contingent—fifty men-at-arms according to one treatise, but more usually twenty or thirty if the lists of protections are to be believed.[21] That eminence on the field of battle carried social implications is suggested by the summons of bannerets to parliament; but the summons of knights such as Sir John de Cobham several years before elevation to the rank of banneret reminds us that military rank and social status did not automatically coincide.[22] By the later years of Edward III's reign it seems that bannerets could usually count on being summoned to parliament, and Tout even went so far as to suggest that the bannerets threatened to emerge 'as an order of gentility between baron and knight'.[23] However, there was little chance of their order becoming hereditary, and therefore permanent, so long as the issue of a summons was decided by the King's favour. For example, Sir Roger Beauchamp, summoned to parliament from 1363 to 1379, Sir Richard Stafford, summoned from 1371 to 1379, and Sir Guy Brien, summoned from 1350 to 1389, were three bannerets whose heirs were never to enjoy a summons.[24] But even though a banneret could not pass on a dignity to his heirs male, the notion had gained acceptance that he was a lord of parliament. An interesting episode in 1383 helps us to understand the status of the banneret at the beginning of Richard II's reign. On learning that Sir Thomas de Camoys had been elected one of the knights of the shire for Surrey, the King wrote to the sheriff of Surrey on 8 October ordering a re-election.[25] He said that Sir Thomas was a banneret, like several of his ancestors, and that it was not the practice to choose bannerets as knights of the shire. Although the letter implies that the Camoys family had enjoyed the favour and standing to rank as bannerets over

[21] The figure of fifty men-at-arms is given by Du Cange, *Glossarium ad Scriptores Mediae et Infimae Latinitatis*, i (Paris, 1733), col. 976, who quotes Lauriere, *Glossarium Juris Gallici*, but this is hardly borne out by an inspection of rolls which contain lists of protections, such as C.76/12, C.76/15 or C.76/38. Practice in the French and English armies may however have differed.
[22] Sir John de Cobham was summoned to parliament from 24 November 1350 (*G.E.C.*, iii, 344), but he was not raised to the rank of banneret until 6 April 1354 (*Cal. Pat. Rolls 1354–8*, p. 27).
[23] Tout, *Chapters in the Administrative History of Medieval England*, iii, 291 n. 1.
[24] Ibid., p. 296 n. 2.   [25] *Cal. Close Rolls 1381–5*, p. 398.

several, though not all, recent generations, the last member to be summoned to parliament had been Sir Ralph, from 1315 to 1335.[26] Sir Thomas, who had succeeded to the family estates in 1372, received summonses to parliament from 1383, when he was accordingly disqualified from membership of the Commons, until 1420, the year before his death.[27]

How then did a knight become a banneret? Was he invested by the King at a formal ceremony? Chandos Herald tells us that on the eve of the battle of Najera in 1367 Sir John Chandos brought his banner to the Black Prince saying: 'Sire, I have served you in the past and everything whatsoever God has given me, comes from you, and you know well that I am wholly yours and will be always; and if it seems to you time and place for me to raise my banner, I have enough fortune of my own that God has given me to hold, wherewith to maintain it. Behold it, I present it to you.' The Prince, with King Pedro the Cruel and the Duke of Lancaster, then unfurled the banner and returned it to him.[28] Chandos had been created a banneret in 1360, when he received the estate of Saint Sauveur-le-Vicomte to support the rank, and in approaching the Black Prince on the eve of Najera he was simply asking to display his banner for the first time in battle.[29]

On some occasions, apparently when it was necessary to supplement the new banneret's income with a grant of lands and rents, any such formal ceremony that there may have been was accompanied by the issue of letters patent. These grants afford us the only indication we have of the level of income expected of a banneret. When Sir John de Cobham was raised to the rank on 6 April 1354 he received a grant of 100 marks *per annum* from the issues of the county of Norfolk that he might better support the dignity.[30] As he probably received landed revenues of twice that figure already, it would seem that a banneret was expected to enjoy an income of at least £200 and perhaps more: when Sir

---

[26] *G.E.C.*, ii, 506–8.

[27] Thomas was knighted by May 1371 (*Cal. Pat. Rolls 1370–4*, p. 87). He saw service in France in the company of William, Lord Latimer (*Cal. Pat. Rolls 1377–81*, p. 569).

[28] Chandos Herald, *Life of the Black Prince*, ed. M. K. Pope and E. C. Lodge (Oxford, 1910), pp. 95–6.

[29] Ibid., p. 213.   [30] *Cal. Pat. Rolls 1354–8*, p. 27.

Reginald de Cobham of Sterborough was raised to the rank of banneret in 1338 the King undertook to provide him with 400 marks yearly in lands and rents.[31]

To trace the later history of the bannerets would take the story far outside the scope of this study. Suffice it to observe that although the word is still used in the 1420s[32] and indeed as late as the reign of Henry VIII, the bannerets never succeeded in emerging as a rank of the peerage. Some rose to the baronage, others sank into the knightly class. It seems safest therefore to interpret the survival of the word into Tudor times as antiquarian usage, rather like the continued description of the esquires as noble and gentle in the seventeenth century long after nobility and gentry had separated.

About the knights bachelor we need say less. Knights fees had initially been created with a view to the provision by tenants-in-chief and influential sub-tenants of their *servitium debitum* in the feudal host. The typical fee of Anglo-Norman England was very small, no larger than $1-1\frac{1}{2}$ hides according to the most recent calculations.[33] But inflationary pressures had effected a reduction in the numbers of those who could support the arms of a knight, and the survivors were the better endowed members of their class. In the thirteenth century the articles of the eyre still defined a knight as the holder of a knight's fee, but distraint which had become an accepted practice in Henry III's reign employed an economic and not a tenurial criterion to decide who should be knights.[34] By the reign of Edward II, when distraint had settled into a routine, the level was fixed by convention at an annual income of £40.[35] Although there is little evidence to suggest that knighthood had acquired aristocratic overtones by 1300 which it did not have in 1100, the economic difficulties of the intervening period had slimmed the ranks of those who could afford to be *milites*.

---

[31] *Cal. Pat. Rolls 1338–40*, pp. 105–6.

[32] A. R. Wagner, *Heralds and Heraldry in the Middle Ages* (2nd ed., Oxford, 1956), pp. 59–64.

[33] S. Harvey, 'The Knight and the Knight's Fee in England', *Past and Present*, 49 (1970), 1–49.

[34] See below, pp. 36–47.

[35] The exceptions were two distraints ordered at the level of £50 in 1316 and 1319.

The knights and esquires made up the cavalry of the English armies in the middle ages. They were the *homines ad arma* or men-at-arms. A valuable source for the meaning of this and other terms is the list of knights summoned county by county to a great council on 30 May 1324.[36] The returns which the sheriffs compiled list not only the knights but also the men-at-arms of equivalent or near equivalent rank. The Lincolnshire lists are among the most detailed. After naming the knights in the three divisions of his county, the sheriff gave the names of sixteen men whom he described as 'the other men-at-arms' in the county of Lincoln. The sheriff concluded his return by saying that these same men, whom he now styled *armigeri*, were with Henry de Beaumont, Thomas de Wake, and William de Kyme, and that if it was desired to have the names of the other *homines ad arma* enquiry should be made of the knights of the county. The sheriff seems to imply therefore that his list of *armigeri* is incomplete. The *armigeri* and knights together he identifies with *homines ad arma*. The same identity is assumed by the sheriff of Sussex.[37] A strange variation in terminology produced by the sheriff of Norfolk and Suffolk also points to the inclusion of the *armigeri* among the *homines ad arma*. After listing the knights of the two counties that comprised his bailiwick, he named the *armigeri ad arma* and finally the *other* men-at-arms. The unconventional *armigeri ad arma*, which was also used by the sheriff of Warwick, referred to those men-at-arms who had not yet assumed knighthood.[38]

Homines ad arma, then, embraced both the knights and the *armigeri*, though the superiority of the knights, we must remember, was recognized in the rate of pay they received, which was twice that of the other men-at-arms. There is some evidence, fortunately, to connect these ranks of the cavalry with various levels of income. In the returns of 1324 the sheriff of Cornwall testified that the knights and men-at-arms in his bailiwick all enjoyed incomes of £40 a year from lands or rents.[39] Now, as the level of distraint was all but fixed at £40 by 1324 the sheriff seems to be identifying the men-at-arms simply with the knights. The sheriff of Lancashire, however, was a little clearer: he said that all the men-at-arms he had listed in addition to the knights, 51 in

[36] *Parl. Writs*, ii, ii, 637–57.   [37] Ibid., 644–5, 648.
[38] Ibid., 642, 640.   [39] Ibid., 655.

number, had incomes of £15 excepting those who had less.[40] If £40 had gained acceptance as the minimum income for a knight, then the sheriff of Lancashire regarded £15 or more as the income of the other men-at-arms—in other words of the *armigeri*. But he seemed unsure where to draw the line. He implies that there were some men-at-arms, surely very lightly armed, who had incomes of less than £15. All the evidence so far quoted dates from Edward II's reign. But during the reign of his son it seems that the man-at-arms came to be a more substantial figure. In 1345, when the Crown embarked on a plan to revise the provisions of the Statute of Winchester, an attempt was made to levy troops for service in France according to the value of lands. A man with land to the value of 100s. was to be a mounted archer, with £10 to be a hobeler and with £25 to be a man-at-arms.[41] The income of £15 deemed sufficient for a man-at-arms in 1324 was evidently no longer adequate twenty years later.

The term *homines ad arma* was not generally employed to describe a rank of society; it implied a military category identified in 1324 with those who enjoyed incomes in excess of £15 and comprising the knights and others who could be described by a number of terms of which *armiger*, employed in the lists of 1324, was but one. In the twelfth century there had been any number of words to describe apprentice knights or men-at-arms who were not knights, some of which were already little used by Edward I's time. *Tiro*, for example, seems to have fallen by the wayside altogether.[42] *Domicellus* and its French equivalent were occasionally used in the fourteenth century to describe the ranks of a household retinue. In an indenture made in 1383 by which Lady Alyne Lestrange agreed to maintain her son John and his wife in her own household for £50 a year, John's retinue is said to be composed of *un esquier un damoisele deux vadletts un norice et un garcon*. Some idea of the relative status of these retainers is given by the cost of board and lodging, fixed for the esquire and *damoisele* at 4d. a day, for the *vadlet* and *norice* at 3d. and for the page at 1d.[43] The use of *domicellus* in a household context is

[40] Ibid., 639.   [41] *Cal. Pat. Rolls 1343–5*, p. 427.

[42] A *tiro* was a knight recently decorated with a sword. The latest and rather isolated use quoted by Du Cange, *Glossarium ad Scriptores*, vi, col. 1366, is from Elmham, *Vita Henrici Quinti*.

[43] *Collectanea Topographica & Genealogica*, v, 180–1. For the identity of

illustrated again in the will of William Strete (1383) who describes himself as *dommicell' de Anglia*.[44]

By the fourteenth century, however, we find that other terms were more commonly employed in the sources. *Scutifer* was one word, found primarily in a military context, which could describe those who were not knights. In origin it meant a shield bearer, but it came to be used like the other terms to describe men-at-arms below the rank of knight. In letters of protection of 1320 *scutifer* was used as a synonym for *armiger* to describe the followers of Sir Maurice de Berkeley.[45] The word does not appear in the sheriffs' returns of 1324, and it was not often used in the second half of the century; a few examples, though, may illustrate its application at that time. In 1374 Laurence Sebrok *esquier* made an indenture of war with Edward III to serve at sea for six months; in a list of those who served in that expedition Sebrok is described as *scutifer*.[46] The word could describe, too, not only the rank below that of knight but also those whose wealth made them potential knights like Arnald Savage of Bobbing (Kent), a *scutifer* in the 1380s and later a knight and speaker of the House of Commons.[47] Unlike *armiger* and *vallettus*, *scutifer* did not change in meaning in the course of the century.

The term *serviens*, or sergeant, also had military roots, though it came to be applied more widely in the later middle ages. In war, as J. E. Morris observed, *serviens* meant simply a soldier, and *serviens ad arma* a mounted soldier.[48] It often implies a man-at-arms of rather lowly standing who was attendant upon or serving in the place of another, usually a knight.[49] In the feudal host the service of two *servientes ad arma* was reckoned to be the equivalent

---

domicellus with scutifer see Du Cange, *Glossarium ad Scriptores*, ii, col. 1591. I am grateful to Dr Lionel Butler for drawing my attention to the survival of the word *domicellus*.

[44] *Collectanea Topographica & Genealogica*, iii, 100. William Strete held several manors in Cambridgeshire and Kent, probably as a feoffee. He held office as butler in the King's household (*V.C.H. Cambridgeshire*, v, 201).

[45] Smyth, i, 228.   [46] E.101/68/6/136; E.101/33/15 m.l.

[47] A protection was granted to Arnald Savage *scutifer* in 1383 (C.76/67 m. 14). Three years later he was a knight (C. 76/70 m. 28), probably dubbed during the Scottish campaign.

[48] J. E. Morris, *The Welsh Wars of Edward I* (Oxford, 1901, repr. 1968), p. 50.

[49] See for example *Chronicles of Robert of Brunne*, i, ed. F. J. Furnivall (Rolls Series, 1887), 31.

of that of one knight.[50] Thus the word *serviens* came to be used in a sense very close to the other terms like *armiger* and *vallettus* which described *homines ad arma* of the £15–£20 level. There is evidence to indicate that the word, at least in its Anglo-French rendering, was used in a non-military context in the fourteenth century. In a petition dating from about 1330 the communities of Hampshire, Wiltshire, Berkshire, Dorset, and Gloucestershire asked for a commission to enquire of the knights, *serjauntz* and merchants of each of these counties whether the wool staple should be located at Winchester or Southampton.[51] Here the sergeants are seen to be men with a stake in the county's affairs, alongside the knights and merchants.

Nevertheless, neither *scutifer* nor *serviens* was widely used in a non-military sense to describe social status. In the early four-teenth century *vallettus* was the word used most often to denote the rank below that of knight. It had long been applied to the young son of a knight who had not yet been dubbed, but once evasion of knighthood became common it lost any exclusive connection with youth. In Edward I's reign the *vallettus* was simply the holder of a knight's fee who had not yet assumed knighthood. At the turn of the century the word is found in the horse inventories where it describes the men-at-arms who made up the retinues of the earls and bannerets. In 1301, for example, Sir Maurice de Berkeley led a contingent made up of two other knights and five *valletti*.[52] Of the five only Geoffrey de Hauteville seems to have come from a family with the resources to support knighthood.[53] Reginald Brun, Thomas de Bingham, William Sturmyn, and John Roges, on the other hand, seem not to have been country landowners. Nothing can be learned of their income from land; but it is significant that none of these men appears in the lists of tenants of fees and lords of vills drawn up in 1303 and 1316. *Vallettus*, therefore, like *armiger*, *scutifer* and *serviens ad arma*, embraced not only those with the wealth to support knighthood but also the far larger number of lesser men-at-arms.

Vallettus appears to have become the most popular style for describing landowners who were not knights. The evidence for a

[50] Morris, op. cit., p. 54.   [51] S.C.8/73/3619.   [52] E,101/9/23.
[53] He held half a fee in Norton Hauteville (Somerset) in 1303; he was returned as a lord of the manors of Newnham Murren and Crowmarsh Gifford (Oxon.) in 1316 (*Feud. Aids*, iv, 171, 307).

clear statement to this effect is admittedly thin, for status is rarely
given in such sources and petitions or in the close and patent rolls
of Chancery. Only in the departments which dealt with the
performance of military service, it seems, were details of rank
considered worth recording. Nevertheless, a few examples
indicate its use as a description of civilian status. Thomas de
Berkeley, lord of Coberley, described himself as a *vallettus* when
he petitioned for redress in 1322.[54] In the same year Worcestershire and Devon sent one *vallettus* and Middlesex, Herefordshire
and Leicestershire two *valletti* each to the November
parliament.[55] In the fourteenth century *vallettus* was not only a
description of social status, it was a term of service too. It is
obvious from requests for protections that *vadlet* was the favoured
term to describe retainers of magnates, the standing of whom it is
difficult in the absence of corroborative evidence to define. In this
connection the Berkeley accounts are of some interest, for they
anticipate a distinction that was to become apparent later.
According to Smyth, the family historian, in the retinue of the
second Thomas de Berkeley (1281–1321) there were 'theis
degrees of servants, Milites, Armigeri, Valletti, garciones, and
pagetti'.[56] Here the *vallettus* is distinct from and inferior to one
who could be described in the vernacular as an esquire.

The difference between the terms *armiger*, *vallettus*, *scutifer* and
so on was not one of meaning but of notarial application. *Serviens
ad arma* was used in the marshal's registers of feudal retinues,
scutifer in the wardrobe books of the King's household and in the
pay rolls, and *vallettus* in the horse inventories and sometimes too
in letters of protection.[57] Each department had its own chosen
word to describe men-at-arms who were not knights. Only
armiger is not identifiable with the practice of a specific office.
These terms, employed in different circumstances to refer to the
same people, can in fact be shown to be largely synonymous. We
have already noticed the identity of *armiger* with the phrase *alii
hominum ad arma* which appears in the lists of 1324. Now the word
armiger can be defined a little more precisely in the light of a letter

---

[54] S.C.8/265/13238.   [55] *Parl. Writs*, ii, 277–8.
[56] Smyth, i. 166.
[57] This was first noticed by Morris, op. cit., p. 51. He overlooked, however,
the use of *scutifer* in the wardrobe book, for examples of which see C.47/4/3 m.
29, E. 101/398/9 m. 27d and E. 36/203 m. 120.

sent by the bishop of Hereford on 12 July 1303.[58] When the
bishop was required to provide the *servitium debitum* from five
knights' fees, he responded by sending one knight, Sir Nicholas
de Valers, and eight other men-at-arms whom he described as
armigeri.[59] Thus the service of two *armigeri* was reckoned to be
equivalent to that of one knight. In the same year, 1303, Sir
Stephen de la More arranged for the military service due from
the half of one knight's fee which he held at Oldland to be
performed by a *vallettus*, John de Pencoyt.[60] Just as the bishop of
Hereford reckoned the service of one knight to be the equivalent
of two *armigeri*, so Sir Stephen de la More took it to be the
equivalent of two *valletti*; both stood for half a knight. Moreover,
J. E. Morris concluded that in Edward I's armies *servientes* and
scutiferi were men of the same class, two being the equivalent of a
knight;[61] thus both terms could be used interchangeably with
armiger and *vallettus*. In letters of protection of Edward II's time
scutifer appears to be synonymous with *vallettus*, and in the royal
Wardrobe Book of 1300 *scutiferi* in the text are called *valletti* in the
margin.[62]

In the shadowy world where the ranks of the knights merged
into those of the rich freeholders below them, any social
stratification there might have been between, say, the 30 librate
holder and the 10 librate holder was certainly not reflected in
social nomenclature. Words such as *armiger* and *vallettus*, difficult
to define in economic terms, in a military context were
synonymous. There was no stratification of landed society below
the rank of knight in 1300. In this way the lesser landowners
resembled their superiors. But just as a graded parliamentary
peerage emerged in the course of the late middle ages, so too over
the same period the equality enjoyed by the words *armiger* and
vallettus gradually gave way to an ordered hierarchy.

In tracing the fortunes of either the *vallettus* or the *armiger* the
historian is confronted by the dearth of mid-century evidence.
Only a few terminal dates can be suggested. In 1322 a country
landowner like Thomas de Berkeley of Coberley could describe

[58] *Reg. Ricardi de Swinfield*, ed. W. W. Capes (Canterbury & York Soc., 6,
1909), p. 392.
    [59] C.47/5/6.   [60] C.47/5/6.   [61] Morris, op. cit., p. 54.
    [62] Smyth, i, 228; N. Denholm-Young, *History and Heraldry* (Oxford, 1965),
p. 21 n. 6.

himself as a *vallettus*; in the 1360s, to judge from the social hierarchy delineated in the Commons petition for the sumptuary laws, he probably could not.[63] According to the preamble of that petition, serving men (*garceons*) wore the clothing of tradesmen (*gentz de Mestire*), tradesmen that of *valletz*, *valletz* that of esquires and esquires that of knights. At the beginning of the century *vallettus* was regarded as synonymous with the Latin *armiger* or French *esquier*. By 1363 the words have parted company. The compilers of the petition saw the *vadlet* as on the lowest rung of gentle society, below the *esquier*, but above the traders.

The complexity of gentle society was recognized in the schedule for the graduated poll tax granted in 1379.[64] A bachelor knight or an esquire who ought by statute to be a knight was to pay 20*s.*; an esquire of lesser estate 6*s.* 8*d.* and an esquire not possessing lands, rents or chattels who is in service or has been armed, 3*s.* 4*d.* The meaning of the word esquire is here being stretched to its uttermost, but the employment of the French *esquier* permitted the clerks to avoid difficulties of describing rank that might have arisen had one of the Latin terms been used. Nevertheless, who were these mysterious esquires not in possession of lands? The schedule suggests that they may have been younger sons who had returned from the wars in France and whose plight must have caused some concern in England, though more likely after than before 1379, when the *chevauchees* still guaranteed some employment for the professional soldier. Equally, they could have been the household retainers of magnates, perhaps the disorderly element of whom the Commons were to complain so vehemently in Richard II's reign.

The word *vadlet* did not appear in the poll tax schedule at all, but other evidence suggests that it was used mainly to describe men who would have paid no more than 3*s.* 4*d.* Thus the ordinance of May 1390 said that *valletz* called *yoman* archers and others of lower estate than esquire should not carry livery unless they were household familiars.[65] A petition of 1397 which repeated this demand spoke of *valletz* called simply *yomen*, not *yoman archers*.[66] The *vadlet* was now condemned as a man of low status who had recently been behaving in a disreputable manner;

[63] S.C.8/265/13238; *Rot. Parl.*, ii, 278.
[64] *Rot. Parl.*, iii, 58.   [65] *Stat. Realm*, ii, 75.
[66] *Rot. Parl.*, iii, 345.

he was relegated below the esquire. The ranks of society at the
end of the century were listed in a petition of 1400 which called
for a knight to forfeit £40 for offending against the Statute of
Liveries, an esquire £20 and a *yoman ou vadlet* £10.[67] Mildred
Campbell, however, questioned 'whether or not the word
yeoman should be employed as the English equivalent of *vadlet* or
vallettus in documents of the thirteenth or fourteenth centuries
when these words are used to designate the rank or status of a
social class or group'.[68] In 1300, when they were largely
synonymous, *vallettus, armiger* or *scutifer* could not be rendered in
the vernacular by *yoman*, but in 1400 when these words had
parted company *vadlet* was the one term which could be
translated by *yoman* not only in the personal sense but also as the
designation of a rank of society. It is the change in meaning of the
words over a long period and not the context in which they are
used that reconciles the conflicting strands of evidence. But the
hierarchy of knight, esquire, yeoman, delineated in 1400 did not
prove adequate for long. County society had become too
complex to be dismissed as lightly as that, and by Henry V's reign
a new term was needed to describe those who were too wealthy to
be called yeoman, yet too poor to rank as esquires.

But that takes the story far beyond the fourteenth century. In
the meantime, once *vadlet* or *vallettus* had parted company with
armiger, it was the latter which assumed exclusive identity with
esquier. The *armiger* of 1400 had not so much risen in an economic
sense as benefited from the exclusion of those who had formerly
been his peers. In 1344 *armiger* still embraced those whose
incomes were as little as £5. Such is the implication of a list of
landowners in his bailiwick compiled by the sheriff of Cornwall.[69]
By 1363, however, the distinction between the knight and the well-
to-do *esquier* was seen as one of social status rather than wealth.
The sumptuary laws divided the *esquiers* into two groups: esquires
and *toutes maneres de Gentils gentz desouth lestat de Chivaler* whose
incomes were below £100 and those with £200 or more. The
latter overlapped with their superiors as the ensuing clause
showed. This stipulated the manner of dress for knights who like

[67] Ibid., 478.
[68] M. Campbell, *The English Yeoman* (London, 2nd ed., 1960), p. 390.
[69] C.47/2/41 m.5. The sheriff named thirty-two *armigeri*, eleven enjoying
incomes of £20 or more, the remainder £10 or £5.

the esquires, were divided into two groups: those with incomes of up to 200 marks and those with incomes of between 400 marks and £1,000. The distinction between the knights and esquires was becoming so imprecise that legislation was needed to maintain it.

In the poll tax returns, by contrast, the *armigeri* seem not to be identified with any income bracket. In the extant returns for Gloucestershire four *armigeri* are named: Thomas Ludlow of Berrington and Robert Somerville of Aston Somerville, who were lords of manors, and Thomas de Bradewell of Broadwell and Nicholas Cole of Littledean, who were not.[70] The latter seem to have belonged to the class of lesser landowners who were doing well for themselves in the post-Black Death world. Thomas de Bradewell, for example, who resided on a manor of Evesham Abbey, may have benefited from a policy of demesne leases.[71] The evidence hardly permits any estimate to be made of the income of these four *armigeri*: the only clue is provided by the amount that each paid in tax, and this is unlikely to prove a reliable guide in view of the widespread evasion that is known to have been practised. Bradewell paid the highest sum, 6s., Robert Somerville 4s. and Nicholas Cole 3s. 4d.; the amount paid by Thomas Ludlow is illegible. In practice, both franklins and *armigeri* seem to have been paying the same amount; of the thirty franklins whose names appear in the returns for south and east Warwickshire some were assessed at 6s. 8d., most at 3s. 4d.[72]

The two Gloucestershire *armigeri* who were not manorial lords were men who in poll tax returns for other counties such as York might have been called franklins or *firmarii*. John de Scarborough, a *firmarius* of Grassington (Yorks.), who paid 3s. 4d. may well have come from a similar background to Bradewell.[73] Both were office holders. The latter held the shrievalty, the former was a collector of parliamentary subsidies. Though the

[70] E.179/113/31 mm. 1, 3, 8d; E.179/113/35A m. 15.

[71] Thomas was a member of the family of de Bradewell who held an estate which later became the sub-manor of Nethercourt (*V.C.H. Gloucs.*, vi, 51–8). See below, pp. 236–43, for a further discussion of the evidence for demesne leasing.

[72] R. H. Hilton, *The English Peasantry in the Later Middle Ages* (Oxford, 1975), p. 26.

[73] *Yorks. Arch. & Top. Jnl.*, vii, 149. He was a collector of subsidies in 1382 (*Cal. Fine Rolls 1377–83*, p. 337).

poll tax returns are difficult to interpret, the various strands of evidence can probably be reconciled. In an age of high social mobility such as the later fourteenth century, terminology can hardly be expected to have been uniform right across the country. Men of broadly similar means were being described interchangeably as franklins, sergeants, *firmarii* or *armigeri*. Even if they were not manorial lords, men like Bradewell in Gloucestershire or Scarborough in Yorkshire filled a role in local society similar to that of the knight. Professor Hilton has pointed to the lack of resident gentry in the majority of villages—only thirteen in 135 vills in the Cotswolds and Avon Valley of Gloucestershire—and suggested that the franklins were playing 'a substitute role for the gentry at the end of the fourteenth century'.[74] But it was not only the franklins. *Armiger* in the 1379 returns, though not yet identifiable with a given level of income, described a man who was of some importance locally.

Vallettus and *armiger*, then, were no longer synonymous, and it was the latter which took precedence. This parting, which pointed the way towards a more stratified society, betrayed the growing importance of those who could still be described as *armigeri*. Evidence of quite another kind led Denholm-Young to a similar observation when he spoke of 'the remarkable rise of the squirearchy'.[75] According to his argument, based on heraldry, the arms of the early-fourteenth-century *armigeri* were for use against the enemy, and were not heraldic: but by the time of Sir Robert Laton's roll of arms, *c.*1370, the esquires had become 'gentlemen of coat armour'.[76] Denholm-Young was speaking largely from his knowledge of the rolls of arms, but the heraldic evidence is both more complex and more difficult to interpret than he was prepared to allow.

As soon as we begin to look at heraldry on seals, it becomes difficult to accept a chronology based solely on the rolls. In 1355 Matthew de Bitton of Hanham (Gloucs.) was using a seal which bore the arms of his family, *ermine a fess gules*.[77] His ancestors had been knights, as his son was to be, but in 1366, when he was

---

[74] Hilton, *English Peasantry in the Later Middle Ages*, pp. 26–7.

[75] N. Denholm-Young, *The Country Gentry in the Fourteenth Century* (Oxford, 1969), p. 4.

[76] Ibid., p. 5.

[77] *Herald & Genealogist*, iv, ed. J. G. Nichols (London, 1867), p. 320.

distrained, Matthew himself had still not assumed knighthood. Earlier still, in 1317, Robert de Langley of Wolfhamcote (Warwicks.), an esquire who was the younger brother of a knight, was using a seal identical in all respects to the seal of a knight.[78] It is not surprising that a member of a knightly family who chose to remain an esquire should wish to continue using the family arms on his seal. But the Statute of Arms of *c.*1292 had laid down that in tournaments each esquire was to wear a cap displaying the arms of the lord whom he served.[79] This merely restated the ancient belief that esquires had no arms of their own, only those of their lord. Before 1300, then, it would be exceptional to find the sons making use of their family seal before they had themselves been dubbed. When they needed to authenticate a charter esquires would use not a seal displaying a shield of arms but a signet, little different from the kind that peasants were using for their own transactions, which carried a simple emblem or device.[80] For example, when Andrew, son of Sir John Curpel of Fincham (Norfolk) sealed a deed late in the reign of Henry III or in the early years of his successor, he used what was in effect a signet, not a heraldic seal.[81] In 1283 William, son of Sir William de Wauncy of West Barsham (Norfolk) was using a seal with decorative border and no inscription which bore *a lion rampant*, a device quite different from the usual Wauncy arms, *gules, six gauntlets argent*.[82] The process by which esquires gradually

[78] Shakespeare Birthplace Trust Record Office, Stratford-upon-Avon, Willoughby de Broke MSS 871. For Robert de Langley see P. R. Coss, *The Langley Family and its Cartulary* (Dugdale Soc. Occasional Papers no. 22, 1974), pp. 17, 24–5.

[79] N. Denholm-Young, 'The Tournament in the Thirteenth Century' in *Studies in Medieval History Presented to F. M. Powicke*, ed. R. W. Hunt, W. A. Pantin and R. W. Southern (Oxford, 1948), pp. 257–63, argues that the printed version of the *Statuta Armorum* is a petition of *c.*1267 and that a statute based on it was enacted in 1292.

[80] See for example the discussion of the Gloucester Abbey leases in Hilton, *English Peasantry in the Later Middle Ages*, pp. 154–60.

[81] *Engravings from Ancient Seals . . . in the Muniment Room of Stowe Bardolph*, ed. G. H. Dashwood, ii (Stowe Bardolph, 1862), plate i, no. 2.

[82] Ibid., i (Stowe Bardolph, 1847), plate xii, no. 8. According to *Herald & Genealogist*, v, ed. J. G. Nichols (London, 1870), 58, there is evidence that members of the Wauncy family bore an eagle or a falcon as well as their more usual charge of *six gauntlets*, but an obvious device like *a lion rampant* must have been one adopted by many families other than some of the Wauncys.

adopted seals bearing heraldic charges rather than arbitrary emblems is an ill-charted and probably uneven one which merits more detailed consideration than can be given here. Esquires from knightly families who simply did not wish to assume the superior rank would of course wish to employ a seal which bore the family arms, as we have seen that Matthew de Bitton did:[83] a coat of arms was a piece of property which could be passed on from one generation to the next. But the use of heraldic seals seems also to have been adopted by humbler, non-knightly families. Some of them quite simply imitated the arms of the lord of whom they held their land. Thus the Talbots, who held a knight's fee at Fincham (Norfolk) of the Wauncy family, assumed an heraldic charge, *six gauntlets, in the order three, two, one*, which directly followed that used by the chief lord of the fee.[84] To take another example, we find that in the early fourteenth century Edmund de Combe, who held a single manor in Fincham, was the first of his family to employ a heraldic seal, carrying the device, *a lion rampant surmounted by a bend*. This is so similar to the arms of Combe of Sussex, *a lion rampant debruised by a fess*, that a common origin for both charges must be supposed.[85] In the light of such evidence it is difficult not to associate men of this rank with the esquires who were ordered by statute to display the arms of the lord they attended in tournaments. The adoption by feudatories of the arms of a chief lord is no doubt only a partial and inadequate explanation of the increasing use of heraldic seals by esquires in the first half of the fourteenth century. But this subject has been little studied in England, and we must turn for comparison to France where it is at least interesting to see that by the end of the thirteenth century esquires had given up signets in favour of seals which bore a coat of arms.[86]

[83] Matthew de Bitton was distrained for knighthood in 1366. See below, p. 45.

[84] This is the coat of arms employed by Thomas Talbot on his seal in 1440–1. According to the Parliamentary Roll of Arms (*c.*1308) the arms of de Wauncy were *gules, a vi gauns de argent* (*Herald & Genealogist*, iv, ed. J. G. Nichols (London, 1867), 330–1. F. Blomefield, *County of Norfolk*, vii (London, 1807), 345–6 gives the descent of the Talbot manor in Fincham.

[85] *Engravings from Ancient Seals . . . in the Muniment Room of Stowe Bardolph*, i, plate x, no. 4. For the arms of the Combes of Sussex see *Herald & Genealogist*, v, 57. Blomefield, *County of Norfolk*, vii, 347, gives a pedigree of the Combes of Fincham.

[86] P. Adam-Even, 'Les Sceaux d'ecuyers au xiii^e siecle', *Archives heraldiques suisses*, lxv (1951), 19–29. I am grateful to Mr M. H. Keen for referring me to this important article.

Although the rolls of arms upon which Denholm-Young relied so heavily do not after all show that the esquires became armigerous in about 1370, it is still significant that the arms of esquires which were not emblazoned on the Parliamentary, Carlisle or Dunstable Rolls should appear for the first time on a roll of arms in about 1370. Even if they were not newly armigerous they were regarded with a growing respect which is attested by the remarkable grant of arms, the earliest made by a king of England, to John de Kingston on 1 July 1389.[87] Learning that Kingston had been challenged by a French knight, Richard II received him into the estate of gentleman (*Gentile Homme*), and made him an esquire with the right to bear the arms *Argent, ove une Chapeure d'Azure, ovesque une Plume d'Ostrich, de Geules*. By 1390 the esquires had inherited some of the chivalric aura that had long surrounded knighthood. The grant, for example, was couched in the form of an ennoblement. The rank of esquire was seen as a social distinction, and it could apparently, like knighthood, be conferred by the King. Moreover, the creation or acknowledgement of gentility at the same time as the grant of arms suggests that gentility was coming to be identified exclusively with the armigerous.[88]

Social changes of some complexity, by no means confined to England, were at work in the thirteenth and fourteenth centuries. Whether the process is interpreted as a rise in the status of esquires or as a devolution of privilege once enjoyed only by the knights, the effect was still to bestow respectability on the squirearchy. To this background it is worthwhile linking the heraldic with the semantic evidence which we discussed earlier. We have seen that the process of stratification, signalled by the separation of *armiger* from *vallettus*, commenced in the first half of the fourteenth century, in other words around the time that esquires began using heraldic devices on their seals. *Armiger*, therefore, may well have survived as the commonest Latin translation of *esquier* because it could be identified with the armigerous esquires; and these were likely to be the esquires who had need of arms on active service or who were the sons of knights.

[87] *Cal. Pat. Rolls 1388–92*, p. 72; A. R. Wagner, *Heralds and Heraldry in the Middle Ages*, p. 123.

[88] On the growing identity between the armigerous and the gentleborn see also below, pp. 248–9.

The entry of the esquires into the ranks of the armigerous, with
the consequent recognition of their noble and gentle blood,
cannot be divorced from the original military function of
heraldry. The increase in the cost of warfare, as significant in the
fourteenth century as it had been in the thirteenth, meant that a
mounted man-at-arms in Edward III's reign had to be an esquire
of some consequence and no longer a near landless *vallettus*. For
example, the elaboration of armour helps to explain why a man-
at-arms needed an income of £25 in 1345 when £15 had been
sufficient in 1324.[89] Moreover, in the administration of the shires
esquires had come to be accepted as the equals of the knights
simply because there were not enough knights willing to
undertake the burden. They were performing the duties which
fell to the knights: they sat in parliament and they held all the
local offices. Some, of course, were rich enough to be knights but
preferred not to accept what they saw as an honour of dubious
value. The fifteenth century *armiger* yielded nothing to the knight
in wealth and distinction, as the careers of men such as John
Greville and William Fynderne showed.[90]

On what authority the esquires had first assumed their arms is
not known—perhaps on none but their own.[91] In a period of
almost continuous foreign warfare it would have been very
difficult to limit the assumption of arms, particularly by men on
active service. In his book on the laws of war, probably written
about 1440, Nicholas Upton said that 'in these days we see openly
how many poor men through their service in the French wars
have become noble, some by their produce, some by their energy,
some by their valour and some by other virtues which, as I have
said above, ennoble men. And many of these have upon their
own authority taken arms to be borne by themselves and their

[89] The elaboration of early-fourteenth-century armour is illustrated in the
will of Sir Fulk de Pembridge (1326) who left what amounted to a full suit of
armour to his three elder sons and two hawberks to his youngest. The eldest son
received a hawberk, a haketon, an aventail and bascinet, a tournament helm, a
pair of coutes, two pairs of greaves and three pairs of cuisses (thigh armour). Not
only the complexity but also the sheer quantity of armour which Sir Fulk
bequeathed is noteworthy (Brit. Lib. Stowe Ch. 622).

[90] J. S. Roskell, *The Commons in the Parliament of 1422* (Manchester, 1954), pp.
182–3, 187–8.

[91] For a discussion of the right to bear arms see below, pp. 27–9 & n.

heirs'.[92] Upton was probably being unduly disparaging: many such men were not all that poor. But what he said of the fifteenth century may have been equally true of the fourteenth. The newly armigerous probably embraced not only the sons of knights who were not knighted but also the humbler men-at-arms, in the £20–£30 class perhaps, who did not themselves qualify for knighthood.

Suggestions such as these can only be in the nature of guesswork. What does at least seem fairly certain is that the 'rise' of the *armiger* and the 'decline' of the *vallettus* had been set in motion long before the Black Death upset the ordering of fourteenth-century society. We cannot therefore escape by interpreting complex social changes as simply the product of a crude economic determinism. Nevertheless, the effect of the demographic catastrophe may well have been to prolong and extend the process of 'gentrification' by which the status of the esquires had been enhanced earlier in the fourteenth century. Just how far the composition of landowning society had shifted between 1086 and 1400 is one of those difficult questions to which no firm answer can ever be given, but it is at least possible that the economic conditions of the later fourteenth century favoured the advancement of the smaller landowners at the expense of the greater lords who were more dependent on hired labour.[93] These smaller proprietors would have been the men described as *franklins*, *sergeants* or *firmarii* in the poll tax returns. But can they also be identified with the esquires with incomes of below £100 whom parliament prohibited from wearing cloth of gold, silver or silk—implying that they were wearing just such garments? These must have been very substantial men indeed. The most we can say is that the later fourteenth century saw unprecedented social mobility, and that the old hierarchy had first to be buttressed— by the legislation of 1363—and then extended downwards.

Once again this is revealed in a changing vocabulary. The words franklin and *firmarius* did not earn a lasting place in the social order. As the Commons observed in 1400, it was not franklins but esquires and then *vadlets* who followed the knights. Yet neither did the term *vadlet* (or valet) gain ultimate acceptance as the designation of a rank of society. We can easily

[92] Wagner, op. cit., p. 125.   [93] See below, p. 241.

speculate why: franklin was inappropriate because it denoted only free not gentle blood, and valet because it parted company with 'yeoman' to become a term in the vernacular implying service. A fresh term was needed to describe the lowest rank of gentle society. This was provided in the fifteenth century when the vernacular translation of the phrase *gentil homme* was adopted to describe both the personal status of a man and the rank of society to which he belonged.[94] It might be argued, however, that we are witnessing no more than the supersession of French by the vernacular as the language of the nobility, and that 'gentleman' in the fifteenth century simply described those who would have passed for *gentilhommes* a century before. This objection would be unfounded. *Gentilhomme* or *generosus* had described the condition of birth of all those embraced by noble society; it did not designate a separate rank within the nobility. After 1415, on the other hand, 'gentleman' in the vernacular is employed for the limited purpose of denoting the lowest order of the gentleborn. An earl, for example, though *noble et gentil* in 1300, would have felt insulted if described as a 'gentleman' in 1415.

The franklins survived, but it was as gentlemen that the lowest of the gentleborn entered the ranks of landed society. Thus the freedom of the franklin was judged to be inferior in social esteem to the gentility of the gentleman. Now Sitwell once suggested that *gentil* originally conveyed the idea of freedom as opposed to serfdom; that a gentleman was not a person of heraldic status but a freeman whose ancestors had always been free.[95] This statement, as Sitwell himself recognized, cannot be accepted without qualification for there were many free men in the rural economy who were never of gentle blood. But in the fourteenth century it was nevertheless possible to speak of gentlemen and freemen almost in the same breath:

> Lithe and lysten, gentylmen
> That be of freebore blode.[96]

---

[94] It could also be employed in a military context: in the Maine ordinances of the Earl of Shrewsbury 'gentlemen' are identified with the men-at-arms (Sir N. H. Nicolas, *History of the Battle of Agincourt* (London, 1833), Appendix p. 43).

[95] G. R. Sitwell, 'The English Gentleman', *The Ancestor*, i (1902), 103.

[96] The opening line of *A Geste of Robyn Hode* (F. J. Child, *The English and*

All gentlemen therefore were free; but not all freemen were gentlemen. The gentleman, like the knight and the esquire, was born of gentle blood, the franklin only of free blood.

To the distinction that was conferred by gentle birth on knights, esquires and gentlemen we must add the growing identity between gentle blood and armigerous rank. Just what quality, if any, was enjoyed by the armigerous raises the whole question of the right to bear arms. If, as Sitwell claimed, anyone was entitled to adopt a coat of arms, and without authorization, then armigerous rank could hardly have conferred any honour at all.[97] There are signs, however, that even if such had once been the case the unrestricted right to bear arms was being curtailed by the reign of Henry V. It is to this period that we can trace the beginnings of a well-developed system of heraldic administration under the office of Garter Principal King of Arms, created in 1415. Two years later, in 1417, at Caen Thomas, duke of Clarence, issued letters which determined the relative precedence of the heralds and sergeants-at-arms, and by an important series of (undated) ordinances defined the duties of the Kings of Arms.[98] That some control over the unrestricted adoption of arms may have been the purpose behind all this activity is suggested by the letters which Henry V issued on 2 June 1417 ordering the sheriffs of Hampshire, Wiltshire, Sussex

---

Scottish Popular Ballads, iii (New York, 1956) p. 56). J. C. Holt, 'The Origins and Audience of the Ballads of Robin Hood', *Past and Present*, 18 (1960), 90, believes that these lines are the work of the compiler of the ballad, and therefore date from the late fourteenth or early fifteenth century. The reference to Robin Hood in Langland's *Piers Plowman* shows that the ballads were circulating by the 1370s.

[97] Sitwell, op. cit., pp. 77–88. If the adoption of coats of arms was totally unregulated, however, it is a little difficult to understand why there was so little overlap. The number of recorded cases of disputed ownership of arms heard in the Court of Chivalry can, after all, be numbered in single figures. Perhaps the Constable or the Marshal exercised some jurisdiction over the assumption of arms? On the other hand, if it were indeed the case that knights and esquires tended to derive their own coats from the arms of the lords from whom they held their lands, then the absence of conflicting claims to the same coat of arms becomes more understandable. We know from the grant made in 1442 by Humphrey, Earl of Stafford, that as late as the fifteenth century, when closer regulation of the granting of arms was beginning, that the greater nobles still maintained their own heralds (Sitwell, op. cit., p. 83).

[98] Wagner, *Heralds and Heraldry in the Middle Ages*, pp. 59–64.

and Dorset to proclaim that whereas on recent expeditions abroad many persons had assumed arms and tunics called 'Cotearmures' none should use coats of arms except by authorization or ancestral right; and that all except those who had borne arms with the King at Agincourt should on a certain day declare their arms and by whose grant they had them.[99] It seems to have been in the early fifteenth century therefore that a serious attempt was made to bring the granting of arms under the supervision of the heralds. And the lowest rank of society whom they recognized as armigerous was that of gentleman. If the growing power of the Kings of Arms effected some control over the adoption of coats of arms, it may paradoxically at the same time have encouraged the process of 'gentrification', if such it may be called, because those who aspired to the rank could now approach a herald empowered to confer gentle status. Still more, Clarence's ordinances instruct Garter and the Kings of Arms in their respective provinces to seek out those of noble and gentle estate, and to ascertain those who ought to bear coats of arms.[100]

How soon the gentlemen were recognized as belonging to the armigerous is hard to say. Possibly the earliest evidence on this point comes from 1446 when John Wryxworth, Guienne King of Arms, confirmed the entitlement of John Oxenden, gentleman, to the arms, *Argent, three oxen sable armed with gooldys, a chevron of the same*.[101] Now John was already using this coat of arms before 1446, for it was in response to a request from him that Guienne issued the letters to confirm 'the right armes of the said John as their progenitors tyme out of mynde have borne them'. It is more

---

[99] *Cal. Close Rolls 1413–19*, p. 433.

[100] 'Item nous voulons et estroictement chargeons et commandons que Jarretiere (Garter) generalement et tous autres Roys d'armes en leur propre province d'oresenavant facent leur debvoir diligentement d'avoir congnoissance de tous les estatz nobles et gentilz habitantz et demourantz en icelle, les noms des ditz estatz et nobles et principallement de ceulx qui doibvent porter cotes au service nostre Souverain seigneur, son lieutenant ou Commissaires de Cestuy Royaume, et que tous leurs noms et armes soient registrez et les noms de leur yssue avecques leur vraye difference pour record et perpetuelle memoire sur paine'. (The ordinances, of which this clause is the fourth, are printed in Wagner, *Heralds and Heraldry in the Middle Ages*, pp. 136–8).

[101] 'Visitation of the County of Kent', ed. J. J. Howard, *Archaeologia Cantiana*, vi. (1866), 277.

than likely, then, that gentlemen could have been among those assuming arms on their own authority back in the reign of Henry V.

As the gentry were becoming separated from the franklins, so too were the magnates becoming separated from the gentry, and by the mid fifteenth century the hereditary nobility were identified with the parliamentary peerage. According to K. B. McFarlane, 'nobility had parted company with gentility, the quality with which those rejected were still permitted to be endowed'.[102] However, stratification had by no means gone so far as to effect so rigid a separation. On 13 August 1442 Robert Whitgreave, a teller of the Exchequer and retainer of Humphrey, Earl of Stafford, was granted a coat of arms by his good lord who described him as a 'noble man', yet Whitgreave was a mere esquire.[103] The heralds regarded noble and gentle as synonymous still in the 1450s, when a grant of arms constituted an ennoblement admitting the recipient to the company of 'ancient, gentle and noble men'.[104] Although the identity of the magnates with the House of Lords was assumed by the end of the middle ages, the divergence in meaning between noble and gentle, which ratified the process of stratification, was the product of not this but of a later period.

The late middle ages, to recapitulate, saw the emergence of the social order that characterized England in the age of the Tudors. In 1300 there had been no clearly established order of precedence in gentle society below the rank of knight. A century later *scutifer* and *serviens* had fallen into near disuse, and *armiger* was the preferred translation for *esquier* to describe the order immediately below that of the knights. Thus by 1400 the ranks of society were said to be knight, esquire, valet; but such was the rapid decline in the standing of those to whom valet could be applied that less than a quarter of a century later the hierarchy had become knight, esquire, gentleman. The smaller, non-knightly landowners, whose status had been uncertain a century earlier, were now clearly recognized to belong to gentle society, their superior birth confirmed by possession of a coat of arms.

[102] McFarlane, op. cit., p. 275.   [103] Ibid., p. 6.
[104] Wagner, op. cit., pp. 77–8.

iii

As Sitwell observed, 'there were no gentlemen in the middle ages. There were knights, esquires and *valletti*'.[105] The term 'gentry' is no more than a convenient modern description of those who should more properly be called knights and esquires. These minor lords, whose estates were generally rather localized, were identified with the shire where they lived, and a number of fourteenth-century sources list them county by county. One of the most comprehensive of these is the Parliamentary Roll of Arms, dating probably from 1308.[106] This gives the names of the earls and knights of the King's household, followed by a list of the other knights and their arms county by county. With fifty-five Gloucestershire ranks fourth after Norfolk, Suffolk and Lincolnshire. Gloucestershire's eminence seems all the more pronounced when comparison is made with neighbouring counties: Wiltshire and Hampshire have thirty-three, Hereford twenty and Oxfordshire and Berkshire only twenty-three and thirteen respectively. Although the conclusion that Gloucestershire was better endowed with knights than many neighbouring counties is confirmed by other sources, the reliability of the Parliamentary Roll is open to question. Of the fifty-five knights in the Gloucestershire list as many as twenty-four seem to have held no land in the county at all. For example, three members of the Northumberland family of Felton are named. The Lestranges, also listed under Gloucestershire, were unknown there. And just as names occur of men unconnected with the shire, so are there some surprising omissions of knights with clear Gloucestershire affiliations: Sir Nicholas de Kingston, Sir Nicholas de Bathonia and Sir Thomas Boteler of Badminton are all absent. Other knights appear under the wrong county: Sir Richard de Croupes, whose only manor was Whittington (Gloucs.) was listed under Somerset and Dorset. Such discrepancies would be understandable if the Parliamentary Roll had been compiled not, as lists made for fiscal purposes were, from returns sent in by sheriffs, but at the King's court by heralds whose knowledge of the county communities was limited.

[105] Sitwell, op. cit., pp. 64–5.
[106] *Parl. Writs*, i, 418–9. For a discussion of its date see N. Denholm-Young, *Collected Papers* (Cardiff, 1969), pp. 121–32.

A list of archbishops, bishops and other lords summoned to provide military service in 1300 offers a more reliable guide to the landowners of Gloucestershire at the beginning of the century.[107] They are divided into 20 and 40 librate holders. Sixty lords who held 20 librates were named, of whom eight were magnates, another twenty ecclesiastical lords and thirty-two knights or esquires. Of those who held lands or rents in the county to the value of £40 or more four were magnates, ten ecclesiastical lords and thirty-two knights or esquires. In 1300, then, about sixty-four knights and esquires were summoned. Unfortunately, the list suffers from the twin drawbacks of failing to note rank and of not distinguishing the resident from the non-resident lords. We can be sure that none of the earls lived permanently in Gloucestershire; but for sheer lack of evidence it is difficult to identify the favoured manor houses of the smaller landowners. A licence to crenellate can be taken to indicate which house a lord regarded as his principal residence, but only three Gloucestershire knights obtained such licences in the fourteenth century.[108] Where a knight held manors scattered across several counties his place of residence has usually to be inferred from circumstantial evidence. For example, men usually held office in the county where they resided. The Russels, who held Dyrham and Aust in Gloucestershire seem to have lived in Dorset or Hampshire until the 1370s when Sir Maurice, later to be sheriff of Gloucestershire, moved to Dyrham where he lived until his death in 1416.[109]

For these reasons it is more than useful to have a list in which lords who were resident in Gloucestershire are named separately from those who simply held land therein. In 1322 the sheriff of Gloucester was ordered to make a return of those men-at-arms in his bailiwick aged between sixteen and sixty who were able in body and could wield arms.[110] As he seems to have omitted the magnates, lay and ecclesiastical, except for Henry of Lancaster, the list is primarily one of gentry. The sheriff named twenty-eight men-at-arms who were resident in the county. A few are

[107] Brit. Lib., MS Harley 1192, fos. 49–50.

[108] Cal. Pat. Rolls 1292–1301, p. 430; 1307–13, p. 346; 1334–38, p. 33.

[109] Maurice's father, Ralph Russel, demised the manor to him and his wife in 1369 (Cal. Pat. Rolls 1367–70, p. 281). For his brass at Dyrham see C. T. Davis, The Monumental Brasses of Gloucestershire (repr. Bath, 1969), pp. 25–8.

[110] C.47/2/23 m. 36.

identified as knights, but others, known from other sources to have been dubbed by 1322, are not so described. The sheriff goes on to list another thirty-four men-at-arms who held land in the county but who were non-residents. Twenty-four of these were *milites* and ten *armigeri*. The importance of this list is to show that fewer than half of the gentry with landed interests in Gloucestershire actually lived in the county. Moreover, as the list of non-resident landowners indicates, the number of knights was much lower than the number of men-at-arms. It was this discrepancy that led the Crown to compel those men-at-arms to assume knighthood who had the means to support the rank. In 1324, for example, two years after this list was compiled, a distraint was ordered, and the sheriff of Gloucester returned that fourteen men who held lands in his bailiwick were eligible to become knights. Of these John de la Mare, John de Bitton, Thomas de Berkeley of Coberley, William de Whittington and William Walsh were probably resident in the shire, and all except Whittington had been included in the 1322 list. Some at least, then, of the men-at-arms were eligible to be knights. For quite another reason the number of able-bodied knights was likely to be smaller than the number of families that had means to support knighthood. Some knights and esquires were too old to merit inclusion in the list. Some estates were held by widows, others by minors. According to the list of those summoned to serve in 1300, for example, two estates were held by widows in dower and three more by minors in wardship. The absence of several well-known names from the 1322 list is probably explicable in these terms. Although age is often difficult to estimate with accuracy, it is likely that Simon Basset and Peter le Veel were still too young to wield arms. No doubt oversight led to other omissions from the sheriff's return. In all it seems that there were some thirty-five to forty families in Gloucestershire from whom knights could be drawn, but hardly more than about twenty-five actual knights are attested by contemporary sources.

Some support for this estimate comes from the list of Gloucestershire knights summoned to the great council of 1324. The names of forty-five knights are legible, and if those which are faded are taken into account the total would rise perhaps to fifty.[111] As twenty-seven of these are also listed under another

[111] C.47/1/10 m. 3, printed in *Parl. Writs*, ii, 655–6.

county probably no more than about twenty were residents of Gloucestershire. Four knights who almost certainly lived in the shire—Reginald de Abenhall, William de Wauton, Richard de Croupes and Nicholas de Bathonia—were omitted. Their inclusion would raise the total to twenty-four knights. This estimate is consistent not only with the list of 1322 but also with the evidence given by a narrative source. According to the Gloucester Abbey chronicle, when Abbot Gamage entertained the justices of trailbaston to dinner in 1305 he invited about seventy guests, including the Priors of Llanthony and St. Oswald's, thirty knights and 'all the more honourable persons of the county.'[112] The visit of the King's justices was made the occasion for a gathering of the local worthies, both secular and ecclesiastical.

If the early-fourteenth-century county community was led by these thirty knights, it nevertheless embraced landowners deemed worthy of invitation to the abbot's feast who could not have supported knighthood—'the more honourable presons' to whom the chronicler referred. These would have been the esquires whose incomes were assessed a generation later, when Edward III attempted to levy troops according to the value of men's lands. In 1344 a commission was appointed in each county to find the names of all laymen with incomes of £5, £10, £25, 100 marks, £100 and so on up to £1,000.[113] Many of these lists of county landowners still survive. The Gloucestershire commissioners made two returns, one listing sixty-five lords, the other as many as 177, of which the second return is the more valuable.[114] The opening names are those of the earls and barons who held land in the shire. Of these Thomas de Berkeley was said to enjoy the highest income—£400—while the other magnates held land in the county varying in value from £10 for the earl of Northampton to £300 for the earl of Hereford. The 168 names which follow appear to be in no form of order. One knight only, whose name is unfortunately illegible, enjoyed an income of £100 and another, Maurice de Berkeley of Uley, of 100 marks. Seven knights drew £40 from their Gloucestershire lands and Thomas de Breouse and William Tracy £30 and 30 marks respectively.

---

[112] *Historia et Cartularium Monasterii Sancti Petri Gloucestriae* ed. W. H. Hart (Rolls Series, 3 vols., 1863–7), i, 38.

[113] *Cal. Pat. Rolls 1343–5*, pp. 414–6.

[114] C.47/2/52; the longer return is C.47/2/58/37.

Seventeen men enjoyed incomes of £20, four of 20 marks, forty-nine of £10, six of 10 marks and eighty of £5. The reliability of this list, as of others compiled for the needs of medieval government, can be called into question. For example, in 1344 Thomas de Berkeley's income was nearer £1,000 than £400, and William Maunsel who held two manors in the county would surely have enjoyed an income in excess of the £10 with which he is credited.[115] The incomes of John de Acton, Thomas de Rodborough, William de Cheltenham and Ralph de Abenhall all look suspiciously low. But even if most of the figures verge on the low side, the list may reflect relative positions in the county hierarchy accurately enough. Moreover, it brings to light the large number of 'lesser gentry' who are more often than not hidden from the historian's gaze: nearly half of those listed were credited with incomes of a mere £5. But this list suffers from limitations common to others of the fourteenth century for it distinguishes neither social rank nor place of residence and the incomes given are those from lands held in Gloucestershire only. Some lords, like Thomas de Berkeley of Coberley and John Chidiok whose incomes from Gloucestershire were said to be only £10 drew much larger incomes from their lands elsewhere.[116] If the estimates of income in this list are accepted for the moment, the leading 'gentry' families of the shire, from whom the office holders would be drawn, were those with lands and rents worth between £10 and £100. Of the sixty-nine men whose incomes come within that range at least twenty lived in other counties. In the 1340s, then, the resident 'gentry' of Gloucestershire numbered about fifty families, most though not all of them having the means to support knighthood. The 'actual' knights numbered perhaps thirty. Such an estimate is compatible with the evidence of the lists from the beginning of the century.

After the 1340s there are no more lists of county landowners until the income tax of 1436, returns for which survive for sixteen counties, though not, unfortunately, for Gloucestershire. As the county has been hardly any luckier with the poll tax returns,

[115] Smyth, i, 306.
[116] Those other men whose incomes look low, such as Abenhall, Cheltenham and Rodborough, all held the bulk of their estates within the county. Thus, if some of the low returns can be explained by lands being held elsewhere, many others cannot.

which are too fragmentary to be of any general use, our knowledge of the composition and number of the lesser landowning class in 1400 is dangerously patchy. However, the suggestion that after Edward III's reign the ratio of knights to men-at-arms steadily decreased may well be true.[117] Whereas nearly thirty knights lived in Gloucestershire in 1344, there are references to only half that number in the county in 1400.

These calculations possess more than a purely local interest in view of the Crown's concern to halt what was seen in the thirteenth century as a decline in the number of knights. Professor Hilton, however, did not believe that there was such a shortage. In the West Midlands, he said, 'we find that . . . during the three decades of Edward I's reign there were at least two hundred families from which knights were dubbed, the majority coming from Gloucestershire, Warwickshire providing more than sixty and Worcestershire about fifty'.[118] But the implication that there were ninety knightly families in Gloucestershire is hardly borne out by the evidence of the county lists. These suggest that Denholm-Young's more cautious estimate that there were no more than about 1,250 actual knights and 500 fighting knights in the whole of England may be nearer the truth.[119] Indeed, were there so many knights available for service as Hilton supposed, it is difficult to understand why the Crown ever needed to resort to distraint for knighthood.

[117] M. Powicke, *Military Obligation in Medieval England* (Oxford, 1962), p. 178.
[118] Hilton, *Medieval Society*, p. 54. Hilton said that he was 'taking the various sources in combination', by which he means the Parliamentary Roll of Arms, deeds, records of itinerant justices and the Chancery enrolments.
[119] Denholm-Young, *Collected Papers*, pp. 85–7.

II

MILITARY SERVICE

i

According to the social theory propounded by clerical writers in the middle ages, society was divided into three orders or estates. Those who worked, the peasants, supported the other two orders, the clerks, whose office it was to pray, and the knights, who were to fight.[1] It was the knights who were the elite of medieval armies, summoned and organized quite separately from the levies of foot, and their superiority over the other men-at-arms recognized in the pay differential.

J. E. Morris calculated that no more than 228 knights and 294 *servientes*, representing 375 knights or only an eighteenth of the maximum nominal strength of the English cavalry, took part in the Welsh War of 1277.[2] The suggestion that a serious discrepancy existed between the nominal strength of the cavalry and the number of fighting knights (*strenui milites*) was taken up by Denholm-Young who suggested that the latter totalled no more than 500.[3] This was why King Edward I needed to employ propaganda to inspire the nobility and knights with an enthusiasm for his wars, just as Edward III was to do later when he claimed the throne of France. In so far as he succeeded in harnessing magnate interests to his own, Edward III was arguably the more sucessful, for little difficulty apparently was experienced in raising armies to join in military adventures that were popular and which offered the prospect of winning ample booty in foreign fields. But Professor Postan has shown how shortage of evidence for the careers of all but a handful of captains justifies a sceptical approach to the notion of massive

---

[1] For the three-fold division of society into *bellatores*, *oratores* and *laboratores* see *Langland's Piers the Plowman*, ed. W. W. Skeat, iv (Early Eng. Text Soc., old series 30, 1873), 157.

[2] J. E. Morris, op. cit., p. 45.

[3] N. Denholm-Young, *Collected Papers*, pp. 85–7.

profits won during the Hundred Years War.[4] From the surviving documentation it is possible to gain some idea of the measure of support which the wars attracted among the knights and esquires, but none at all of the extent or distribution of the profits which the campaigners brought home. That can at best only be inferred indirectly from the popularity of the wars. And once attempts to extend military obligation had ceased, it was upon the popularity and profitability of war that the King's ability to assemble an army ultimately depended. Thus some impression of the popularity of warfare in the fourteenth century may be given by a study of the military service performed by the landowning class of one shire; and this may also serve to illuminate the Crown's reasons for resorting to compulsion to augment the number of knights.

Morris's calculations certainly support the view that the military strength of England was suffering by Henry III's reign from a decline in the number of knights. That there was a discrepancy between the number of knights and the number of families with the means to support knighthood there can be no doubt. In the 1320s there were some twenty-five knights in Gloucestershire, and by the 1340s the figure stood at about thirty, perhaps as a result of sucessive writs of distraint; yet between thirty-five and forty-five families holding 40 librates or more were living in the county.[5] The fears which led the Crown to issue writs of distraint had some foundation, therefore. Less obvious is the precise purpose which the writs were intended to serve. They merely ordered the sheriff to proclaim that all who had held lands and rents to a certain value for at least three years and were not yet knights should take up that rank by a certain date lest they should incur a penalty. No reason for the distraint was ever given. Denholm-Young suggested that under Henry III distraint was no more than a fiscal device, 'an excuse for collecting fines *pro respectu milicie*—for respite of knighthood'.[6] Such a view does not accord well with Denholm-Young's own belief that there was a shortage of knights in the thirteenth century: if there were

---

[4] M. M. Postan, *Essays on Medieval Agriculture and General Problems of the Medieval Economy* (Cambridge, 1973), pp. 63–80, reprinted from *Past & Present*, 27 (1964).

[5] See above, pp. 30–5.

[6] Denholm-Young, *Collected Papers*, p. 91.

insufficient knights for military and administrative purposes, as Denholm-Young has himself shown,[7] then distraint must have been undertaken with the serious intent of augmenting the number. Henry III's government is certainly open to the reproach that it frustrated its own object by the practice of respite of knighthood: as distraint was ordered more often, so remissions became more common.[8] But every medieval government was obliged to temper its policies according to the needs of patronage and sheer practicality. However ineffective may have been its application, distraint was surely intended to be more than a mere fiscal device. If the intention was simply to raise money, the evidence hardly suggests that there was 'an appreciable income' to be raised by sales of remissions.[9]

It may be more plausible, then, to suggest that the purpose of distraint was to replenish the ranks of those who administered the shires rather than to fill the King's coffers. So long as it was resolved to use only the knights to run the shires it was necessary somehow to ensure an adequate supply of such men. Distraint may have served this purpose. But right from the early decades of the fourteenth century *valletti* were performing the local duties that fell to the knights, and there was never any attempt in this period to limit office holding to the knights alone.

The timing of the writs point to another explanation. The first general distraint of knighthood, on 16 November 1224, appears to have been issued as part of the preparations for an expedition to Gascony planned for the following year.[10] The order of 25 July 1240, too, seems to have been associated with a Gascon expedition. The final overseas expedition of Henry III's reign, that of 1253, involved at least two writs of distraint with probably an attempt at a third.[11] The planning of a military expedition in the thirteenth century was often coupled with the issue of a writ of distraint for the obvious purpose of increasing the pool of knights available for service. Knights had better and stronger horses, and we may suppose that their armour was more elaborate.[12] As Powicke has shown, distraint was linked especially with foreign

---

[7] Ibid., p. 88   [8] Ibid., p. 90   [9] Ibid., p. 91
[10] M. R. Powicke, *Military Obligation in Medieval England*, p. 72
[11] Ibid., p. 75.
[12] See for example the horse inventories for the Falkirk campaign printed in H. Gough, *Scotland in 1298* (Paisley, 1888), pp. 161–237.

military service in this early period: indeed, the fines of those were remitted who would join the King in Gascony.[13]

In the fourteenth century distraint was still used to augment the reserve of troops for war. The writ of 1316 was issued in connection with campaigns in Scotland, and that of 1325 in connection with the Gascon expedition. The reopening of the Scottish wars by Edward III was accompanied by the issue of writs of distraint in 1333 and 1334. There seems little reason to doubt the strength of the government's determination in these two years: four months after the writ of 20 March 1333 those sheriffs who had failed to make returns were rebuked for their negligence.[14] However, after the writ of 20 December 1334 no further attempt at distraint was made until 1341 in the aftermath of the expedition to the Low Countries. The writ of 1344, although apparently not connected directly with any military activity, may well have been a part of the scheme to extend military service: a renewed measure of compulsory knighthood would have complemented the attempt to revise the provisions of the Statute of Winchester. Towards the end of Edward III's reign, however, distraint was pervaded by an air of unreality. It probably came to be seen by the Crown as no more than a small but still useful source of revenue from fines. In Richard II's reign no writ appears to have been issued after that ordered on 20 November 1377, occasioned perhaps by the coronation of the new King.

The early years of Edward III's reign were something of a turning point. The writs for distraint of 1333 and 1334, like earlier ones, were part of the preparations for military action against an enemy. But after the 1340s distraint was rarely used as an instrument for the provision of knights for an expedition.[15] For one thing the organization of war had changed. Compulsory knighthood had been initiated at a time when the feudal levy had still formed the nucleus of the King's army, even if the system had been supplemented by the granting of fief-rentes.[16] But the feudal

[13] Powicke, *Military Obligation*, p. 74.

[14] *Cal. Close Rolls 1333–7*, p. 144.

[15] The distraint of 1356 followed the battle of Poitiers; thus it could hardly have been intended to produce knights for that campaign. The 1366 distraint, however, may have been associated with the Najera expedition.

[16] Powicke, *Military Obligation*, p. 167.

retinues of the tenants-in-chief hardly matched the notional *servitia debita* required of them, and Henry III's government had to acquiesce reluctantly in a reduction in military service. The process of commutation combined with the unpopularity of overseas expeditions and the poor leadership of Henry III to produce an unwillingness to take up knighthood which was combated by the policy of distraint. Even though the vigorous kingship of Edward I contrasted with that of his father, orders of distraint were still necessitated by the immense strain which the wars in Scotland and Wales imposed on the resources and manpower of the realm. Nor did the problem of obtaining knights disappear under Edward II, when the disastrous progress of the war against the Scots must have dissuaded many knights from serving. But once warfare on the border was superseded by the more attractive prospect of campaigns in France the conditions changed, and for the remainder of the middle ages armies were raised by the contractual system. Objections to service overseas did not disappear immediately, but the acceptance of pay and the experience of campaigns like those of Crecy and Poitiers dispensed with the objection that captains and knights would be out of pocket as a result of service abroad.

Yet even in the heyday of chivalry in Edward III's reign some of those eligible still refused to assume knighthood. It was an honour which they found it best to decline. The sheriffs' returns give the impression that the great majority of those who qualified were already knights, but the accuracy of this evidence is difficult to estimate. Easily corruptible as they were, sheriffs might have been tempted by bribes to omit certain names. On one occasion at least, in 1369, the Exchequer knew that the information it received was incomplete. Following the order for distraint issued in 1366 the sheriff of Norfolk and Suffolk had returned a seemingly exhaustive list of thirty-three men who held lands and rents to the value of £40 *per annum* and who were not yet knights. Yet, the sheriff was told, it had come to the notice of the Exchequer that as many again were eligible for knighthood. After this rebuke the sheriff added another ten names to his list.[17] That the sheriff of Norfolk could find a total of forty-three men who had not assumed knighthood hardly accords with the view

[17] E.159/145 Recorda m. 26d (Easter term).

that most of the £40 class were already knights.[18] He was not the only sheriff to be rebuked for negligence. In 1369 William Crook, attorney of the sheriff of Gloucester, appeared at the Exchequer to be told that there were others in his county eligible for knighthood. The sheriff had listed only two names initially— Matthew de Bitton and John Giffard of Weston—but unfortunately it is not known if he added others subsequently.[19]

Although the returns to orders for distraint were subject in their compilation to the influences of favour and friendship which pervaded all levels of medieval administration, it would be wrong to reject altogether the evidence which they have to offer. Even if the machinery of the Exchequer was slow in moving into action—three years after the 1366 writ was issued in the above case—the fact remains that the negligent sheriffs were finally brought to account. Had the Exchequer suspected on other occasions that returns were inaccurate, it would no doubt have taken the appropriate action: as Powicke has observed, Exchequer supervision was sufficiently strict to prevent extreme corruption.[20] Moreover, omission was not the only sin of which sheriffs were capable. In 1356 the sheriff of Gloucester included the names of several men who claimed that they did not hold lands or rents to the value of £40. The objections of John de Morhall were upheld when subsequent inquests found that his lands and rents in five counties were worth only £25 16s. 4d.[21] In such calculations reprises, outgoing rents and lands held in dower were exempted.[22] In 1356 for the first time the sheriff of Gloucester returned the names of burgesses whom he considered eligible for knighthood. The return itself is lost, but Walter de Frampton, John de Wycombe, and Richard Hurel, three burgesses of Bristol, subsequently pleaded in Exchequer that they did not hold lands of sufficient value.[23] The inclusion of burgesses in 1356 and 1366, and the possibility that there was a distraint at the level of £15 in 1353, suggest that there may have been a

---

[18] Powicke, *Military Obligation*, pp. 174-5.

[19] E.159/145 Recorda m. 26d (Easter term).

[20] Powicke, *Military Obligation*, p. 175.

[21] E.159/133 Recorda (Easter term).

[22] Powicke, *Military Obligation*, p. 177. Reprises comprised rent-charges and annuities payable from the issues of the manor.

[23] E.159/133 Recorda.

shortage of knights in the aftermath of the Black Death.[24] Equally it may simply have been a fiscal measure to induce those distrained to purchase exemptions. One thing at least seems clear: by the 1350s compulsory knighthood has ceased to have any military significance. Burgesses were distrained not to take up active service but to fine for exemption.

Some sheriffs may have been negligent, but the evidence suggests that limited information was a more important constraint on the integrity of their returns. Many potential knights whose estates were scattered across several counties did not have lands or rents to the value of £40 within the bounds of just one shire. In such cases the sheriff stated the value of the defaulter's lands within his own bailiwick and listed the other counties where lands were held.[25] Moreover, the sheer difficulty of estimating the value of an estate is testified by the litigation in Exchequer which followed each distraint. Sheriffs were not only unsure of the value of their neighbours' lands but sometimes also showed that they had little idea whether they were knights or not. Ralph Bluet, named by the sheriff of Gloucester in his return in 1333, appeared at the Exchequer to say that he had already been knighted by Gilbert Talbot while serving in Scotland.[26]

If it is reasonably clear that until the 1330s the Crown issued writs of distraint to increase the supply of knights for war, it is less apparent why some of those who qualified were so anxious to avoid knighthood. One suggestion is that it had become too expensive: the cost of a knight's equipment, said Denholm-Young, far outstripped the general rise in the level of prices in the thirteenth century. Once distraint was fixed by custom at £40, lower than it had been on occasions, people began to think of evading knighthood.[27] Powicke suggested, too, that the cost of the ceremony of knighting may have been regarded as excessive by some who found it preferable to fine for respite.[28] An episode in the *Gest of Robin Hood* supports the suggestion that compulsory knighthood embraced men too poor to support the rank.

[24] Cf. Denholm-Young, *The Country Gentry*, p. 17n.
[25] See for example C.47/1/12m. 8d; E.198/3/18.
[26] E.159/112 m. 103d.
[27] Denholm-Young, *Collected Papers*, p. 91.
[28] Powicke, *Military Obligation*, pp. 69–70.

Commenting on his sorry condition, Robin says to Sir Richard atte Lee

> I trow thou wert made a knight of force
> Or else of yeomanry

to which Sir Richard retorted that his ancestors had been knights for a hundred years.[29] Knights by distraint, then, were sometimes characterized in contemporary literature as men who lacked the means to support their rank. This view is not without foundation. John de la Boxe and Richard de Bagingdon, two of the six men whom the sheriff of Gloucester named in his return to the writ of 1333, almost certainly drew incomes of less than £40. John held only a quarter of a knight's fee at Box in Bledislowe Hundred, hardly an estate to provide him with the income of 20 marks which it was said that he enjoyed from his Gloucestershire lands.[30] The sheriff said that he held other lands in Hampshire or Somerset, but there is no evidence to support this. Richard de Bagingdon held a quarter of a fee at Wootton (Heref.) and a manor at Baunton (Gloucs.), the latter said to be worth £10; together these estates would barely have qualified him for knighthood.[31] But the inclusion in the sheriff's return of men whose means were probably inadequate was rather unusual. Only in 1324, when John de la Mare was distrained, probably unsucessfully, had the sheriff previously named a man whose means were insubstantial. Much later in the century mere 20 librate holders and burgesses were included, but with the purpose largely of compelling them to fine at the Exchequer. In the period of most intense distraint up to the 1330s there is surprisingly little correlation between distraint and inadequate means. John de Berkeley of Dursley, distrained in 1326 and 1333, could not plead poverty when he held three manors in Gloucestershire, one of which was the town of Dursley.[32] Nicholas Burdon, who was distrained in 1324, 1326, 1333 and 1334, held manors at Oldbury-on-the-Hill and Didmarton (Gloucs.), Poulshot and Yatesbury (Wilts.), and Kingsteignton (Devon).[33] The names which the sheriff at Gloucester listed in his

[29] Ibid., pp. 173-4.   [30] C.47/1/19 m. 9; *Feud. Aids*, ii, 251.
[31] *Feud. Aids*, ii, 270, 376   [32] *Gloucs. Inqs. Post Mortem*, v, 320-1.
[33] C.I.P.M., iv, no. 20; *Feud. Aids*, ii, 269, 282; v, 212.

return in 1326 are not those of men fallen on hard times. In
addition to John de Berkeley he named another thirteen men,
most resident outside Gloucestershire, whose lands and rents
within and without the county came to £40.[34] Three of these—
Thomas de Berkeley of Coberley, Nicholas Burdon and Matthew
Fitzherbert—held lands in three counties.[35] The others who held
in two counties only were still men of some consequence like John
de Grey of Rotherfield and William de Lisle.[36] In view of the
sheriff's admitted paucity of information it is possible that some
of these had already assumed knighthood, but the relative wealth
of the alleged defaulters is sufficient to throw doubt on the view
that those distrained were men who could not afford to become
knights.

Another clue is provided by looking at the local careers of the
men who were distrained. In the first thirty years of the century
the names that recur in the sheriff of Gloucester's returns are
those of John de Bitton, William Whittington, Thomas de
Berkeley of Coberley, William Walsh, Nicholas Burdon and John
le Boteler of Llantwit.[37] Of these only John le Boteler was active
in local affairs prior to distraint. He never held any of the major
offices in Gloucestershire, but between 1322 and 1327, perhaps
because of his eminence as a steward of the younger Despenser,
he was often a justice of oyer and terminer.[38] William Walsh
served as a commissioner of array on just two occasions, in 1322
and 1324.[39] The others did nothing. The later evidence gives the
same impression. John de Berkeley, distrained in 1326 and 1333,
John FitzNichol and John de Brokenburgh in 1344 and Matthew
de Bitton and John Giffard of Weston in 1366 played no part at
all in the life of the shire before being pursued to take up
knighthood.[40]

[34] C.47/1/12 m. 8d.

[35] In addition to lands in Gloucestershire Thomas de Berkeley held estates in
Worcestershire and Oxfordshire, Nicholas Burdon in Wiltshire and Devon and
Matthew Fitzherbert in Hampshire and Yorkshire.

[36] John de Grey of Rotherfield, who was summoned to parliament from 1338
to 1357, in fact held manors in five counties (*G.E.C.*, vi, 145).

[37] C.47/1/7 m. 31; C.47/1/8 m. 7d; C47/1/11 m. 3; C.47/1/12 m. 8d.

[38] *Cal. Pat. Rolls 1321–4*, pp. 153, 257, 311, 368, 380, 443, 449, 452; *1324–7*, pp.
64, 233.

[39] *Cal. Pat. Rolls 1321–4*, p. 73; *1324–7*, p. 27.

[40] It is doubtful whether Brokenburgh actually lived in Gloucestershire.

Not all of those who were named responded by becoming knights. In 1335 John le Boteler of Llantwit obtained an exemption from so doing on the grounds that he was upwards of seventy years of age.[41] A little later John FitzNichol sought a similar way out: given respite in 1342 and 1346, finally in 1347 he was granted exemption for life at the request of Sir Reginald de Cobham of Sterborough.[42] It is less easy to say whether those who did not purchase an exemption actually assumed knighthood. Most, it seems, did; but William Walsh, Nicholas Burdon, John de Brokenburgh and Matthew de Bitton who are never subsequently referred to as knights may well have practised successful evasion.

Apart from John le Boteler, the landowners who did not take up knighthood continued to lead uneventful lives. But it is significant that many of those who were pressed into assuming the title now held local office for the first time. Of the six men named regularly in returns in the first three decades of the century at least three were successfully distrained. John de Bitton, knighted by 1331, never held any local office; but he is untypical. Thomas de Berkeley of Coberley, who remained in the background in the 1320s, had finally taken up knighthood by 1330 when he became sheriff for the first time. During a career in local politics which lasted into the 1350s he held all of the major offices in the shire.[43] William de Whittington, distrained in 1312, 1316 and 1325, was knighted by 1327 and represented Gloucestershire at the Lincoln parliament in September 1327. Subsequent to later writs of distraint two more Gloucestershire esquires were pressed into assuming knighthood. John de Berkeley of Dursley, named in 1326 and 1333, received the honour in the Scottish campaign of 1333. Thereafter he played a more active part in the life of the shire, as a commissioner of array in 1337, a chief taxer in 1346 and 1347 and a knight of the shire in March 1340.[44] In 1366 John Giffard and Matthew de Bitton were

---

[41] *Cal. Pat. Rolls 1334–8*, p. 157.

[42] *Cal. Pat. Rolls 1340–3*, p. 515; *1345–8*, p. 121, 342. Sir Reginald de Cobham of Sterborough was Thomas de Berkeley's son-in-law (*G.E.C.*, iii, 353).

[43] Sir H. Barkley, 'The Berkeleys of Coberley', *Trans. Bristol & Gloucs. Arch. Soc.*, xvii (1892–3), 111–121.

[44] Sir H. Barkley, 'The Berkeleys of Dursley', *Trans. Bristol & Gloucs. Arch. Soc.*, ix (1884–5), 227–76.

distrained. The former assumed knighthood, the latter almost
certainly did not. The former went on to sit in parliament in
1373, 1376 and 1379, the latter held office only as a taxer in 1374,
the year of his death. Matthew's unwillingness to hold public
office had been demonstrated as early as 1350 when he sought to
be discharged from a commission to collect a subsidy to which he
had been appointed.[45]

There is more than a suggestion, then, that reluctance to
assume knighthood may have been connected with a reluctance
to assume public office. To judge from the careers of those who
were successfully distrained their fears may have been justified. It
had long been the ideal of medieval government for the shires to
be run by local knights. As early as 1194, for example, when four
coroners were first appointed in each shire, three were to be
knights and one a clerk.[46] Knights were required to sit on the
grand assize still in the fourteenth century. Esquires, of course,
were already sharing the burden of local administration, just as
they were sitting in parliament as early as in the 1320s; but a
knight would be expected to play his part in the affairs of the shire
even if the Crown could hardly compel him to hold office against
his will. A 40 librate holder who preferred to eschew public life
would be well advised to remain an esquire. In this connection
the career of Peter de la Mare, a retainer of Henry of Grosmont, is
instructive. In 1326 Peter was granted a respite from taking up
knighthood.[47] In 1332 he was appointed a keeper of the peace in
Wiltshire, but in the following year obtained an exemption for
life from serving on juries or holding office against his will.[48] In
consequence he did not sit on any commissions again until the
1340s. Peter de la Mare was reluctant to be tied down in
Gloucestershire and Wiltshire because his employment in
Grosmont's retinue frequently took him abroad. Moreover, he
was not averse to military service: he had served in Gascony and
Scotland by 1333, and it was no doubt to claim the higher rate of
pay that he finally became a knight in 1337, safe in the knowledge
that his exemption would prevent his appointment to offices and
commissions in his shire.[49] As de la Mare had to acquire an

[45] Cal. Close Rolls 1349–54, p. 184; 1369–74, p. 527.
[46] R. F. Hunnisett, The Medieval Coroner (Cambridge, 1961), p. 1.
[47] Cal. Pat. Rolls 1324–7, p. 247.   [48] Cal. Pat. Rolls 1330–4, pp. 294, 296.
[49] J. Barnes, Life and Times of King Edward III (Cambridge, 1668), p. 113.

exemption, evasion of knighthood in itself was evidently insufficient to escape office-holding; but his later career suggests
that it was for that reason that he was unwilling to become a
knight.

No explanation for the reluctance to take up knighthood can
ever be wholly convincing, for there is none that fits all the facts.
In the thirteenth century opposition to military service may have
been at the root of the problem, but it is doubtful whether this was
any longer so in the fourteenth. Peter de la Mare was just one of
many *valletti* who performed active service, even though he could
claim only half the daily wage to which he became entitled as a
knight. John Giffard of Weston, named in the distraint of 1366,
was still an *armiger* when he served in Gascony three years later.[50]
While it was undoubtedly in connection with military preparations that the Crown issued writs of distraint, at least until the
1330s, there is little evidence to suggest that unpopularity of
active service led to widespread evasion of knighthood; and once
armies came to be raised by contract such fears would have been
superfluous anyway.

It is usually accepted that England experienced little difficulty
in fielding armies in France after the attempts to extend military
obligation had ceased. The reign of Edward III 'witnessed a
quiet revolution in the administration of war' in which the
contractual system finally triumphed. Warfare became a 'kind of
joint stock enterprise of the king and his subjects'.[51] Like the
chroniclers who celebrated the world of chivalry, modern
historians pointing to the profits of war readily cite the careers of
great magnates or captains of retinues like Sir John Chandos.
This is hardly surprising, and it is scarcely possible even to begin
to redress the balance. The evidence just does not survive to
indicate how the knights fared, or whether they left the field of
battle better or worse off financially. Even a more simple question
is difficult to answer: just how many of the knights actually
performed active service? We must make some attempt to answer
this question, but before so doing it is necessary to glance at the
sources.

[50] E.159/145 Recorda m. 26d; C.61/82 m. 7.
[51] M. H. Keen, *England in the Later Middle Ages* (London, 1973), p. 148.

ii

From the enrolments of letters of protection and general attorney lists can be compiled of the knights and esquires who served in war. Although the rolls of Chancery are replete with protections, they are not totally reliable for evidence of service. Such letters were issued only on request. Those that were issued were certainly enrolled; but they were not requested by or for all of those who went on active service. For example, William Maunsel and Nicholas de Kingston, known to have been on the Scottish Marches in 1298, did not obtain protections.[52] Nor did Ralph Bluet, who was serving in Gilbert Talbot's retinue in the north in 1333 or earlier.[53] Whether these two cases were exceptional is hard to say. A knight likely to be away for some time would surely have thought it wise to secure his interests by seeking a protection, which at the cost of only 2s. was cheap to obtain.[54] Moreover, a captain who wrote to Chancery for protections for his men was hardly likely to include some and not others. On the contrary, the long lists of those in receipt of protections included many menial servants and officials in addition to the military retinue. Captains also requested protections, which were enrolled, for men who failed to perform the service they promised. In 1382 Gilbert Denys's letters of protection were revoked two months after issue when Sir John Devereux, captain of Calais, testified that he had still not crossed the Channel.[55] Protections, therefore, issued as they were prior to the commencement of a mission, only give evidence of intended service. If they were issued to some who never performed service and not issued to some who did, they may be a source inaccurate in detail but still indicative of the total number of men-at-arms in an army. And by the later decades of the century they can be supplemented by the retinue rolls which commanders sent into the Exchequer when settling their accounts.

Appendix III, in which those Gloucestershire knights and esquires who participated in expeditions in this period are listed, summarizes the evidence from these sources. It is best to begin

[52] K. B. McFarlane, 'An Indenture of Agreement between two English Knights', *Bull. Inst. Hist. Res.*, xxxviii ((1965), 200–10.

[53] E.159/112 m. 103d.

[54] P. Chaplais, *English Royal Documents* (Oxford, 1971), p. 22.

[55] *Cal. Pat. Rolls 1381–5*, p. 111.

with the Falkirk campaign of 1298 for which the horse inventories give as complete a list as can be obtained for any
campaign.[56] Fourteen knights and *valletti* out of possibly thirty-
five to forty men-at-arms in Gloucestershire fought at Falkirk.
There is nothing to suggest that the four other men who were
summoned from the shire performed their service. Giles de
Berkeley of Coberley certainly did not because he had died four
years previously, and William de Berkeley of Dursley was
probably very old.[57] No extenuating circumstances can be
adduced to explain the probable absence of the remaining two,
Peter Crok and John de Wilington. Nevertheless, the numbers
present on the Falkirk campaign were still very impressive, and
by the winter two more knights from Gloucestershire, Nicholas
de Kingston and William Maunsel had arrived on the Scottish
border.[58]

For the next major campaign, that of 1300, Edward I
summoned the 40 librate holders to follow him in Scotland. The
commissioners listed thirty-two landowners in Gloucestershire
who were eligible for service.[59] Of those in the list known to have
resided in the county only five attended; but if other Gloucestershire men-at-arms, not listed in the summons and known to have
served, are included, then the total rises to ten. Again it must be
emphasized that not all the knights or rich *valletti* in the county
were available for military service, and one who was
summoned—William de Berkeley of Dursley—died in the same
year. The remaining campaigns of Edward I's reign attracted
slightly less support: in 1301 and 1303 eight Gloucestershire
knights and *valletti* attended, in 1307 nine and in 1310–11 eight.
Of the eight who fought at Bannockburn, mainly retainers of the
Berkeleys and of the earl of Pembroke, Sir John de la Rivere was
killed and at least three others, Sir John and Henry de Wilington
and Henry de Hatherley, were captured.[60] Sir John must soon
have been released because on 30 August 1315 he was told by the
King to remain on the Scottish border during the coming

[56] H. Gough, *Scotland in 1298* (Paisley, 1888), pp. 161–237. See also pp. 84–8.
[57] *C.I.P.M.* iv., no. 458; Sir H. Barkley, 'The Berkeleys of Dursley', 253.
[58] K. B. McFarlane, 'An Indenture of Agreement'.
[59] *Parl. Writs*, i. 338.
[60] J. R. S. Phillips, *Aymer de Valence, Earl of Pembroke, 1307–24* (Oxford, 1972),
p. 75; *Trans. Bristol & Gloucs. Arch. Soc.*, xxi (1898), 10–11; C.71/6 m. 4.

winter.[61] When hostilities were resumed in 1318 with the siege of Berwick, ten Gloucestershire knights and *valletti* received protections, suggesting an attendance higher than in any other campaign until the outbreak of the Hundred Years War. Not more than four or five men-at-arms from the county were present in any year during the Scottish wars of the 1330s. If it is not always possible to say for certain who did attend these expeditions, a list of lords who proferred substitutes in 1323 identifies some of those from Gloucestershire who did not.[62] Among them may be numbered Sir John de Guise, John FitzNichol, David le Blount, Sir William Tracy, John de Berkeley of Dursley, Thomas de Berkeley of Coberley and Sir Thomas Boteler of Badminton. But as each of these men, with the exception of David le Blount, either had fought or was to fight in at least one campaign, the list does not reveal the presence of a hard core of local knights or esquires who were shunning military service.

The story of dwindling participation in warfare in the 1330s was brought to a halt with the outbreak of the Hundred Years War. The army which Edward III led to Flanders included nine Gloucestershire knights. Despite the frustrations which that army endured Edward was able to engage considerable support again in 1340 when he set sail from the Orwell: on the campaigns that year which led to the truce of Esplechin eleven knights and *valletti* from the shire were present.[63] The same number crossed to Brittany in the three expeditions of 1342, most of them accompanying the king himself in October.

The next army to cross the Channel was that which defeated the French on 26 August 1346 at Crecy and which reduced Calais in the following year. Numbering perhaps some 10,000 on the battlefield, it had swelled by the end of the siege to become the largest English army fielded in France in the fourteenth century. By 1347 there were about 32,000 men encamped around the walls of Calais, of whom 2,500 were heavy cavalry.[64] Nine

[61] *Parl. Writs*, ii, ii, 458. [62] C.47/5/10.
[63] H. J. Hewitt, *The Organisation of War under Edward III* (Manchester, 1966), p. 31, points out that though the Flanders campaigns have been condemned as fruitless, this may not have been the opinion of the knights who took part and shared the loot.
[64] A. E. Prince, 'The Strength of English Armies in the Reign of Edward III', *Eng. Hist. Rev.*, xlvi (1931), 353–71.

5

Gloucestershire knights and *valletti* were issued with protections for the Crecy campaign. When it became clear that the siege at Calais was to be prolonged, the English army was strengthened by reinforcements from home and by the arrival of Lancaster's retinue from Gascony. Thus at the height of the siege as many as seventeen knights and *valletti* from Gloucestershire out of a possible thirty-five to forty-five were present; three of these knights, Ralph de Abenhall, Ralph de Wilington and Maurice de Berkeley of Uley died in the wave of dysentry that swept through the English ranks.

Though scarcely half the knights and esquires of this one county took part, the participation which the campaign of 1346-7 inspired was, it seems, never exceeded in the fourteenth century. The evidence, though perhaps incomplete, would suggest that on the Poitiers campaign of 1356 only six Gloucestershire knights were present. The whole of the Black Prince's expeditionary force may have numbered no more than 2,600, however.[65] On the Rheims campaign Edward III led an army of 12,000 which included eight Gloucestershire knights. The resumption of war after 1369 witnessed a series of English *chevauchees* which inflicted damage on the French countryside without engaging the enemy in battle. The forces now were hardly comparable in size with the armies assembled earlier in the century, but some of the expeditions attracted a following among the gentry that was surprisingly high. In 1372, for example, eight Gloucestershire knights and esquires intended to serve in Brittany, although the expedition that finally sailed was much depleted. Towards the end of 1374 protections were issued in favour of three knights and three esquires from Gloucestershire who were going on the expedition to Brittany, mostly in the retinue of Thomas de Berkeley. About the same number of men from the county were present on Buckingham's *chevauchee* of 1380-1 and on Richard II's expedition to Ireland in 1394.[66] Campaigns became less

[65] Ibid., 366.

[66] The numbers attending these later campaigns, being on the low side, suggest that Gloucestershire may not be typical of other counties. Of the two leading magnates who would recruit in the shire, Sir Edward Despenser died in 1375 leaving a son who was a minor and Thomas de Berkeley (1368–1417) did not often see active service in these years. In localities where leading commanders recruited heavily the proportion of men-at-arms who saw foreign service in the late 1370s may well have been higher.

frequent. Knights were in lower demand now; and, as Powicke observed, the ratio of knights to men-at-arms decreased, as men-at-arms as a whole declined in relation to mounted archers.[67]

iii

If we turn now to look at the implications for English local administration, one generalization that can safely be made is that the wars of the fourteenth century did not leave the shires denuded of knights. When Edward I was making his heaviest demands in the cause of the Scottish wars scarcely more than a third of the available men-at-arms in Gloucestershire answered his call; only in 1347 for the siege of Calais did at least half of them perform active service. After the renewal of war in 1369 no more than seven men-at-arms from the county were present on any campaign. Perhaps only three or four of these would have been knights, but in view of the decline in their number over the course of the century the proportion of knights who saw active service may have remained constant; as a proportion of all the available men-at-arms, however, the *strenui milites* may have become fewer.

On the evidence of the protections and retinue rolls the English armies of the middle ages were constantly shifting and changing in composition; but the instability induced by this high turnover was balanced by the constant presence of a core of knights who could always be relied on to attend. It is noticeable throughout the century, and most of all during the Scottish Wars, that a small number of knights were on active service for campaign after campaign. Between 1298 and 1400 a dozen knights from Gloucestershire fought in four campaigns or more (Table I). If the great majority of the gentry had at least some experience of active service, only a few made an active profession of arms. Such evidence reminds the historian how dangerous it is to regard the knightly class as synonymous with the *strenui milites*. It would be going too far to say that there was a demilitarization of the

---

[67] Powicke, *Military Obligation*, p. 178; J. W. Sherborne, 'Indentured Retinues and English Expeditions to France 1369–80', *Eng. Hist. Rev.*, lxxix (1964), 645, says that in 1359–60 indentures provided for about 680 knights out of a total of 870 men-at-arms and in 1373 for about 380 knights out of 2,022 men-at-arms.

TABLE I
Military Careers of Twelve Gloucestershire Knights, 1298–1400.

	Campaigns	Dates
Stephen de la More	5	1298–1311
Nicholas de Valers[1]	5	1298–1311
John de la Rivere	5	1298–1314
Richard de la Rivere	6	1298–1324
William de Wauton	10	1298–1327
Peter de la Mare	5	1322–1342
Maurice de Berkeley of Uley I	6	1334–1347
Simon Basset	8	1336–1360
Robert de la Mare	5	1338–1360
Peter le Veel[2]	14	1349–1381
Gilbert Giffard	4	1370–1373
Maurice de Berkeley of Uley II	4	1380–1395

[1] On 2 March 1291 letters of protection for two years from Michaelmas were issued to Nicholas de Valers, then a *vallettus* of the King's household, going to the Holy Land (*Cal. Chancery Warrants 1230–1326*, p. 30). Since 1291 saw the fall of Acre and the end of the Latin kingdom of Jerusalem, Valers is more likely to have intended to go as a crusader than as a pilgrim. The letters of protection of course prove only that he intended to set out, not that he actually went.
[2] He seems to have served in Gascony almost continuously, 1362–7.

knightly class in the course of the fourteenth century, but the prospect of active service does not seem to have exercised an appeal that was any more than intermittent.

An analysis of the ties contracted by the knights who took part in four or more campaigns suggests one reason why it was these twelve who saw active service most often: at least ten of them were retainers.[68] By the fourteenth century it was the practice for lords to recruit the knights, men-at-arms and archers they had contracted to provide by themselves sub-contracting, and in assembling his host a noble captain would naturally call on the services of his life retainers. Though they often numbered no more than a small fraction of the total force contracted, it was nevertheless they who accompanied their lord regularly on campaign after campaign.[69] Of the twelve knights only Stephen de la More and Nicholas de Valers seem to have been

[68] The evidence on which this statement is based is tabulated below, Appendix III.
[69] N. B. Lewis, 'The Organisation of Indentured Retinues', *Trans. Roy. Hist. Soc.*, 4th ser., xxvii (1945).

unattached. Never appearing regularly in the company of a single magnate, they were probably professional soldiers who contracted to serve any captain raising a troop: there was, no doubt, ample need for their services in the years at the turn of the century when Edward I was striving to reduce Scotland by the mobilization of massive armies.[70]

A few of the most active *strenui milites*, then, were not retainers; but the majority were. They entered magnate service when young, no doubt in search of a career that would bring rewards greater than could be earned by staying at home. Just how young some of them were is indicated by the length of their military careers, which for six of the twelve knights spanned more than a couple of decades. Sir William de Wauton accompanied the Berkeleys on expeditions over a period of thirty years. A retainer's interest in seeking personal fortune on the battlefield coincided with that of his lord who expected his indentured knights to comprise the core of his retinue on active service. It is clear that some at least of those retainers attended with great regularity. Other retainers, perhaps, were office-holders whose commitments did not allow them to leave the county so often. On the other hand, there are a few indications that the wars siphoned off knights who were currently serving as sheriffs or keepers of the peace. We must turn, then, to the effects of warfare on the workings of local administration.

There is some justification on *a priori* grounds for believing that a major campaign was likely to drain off just those knights and esquires who carried the burden of local administration in the shires.[71] As a result of the workings of patronage at court and in the King's administration, retainers of influential magnates were likely to be prominent among the local office-holders;[72] and these rather than unconnected knights were the men likely to be engaged most often on military service. But in practice the case for identifying the *strenuus miles* with the administrator is not quite so straightforward.

Five of the dozen knights who took part in four or more campaigns shared little of the administrative work of the shire at

[70] Both knights had earlier served in Wales in 1294–5 (C.67/10 mm. 3, 5).
[71] This is the argument of M. M. Postan, *Medieval Agriculture and General Problems*, pp. 67–8.
[72] See below, ch. IV.

any time in their lives.[73] In the years when he was regularly serving in Scotland, Sir Stephen de la More's administrative work did not extend further than the supervision of arrays;[74] and even after he had retired from the fray the only burdens he undertook were those of representing his county in parliament in 1316 and at a great council in 1324.[75] His lack of interest in local affairs was shared, among his soldier contemporaries, by Nicholas de Valers and Richard de Croupes. Towards the end of his life the latter secured his position by obtaining an exemption from office holding.[76] During the Hundred Years War many of the most regular campaigners from Gloucestershire were men who held no local offices at any time in their lives. In the opening phase of the war, between 1338 and 1347, twenty-six men-at-arms from the county went to fight abroad. Of these, four had held or were to hold the office of sheriff, and five were at some stage appointed keepers of the peace; but eight, of whom at least three were knights, never accepted any office in the shire at all.[77] Over the period 1369–81, when twenty-one Gloucestershire men-at-arms fought in France, the proportion of office-holders was rather higher. Nine of them had held or were to hold the shrievalty, and twelve were J.P.s. But in the same group there were six, at least three of them knights, who shunned office-holding altogether.[78]

The *strenui milites*, then, cannot be identified exclusively with the men who shouldered the burden of local administration. But this is not to suggest that the sheriffs, escheators and keepers of the peace were men devoid of military experience. A few certainly, like William de Cheltenham and Robert Palet, two magnate stewards who sat on the bench, never saw active service. But at least twenty-nine of the forty-seven men who held the shrievalty in Gloucestershire in the fourteenth century had been on one

[73] Maurice de Berkeley of Uley (d. 1347), Maurice de Berkeley of Uley (d. 1401), Gilbert Giffard, Stephen de la More, Nicholas de Valers.

[74] *Cal. Close Rolls 1302–7*, p. 505; *Cal. Close Rolls 1313–18*, p. 563.

[75] *Members of Parliament*, p. 53, Moor, iii, 198.

[76] *Cal. Pat. Rolls 1330–4*, p. 459.

[77] The eight were William de Careswell, Roger de Bradeston, John de Bitton, Peter Corbet, Ralph Bluet, High Pauncefot, Hugh de Rodborough, and Henry le Veel.

[78] The three knights were John Bitton, Maurice Berkeley of Uley, and John de Wilington.

campaign or more. Of the thirty-one men (including magnates, but excluding justices of the central courts) appointed to commissions of the peace between 1300 and 1360 at least twenty-one had seen active service. Few of these men, however, appear to have fought in many campaigns. Sir Simon Basset was exceptional. His military employments, stretching over twenty-four years, included at least eight campaigns. During his tenure of the shrievalty from 1341 to 1350 he took part in the expedition to Brittany in 1342 and the Crecy/Calais expedition four years later. Perhaps it was his neglect of the shrievalty that led to Basset's sudden departure from Calais: on 23 January 1347 the King pardoned him on condition that he return there as soon as his duties should permit.[79]

Military service no doubt prevented a few other knights from performing their duties, but the evidence hardly goes so far as to suggest that local administration in England was much affected by the demands of war. It would be wrong always to think of the knight who fought in the English armies as one who combined the life of the soldier with that of the landed gentleman. A knight or esquire whose early years were passed in Scotland or France would not take up local office until he had settled down in the shires for good. McFarlane showed how William Maunsel and Nicholas de Kingston only became local administrators when they had ceased to be soldiers.[80] A contemporary of theirs, William Gamage, who had fought at Falkirk, did not hold office until the early years of Edward III. Sir Peter le Veel only became a keeper of the peace and sheriff of Gloucester in the 1370s when his active military career, already of twenty years standing, was nearing its close.

Thus many who took up arms were young men. While one generation was seeking glory on the battlefield, the other was carrying the burden of local affairs. When John Tracy was knighted at Calais in 1347 his father, Sir William, was still serving as a justice of oyer and terminer back in Gloucestershire. Also present at Calais was Hugh Pauncefot who did not succeed to the estates of his childless elder brother, Grimbald, until 1375. On the expedition to the Low Countries in 1338 Sir Peter de la Mare

---

[79] G. Wrottesley, *Crecy and Calais* (London, 1898), p. 109.
[80] McFarlane, 'An Indenture of Agreement', pp. 208–9.

was accompanied for the first time by his son, Robert, still in his early twenties.[81] But if these young men were lucky enough to return home and to enter into their inheritances, others were not so fortunate. The careers can be traced of at least five young men from Gloucestershire who met early deaths, perhaps on the battlefield (Table II). Despite the absence of any corroborative evidence, it seems not unreasonable to assume that the three who received protections for the last time in 1347— Henry, son of Henry de Wilington, Roger de Bradeston and Thomas, son of John le Boteler of Llantwit — met their deaths at the siege of Calais, as did so many English knights. Peter, son of Peter le Veel, who accompanied his father in the Black Prince's retinue regularly over a period of fifteen years, disappears from the scene after 1370 and is not named as an heir on his father's death.[82] When discussing the undoubted attractions of war, therefore, it is appropriate also to recall the casualties. It would be wrong to think that the losses among the gentry families were confined to the established knights who lost their lives in battle, for there may have been many others like these five men: such knights or esquires, who perhaps did not yet hold lands in their own right, would have had little need of protections, and would therefore be the least likely to leave their mark on the records of Chancery.

One effect of the wars on English local administration, albeit only an indirect one, was to thin the ranks of those who later in life would have filled offices and commissions in the shires.

Nevertheless, if the near-continuous warfare of the period succeeded in disrupting the smooth operation of local administration, a case has yet to be produced in support of that view. It is an oversimplification to say, as Postan does, that a very large proportion of the administrative class of the shires was repeatedly drained off for service in France.[83] Knights were certainly not numerous. But the wars did not drain off sufficient of them to leave the counties denuded of men qualified to carry

[81] W. A. Shaw, *The Knights of England*, ii (London, 1906), 8; Wrottesley, op. cit., p. 192; C.76/12 m. 8; *C.I.P.M.* ix, no. 399.

[82] The descent of the Veel family after Sir Peter's death in 1391 is confused, but he seems to have left three adult sons, Thomas, Henry and Robert (*Cal. Close Rolls 1381–5*, p. 442; *Cal. Pat. Rolls 1391–6*, p. 245; *1385–9*, p. 69).

[83] Postan, *Essays on Medieval Agriculture*, pp. 67–8.

TABLE II
The military careers of five Gloucestershire knights and esquires who died before succeeding to the family estates.

	Date of Expedition	Source
Henry, son of Henry de Wilington	1338	C.76/12m. 3; C.76/13m. 2
	1340	C.76/15m. 21
	1341	C.76/16m. 6
	1343	C.76/18m. 16
	1347	C.76/24m. 3
Roger de Bradeston knight	1338	C.76/12m. 6
	1340	C.76/15m. 24
	1345	C.76/20m. 8
	1347	C.76/24m. 13; C.76/25m. 10
Thomas, son of John le Boteler of Llantwit	1347	C.76/24m. 8
Peter, son of Peter le Veel, knight	1355	C.61/67m. 8
	1359	C.76/37m. 3
	1369	C.61/82. 5
	1370	C.61/83m. 7
Edward Berkeley knight[1]	1359	Smyth, i, 257
	1362	C.61/75 mm. 3, 4
	1363	C.61/76m. 6

[1] He was described as son of Sir Maurice de Berkeley, presumably Maurice of Uley who died in 1347 (C.61/76m. 5).

on the process of government; neither are there noticeably more knights holding office in time of peace. Although the cavalry was drawn from the ranks of the 'gentry' families, the professional men-at-arms cannot be identified with the men who held the shrievalty and who sat on the bench. The fourteenth-century cavalry was as likely to be composed of young knights, but recently dubbed, as of well-established veterans like Sir Richard de Croupes or Sir Simon Basset. The head of the family, probably well past the age of military employment, stayed at home to carry on the work of administration; his sons or younger brothers, attracted by the lure of war in foreign fields, departed to win their spurs in battle. The King's government, then, was maintained in spite of the strains and stresses of war. The effectiveness of that government may have been reduced; but there were still sufficient knights and esquires in the counties to ensure that the offices and commissions were not left vacant.

III

LORDS AND RETAINERS

Among his most regular followers on active service, then, a lord would number his life retainers. If they formed but a small proportion of the total contingent, nevertheless they were the most likely to follow him on campaign after campaign. Bound as they were to serve in both peace and war, they were simply fulfilling the terms of the indenture. But duty and service coincided with self-interest; and it is very likely that they welcomed the opportunity which active service offered to seek profit and adventure. These liveried retainers were but one element in a sophisticated magnate household which was composed of a large staff of domestic servants and officials. Socially the knights and rich esquires would be the most substantial members of the retinue, taken in its broadest sense, and their attendance was required only when the lord wished to ensure a respectable following around his person. Yet it was not their function simply to bask in the reflected splendour of their patron. The life retainers overlapped with the domestic servants, and the ranks of the magnate household were not so sharply distinguished as to preclude the former sharing with the latter the responsibilities of administration and estate management.

The nature and purposes of retaining by indenture have been examined in some detail by N. B. Lewis and K. B. McFarlane.[1] More recently the biographers of Henry of Grosmont, Thomas of Lancaster and Aymer de Valence have shown how the power of a magnate in politics was connected with, and in some ways dependent on, the following he attracted among the gentry.[2]

---

[1] N. B. Lewis, 'The Organisation of Indentured Retinues in Fourteenth Century England', *Trans. Roy. Hist. Soc.*, 4th series, xxvii (1945), 29–39; K. B. McFarlane, 'Bastard Feudalism', *Bull. Inst. Hist. Res.*, xx (1945), 161–81.

[2] K. Fowler, *The King's Lieutenant: Henry of Grosmont* (London, 1969); J. R. Maddicott, *Thomas of Lancaster, 1307–22* (Oxford, 1970); J. R. S. Phillips, *Aymer de Valence, Earl of Pembroke, 1307–24* (Oxford, 1972).

Valuable though an analysis of a single retinue may be, this is really an approach suggested by the uneven nature of the surviving sources, for only a few retinues are copiously documented. The Muniment Room at Berkeley, to take one example, still contains some, though by no means all, of the account rolls and charters which Smyth used to write his account.[3] Because the accident of Bolingbroke's usurpation in 1399 caused the preservation alongside the public records of the Lancastrian archives many of our assumptions about 'bastard feudalism' are still coloured by our detailed knowledge of John of Gaunt's retinue, which was quite exceptional in its size. But a perusal of the protections enrolled in Chancery will permit at least a partial reconstruction of the retinues of other—and lesser—lords, which will help to redress the present imbalance in our knowledge. Protections were sought less often in Richard II's reign when the wars petered out, but petitions, correspondence, letters of attorney and cases recorded on the court rolls still reveal much about the connections between magnates and their retainers.

Now that the organization of the retinue has been adequately charted the need is to examine 'bastard feudalism' in a wider perspective. This can best be achieved by turning from the individual retinue to study the pattern of retaining in an area such as a county. One objective of such an approach will be to estimate approximately the proportion of the gentry who were retained. No authoritative estimate can ever be formulated because of the sheer impossibility now of compiling an exhaustive list of retainers; but the evidence, though scattered, is probably sufficient to justify the exercise. The question, moreover, is one of some importance. This is the period when the gentry were beginning to assert themselves in parliament; and an attempt to measure the extent of retaining will indicate how far the independence which the Commons showed in parliament was rooted in the presence there of a body of knights who were independent of any formal ties with the nobility. But first of all a description must be attempted of the retinue of the Berkeleys and of the estates from which this family, so important in the

---

[3] J. Smyth, *The Berkeley MSS: i and ii, The Lives of the Berkeleys: iii, The Hundred of Berkeley*, ed. J. Maclean (Gloucester, 1883–5).

history of Gloucestershire, drew their wealth in the fourteenth century.

The Berkeleys traced their descent from Robert Fitzharding, a prosperous merchant of Bristol, who was rewarded for his financial backing of the Angevins with a grant of the manor of Berkeley and its members by Henry of Anjou in 1154. These lands lay at the heart of the Berkeley inheritance for the rest of the middle ages; although many of Robert's descendants, in particular Thomas III (1326–61), were active in the land market, newly-purchased manors in Wiltshire and Berkshire were used principally to endow younger sons. The patrimony of the Berkeleys comprised two distinct blocks of lands on the east bank of the river Severn. The town of Berkeley with its members, often known as Berkeley Harness, comprised about a dozen manors stretching across the Vale to the market town of Wotton-under-Edge under the Cotswold escarpment. Berkeley Harness seems to have been synonymous with the hundred of Berkeley, which conferred jurisdictional power on the lord at Berkeley Castle. Outside the hundred the Berkeleys also held in Gloucestershire the manors of Upton St. Leonard near Gloucester and Aure on the west bank of the Severn.

Further south, in Somerset, they held the manors of Portbury, Bedminster and Redcliffe with their appurtenant hundreds. Robert Fitzharding had purchased these manors, which lay on the southern outskirts of Bristol, from Henry II's uncle, Robert, earl of Gloucester. But the resentment of the burgesses of Bristol at the subjection of Redcliffe to the court of the Berkeleys led to violence so often that the family were probably not always able to tap the wealth of these lucrative manors. In 1305 Maurice de Berkeley complained that a gang had sacked his house in Bedminster while he had been serving with the King in Scotland.[4] Shortly afterwards the citizens of Bristol complained in their turn that the Berkeleys had enforced suit of court in Redcliffe, beating up those who had refused to attend. Trouble flared up again in 1330 when Thomas de Berkeley complained of an attack by the burgesses of Bristol on his bailiffs at Redcliffe, but the absence of any subsequent complaints by either side suggests a relaxation of tension.[5] The only manor which did not fit into

[4] Smyth, i, 196.
[5] Ibid., 200.

this pattern was that of Great Wenden in Essex, which the second Maurice de Berkeley (1243–81) acquired by marriage. But in 1368 the picture was transformed by the marriage of Thomas IV to Margaret, daughter and heiress of Warin, Lord Lisle, by which the Berkeleys acquired two dozen manors in Wiltshire, Buckinghamshire, Oxfordshire, Northamptonshire, Devon and Cornwall.[6] However, this sudden expansion in the family's territorial power lasted only for the lifetime of this lord. When Thomas IV died in 1417, and the Berkeley inheritance was divided between his daughter Elizabeth, wife of Richard, earl of Warwick, and his nephew James, who succeeded to the title, the long dispute began between the heir male and the heir general that culminated in the battle of Nibley Green on 19 March 1470 between William, Lord Berkeley, and his unsuccessful rival, Lord Lisle.

In the fourteenth century these difficulties lay in the future. Until 1417 the Berkeleys were remarkably successful in producing male heirs, and the estates were able to enjoy a continuity in administration rare in the middle ages; it was broken only by the forfeiture to the Crown that followed Maurice de Berkeley's participation in the rebellion of the Contrariants in 1321–2. The accounts preserved in Berkeley Castle provide some insight into the administration of the Berkeley estates and household at the time of the restoration to his inheritance of Maurice's son, Thomas, at the beginning of Edward III's reign. It will be best to sketch briefly this administration before considering the income of the Berkeleys.

The financial system operated at two levels. In each manor was a reeve who accounted for its issues. At the higher level all issues from the manors passed through the hands of the receiver. He then allocated sums of money to the other departments such as the wardrobe, which maintained the private establishment of the lord. The workings of this administration are revealed in the account roll of Thomas de Shipton, keeper of the wardrobe, for the period 24 April–8 September 1328.[7] In those four and a half months the wardrobe received an income of £156 6s. 0¼d., of which £143 0s. 1¼d. was a block grant from the receiver.

---

[6] Smyth, ii, 1–5.

[7] Berkeley Castle S(elect) R(oll) 60, extracts from which are printed in Jeayes, pp. 283–5.

Expenditure over the same period mounted to £157 19s. 5½d. Although this exceeds the allocated income by a small margin, it would be incorrect, in the absence of a continuous series of accounts, to assume that Thomas de Berkeley was facing problems of insolvency. Medieval accounts were designed to establish liability, not to estimate profit or loss.

Perhaps the most important figure in the administration of any great medieval estate, lay or monastic, was the steward. It was his duty to supervise the management of the estates, preside over hundred and manorial courts and perform many other duties that varied from one estate to another.[8] Unfortunately the names survive of only six of the stewards who served the Berkeleys in the course of the fourteenth century; but some idea can still be gained of the kind of men who held this important office.[9] Henry de Rockhill, steward of Maurice de Berkeley in the 1320s, must have been a man trusted by his master, who appointed him one of his executors.[10] Nothing else is known about him; but he may be presumed to have come from Rockhill near Keynsham. By 1327 he had been succeeded by Sir Thomas de Rodborough of Rodborough, a local knight who had been associated with the Berkeleys for at least nine years.[11] In 1332 the office had passed to the ubiquitous William de Cheltenham, who looms so large in the history of Gloucestershire in the middle years of the century; John de Cheltenham, who was steward in 1339, was probably his brother.[12] How long William served as steward is impossible to say, although he is found in the service of the Berkeleys as a retainer or attorney for more than twenty years. He ended his career as a country gentleman; but his origins are shrouded in obscurity, and he derived his considerable influence solely from the trust which his lord, Thomas de Berkeley (1326–61), chose to place in him. Rewards were heaped upon him.[13] The lands with which he was endowed lay on both sides of the river Severn, but it

---

[8] On the duties of a steward at the end of the thirteenth century see N. Denholm-Young, *Seignorial Administration in England* (Oxford, 1937), pp. 66–85.

[9] See below, Table III p. 65.   [10] Smyth, i, 273.

[11] Berkeley Castle S. R. 39 (account of the steward of Berkeley, January–Michaelmas, 1327). Rodborough had taken part in the raid by the Berkeleys on Painswick in 1318 (Phillips, *Aymer de Valence*, p. 266).

[12] Just. 3/127 m. 25; S.C.1/39/90.

[13] Smyth, i, 342. See also below, pp. 157–8.

TABLE III

Stewards of Secular Estates in Gloucestershire

Walter de Nas	Earl of Pembroke	1321	Phillips, *Aymer de Valence*, p. 291.
John le Boteler of Llantwit	Hugh Despenser the Younger	*c.*1322–6	S.C.8/72/3571, 3572.
Henry de Rockhill	Maurice de Berkeley	1326	Smyth, i, 273.
Sir Thomas de Rodborough	Thomas de Berkeley	1327	Berkeley Castle, S.R.39.
William de Cheltenham	Thomas de Berkeley	1332	Just. 3/127 m. 25.
Andrew Crokesford	Hugh Audley	1335	Just. 3/127 m. 18d.
John de Cheltenham	Thomas de Berkeley	1339	S.C.1/39/90.
William de Tytherington	Lord Stafford	1339–41	Stafford Rec. Office, D'641/1/2/126–7.
John Clyve	Thomas de Bradeston	1348	Just. 3/131 m. 6d.
John de Weston	Earl of Stafford	1349–60	Stafford Rec. Office, D.641/1/2/132–5.
Robert Palet	Edward Despenser	1367	K.B.27/429 m. 21.
John Sergeant	Thomas de Berkeley	1378	Just. 3/60/4 m. 21d.
Sir Thomas FitzNichol	Earl of Stafford	1388–9	Just. 3/180 m. 16; Stafford Rec. Office, D.641/1/2/152.
Thomas de Bridges	Lady Despenser	1378–95	K.B.27/471 Rex m. 9d; Just.3/180 m. 26.
	Earl of Warwick	1391–5	Just.3/180 mm. 21d, 26d, 27.
Richard Ruyhall	Earl of Warwick	*c.*1390	C.115/K.2/6684 f. 166.
	Thomas de Berkeley	1388–95	Just. 3/180 mm. 16, 27.
John Couley	Thomas de Berkeley	1393	Just. 3/180 m. 24d.

seems probable that he resided at Pucklechurch, near Bath, for he founded a chantry there, in St. Andrew's Church.[14] By the time of William's death the Cheltenhams could be counted among the gentry families of the shire, and in May 1360 Maurice de Cheltenham followed in the footsteps of his father by being

[14] *Cal. Pat. Rolls 1334–8*, p. 559.

elected to serve as a knight of the shire in parliament.[15] Two stewards who are known to have served the fourth Thomas de Berkeley (1368–1417) present contrasting backgrounds. John Couley, who held the office in 1393, was in the tradition of the earlier steward.[16] He was probably a descendant of an earlier John de Couley who held an estate of 200 acres at Coaley in the hundred in 1325.[17] On the other hand, Richard Ruyhall, who succeeded Couley as steward, came from a well-established gentry family of Worcestershire.[18] He was also retained by the earl of Warwick, and his growing prosperity was reflected in his purchase of the manor of Dymock (Gloucs.).[19] If most of the professional administrators employed by the Berkeleys, then, were drawn from below the ranks of the gentry, the careers of Rodborough and Ruyhall serve as a reminder that the chivalric classes who performed public duties for the King also performed private administrative duties in the service of the magnates.

Like all magnates with a position in society to maintain, Thomas de Berkeley employed a large number of those whom John Smyth, the family historian, calls 'menial servants'—full-time domestic servants in the household. We can uncover something of the background of men like William Curteys (c.1318–38), Robert Groundy (c.1339–44) and John de Melksham (c.1329–38), who witnessed charters and were evidently in frequent attendance at Berkeley Castle.[20] Of these three Robert Groundy paid 1s. 7¾d. in the parliamentary subsidy of 1327—he is shown as a resident of the town of Berkeley—and John de Melksham 3s. 4¼d. under the village of Cam in the hundred of Berkeley.[21] The evidence is not such as to suggest that these were substantial county landowners. From a similar background, though perhaps slightly richer, was John Chaumpeneys, one of the three men whom Maurice de Berkeley appointed as his

[15] Cal. Pat. Rolls 1358–61, p. 211.

[16] Just. 3/180 m. 24d.   [17] Gloucs. Inqs. post Mortem, v, 191.

[18] Just. 3/180 mm. 16, 27. In Worcestershire the Ruyhalls held the manors of Birtsmorton, where they resided, Cowleigh, Cannow, Queenhill and lands in Ryall (V. C. H. Worcs., iii, 489, 491, iv, 31, 140).

[19] C.115/K.2/6684 (Reg. William de Cheryton, Prior of Llanthony). For his purchase of Dymock see C.P.25(1)/78/81/78; Gloucs. Inqs. post Mortem, vi, 249.

[20] Berkeley Castle select charters, Bod. Lib. microfilms, book 10, fos. xxxii, xxxvd, slv, lxxxiid, lxxxiii, ccxxx.

[21] Gloucs. Subsidy Roll, p. 26.

executors in 1326.[22] In 1327 he paid 3s. 8½d. under Cowhill, and the very considerable sum of 18s. 10d. under Kingsweston and Elberton.[23] Some of these men held office in the hundred of Berkeley as well as in the household. In 1347 Robert Groundy was the bailiff and John Clyve the constable in this hundred where Thomas' servants discharged the duties performed elsewhere by men who answered to the sheriff.[24]

The account rolls of manors in the hundred of Berkeley for the closing years of Edward II's reign which illuminate the workings of the administration of the Berkeley estates are also the main source for the landed income of the lords of Berkeley. The changing economic fortunes of the family cannot be traced in detail over the course of the century, but it is sufficient here to look in some detail at the revenues at the close of Edward II's reign, and turn for purposes of comparison to the few accounts which survive from the later decades.

The reeves' accounts of 1326–7 for the manors of Alkington, Ham, Hurst and Slimbridge, and of 1325–6 for Hinton, afford a valuable insight into the agrarian economy of the Vale. It was a world of scattered hamlets, which was imperfectly manorialized. The land of the Vale was fertile, and the prosperity of the area found expression in the high values of the manors recorded in the accounts. Alkington was worth annually £89, Hinton £106, Hurst and Slimbridge together £108, and Ham no less than £214.[25] Contemporary tax returns, those of the subsidy of 1327, reveal the hundred populated by freeholders, well below the rank of knight or esquire, paying sums of 7s. or 8s. in many cases; one Walter de Symond of Hill, close to Berkeley, paid as much as 10s.[26] Of the gross income of £51 10s. 2¼d. which Thomas de Berkeley received from rents and aid at Alkington in 1326–7, the rents of free tenants accounted for £44 16s. 2d.[27] Moreover it was rent and aid, not sales of demesne produce, which formed the largest single item on the account of each manor; the demesnes were never very large. In the last year of Edward II's reign the revenues from these manors in the hundred amounted to £542 19s. 0d. If we include the towns of Wotton-under-Edge and

[22] Smyth, i, 273.
[23] *Gloucs. Subsidy Roll*, pp. 27, 45.   [24] Just. 3/131 mm. 6d, 9d.
[25] Berkeley Castle S.R.s 41–5. These figures exclude foreign receipts.
[26] *Gloucs. Subsidy Roll*, p. 26.   [27] Berkeley Castle S. R. 41.

Berkeley—valued respectively at £92 12s. 1d. and £26 13s. 11d.
in the inquisitions taken when Maurice's rebellion brought the
estates temporarily into royal keeping—then the lands in the
hundred can be estimated to be worth £661.[28] The gross overall
value of the Berkeley estates, including the Somerset lands
and jurisdictional profits, may well have approached £800 a
year when the young Thomas was restored to his inheritance
in 1327.

According to Smyth the revenues of the Berkeleys continued to
rise until the middle of the century. He says that in 1335 there was
a clear income of £659 7s. 0d., in 1345 of £977 16s. 5d. and in
1346 of £1,150 18s. 8d.[29] This sustained increase was the result of
the many purchases of land made by the third Thomas de
Berkeley (1326–61) to provide for his younger sons. Unfortunately Smyth does not quote any figures from the receivers'
accounts for later than 1346; but he did notice the changes which
overtook agrarian organization in the later fourteenth century.
'Then began the times to alter, and hee with them . . . and then,
instead of manuring his demesnes in each manor with his own
servants, oxen, kine, sheep . . . under the oversight of the reeves
of the manors . . . this lord began to joyst and tack in other men's
cattle into his pasture grounds by the week, month and
quarter'.[30] At Ham this change had taken place by 1385–6, when
leases of demesne lands were worth £5 19s. 4d.[31] On the Berkeley
estates, where the demesnes had never been very extensive, the
abandonment of direct cultivation did not entail a fundamental
readjustment of the relationship between lord and tenant. Rents,
as ever, remained the most important source of revenue, but in
the post-Black Death world, when lords were in a weaker position
than earlier, there was no certainty that they would be collected.
At Ham in 1385–6 rents totalled £64 5s. 1d.; however, the
account opens with £38 15s. 10d. of arrears carried forward from
the previous year's account. In the absence of a continuous series
of such accounts it is impossible to say whether such arrears were
being allowed to accumulate. But if they were not, there is no
reason to believe that the Berkeleys were being compelled to live
in straitened circumstances by Richard II's reign: the manor of

Ham, worth £208 14s. 9d., including arrears, was just as lucrative as it had been half a century before.[32] Moreover, by this time of course the income of the Berkeleys was augmented by the acquisition of the Lisle inheritance.

This brief account of the landed wealth of the Berkeleys has attempted to do no more than identify the foundations of the power of the family, and to demonstrate that although they were never raised above the rank of baron in this period, they possessed the landed wealth to support a retinue of some size and magnificence. The names of the retainers to whom fees and liveries were granted would have been recorded on a livery roll, but unfortunately none survives in the Berkeley muniment room. But we do know how many knights and esquires were retained at the height of the family's power and influence in the middle ages. Smyth, the family historian, says that in the time of the third Thomas de Berkeley (1326–61) the retinue contained twelve knights and twenty-four esquires.[33] This retinue can be compared with that of another West Country magnate: a livery roll dating from about 1385 shows that the earl of Devon's retinue was composed of five members of the Courtenay family, seven knights and forty esquires.[34] The retinue of a Gloucestershire baron may, then, have rivalled that of one of the poorer earls in size; but it is possible that the changing economic fortunes of the nobility had compelled the Courtenays to reduce their commitments in fees and liveries by the 1380s.

In the absence of any livery rolls, the retinue has to be studied through indirect sources; but there are sufficient of these for the early decades of the fourteenth century to construct a fairly detailed picture of the knights of the Berkeley family, and it is only later that it becomes less complete. Relying mainly on letters of protection Dr J. R. S. Phillips identified six retainers who were with the second Thomas de Berkeley and his son Maurice between 1297–99 and 1313–15: Sir Thomas de Berkeley junior, John de Berkeley, Sir William de Wauton, Geoffrey de Hauteville, Sir Thomas de Gurney and William de Gamage.[35] These men regularly accompained the Berkeleys on campaigns in Scotland. Prominent in the protections too, though unnoticed

[32] Cf. Berkeley Castle S.R. 42. In 1326–7 Ham had been worth £214.7.7.
[33] Smyth, i, 304.   [34] Brit. Lib. Add Roll 64320.
[35] Phillips, *Aymer de Valence*, p. 305.

by Dr Phillips, is Sir John Maltravers junior of Lytchett (Dorset),
who was taken prisoner with the Berkeleys at Bannockburn in
June 1314.[36] Since they were appointed keepers of the imprisoned Edward II both Gurney and Maltravers were presumably
still in the service of the Berkeleys in 1327. Berkeley retainers who
were not prominent in military service can be identified from
other sources. One petition of around 1312 names John le Boteler
of Llantwit and Walter Torel as Berkeley retainers, and another,
from the time of the 1322 rebellion, states that Henry Fitzwilliam
wore the robes and livery of Maurice de Berkeley.[37] Their
appearance as witnesses to charters, and intermittently too in
protections, suggests that John de St. Lo and John de Clivedon
were two more retainers of the family.[38] Another contemporary,
finally, was Sir John de Bitton, who made bequests to his lord,
Thomas de Berkeley, in his will, made in 1313.[39]

If the Berkeleys retained up to a dozen knights in the middle of
the fourteenth century, these men may well represent the full
complement of knights indentured in the reign of Edward II. It
would be expedient now to look more closely at this group of men
and their links with the house of Berkeley, before identifying the
retainers who were serving later in the century.

The retinue mirrored the location of Berkeley power and
influence. Five of these families lived at Berkeley, or in its
immediate vicinity. Thomas de Berkeley junior and John de
Berkeley were, of course, younger members of the family; while
William de Wauton lived at Cromhall, John le Boteler at
Hardwicke, and Henry Fitzwilliam at Olveston, all within a few
miles of their lord's castle.[40] William de Gamage, too, was a
Gloucestershire man; but he was the only retainer in this period
to come from west of the river Severn, where the Berkeleys held

[36] C.81/1720/95, 96, 97; *Cal. Pat. Rolls 1317-21*, p. 432.
[37] S.C.8/323/E563; S.C.8/41/2027.
[38] Bob. Lib. microfilms bk. 10, fos. ixd-x, xd, xliii-xliiid; C.81/1720/91, 93;
C.67/16 m. 6.
[39] Somerset Record Office, D/D/B Register 1, fo. 69a (Bishop Drokensford's
Register).
[40] In 1322 Sir William de Wauton held Alkerton (*V. C. H. Gloucs.*, x, 129) and
Cromhall (Sir R. Atkyns, *The Ancient and Present State of Gloucestershire* (London,
2nd edn., 1768), p. 196). For Boteler's house at Hardwicke see *V. C. H. Gloucs.*,
x, 182. Fitzwilliam was the second husband of Isabel, widow of Peter Crok of
Olveston (S.C.8/41/2027).

the manor of Aure.[41] The lands of two more of the retainers, like those of their master, extended on both sides of the river Avon. Sir John de St. Lo, who held land in several south-western counties, was probably drawn within the orbit of the Berkeleys because Clifton, his one manor in Gloucestershire, lay on the outskirts of Bristol.[42] Sir John de Bitton held three manors in Somerset, and resided at Barre Court on the southern edge of Gloucestershire.[43] Sir Thomas de Gurney came from Inglescombe (Somerset), still well within the territorial influence of the Berkeleys.[44] This picture of a retinue composed of local knights is, however, broken by a few exceptions which testify to the wider appeal exercised by the Berkeleys. Geoffrey de Hauteville, whose name appears frequently in the protections, probably came from Oxfordshire, where he held two manors; in Somerset the family held the manor of Norton Hauteville, but by 1316 this had passed from Geoffrey to one John de Hauteville.[45] Sir John Maltravers of Lytchett (Dorset) hailed from more distant parts, but from furthest afield of all came Odo de Bodrugan, a Cornish knight in the service of the Berkeleys around 1330.[46] Although the lords of Berkeley were of sufficient renown to attract men from so far off, in this period nine of their household knights were drawn from Gloucestershire and Somerset, if junior members of the family are

---

[41] William de Gamage was lord of Ley, in Westbury-on-Severn (*Feud. Aids*, ii, 268). He is omitted in the incorrect descent of the family in *V. C. H. Gloucs.*, x, 86. He died in 1346 holding lands in Oxfordshire too (*Cal. Fine Rolls 1337–47*, p. 479).

[42] John de St. Lo held the manors of Clifton (Gloucs.), Newington and Publewe (Somerset), Little Cheverell and Hardenhuish (Wilts.) (*Feud. Aids*, ii, 248; iv 323, 328; v, 204, 208).

[43] The Bittons held Norton Malreward, Chilcompton and Hinton-with-Camel (*Feud. Aids*, iv, 325). For the descent of the family and their residence at Barre Court see H. T. Ellacombe, *History of the Parish of Bitton* (Exeter, 1881–3).

[44] The descent of the various branches of the Gurney family is traced in J. Batten, 'Stoke-sub-Hamden', *Trans. Somerset Arch. & Nat. Hist. Soc.*, new ser., xx (1894), opp. p. 270. Sir Thomas de Gurney, the regicide, held Inglescombe and Farringdon, and died in 1333 at Bayonne.

[45] *Feud. Aids*, iv, 171, 307.

[46] Berkeley Castle S.R. 39, 62. One Nicholas de Bodrugan appears in the company of Sir Maurice de Berkeley, probably in 1346 (C.81/1720/93). Odo de Bodrugan died in 1331 holding the manors of Restronguet, Tregrean, Bodrugan, Trethak, Tremodret, Trerim, Little Lantyan and Looe (*C. I. P. M.*, vii, no. 385).

included too. These men found it prudent to seek the good lordship of the most important magnate in the area, just as he found it in his interest to strengthen the ties which bound the local gentry to him.

When we come to the time of Thomas III (1326–61) and his son Maurice (1361–8) the retinue is less well documented; but what information there is suggests that the retainers were still largely local men. The service to the Berkeleys of three generations of the Tracy family spanned three-quarters of a century until the 1390s at least.[47] The Tracys held two manors in Gloucestershire at opposite ends of the county, Toddington in the north and Doynton in the south.[48] From Somerset came Sir John Palton who served with the Berkeleys on campaigns in the 1340s.[49] Ralph Walsh, lord of the manor of Woolstrop in Quedgeley and of other manors in South Wales, is described as Berkeley's receiver in an account of 1373–4.[50] Sir Richard Acton, one of the retainers sent to escort the young Thomas IV to Berkeley where his father lay dying in 1367, was a Somerset knight who held lands at West Bagborough and Chelvey. According to Smyth, Acton was accompanied on that journey by Sir Nicholas Berkeley of Dursley, now a retainer of the family with whom his father, Sir John, had once been at loggerheads.[51] One retainer from a little further afield was Robert Dabetot, a Worcestershire man who is found serving Thomas de Berkeley in the 1330s.[52]

For the retainers of Thomas IV (1368–1417) there are a few more sources. One of his stewards enjoyed the standing of a

[47] Smyth, i, 305; K.B. 27/536 Rex mm. 21–21d.

[48] In 1316 Tracy was returned as lord of Doynton (*Feud. Aids*, ii, 269), but Toddington was omitted. He also held Burgate and the hundred of Ford (Hants.). For this family see Lord Sudeley, 'The Tracys of Toddington', *Trans. Bristol & Gloucs. Arch. Soc.*, 88 (1969), opp. p. 136.

[49] C.76/20 m. 8; C.76/22 m. 3. In 1346 John de Palton held manors in Croscombe, Priestleigh, Barton, Whiteoxmead and East Horrington (Somerset) (*Feud. Aids*, iv, 350).

[50] Berkeley Castle, General Series Account Rolls, account of William atte Nasche.

[51] Smyth, ii, 3.

[52] Dabetot held the manor of Hindlip which he released to the earl of Warwick (*V. C. H. Worcs.*, iii, 398–9); Berkeley Castle S.R. 39. See also below, p. 157.

country esquire: Richard Ruyhall, who has already received notice, held the manor of Birtsmorton (Worcs.) and later acquired Dymock, in the west of Gloucestershire.[53] Those whom Thomas appointed as his feoffees on 24 June 1417 were likely to be among the men whom he favoured: Sir Walter Pool, Sir Gilbert Denys, Thomas Knolles, citizen of London, Thomas Rugge, John Grevell, Robert Greyndour and Thomas Sergeant were, with one exception, gentlemen of Gloucestershire and Somerset likely to be in the retinue.[54] Pool acquired extensive interests in south Gloucestershire by his marriage to Elizabeth, daughter of the second Sir Thomas de Bradeston of Winterbourne.[55] Denys inherited the lands of the Corbets of Syston by his father, and his wife brought him a moiety of the lands of the last of the Russels of Dyrham.[56] Thomas Rugge lived at Charlcombe, north of Bath. Apart from Thomas Knolles, all the others were Gloucestershire men. There is no evidence by which any of these feoffees can be identified directly as retainers of lord Berkeley: he may have enfeoffed them simply because they were neighbours well known to him. But sufficient evidence has already been examined to show that it was precisely neighbours like these, living under the shadow of Berkeley Castle, who were likely to be found in the retinue. In one respect, however, the membership of the retinue changed in the time of Thomas IV. Now that his marriage had brought him the Lisle inheritance, Thomas began to retain men in the counties where the Lisles had once held sway; in 1413, for example, he granted to Robert Shottesbrooke, an esquire from Berkshire, a fee of £14 *per annum* assigned on the manor of Orcheston (Wilts.).[57] It is likely, then, that the composition of the retinue came to reflect the wider territorial power enjoyed by the house of Berkeley in these years.

It is worthwhile to emphasize, though, that the retinue was not the only instrument through which the influence of the Berkeleys was exerted in Gloucestershire. In the Vale itself the power of the lord of Berkeley was augmented by the liberty which he held. Most of the hundreds in Gloucestershire which had passed into

[53] See above p. 66.   [54] Jeayes no. 581.
[55] R. Austin, 'Notes on the Family of Bradeston', *Trans. Bristol & Gloucs. Arch. Soc.*, 47 (1925), 279–86.
[56] *Cal. Pat. Rolls 1417–22*, p. 175.
[57] Smyth, ii, 21.

private hands were held by monasteries, such as Cirencester, but the hundred of Berkeley was held by the lord at Berkeley Castle; nearly all the manors within it were held by one or other of the branches of the Berkeley family.[58] The eminence of the family at the castle is known to have led to disputes with the elder branch seated at Dursley. When Henry II had granted the castle and lordship of Berkeley to Robert Fitzharding of Bristol, the dispossessed de Berkeleys moved to Dursley, a few miles to the east, where they were still subject to the jurisdiction of the lord of the hundred of Berkeley. This was very much resented by a fourteenth-century member of the Dursley branch, Sir John de Berkeley. In a petition of about 1330 he complained bitterly of the franchise of writs within the hundred which, he alleged, the lord of Berkeley had newly procured 'par eide et mautenaunce de Sire Roger de Mortimer nasgaires un des conseillers le Roi.'[59] Nothing is heard of these disputes, however, after the lifetime of Sir John.

Unlike Sir John most of the local gentry accepted the hegemony of the Berkeleys. Whether they were formally indentured retainers or not it seems that their lives centred on the castle with some willingness. They were constantly going to and from Berkeley. Deeds and charters recording transfers of land within the hundred were witnessed and preserved at the castle, and their witness-lists serve to show who were the most frequent visitors to the castle. Generations of the Bassets of Uley, for example, are found in this capacity.[60] One member of that family, Sir Simon Basset, sheriff of Gloucestershire from 1341 to 1350, was retained as a household knight of King Edward III.[61] Nevertheless, the indications of a connection with the Berkeleys are clear. If Smyth's pedigree can be trusted, Basset's grandmother (or great-grandmother) was Margaret, daughter of the first Thomas de Berkeley (1220–43).[62] Simon's name frequently appears in

---

[58] See for example *Feud. Aids*, ii, 265. The FitzNichols of Hill and Nympsfield were also a junior branch of the main family. Thomas de Berkeley of Berkeley acquired the manors of Beverstone and Kingsweston from Thomas Apadam in 1330.

[59] S.C.8/157/7832, printed below Appendix one, no. 2.

[60] Bod. Lib. microfilms bk. 10, fos. iii, ix, xxvii, xli, lvii, lviiid.

[61] *Cal. Mem. Rolls 1326–7*, p. 379; E. 36/204/86.

[62] Smyth, i, 121. The Bassets held a manor at Uley, where they were buried in

surviving accounts in the muniment room; and he went on a
campaign to France in the retinue of Sir Maurice de Berkeley.[63]
Members of the neighbouring family of le Veel of Charfield are
frequent witnesses of Berkeley charters, although they did not,
from the absence of evidence in protection lists, join the Berkeleys
on active service.[64] After the marriage at Charfield of the third
Thomas de Berkeley to Katherine, widow of Sir Peter le Veel, the
connection became firmer.[65] While formally a retainer of the
Black Prince, the second Sir Peter le Veel must have enjoyed the
favour of the baronial house in the way that the Bassets did. It is
clear then that the influence of the lord of Berkeley cannot simply
be measured in terms of the number of household knights in his
pay. The web of baronial power was more intricate and far-
reaching than that. Thus it is interesting to note by way of
comparison that in their private war with the Nevilles in the
1450s, the Percys' leading supporters among the local gentry
were not necessarily retained by indenture.[66] In this respect the
workings of power and influence locally on the Scottish Marches
in the fifteenth century differed little from the conditions in
Gloucestershire in the fourteenth.

   Much of this can be explained in terms of geography. Families
like the Veels, Bassets and Sergeants had little option but to co-
operate since they lived within the orbit of Berkeley Castle. An
indenture would merely have added formality to the connection.
It is interesting to see, however, that two of these men already
received retaining fees. Simon Basset and Peter le Veel were
retainers of distant lords, the King and the Black Prince
respectively, who might be able to wield only limited influence
within the shire to the advantage of their dependants. This was
not necessarily a substitute for the good lordship of Thomas de
Berkeley. Local gentry therefore were linked to him not only by
deeds of indenture but also by common interests.

   In the middle years of the century another local retinue

---

the North Chapel of the church ('Uley Old Church', *Gloucestershire Notes &
Queries*, v (1891–3), 105).
   [63] Smyth, i, 251.
   [64] Bod. Lib. microfilm bk. 10, fo. xiv; Jeayes nos. 461, 493.
   [65] *G.E.C.*, ii, 130.
   [66] J.M.W. Bean, *The Estates of the Percy Family, 1416–1537* (Oxford, 1958),
p. 97.

centred upon the person of a successful captain in the French
wars who was a neighbour and ally of the Berkeleys. Sir Thomas
de Bradeston's importance derived not from the long-standing
territorial importance of his family in the county but from his
career as a soldier and counsellor to Edward III. Indeed, the
origins of his family are obscure. They probably lived at
Breadstone, near Berkeley, and one Robert de Bradeston often
witnessed charters at the castle in the opening years of the
century.[67] The family fortunes were founded by Thomas who
rose to be a King's banneret, and was summoned to parliament
from 1347 to 1360, the year of his death.[68] But Thomas was the
only member of the family to be so honoured; by the end of the
century the Bradestons had settled down to be country gentry at
the manor of Winterbourne which had been Thomas's seat.
From the protections it is possible to identify some of the knights
who were regular followers of Bradeston. Many of the permanent
retainers, such as the brothers John and Robert de Apperley,
came from Gloucestershire, or from Somerset;[69] and those who
resided elsewhere usually had connections with Gloucestershire.
John de Eylesford who resided at Tullington (Heref.) inherited a
manor in the village of Westbury (Gloucs.); while from Wiltshire
came Walter de Pavely whose sister Thomas de Bradeston had
married.[70] More familiar, though, are the knights whose names
appear also in the retinue lists of the Berkeleys: Sir John de
Palton, the Somerset knight who fought in the retinue of Maurice
de Berkeley in the 1340s, transferred to Thomas's company at the
siege of Calais in 1347 after Maurice's death there on 12
February.[71] Sir Edmund de Clivedon and members of the
Gurney family also appear under both lords, while William de
Cheltenham often acted as Bradeston's attorney.[72] Bradeston's
retinue was as closely linked to that of the Berkeleys in the middle
years of the century as that of the Berkeleys themselves had been

[67] Bod. Lib. microfilms bk. 10, fos. xvd, xxixd, xxxv, xxxviii, xli, xliid, slviii.
[68] R. Austin, 'Notes on the Family of Bradeston', 279–86; G.E.C., ii, 273.
[69] C.81/1721/26, 27, 30, 31.
[70] C.81/1721/26, 27, 30, 31; C.76/22 m. 5; C.81/1760/69. For the lands which
a later John de Eylesford held in 1396 see Gloucs. Inqs. post Mortem, vi, 194–5.
[71] In 1346 John de Palton was in Maurice de Berkeley's retinue (C.76/22
m.3); after Maurice's death at Calais on 12 February 1347 he was to be found in
the retinue of Bradeston (C.76/24 m. 4).
[72] C.81/1721/26–28, 30, 31; C.76/18 m. 13.

to Aymer de Valence between 1297 and 1317.[73] But the overlap
was not confined to the military followings of the two lords, for
John Clyve, Bradeston's steward in 1347, was at the same time
constable of the liberty of Berkeley.[74] The evidence permits us to
trace something of the personal friendship between Sir Thomas
and Sir Maurice de Berkeley which lay beneath these administrative connections. Both Bradeston and Sir Maurice de Berkeley
were King's bannerets.[75] Of this Maurice, says Smyth, 'Also was
Thomas de Bradeston his unseparable companion in Armes'.[76]
After Maurice's death before the walls of Calais in 1347 Thomas
erected to his memory the great east window of St Peter's Abbey,
Gloucester, which has been dated on heraldic grounds to c.1348–
50.[77] The Berkeleys were always able to rely on the friendship
and co-operation of this veteran of the French wars; but there is
no evidence to suggest that this relationship ever took the form of
an indenture. Perhaps there was no need.

Bradeston did not enjoy the jurisdictional power wielded by
the Berkeleys. But the mischief that could be done by even a
minor magnate is shown by a petition against Bradeston in the
name of the people of the King's Barton by Gloucester. After
narrating a blood-curdling crime said to have been committed by
his *vadlet*, Piers de St. Comb, the petitioners complain of Lady
Bradeston and her steward, Hugh Arlos, who were said to have a
hand in every dispute in the county; if Bradeston were not so close
to the King a thousand petitions would be presented against him.
At court he is like a little saint, in his own country, like a raging
lion.[78] On the one hand, the warmth of his friendship with
Maurice de Berkeley is testimony of the qualities which Thomas
undoubtedly possessed; on the other, he and his wife permitted,

---

[73] Thomas de Berkeley and his son Maurice had been retained by Aymer de
Valence (Phillips, *Aymer de Valence*, p. 261).

[74] Just. 3/131 mm. 6d, 9d.

[75] E.36/203 f. 119; E.36/204 f. 86. Thomas de Bradeston was a *scutifer* of the
King's household in 1328 (*Cal. Mem. Rolls 1326–7*, p. 374). By 1334 he was a
knight (Brit. Lib. MS Nero C. viii fo. 223). In July 1330 Sir Maurice de
Berkeley was retained to stay with the King for life, supplying fourteen men-at-
arms in time of war (*Cal. Pat. Rolls 1327–30*, p. 530).

[76] Smyth, i, 254.

[77] C. Winston, 'An Account of the Painted Glass in the East Window of
Gloucester Cathedral', *Archaeological Journal*, xx (1863), 326.

[78] S.C.8/97/4826, reproduced in Appendix I, no. 3.

even if, on the most generous interpretation, they did not actively
encourage, thuggery and violence. The contrast is stark; but it is
far from unique in the history of the middle ages.

The composition of their retinue was a reflection of the
territorial power of the house of Berkeley. If most of their
household knights were drawn from Gloucestershire and
Somerset, yet such was the prestige of the family, several of whom
achieved distinction in the French wars of Edward III, that they
attracted the service of men from further afield. But the picture
has to be put in perspective: it is worth emphasizing that at no
time were more than eight or nine knights in Gloucestershire
likely to have been feed retainers of the Berkeleys, when upwards
of forty gentry families resided in the shire. To whom, then, did
other knights and esquires turn if they sought the favour and
protection that went with the receipt of a magnate's livery? This
question takes us away from the Berkeleys to consider as a whole
the structure of retaining in fourteenth century Gloucestershire.
The evidence upon which this analysis is based is tabulated in
Appendix III.

The evidence suggests that it was usually to a local lord that a
knight would turn. Of the lords who were resident in Gloucestershire in this period, Thomas de Bradeston and the Berkeleys have
already been noticed. But in the first two decades another
important family was that of Giffard of Brimpsfield.[79] John
Giffard played an active part in the baronial wars of Henry III's
reign, and through marriages to two wealthy wives in succession
he acquired wide estates in Gloucestershire and Wiltshire. The
family became extinct on the execution of his son, John 'the
Rich', after the battle of Boroughbridge in 1322. After the failure
of the rebellion in 1322 a retainer of his, Thomas de Brocworth,
complained that he was being falsely indicted for involvement
simply because he received robes from the contrariant, John
Giffard.[80] No doubt, Brocworth was only one of several Gloucestershire men who had been dependants of Giffard, but his is the
only name to have come down to us.

Other magnates who took Gloucestershire men into their pay
were the lords of the Welsh Marches. At Goodrich, across the

---

[79] For this family see H. M. Cam, *Liberties and Communities in Medieval England*
(Cambridge, 1944), pp. 128–31, where a pedigree is given.
[80] S.C.8/112/5564.

river Wye from Gloucestershire, was the castle of the Talbot family who inherited Aymer de Valence's estates in the county.[81] Richard Talbot, steward of Edward III's household from 1345 to 1349, married Elizabeth, daughter of John Comyn by Joan, Aymer de Valence's sister.[82] One of their retainers in Gloucestershire, Sir Ralph Bluet of Daglingworth, appears to have served both Richard Talbot and his father Gilbert over a period of at least fifteen years in the 1330s and 1340s.[83] Bluet held land in the Talbots' own county of Hereford, too, and it is noticeable that the estates of three other men in the service of the Talbots, Sir John Greyndour, Sir Ralph de Abenhall and Sir Thomas Moigne, were located in the west of Gloucestershire, where the influence of the Marcher lords was likely to be strongest.[84] John Talbot, of the branch of the family which resided at Richard's Castle, again in Herefordshire, had at least one dependant in Gloucestershire. William Maunsell, whom Talbot asked to be excused from serving on a commission of array in 1352, held the manors of Frampton and Lyppiatt near Stroud.[85]

Some of the Marcher lords were of more than local importance. The Despensers and the Mortimers of Wigmore, themselves extensive landowners in the Marches of Wales, were nevertheless actors on the stage of national politics, sufficiently powerful to draw men from beyond the area of their direct territorial influence. The elder Despenser, who held only a single manor in the county before 1322, had at least one Gloucestershire retainer in William de Dene of Mitcheldean, who was his steward.[86] Despenser's son, however, acquired extensive interests in the county through his marriage to Eleanor, one of the heiresses of Gilbert de Clare, earl of Gloucester, and these in turn were swollen after 1322 by the confiscated lands of the

---

[81] Aymer de Valence had held Painswick, Moreton Valence and Whaddon (Phillips, *Aymer de Valence*, p. 336). The Talbots already held the manor of Longhope in their own right.

[82] *G.E.C.*, xii, i, 611–14.   [83] E.159/112 m. 103d; C76/25 m. 16.

[84] Sir Ralph de Abenhall held manors at Blaisdon, Littledean and Abenhall which passed by marriage to the Greyndour family. Sir Thomas Moigne held Taynton near Newent.

[85] S.C.1/41/105.

[86] *Rot. Parl.*, ii, 406; *Sir Christopher Hatton's Book of Seals*, ed. L. C. Loyd & D. M. Stenton (Oxford, 1950), no. 127.

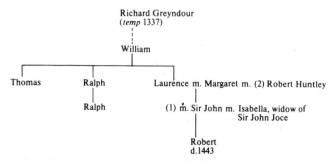

Greyndour of Hadnock

Contrariants.[87] A petition from one Gilbert Masynton of Hardwicke complained of the conduct of John le Boteler of Llantwit, who was described as steward of the younger Despenser in the counties of Stafford, Worcester and Gloucester.[88] According to another petitioner of about 1327, John de Hampton, who served as sheriff of Gloucester from 1318 to 1323, was one of the chief counsellors of Despenser.[89] Despite the debacle of 1326–7, the Despensers still remained influential in Gloucestershire, where their most important manor was Tewkesbury.[90] At the end of the century Thomas Despenser, earl of Gloucester, had a number of retainers in the county, two of whom, John Brouning and Robert Pointz, held office locally during the years of Richard II's 'tyranny'.[91]

It was John of Gaunt in the 1380s and 1390s who drove the biggest inroad into the dominance of local magnates like the Berkeleys, Talbots or Despensers. Although the territorial preponderance of the Duchy of Lancaster lay rather in the Midlands and North, Gaunt held manors in Gloucestershire at Rodley and Minsterworth, west of the Severn, and Kempsford on the border

[87] The lands held in Gloucestershire by the two Despensers are detailed in E.142/33 mm. 1,2.
[88] Rot. Parl., ii, 385.   [89] S.C.8/66/3288.
[90] The Choir of Tewkesbury Abbey, where the Despensers were buried, was rebuilt by them between 1318 and 1320, and 1332 and the 1340s (R. Morris, 'Tewkesbury Abbey, the Despenser Mausoleum', Trans. Bristol & Gloucs. Arch. Soc., xciii (1974), 142–55).
[91] Cal. Pat. Rolls 1391–6, p. 510; Cal. Close Rolls 1399–1402, p. 306.

with Wiltshire. Some of the men whom Gaunt retained in the county held local posts in his administration. Thomas de Bridges, who is also found in the service of Edward Despenser and the earl of Warwick, was lieutenant to Richard de Burley, the duke's steward in Gloucestershire.[92] John Sergeant of Stone, a neighbour of the Berkeleys, was receiver of Monmouth.[93] Several members of the Greyndour family,[94] from Hadnock on the edge of the Forest of Dean, rose in the service of John of Gaunt, and became of some consequence in Gloucestershire. Thomas Greyndour was receiving an annuity of 10 marks from Gaunt in 1364. His brother Ralph accompanied Gaunt on his chevauchee in 1371 and was appointed keeper of Skenfrith Castle, and Ralph's son, another Ralph, held the same post at Whitecastle. Laurence Greyndour, Thomas's second brother, married the heiress of Sir Ralph de Abenhall, and in 1363 took a twelve year lease on part of Gaunt's demesne at Monmouth.[95] Members of some of Gloucestershire's most well-established families, too, are found in Gaunt's retinue. On 5 May, 1381, Thomas de Berkeley of Coberley and John Giffard of Leckhampton entered into indentures with Gaunt, and ten years later they were joined by Maurice de Berkeley of Uley, one of the wealthiest knights in the county.[96]

But Gaunt's prominence was exceptional; only the King could match his capacity to retain men in every shire. At any time the King would have perhaps two or three feed men in Gloucestershire, such as the bannerets Maurice de Berkeley and Thomas de Bradeston or the knights, Simon Basset and John Pauncefot.[97] However, it has already been noticed that some of

[92] John of Gaunt's Register, 1379–83, i, ed. E. Lodge & R. Somerville (Camden Soc., 3rd Series, lvi, 1937), nos. 70, 644.
[93] Ibid., nos. 75, 657.   [94] K.B.27/424 Rex m. 12d.
[95] R. R. Davies, 'The Bohun and Lancaster Lordships in Wales in the Fourteenth and Early Fifteenth Centuries' (Oxford D.Phil. thesis, 1965), pp. 206–8. I am grateful to Professor Davies for permission to use his thesis. The pedigree corrects that printed by Maclean in Trans. Bristol & Gloucs. Arch. Soc., vi (1881–2). See also below, pp. 82, 179–80, 246.
[96] Ibid., nos. 35–6; N.B. Lewis, 'Indentures of Retinue with John of Gaunt, Duke of Lancaster, Enrolled in Chancery' (Camden 4th series, i, 1964), 103.
[97] For Berkeley and Bradeston see above p. 77. Basset had been retained to serve in the King's household by 1330 when he was a scutifer (Cal. Mem. Rolls 1326–7, p. 379). He was a household knight by 1337 (N. B. Lewis, 'A Contract

those retained in the King's household were also in receipt of fees from local lords like Berkeley.[98] If a knight wished to secure his interests locally, he was well advised not only to take a fee from the King but also to join the retinue of the lord who was dominant in the shire. For example, the royal knight, Sir John Greyndour, who was amply rewarded by Henry IV with grants of lands in South Wales, was retained also by Gilbert Talbot and Thomas de Berkeley.[99] To be retained as a household knight of the King was not regarded as an effective substitute for good lordship closer at hand.

The picture then is of a society where the connections were of a predominantly local nature. A lord attracted to his service gentlemen who lived in the area where he was territorially dominant, which even in the case of an important magnate such as the earl of Warwick could be confined to only a few counties. 'Bastard feudalism' consisted of connections between lords and the knights who resided in the locality, superimposed on which was a thin pattern of more distant ties between magnates of the first rank and gentry in nearly every county of England. This suggests that the horizons of most of the knights were surprisingly narrow. Those who were not retained at all scarcely had reason to travel outside their own county except on business; while those who were retainers did not usually have to travel far when they attended their lords in accordance with the terms of their contract. On the other hand, knights called upon to serve in their lords' retinues could find themselves fighting on campaigns in Scotland, France or Gascony. Overall the impression remains that gentle society in the fourteenth century was still very localized. That knights should have looked to neighbouring magnates suggests that they thought in terms of local communities, and that they sought to take advantage of magnate influence which was probably quite important in the politics of the shire. Thus the structure of 'bastard feudalism' invites in its turn a consideration of the interests that bound lord and dependant together.

Army', *Bull. Inst. Hist. Res.*, xxxvii (1964), 10). John Pauncefot appears as a King's knight in the reign of Henry IV (*Cal. Pat. Rolls 1399–1401*, pp. 196, 426).
   [98] See above, p. 75.
   [99] Smyth, ii, 23; *Cal. Pat. Rolls 1396–9*, p. 138; *1399–1401*, pp. 10, 249.

The earliest surviving indenture dates from 1278.[100] But the practice of making life indentures may have antedated that by some years. If the precise origins of retaining by indenture still remain shrouded in mystery, there is reason to believe that its rise in popularity in the later thirteenth century may be connected with contemporary changes in society, notably in military organization. Historians are probably right to seek the ancestry of the life indenture in the contract by which a lord or captain raised a retinue to serve in war for a limited period. From the beginning the feudal host had been supplemented by men who had made an oral or written agreement, and by the late thirteenth century the written contract was being used regularly to embody undertakings for non-feudal service. But it was not the military need alone which led magnates to surround themselves with a permanent body of knights. An annual retaining fee for life was hardly necessary when a short-term contract would suffice. One point of view was put by N. B. Lewis who stressed that: 'the indentured retinue played an important part in, and made a valuable contribution to, the working of . . . the contract army. . . . Its numbers may not have been large in proportion to the total size of any troop, but it was at least a nucleus around which less stable elements could collect'.[101] Equally noticeable, however, is the constantly shifting composition of the contingents that were led off to war. On the evidence of the numerous Berkeley protections from the first twenty years of the century only Thomas de Gurney and William de Wauton could be relied on regularly to serve in war.[102] Many names appear in the lists for only one or two campaigns. Nor were the Berkeleys in any way exceptional: in the expeditionary force which Humphrey de Bohun, earl of Hereford, led in 1371, consisting of thirty-one knights, forty-six men-at-arms and 100 archers, only six of the knights can be identified with fair probability as permanent retainers.[103] Such examples emphasize that a lord with a

---

[100] M. Jones, 'An Indenture between Robert, Lord Mohaut, and Sir John de Bracebridge for life service in peace and war, 1310', *Jnl. Soc. Archivists*, vol. 4, no. 5 (1972), 384–94.

[101] N. B. Lewis, 'The Organisation of Indentured Retinues', pp. 31, 33–4.

[102] C.81/1720/79; C.67/12 m. 5; C.67/14 m. 9; C.67/15 m. 10.

[103] G. A. Holmes, *The Estates of the Higher Nobility in Fourteenth-Century England* (Cambridge, 1957), p. 80.

glittering war record could assemble a retinue on short-term contracts without having to rely unduly on his own permanent retainers.

It is more likely, then, that magnates kept their corps of household knights and esquires with a view to peacetime, not wartime, conditions. K. B. McFarlane was probably near the truth when he said that the purpose of a retinue was 'to secure attendance of a sufficient following about the lord's person when he was resident in England'.[104] Such a requirement was not novel to the fourteenth century. In the reign of King John the abbot of Westminster was travelling around with an entourage comparable to that which accompanied the King himself.[105] The secular magnate, too, in the twelfth and early thirteenth centuries was surrounded by his retinue. His charters were witnessed by the *pares* or military vassals. By the fourteenth century, when the tie of land had weakened, these men were replaced by the knightly retainers whose dependence on a magnate was of a personal not a tenurial nature. Just as the standing of a feudal lord in the twelfth century was measured by the number and quality of his enfeoffed knights, so the reputation of a magnate in the fourteenth century turned on the size and magnificence of his liveried retinue. The importance of aristocratic display in medieval society has long been recognized by historians. The numbers mentioned by Smyth suggest that to the Berkeleys the size of the retinue was regarded almost as an end in itself. In the time of the second Thomas (1281–1321), he says that 'the household and standinge domesticall family of this lord, lodged in house, consisted of 200 persons and upwards'.[106] By the middle of the fourteenth century the retinue of the third Thomas was still larger: 'the knights that had wages by the day and their double liveries of gowns furred were usually twelve, often more, each of them two servants and a garcion page, and allowances for the like number of horses. The esquires that also had wages by the day, each of them one man and a page, and allowance in like manner for their horses, were twenty and fower, often more ... I am confident that the mowthes of his standing house, each day fed, were three hundred

[104] McFarlane, *The Nobility of Later Medieval England*, pp. 104–5.
[105] F. M. Stenton, *The First Century of English Feudalism* (Oxford, 2nd edn., 1961). pp. 72–3.
[106] Smyth, i, 166.

at least: And in greatness of Traine this lord exceeded his grandfather'.[107] At the end of 1367, when Maurice de Berkeley was on
his death bed, a suitable escort was despatched to bring the
young Thomas back from Buckinghamshire: 'attending him
(were) three of his household knights Sir Richard de Acton, Sir
John Tracy and Sir Nicholas de Berkeley and twenty-three of his
household Esquiers (all named in his household account); the
knights were suited in their liveries of fine cloth of ray furred with
minever . . . : And the bridegroom himself was in scarlet and
sattin and a silver girdle'.[108] In another retinue early in the
following century failure to escort a lord was considered sufficient
reason for dismissal: this was the fate of Ralph Brit who
unsuccessfully claimed infirmity as an excuse for his failure to
ride from Dorset to Wiltshire with his lord, Sir Ivo Fitzwaryn,
when so summoned.[109] To a magnate, then, it was perhaps of
most importance that his retainers should be in full attendance
when a distinguished guest was being entertained, or when he
was making a progress of his estates.

Retainers, however, were not there solely for purposes of
ostentation. Sound counsel and some administrative ability were
also qualities which a magnate sought from the knights in his pay.
On most estates the administration hinged on a council consisting
of the lord, his officers and chosen advisers, some of whom would
have been knights.[110] The few scattered references are not clear
enough to show whether the lord of Berkeley had a formally
constituted council, the members of which were sworn by oath
and regularly paid. In 1327 a payment was made for their
attendance at a court to Thomas de Rodborough 'et alii de
consilio' of Thomas de Berkeley.[111] In 1395 William Tracy, the
sheriff of Gloucestershire, and Richard Ruyhall, who is known to
have been Berkeley's steward at approximately that time, were
said to be *de consilio* of that lord.[112] It seems, then, that there was a
council and that one of its members was the steward, but beyond
that it would be rash to generalize. A magnate whose estates were
spread over many counties would of course need to ensure that

[107] Ibid., 304.   [108] Smyth, ii, 3.
[109] McFarlane, *The Nobility of Later Medieval England*, p. 105.
[110] N. Denholm-Young, *Seignorial Administration*, pp. 25–31.
[111] Berkeley Castle S. R. 39.
[112] K.B.27/536 Rex mm. 21–21d.

influential retainers were not confined either to one area, or
employed only in the central departments of his administration.
In an age of slow communications it was impossible to direct a
great lordship effectively from the centre; administration had to
be decentralized. Thus it made good sense to divide a large estate
into bailiwicks, each under the stewardship of one of the local
gentry. Several important magnates, who resided outside the
county, protected their interests in Gloucestershire in this way by
retaining local gentry. John of Gaunt, for example, employed
Thomas de Bridges and members of the Greyndour family in his
administration.[113] The earl of Stafford's steward at Thornbury in
1388 was Sir Thomas FitzNichol from neighbouring Hill.[114] The
gentry, then, played their part in managing the estates of the
greater lords; indeed, they were among the leading beneficiaries
of the bureaucratic and rather top-heavy seignorial administration of the middle ages. It was in recognition of the tasks they
could perform locally and of the influence which they could wield
in the community of the shire that a great magnate like Gaunt
took into his pay knights and esquires who turned to him rather
than to a local lord.

In considering the history of retaining it is often helpful to
make a distinction between the secular and ecclesiastical
magnates. Most of the evidence so far considered relates to the
retinues of the former, but the necessity to protect their interests,
which led secular magnates to pay fees to members of the gentry,
was felt equally by the ecclesiastical corporations which were
such important landowners in Gloucestershire. They paid annuities to office-holders such as the sheriff: in 1310 the Prior of
Bath, who held the manor and hundred of Pucklechurch,
granted to John de Hampton, the sheriff between 1318 and 1323,
an annual pension of 20/- and one esquire's robe.[115] More
generous was the fee of £30 which Richard de Foxcote was
receiving from the Hospitallers at the end of his term of office in
1338.[116] The monks of Battle Abbey in Sussex, it has been noted,
tended to retain 'young men of well-connected gentry

---

[113] See above, p. 81.   [114] Just. 3/180 m. 16.

[115] *Two Cartularies of Bath Abbey*, ed. W. Hunt (Somerset Rec. Soc., vii, 1893),
110–1.

[116] *The Knights Hospitaller in England*, ed. L. B. Larkin (Camden Soc., 1857),
p. 208.

families'.[117] It is impossible to say how much any of the Gloucestershire monasteries spent on considerations like this: the evidence is so intermittent that only examples can be given. But it is clear that every monastery that could afford it took care to secure its interests by the granting of fees to local office-holders.

In the office of steward the monasteries, like the secular magnates, seem principally to have employed men of humbler origin than the knights. For the three Gloucestershire monastic stewards known to have been knighted there were at least seven who were drawn from below the knightly class as the appended table shows.[118] William de Tytherington, steward of Llanthony in 1346, was apparently one of the humbler holders of this office: he was not the lord of a manor. But his appearance as knight of the shire for Gloucestershire in March 1330 points to the importance which he enjoyed as a retainer of Ralph, Lord Stafford. This is the quality which explains how men like William de Cheltenham, steward of the Berkeleys, Robert Palet, steward of Sir Edward Despenser and Thomas de Bridges, a retainer of Despenser, Gaunt and Warwick came to be appointed by monasteries; it was worthwhile securing their services precisely because they already held positions of eminence. Nevertheless, such men, busy with the affairs of their employer and with the demands of county politics, must have had only limited time to devote to the administration of the estates entrusted to their stewardship. In the fourteenth century this office was not yet the sinecure it was to become in the fifteenth when it was to be offered to a local duke or earl. The duties were probably like those required of the steward of a lay magnate. An idea of the nature of the work is given in a letter written in April 1395 at the behest of Thomas de Bridges, steward of Llanthony: 268 sheep belonging to Thomas Batyn had been seized in the Prior's manor of Great Barrington by some felons, and Bridges despatched letters confirming that he had restored them to their owner.[119] However, the most important duty required of the steward was that of holding courts, and there is plenty of evidence to suggest

[117] E. Searle, *Lordship and Community: Battle Abbey and its Banlieu* (Toronto, 1974), p. 419.
[118] On monastic stewards see M. D. Knowles, *The Religious Orders in England*, ii, (Cambridge, 1955), 285.
[119] C.115/K.2/6684 f.171.

TABLE IV

Stewards of Monastic Estates in Gloucestershire

Sir Miles de Rodborough	Bishop of Worcester 1308		*Reg. Reynolds* (W.H.S.), 2.
William de Bradewell	Winchcombe Abbey 1319		*Landboc . . . de Winchelcumba*, i, 289–90.
Robert de Aston	Cirencester Abbey	1321	*Ciren. Cartulary*, i, no. 126.
William de Brocworth	Gloucester Abbey	1329	Just. 3/122 m. 5.
Richard de Hawkeslow	Westminster Abbey	1332	Just. 3/127 m. 25.
William de Cheltenham	Bishop of Worcester 1339		R. M. Haines, *Administration of the Diocese of Worcester* (London, 1965), p. 142.
Richard Vyel	Gloucester Abbey	1346	Just. 3/131 m. 13d.
William de Tytherington	Llanthony Priory	1346	Just. 3/131 m. 13d.
Sir Robert Shareshull	Westminster Abbey	1348	Just. 3/131 m. 6d.
Robert Palet	Gloucester Abbey	1373–5	Just. 3/161 m. 6; *His. & Cart. Mon. Glouc.*, iii, ed. Hart (Rolls Ser., 1867), 250.
John Brouning	Bishop of Worcester 1376		Just. 3/166 m. 4d.
Richard Urdeley	Cirencester Abbey	1388	Just. 3/180 m. 16.
Sir John Cassy	Gloucester Abbey	1389	Just. 3/180 m. 16d.
John Syre	Tewkesbury Abbey	1390	Just. 3/180 m. 26d.
Thomas de Bridges	Cirencester Abbey	1394	Just. 3/180 m. 26d.
	Llanthony Priory	1394–6	C.115/K2/6684 ff. 198d.
	Llanthony Priory	1394–6	C.115/K2/6684 ff. 171, 198d.
Richard Russell	Winchcombe Abbey 1396		Just. 3/180 m. 29.
Richard Ruyhall	Westminster Abbey	1404	Just. 3/189 m. 29.

that he presided over these in person, even if he did not pay attention to the smaller details of administration.[120] It was still worthwhile for monasteries to appoint such magnate retainers who wielded influence both in the sheriff's office at Gloucester and in the inner councils of a noble household, for they had to protect their own interests by fair means or foul; and whatever the esteem in which the religious orders were held in this period,

[120] See for example Just. 3/131 m. 6d; Just. 3/161 m. 6; Just. 3/189 m. 29.

the granting of fees and offices must surely have created a bond of common interest between the monasteries and the local gentry.[121]

No further elaboration is needed to show how the interests of lords, lay or ecclesiastical, were served by retaining local knights and esquires. And there was no shortage of aspiring recipients of magnate generosity in the distribution of fees, for a knight stood to gain many advantages from membership of a retinue. First, there was the financial benefit. One or two retainers were in receipt of very high fees indeed. Sir John de Bures received an annuity of £40 from Thomas, Earl of Lancaster, who had a reputation for paying generous fees.[122] On 9 February 1400, King Henry IV confirmed James Clifford, who was only an esquire, in his fee of £40.[123] Sir John Bromwich, admittedly an important man, received a fee of 100 marks from the Mortimer lordships of Clifford and Glasbury.[124] Such high fees were exceptional: that of Clifford can probably be explained in terms of the new King's anxiety to secure the allegiance of one of Richard II's esquires. Even so, to a poorly endowed knight a more typical fee of £10 or £20 must have been more than welcome; in an age when custom had fixed distraint at the level of £40 a fee could increase a knight's income by half as much again. On the other hand there is some indication that money may not have been the main motive. For every knight like Peter le Veel who held five or six manors and who joined a retinue there is another like Edmund de Croupes of Whittington who held only one manor and for whom there is no evidence of membership of a retinue at all. It would be wrong to overstate the case; the evidence is inadequate, and Croupes may have tried hard to find a good lord. But it does not suggest that the retaining fee itself was the main attraction.

Personal reward was to be found, therefore. But lords had to

---

[121] K. L. Wood-Legh, *Church Life under Edward III* (Cambridge, 1934), pp. 23–5, shows that gentry came into close contact with the affairs of monasteries, too, as administrators of houses temporarily brought into royal keeping. Sometimes the abbot and convent would petition the King for the appointment of men known to be friendly.

[122] G. A. Holmes, *Estates of the Higher Nobility*, p. 135.

[123] *Cal. Pat. Rolls 1399–1401*, p. 36.

[124] *Cal. Pat. Rolls 1381–5*, p. 99.

strike a balance between the largesse expected of men of their standing and the resources they had at their disposal. Largesse, therefore, had to be discriminating. The services given by a man like William de Cheltenham were never overlooked. Thomas de Berkeley conferred on him a fee of £10 6s. 4d. for life; in addition, Cheltenham was granted a rent from lands in Arlingham, the wardship of the heir of John Berkeley of Wick-by-Arlingham, with the profits of that manor, and the manors of Piriton and Little Marshfield.[125] Cheltenham, as a steward, could expect generous rewards in addition to the retainer's fee. Household knights and esquires of the King could expect to pick up wardships or grants of custody: James Clifford, already in receipt of an esquire's fee which Henry IV raised to £40, was granted custody of Braden Forest in Wiltshire.[126] In 1408 the King's knight, Sir John Greyndour of the Forest of Dean, was granted lands and rents to the value of 40 marks yearly forfeited by rebels in the lordship of Newport.[127] Other important retainers might hope to obtain such perquisities indirectly through the intercession of their good lord at court. In general, though, rewards had to be earned.

What may have been of the greatest value to a retainer was the support and patronage of a lord, which he could put to good use in a number of ways. John de Berkeley of Dursley was evidently of the opinion that receipt of Lord Berkeley's livery and robes was the key that opened the door of office-holding in Gloucestershire.[128] Men who are not identifiable as Berkeley retainers were appointed sheriff, and it is possible that Berkeley exercised his influence to the advantage of men, like Sir Simon Basset (sheriff, 1341–50), of whom he approved, but who were not necessarily in his retinue. However, in a system where the King's appointments to offices and commissions were influenced by the wishes of the magnates whose support he needed, one who enjoyed the favour of a lord was more likely to secure local office.

Less excusable was the support which a retainer might receive when involved in litigation in the courts with someone outside the retinue. Magnate interference in the working of the courts, the practice known as 'maintenance', incurred the wrath of the

[125] Smyth, i, 342.
[126] Cal. Pat. Rolls 1399–1401, p. 36.
[127] Cal. Pat. Rolls 1405–8, p. 439.   [128] S.C.8/157/7832.

Commons on many occasions.[129] In 1376 they complained that
J.P.s were often nominated 'par brocage des Meyntenours du
pays qi font grande outrage par lour meyntenance as povres
gentz du pays, et sont communement mayntenours de les
mesfesours'.[130] Support in litigation was probably the quality of
good lordship that a retainer valued most; and as corruption in
the legal system increasingly inclined men to resort to dubious
practice, so maintenance became self-generating and self-
perpetuating. John le Boteler of Llantwit was one retainer who
turned maintenance to his own ends. The Prior of St Oswald's,
Gloucester, petitioned that although a writ of trespass brought by
Boteler was being heard before justices, he had purchased a new
writ for the same trespass to be determined before Maurice de
Berkeley, his own lord. Maurice ignored letters which had been
obtained by Robert Kidderminster, a monk of St Oswald's,
cancelling the new commission, and allowed another retainer,
Walter Torel, to ravage the Priory's lands.[131] An unattached
knight who found himself maliciously indicted by a neighbour in
the pay of a powerful magnate might have little hope of redress
within his own county.

Considerations such as these explain why the gentry found it in
their interests to enter the service of a magnate. It would be
fascinating also to know more about the steps by which a young
knight or esquire set about securing a place in a retinue. In the
fifteenth century it seems that an approach could be made by
means of written correspondence: in reply to a request from Sir
William Stonor in 1478, Lord Strange wrote back, sending a
fee of 40s. until he had made up his mind whether Stonor was
worthy of a permanent fee.[132] In the absence of any similar
correspondence, the evidence for Gloucestershire is only
circumstantial. Seemingly the most odd indenture made by a
Gloucestershire knight is the one which yields most easily to
explanation. On 25 May 1306 Sir John Giffard of Weston agreed
to stay with William Greenfield, Archbishop of York, with two
esquires, two boys and six horses for the lifetime of the

[129] Rot. Parl., ii, 10, 62, 172, 201, 228, 355, 368; iii, 18, 23.
[130] Ibid., ii, 333.
[131] S.C.8/323/E563.
[132] McFarlane, The Nobility of Later Medieval England, p. 109.

Archbishop, who would give him two robes each year.[133] No fee is mentioned. Now John was the nephew of Godfrey Giffard (Bishop of Worcester, 1266–1302) and Walter Giffard (Archbishop of York, 1268–79), to whom Greenfield himself was related, and at Oxford Greenfield had received financial support from Walter.[134] Personal circumstances, then, probably explain this unusual relationship between ecclesiastical lord and dependant. Personal friendship may explain how two contemporaries who were allies and neighbours of the Berkeleys came to be retained to serve in the King's household: Simon Basset seems to have joined as an esquire shortly after, and perhaps through the patronage of, Thomas de Bradeston.[135] Another interesting sidelight is offered by the presence in John of Gaunt's *Register* of two indentures with Gloucestershire esquires. Thomas de Berkeley of Coberley and John Giffard of Leckhampton both entered into indentures with Gaunt on the same day, 5 May 1381.[136] The two men were neighbours, living within four miles of each other; and the coincidence of date suggests that they intended to enter Gaunt's service together, and made a common approach to him. Perhaps there was an agreement, not necessarily written, between these two esquires who wished to advance their careers in the retinue of the foremost magnate of the realm. How long they stayed with Gaunt is not known, but they were not among those who were transferred to the King's sole service after the death of the duke in February 1399. Thomas was then still alive, although it is possible that his companion had died in the meantime. Another Berkeley, this time Maurice, of Uley, joined Gaunt's retinue, on 2 November 1391;[137] no doubt it was helpful when applying to know someone who was already in the retinue.

'Bastard feudalism' has often received a bad press from historians who have considered it a threat to social stability in the

---

[133] *Greenfield's Register*, i, ed. A. H. Thompson (Surtees Soc., cxlv, 1931) no. 385.

[134] A. B. Emden, *A Biographical Dictionary of the University of Oxford*, ii (Oxford, 1958), 820.

[135] Thomas de Bradeston appears as a *scutifer* in the King's household in 1328 and Simon Basset, also as a *scutifer*, in 1330 (*Cal. Mem. Rolls 1326–7*, pp. 374, 379).

[136] See above, p. 81.

[137] N. B. Lewis, 'Indentures of Retinue with John of Gaunt', 103.

late middle ages. It may be worthwhile, then, to consider the question of the stabilizing influence, if any, of 'bastard feudalism' in the light of the Gloucestershire evidence. Examples have been quoted already of men who hedged their bets by accepting fees and robes from the King and from the lord of Berkeley—Sir John Greyndour, for example. Such practice is understandable when corruption and lawlessness were widespread in the localities. Certainly many others did serve more than one lord, but usually in succession and not contemporaneously. In the reigns of Edward I and his son Richard de la Rivere is the one conspicuous exception; while engaged by Aymer de Valence he was also in the service of Henry of Lancaster.[138] Towards the end of the century, however, the picture is very different. Sir John Bromwich is just one for whom the evidence permits a charge of multiple loyalties. Bromwich seems to have started his career in the service of Lionel of Clarence;[139] but after the duke's death he is found in the list of men retained by Gaunt between 1379 and 1383.[140] It was probably to protect his lands in Ireland that Bromwich then decided to join the retinue of Edmund Mortimer, earl of March. After the earl's death in 1381 he obtained confirmation of the indenture whereby he was entitled to receive a yearly rent of 100 marks from the Mortimer lordships during the minority of Edmund's heirs.[141] One can only speculate whether Mortimer's patronage was associated with the appointment of Bromwich as Justiciar of Ireland, in 1379.[142] Unfortunately it is not possible to say how long Bromwich maintained his dual allegiance to both Lancaster and the Mortimers before his death in about 1389.[143] A contemporary of Bromwich, Thomas de Bridges was in Gaunt's retinue at the same time as he was serving the Despensers at Tewkesbury, first as steward, then as receiver.[144] How long he remained with Gaunt is not clear, but in the 1390s he found yet another 'good lord', for he is found as the earl of Warwick's steward of Chedworth between 1391 and 1395.[145] His prede-

[138] Phillips, *Aymer de Valence*, pp. 256–7.
[139] *Cal. Pat. Rolls 1370–4*, p. 87.
[140] *John of Gaunt's Register, 1379–83*, i, 9.
[141] *Cal. Close Rolls 1381–5*, p. 59; *Cal. Pat. Rolls 1381–5*, p. 99.
[142] *Cal. Pat. Rolls 1377–81*, p. 380.
[143] *Cal. Pat. Rolls 1388–92*, p. 100.
[144] K.B.27/471 Rex m. 9d; E.101/511/28; and see above, p. 81.
[145] Just. 3/180 mm. 21d, 26d.

cessor as steward of Chedworth was Richard Ruyhall, who combined this work for the earl of Warwick with his membership of the retinue of Thomas de Berkeley.[146] The Gloucestershire evidence confirms the general impression that by the reign of Richard II men were more disposed to collect fees from a number of lords. The courtier, Sir William Bagot, for example was retained by the King, the earl of Warwick and the earl of Nottingham.[147] If retaining had once contributed a degree of stability, that had largely disappeared by the end of the fourteenth century when allegiance was readily being given to several lords at once.

Before these later decades, though, 'bastard feudalism' can be viewed in a more favourable light. The evidence suggests that retainers adhered to a single lord, and if a transfer of allegiance did occur it was as the result of exceptional circumstances. A couple of examples may be quoted. Before 1322 John le Boteler of Llantwit was in the Berkeley retinue, but with a shrewd sense of where his interests would best be served he then transferred to the service of the younger Despenser.[148] Boteler is thus open to the charge of disloyalty; but the conflict of loyalties which he faced, that is, between King and lord, is one that severed many friendships, notably that between Sir Robert Holand and Thomas of Lancaster.[149] Miles de Rodborough was another knight in these years who served two lords, but definitely not at the same time. In a letter of 1304 Roger Bigod, earl of Norfolk, asked for letters of protection for Miles de Rodborough, then his steward in Ireland.[150] Miles did not rush into a new connection as soon as Bigod died in 1306; but on 20 August 1313, the year before he was murdered, he was admitted as a knight of the King's household.[151] Although the evidence is incomplete, and conclusions can be no more than tentative, there does seem to be an absence for the first half of the fourteenth century at least of those shifting relationships that have led some writers to complain of the unstable nature of 'bastard feudalism'.

[146] Just. 3/180 m. 27; C.115/K.2/6684 f. 166.
[147] A. Goodman, *The Loyal Conspiracy* (London, 1971), pp. 148, 151, 159–64.
[148] S.C.8/323/E563; *Rot. Parl.*, ii, 385.
[149] J. R. Maddicott, 'Thomas of Lancaster and Sir Robert Holand', *Eng. Hist. Rev.*, lxxxvi (1971), 466–7.
[150] S.C.1/28/48.   [151] E.101/375/8 m. 33.

Indeed, there are many examples of very long service to a lord by his retainers. Sir William de Wauton, who accompanied the Berkeleys to Flanders in 1297, was still in their service thirty years later.[152] William de Gamage, who fought at Falkirk in the retinue of the Berkeleys in 1298, was in attendance on the third Thomas de Berkeley in 1329.[153] Sir John de la Rivere had been in the service of Aymer de Valence for seventeen years by the time of his death at Bannockburn in 1314.[154] Moreover, there are a few examples of devoted service by several generations of one family. John Smyth noted with admiration how both William and John Tracy, father and son, had served as knights in the Berkeley household, and in the 1380s and 1390s John's son, another William, added a third generation of service.[155] Similarly, two generations of the de la Mare family served Henry of Grosmont.[156] Places in a retinue were not hereditary, and they could not automatically be passed on from father to son; but loyalty, like merit, was a quality which earned its reward.

Moreover there is another beneficial aspect of 'bastard feudalism' which must not be overlooked. A retainer would look to his lord to assist in the settlement of disputes. In this way their escalation could be avoided. Arguably, this stabilizing influence was less effective by the period of the Wars of the Roses, when the magnates found themselves unable to control their own supporters, but Smyth speaks of the obligations which the third Thomas de Berkeley (1326–61) felt towards his retainers: 'to Acton and Clivedon, two of his servants that contended in a title of land, the better to compose their controversy, he gave twenty pound'.[157] Bitter feelings here were soothed by an act of generosity. The evil of maintenance represented a debasement of the system; but working at its best it could prevent disputes from reaching courts already clogged with litigation.

One aspect of the relationship of lord and retainer remains to be considered: what means were open to the aggrieved party if he

---

[152] C.67/12 m. 3; C.71/11 m. 6; Bod. Lib. microfilms, bk. 10 fos. xxxi–xxxid.
[153] Gough, *Scotland in 1298*, p. 218; Berkeley Castle S.R. 61, 62.
[154] Gough, *Scotland in 1298*, p. 216; Phillips, *Aymer de Valence*, pp. 75, 296.
[155] Smyth, i, 305; K.B.27/536mm. 21–21d.
[156] Fowler, *Henry of Grosmont*, pp. 217, 284 n. 40.
[157] Smyth, i, 346.

felt that the terms of the indenture of retinue had not been fulfilled? About the legal status of the indenture hardly anything is known. Indeed, there is little evidence to show whether failure to honour its terms was generally regarded as actionable at law: for a lord who was not satisfied that a retainer was earning his fee had no need to resort to litigation. He could simply cut off the fee. As McFarlane has shown, in 1402 Sir Ivo Fitzwaryn stopped payment of a fee to Ralph Brit, an esquire of his who declined to accompany his lord on a progress from Dorset to Wiltshire.[158] In an attempt to recover his fee Brit sued Fitzwaryn for novel disseisin. If in theory default might lie with either of the contracting parties, it was in practice really the retainer who would need to invoke the protection of the law against the action of his lord.

New light is shed on the problem of enforceability by a case, heard before the justices of assize at Gloucester in August 1320, which is probably the earliest recorded example of legal proceedings initiated by a retainer against his lord. Sir Nicholas de Kingston of Tortworth alleged that Sir Alan Plokenet of Kilpeck had disseised him of an annual 'rent' of two robes lined with fur which he was to receive for Plokenet's lifetime, assigned on the manor of Syston, near Pucklechurch.[159] Kingston showed a certain writing of Plokenet's, presumably the indenture, and claimed seven years' arrears of his robes, which were said to be worth £5 13s. 4d. per annum. Plokenet did not bother to appear in court, and Kingston was granted the right to distrain on the possessions of his former lord. Kingston had employed the assize of novel disseisin, which entitled a plaintiff to recover a free

---

[158] McFarlane, *The Nobility of Later Medieval England*, pp. 105–6.

[159] K.B.27/246m. 136d, printed below in Appendix 1, no. 1. Alan Plokenet served in Scotland in 1300, 1303, and was summoned regularly thereafter until 1319. He had been knighted in May 1306 at the Feast of Swans. He was summoned to parliament in December 1311. He died shortly before 6 September 1325, and was buried at Abbey Dore (Heref.), of which he had been a benefactor. He was a man of violent temper: when the Bishop of Bath and Wells wrote to summon him to explain why he had buried his mother elsewhere than in Sherborne Abbey, which was her testamentary direction, he is said to have made the messenger eat the letter with the wax. He was twice excommunicated. The family resided at Kilpeck (Heref.). Alan's father had served as a banneret in Wales in 1295 under the Earl of Pembroke (*G.E.C.*, x, 552–5).

tenement of which he had been unlawfully disseised. In 1285 the Statute of Westminster II had extended the definition of what constituted a free tenement to include corrodies and annual payments of grain, food, or other 'necessaries' if these were bound to be paid in some fixed place.[160] By 1320 the definition of a free tenement had widened, presumably as a result of judicial decision, to cover retaining fees, and the assize of novel disseisin was still being used to recover a fee nearly a century later. But the absence of evidence in between suggests that litigation between parties to indentures was not common.

'Bastard feudalism' has been the subject of much critical attention by historians, and the workings of the system are now fairly clear; but no attempt has ever been made to estimate the extent of its hold on society. It remains in conclusion, then, to consider how many of the gentry may have been received within the fold of the indentured retinues.

Appendix III shows those knights and richer esquires resident in Gloucestershire in each generation who were retained, assuming a generation to be about twenty-five years.[161] Taken at face value, the evidence suggests that between a third and a half of the gentry were retained by magnates: 17 out of 45 in 1300, 17 out of 44 in 1325, 16 out of 45 in 1350, 14 out of 40 in 1375 and 16 out of about 37 at the end of the century.

Before considering the implications of these figures, allowance must be made for the incomplete nature of the evidence. The sources here are particularly hard to handle. Because evidence survives to show the connections between lords and some of the gentry, it is easy to argue that other sources must once have existed to illustrate and prove the connections between lords and all of the gentry. This is no more than partly true. It seems likely that the tally of knights retained by the Berkeleys in the opening decade of the century is about complete; but it is fair to add that the retinue is far less amply documented for the time of the fourth Thomas (1368–1417). For other lords likely to have retained some men in Gloucestershire there is very little evidence: John Giffard of Brimpsfield, for example. Some of the sources by which retainers may be identified became less plentiful by the end of the

[160] D. W. Sutherland, *The Assize of Novel Disseisin* (Oxford, 1973), pp. 135–6.
[161] See below pp. 270–92.

century: petitions became fewer, and it seems no longer to have been the practice to enrol protections regularly. For these reasons the lists of retainers in 1375 and 1400 are likely to be more incomplete than those for 1300 and 1325. One other problem must be recognized: the bias in the surviving evidence shows the King, John of Gaunt and the lord of Berkeley enjoying a pre-eminence in retaining that in reality may have been less pronounced. It is easy to lose sight of lesser lords like the Giffards of Brimpsfield simply because evidence of their retinues has not survived in any quantity. Yet these were men of importance in the shire. In local politics a small number of well-placed retainers might count for more than a large number scattered all over the country.

It would be impossible to make an accurate allowance for the margin of error. But it has to be accepted that any figures now compiled will underestimate the number of retainers. Perhaps, then, it may be fair to guess that nearer two-thirds than one half of the gentry were retained in this period. The picture which these rough figures present is not one of a countryside in which rival armies of retainers were confronting each other. Groups of retainers were certainly concentrated in the areas of territorial dominance of their respective lords, but they were not con-centrated in such numbers as to constitute rival armies rubbing shoulders one with another. On the contrary, the retainers lived alongside many independent knights and esquires. In Gloucestershire, the lord of Berkeley, the preponderant magnate in the locality throughout the period, never took from his own county more than about eight or nine of the dozen knights that he retained. The influence of the nearest magnate to the north, the earl of Warwick, seems hardly to have extended into Gloucester-shire at all: in the 1340s he had one retainer from the north of the shire, in the 1390s just two who divided their loyalties between him and two other lords.[162] In the west the Talbots and the Despensers were the nearest lords of any consequence. And between the seats of these magnates lay tracts of countryside where no single lord held sway.

---

[162] Sir Walter Daston, who lived at either Wormington or Dumbleton, was probably a retainer of Warwick (C.67/17m. 39; Wrottesley, *Crecy and Calais*, pp. 32, 238). The two retainers in Richard II's reign were Richard Ruyhall and Thomas de Bridges (C.115/K.2/6684 f. 166; Just. 3/180mm. 21d, 26d).

Such conclusions rest heavily on *ex silentio* arguments. But a document published by K. B. McFarlane reveals the relationship between two knights, who, either by choice or by force of circumstances, were probably independent. On 5 December 1298 Sir Nicholas de Kingston and Sir William Maunsel sealed an indenture of mutual aid by which Nicholas agreed to offer William counsel, to attend upon him and to be prompt with him in all matters both in peace and in war.[163] Sir William agreed to do the same for his colleague. In fact Kingston cannot yet be described as a Gloucestershire knight, for at the time this indenture was sealed his only lands lay in Berkshire. His exchange of lands in Pusey and Compton (Berks.) for William Maunsel's Gloucestershire manors of Tortworth, Redland and their appurtenances is the one documented consequence of their agreement. Because so little is known of the military careers of the two knights, it is difficult to say why they made the indenture. Both knights served in the Scottish wars of Edward I and, since they were not neighbours, it was presumably under these circumstances that they met. Neither appears regularly in the contingent of a single magnate. It is not surprising to find that Maunsel witnesses charters at Berkeley Castle, living as he did not far away.[164] But his name is present in the Berkeley protections only for the Flanders campaign of 1297.[165] There is no reason to believe, then, that he was a retainer of Berkeley or of any other lord. Nor is there any evidence that Kingston was retained. The most likely explanation is that they entered into this indenture, the terms of which are so similar to those of a normal indenture of retinue, as a mutual security pact precisely because they did not have access to the benefits of 'good lordship'.

McFarlane was able to trace nothing further about the subsequent relationship between these two knights. But proceedings which took place before the assize justices at Gloucester twenty-three years later afford eloquent proof that such a mutual agreement was not regarded as an effective substitute for the

[163] McFarlane, 'An Indenture of Agreement', pp. 200–10.
[164] Bod. Lib. microfilms, bk. 10, fos. ii, xiv, xxxd, lviid, lxvi.
[165] C.81/1720/79. Nicholas de Kingston witnessed a charter at Berkeley once, in 1304 (Jeayes, no. 470).

protection afforded by a lord.[166] By 1313 Kingston had become a
dependant of the Herefordshire lord, Sir Alan Plokenet; in that
year Plokenet ceased to pay the fee, and seven years later his
former retainer had come before the justices with an action of
novel disseisin. The terms of the indenture which Kingston had
made with Maunsel in 1298 did not preclude the admission of
either party to a retinue, should the opportunity arise. Kingston
clearly took that opportunity. The terms of the earlier indenture
may still have been operative, since Kingston lived until about
1321, and Maunsel until 1324.[167]

  It is possible, then, to find some evidence in support of the twin
propositions that some of the gentry were independent, and that
membership of a magnate retinue was still regarded by them as
an attractive prospect. The problem, rather, was that there were
too many knights chasing too few places. From the fifteenth
century there is evidence that membership of a retinue was a
prize much sought after. According to a letter in the Stonor
correspondence there was a scramble for a retainer's place on the
death of a certain William Marmion in 1474; when he asked if he
could join Lord Strange's retinue, Sir William Stonor was told
that he would be put on probation.[168] The pressure for places in a
retinue is illustrated too by a letter which Lady Alice wrote in
about 1398 to her son, Thomas, Earl of Kent, informing him that
one William Bawdewyn wanted to enter his service; she had told
Bawdewyn, she wrote, that expense prevented the Earl from
recruiting anyone for at least two years, but Bawdewyn was
evidently so eager that he offered to serve for two probationary
years before being taken on for good. Alice concluded by urging
her son to treat Bawdewyn bounteously.[169] In the Severn basin
area the retinue of the Berkeleys was the magnet that attracted
the local gentry. But the number of knights which the lord of
Berkeley retained in Gloucestershire itself is unlikely to have risen

[166] K.B.27/246m. 136d. See above pp. 134–5. This assize is transcribed
below, Appendix I, no. 1.

[167] For Maunsel's inquisition see *Gloucs. Inqs. post Mortem*, v, 189–90. No
inquisition was taken on the death of Nicholas de Kingston, whose lands passed
to the Veel family.

[168] McFarlane, *The Nobility of Later Medieval England*, p. 109.

[169] *Anglo-Norman Letters and Petitions*, ed. M. D. Legge (Anglo-Norman Text
Soc., iii, 1941), no. 186. I am indebted to Dr J. R. Maddicott for this reference.

above single figures. In a county which contained nearly forty
'knightly' families it can be appreciated, then, that competition
for a place in the retinue was fierce. Most magnates were simply not in the position to accom-
modate all who importuned them. Payment of fees imposed a
strain on the resources of even the most well-endowed magnate.
Just how great this strain could be is shown well by the financial
history of the Percy family. In 1441-2 charges of fees paid to
retainers and estate officials consumed about a third of the earl of
Northumberland's revenues in Cumberland, and in the following twelve years the total increased by about a third again; the
burden on the estates in Sussex was still heavier. By 1461 fees
consumed at least a third and possibly one half of all the gross
revenues of the earl of Northumberland.[170] Most of these were
granted for life. This massive expansion in the granting of fees
coincided with the disturbances in the North which preceded the
outbreak of the Wars of the Roses, and it would be wrong to
suppose that every lord in the fourteenth century would readily
grant fees and annuities on such a scale except perhaps in periods
of similar turbulence like the reign of Edward II. It could be
argued on *a priori* grounds, then, that magnates may have taken
on retainers, for life or at will, in greater numbers in the chaotic
second and third decades than in the more placid years of
Edward II. Towards the end of the fourteenth century the
darkening economic horizons which confronted landowners may
also have influenced the number of retaining fees which they
granted. Monasteries began to adopt a policy of retrenchment.
In contrast to their earlier practice, the monks of the wealthy
abbey of Westminster were distributing very few fees at the end of
the century.[171] The monasteries had little choice but to cut back
on the number of annuitants for they lived entirely on their
revenues from land. Access to royal patronage, however, al-
leviated the predicament of secular magnates who were worried
by a static or falling landed income. It seems unlikely that they

---

[170] J. M. W. Bean, *The Estates of the Percy Family*, p. 94.

[171] For this information I am grateful to Miss B. F. Harvey. For the practice
of retaining royal justices, which came to an end in the reign of Richard II, see
J. R. Maddicott, 'Law and Lordship: Royal Justices as Retainers in Thirteenth
and Fourteenth Century England', (*Past and Present* Supplement, 4, 1978). See
also below, p. 251.

were forced to reduce the size of their retinues. Retrenchment in the short term would have been difficult anyway when so many of the recipients of fees were retained for life. McFarlane argued in addition that there was no secular slump because wealth married wealth.[172] The history of the Berkeley family illustrates his case. Thomas de Berkeley's acquisition of the Lisle inheritance, which followed his childhood marriage to the heiress Margaret Lisle, ensured that his family would not have to worry about any fall in their income from land. Indeed he took into his pay some men who would once have looked to the Lisles. The size of a lord's retinue, then, was not directly determined by fluctuations in the level of landed income, but the revenues at his disposal did impose a rough upper limit: in normal times a lord would probably not wish to spend more than about a third of his gross revenue on retaining fees.

The conclusion that there were numerous unattached gentry is consistent with the evidence afforded by the records of parliament. There were frequent denunciations of maintenance and demands for reform. In 1351 the Commons petitioned the King to keep the peace and to eradicate the maintenance of evildoers and breakers of the peace; the statutes for the keeping of the peace should be strictly enforced.[173] In the reign of Richard II they were more virulent than ever. In the first parliament of 1390 the Commons reminded the King of the complaints they made at Cambridge about the activities of liveried retainers; they were still awaiting a settlement of this question.[174] In 1393 they were complaining that men of little means wore liveries within the realm and practised maintenance.[175] When pressing the King for legislation the Commons were speaking on behalf of gentry angry at the abuse of courts through maintenance, because they themselves were at the receiving end of such abuse. On this issue at least they did not see eye to eye with the magnates; indeed, the desire was to limit their influence.

Such grievances reflect the mentality of a gentry class composed of many independent men who found their interests threatened by the abuse of maintenance. They were not opposed in principle to retaining: many were in retinues, and some at least

---

[172] McFarlane, *The Nobility of Later Medieval England*, p. 59.
[173] *Rot. Parl.*, ii, 228.   [174] Ibid., iii, 265.
[175] Ibid., iii, 307.

of those who were not sought to be. But the opposition to the abuses of magnate power is more understandable once it is accepted that the retainers who benefited and the knights and esquires who suffered came from the same 'class'; and it was that 'class' that was represented in and by the Commons. The advocates of the J.P.s, of sheriffs of substantial means, of the enforcement of the common law, included independent gentry sufficient in number to make their voice heard in parliament.

Any attempt to estimate the place of retaining in fourteenth-century society is bound to be hazardous. It involves, first, an estimate of the value of our surviving sources: for while they highlight the abuses, they rarely show the system working at its best. The picture is one-sided. The term 'bastard feudalism' itself, though a popular and expressive shorthand, is pejorative in tone. It carries the implication that the tie of money between lord and dependant was less stable, more shifting than the tie of land between lord and vassal in the age of classic feudalism. At the close of the century, the careers of Thomas de Bridges in Gloucestershire and Sir William Bagot and John Willicotes elsewhere suggest that retainers were protecting themselves by acceptance of fees from several lords at once; but if this practice continued to grow in the reign of Henry IV it was as a consequence of the political uncertainty of the times. There is simply not the evidence from the twelfth or thirteenth centuries to allow us to say whether social relationships in the later middle ages were more unstable than before. Tenurial links had never been straightforward. The concept of liege homage in Anglo-Norman feudalism had to be introduced because knights held land of more than one lord, and as tenures became increasingly complicated in the twelfth and thirteenth centuries vassalage became unreal. Equally it would be wrong to argue that it was the money fee alone that bound a retainer to his lord; it was. as much a relationship based on common interest.

Little ingenuity would be required to make out a case that gentry feuds, corruption in local government and abuse of magnate power were all aggravated by retaining. Corruption, however, was nothing new. It was ever present under the Normans and Angevins. The holders of local office, the sheriffs and castellans, were generally mightier, and probably therefore more menacing, than they were under the three Edwards. The eyre was developed as a means of controlling official misconduct and lawlessness in the shires, but the hundred rolls of 1274–5 reveal that the scene bore many of the features associated with fourteenth century England. To consider here the allied questions of corruption and lawlessness in the middle ages would be to stray far from the theme of retaining; but while it is safe to admit that some knights owed their continued immunity from the law to the cloak of magnate protection it would be naive to reduce the phenomenon of gentry lawlessness simply to these terms. The failure of the courts of common law to cope adequately with the increasing volume of litigation is probably more important.[176] Fourteenth-century England was a society, the government of which, though highly developed by medieval standards, nevertheless did not command the services of an army of dependent officials; on the contrary, it could do no more than rely for the implementation of its will on the co-operation of the gentry. Corruption and abuse of power, it is scarcely an exaggeration to say, were endemic in such a pre-industrial society. It is hard to believe that sheriffs, escheators and coroners who were not retainers acted with any greater propriety than those who were, or than did the curial sheriffs of a century before.

If 'bastard feudalism' cannot bear exclusive responsibility for the disorderly conditions of the fourteenth century, the evidence condemning it cannot be dismissed out of hand. The difficulty is that our sources document in abundance the abuses of retaining. But we do not know whether John le Boteler of Llantwit, John Poleyn or Piers de St. Combe, Bradeston's *vadlet*, were typical retainers. Are the deeds and exploits of similar evil-doers simply unsung? The evidence which survives, ample though it is, may reveal only the tip of the iceberg. But we must remember that in the fourteenth century there were many more outlets for complaint than ever before. Those who suffered at the hands of the mighty could bring their grievances to the notice of the authorities by any number of means. The eyre, extinct in its traditional form by 1330, lived on in a number of other guises: the justices of trailbaston and the commissions of oyer and terminer, for example. The perambulations of the shires by the Court of King's Bench created the opportunity for local people to come

---

[176] See below, pp. 197–99.

forward with indictments. Petitions reached King, council and parliament in great numbers from individuals and from communities. As the flood of petitions against the Despensers and their dependants showed in 1327, a change of regime could be dangerous for those who had profited too much while the losing side was in power. Certainly intimidation must have ensured that some of the crimes of high-handed retainers never came to light. But in view of the variety of outlets for the aggrieved in fourteenth century England, there is some ground for arguing that were there many more disreputable, lawless retainers, they would have left their mark on the records. The lawless retainer is well-known; but he may be exceptional rather than typical. The wealth of evidence bequeathed by the complaints or indictments against men of the stamp of John le Boteler of Llantwit is an indication that they represent the unpleasant and unacceptable face of bastard feudalism. Evidence of the stabilizing influence of retaining is by its very nature elusive. But Thomas de Berkeley did not omit to resolve the quarrels that arose between his retainers; and the loyal service given to his family by three generations of the Tracy family is also significant.

The legislation of 1390 for the first time began to set acceptable limits to the granting of fees and liveries; and the clamour which led to its publication can be seen as a measure of the influence in parliament and in the shires of men who lived outside the embrace of 'bastard feudalism'.

IV

OFFICE HOLDING AND THE COUNTY COMMUNITY

i

The extent of a magnate's power in the shires depended on his ability to secure the appointment of his own men to local office. Provided that his friends and allies were well placed, he could bend the royal administration in the shires to suit his own interests; for if the King's government was carried into every corner of the land, its impact was nevertheless modified and tempered by the encroachments of bastard feudalism.

The offices and institutions of local government, if not so familiar as the institutions of the central government, have not been completely ignored. Thanks to the survival of the Hundred Rolls, the structure of local government in the age of Edward I is fairly well known;[1] and if the administration of the shires in the fourteenth century has not received the attention which Miss Cam gave to the thirteenth, the ground has at least been turned over. The coroner has been the subject of a monograph, and the history of the shrievalty, though not a well-charted subject once the opening decade of Edward III's reign has been passed, has received detailed study down to 1300.[2] It is only when we try to penetrate behind the façade of the administrative structure that the picture becomes less clear. An appointment to the shrievalty, for example, was of crucial concern to any magnate who wished to influence the politics of his locality, not only for the executive authority but also for the judicial duties which were wielded by this office. Now the formal procedure for the appointment of sheriffs is well-known: they were appointed by the Chancellor, Treasurer and barons of the Exchequer. But in practice it was rarely difficult for magnates to

---

[1] It was analysed by H. M. Cam, *The Hundred and the Hundred Rolls* (London, 1930), who relied largely on the evidence of the Hundred Rolls.

[2] W. A. Morris, *The Medieval English Sheriff to 1300* (Manchester, 1927).

bring pressure to bear for the nomination of their friends and clients.

It is therefore to these informal processes that the historian needs to direct his gaze, for it is still true today, as Powicke said in 1953, that 'we know too little about the distribution of local groups and the relations between them and the very important knights of the King's household or the growing professional class of lay estate agents, monastic stewards and the like'.[3] Thus the purpose here will not be to describe once again the workings of the King's government in the shires but to examine the background of the knights and esquires who filled the offices and commissions and to interpret the local picture in the light of the ideas which the Commons expressed on law enforcement and administration in their petitions to parliament. For such a study the county is the most appropriate medium: it was the unit of local government which was represented in parliament, on which the King's fiscal demands were imposed and within which local loyalties were created and expressed.

ii

The office of sheriff was the oldest and at the same time the most wide-ranging in its responsibilities of all those which carried the King's government into the shires. The sheriff of the Anglo-Norman period was in reality an independent magnate in his shire, needed as much for the military power he could wield on the King's behalf as for his administrative ability, and it was only in the thirteenth century that he was subordinated to the authority of the Crown. This change may have come more suddenly than was once thought: the days of the curial sheriff were numbered once William de Valence, newly arrived at the centre of power, embarked in 1236 on a new policy which would have the effect of reconciling the counties to the court. Local men, not important figures at court, were appointed to the shrievalties. But at this time, too, peripatetic 'professional' sheriffs made their appearance.[4] It was these appointments and the terms on which they were made that provoked the clause in the Provisions of

[3] F. M. Powicke, *The Thirteenth Century* (Oxford, 1953), pp. 539–40.
[4] D. A. Carpenter, 'The Decline of the Curial Sheriff in England, 1194–1258', *Eng. Hist. Rev.*, xci (1976), 1–32.

Oxford relating to the shrievalty; it provides a convenient point of departure for a discussion of the history of this office in the fourteenth century.

The Provisions of Oxford touched on the three problems that were to provoke contention for the next century and a quarter: they said that the sheriff must be a substantial freeholder, a vavasour of the county where he held office, and that he should serve for only one year.[5] These claims embodied an argument that the Commons in parliament were to express for most of the fourteenth century.[6] The landholding qualification reappeared in a clause of the Ordinances of 1311 which at the same time changed the procedure for the appointment of the sheriff. He was to be appointed by the Chancellor, Treasurer and others of the Council who might be present; and only such were to be chosen who were suitable and held sufficient lands that they were able to answer King and people for their deeds.[7] In 1316 the Statute of Lincoln restated explicitly what had only been implied in the Ordinances: that the sheriff should hold in his own county sufficient land to answer the King and his people.[8] These provisions were reinforced by the Statute of York, by an ordinance in 1326 and by the Statute of Northampton two years later.[9] Yet the tedious repetition of these enactments and the frequency of Commons petitions on the same subject in Edward III's reign suggests a continuing failure on the part of the government to appoint to the shrievalty men of sufficient standing. The difficulty which the Crown faced can be appreciated, for it had to reconcile several conflicting needs. One was the desire of the Commons to see the appointment of substantial men drawn from the local community. A second was the desire of the higher nobility to see that their dependants were rewarded with local offices that lay at the disposal of the Crown.

[5] *English Historical Documents, 1189–1327*, ed. H. Rothwell (London, 1975), p. 365.

[6] The demand that the shrievalty should be an annual appointment, because the office had fallen to farmers and unknown people who used it to satisfy their greed, was stated at greater length in the submission which the barons made to Louis IX in January 1264 (*Documents of the Baronial Movement of Reform and Rebellion*, ed. R. F. Treharne & I. J. Sanders (Oxford, 1973), pp. 262–3).

[7] *Stat. Realm*, i, 160.   [8] Ibid., i, 174.

[9] Ibid., i, 258; *Rot. Parl.*, i, 465; *The English Government at Work*, ii, ed. W. A. Morris & J. R. Strayer (Cambridge, Mass., 1947), 48.

A king responsive to the needs of patronage would not lightly disregard a petition from a powerful earl requesting the appointment of some retainer next time a vacancy cropped up. It was no doubt with such processes in mind that the Statute of Lincoln prohibited any steward of a lord from holding the shrievalty.[10] Such men were unpopular with the county communities because they owed their advancement in the local administration not to their links with the shire but to their dependence on a powerful magnate. Finally, a sheriff had to be of sufficient standing, so that if he defaulted his debts could be levied on his lands. In the same way restitution for undue exaction could be made.

These, then, were the arguments on each side. They were evidently rehearsed once again in the parliament of 1340, because in that year a statute was passed reasserting that the sheriff should hold sufficient land in his bailiwick.[11] By 1340 the length of the sheriff's term of office was causing concern too, and the opportunity was taken to reaffirm its limitation to twelve months. For the next three decades, however, this statute remained a dead letter, and numerous parliamentary petitions were submitted calling for observance of the obligations which it had imposed. On the length of the sheriff's term of office, as on the land-holding obligation, there were again two points of view, one that of the Crown, the other that of the Commons. The former was expressed in Walter de Stapledon's ordinance of 1326: if sheriffs were changed frequently the King would not be well served, his mandates not executed and his people harassed in many ways.[12] In other words, a sheriff with experience of his shire would be better qualified to extract money than a man new to his office. The preamble to the statute of 1340, however, expressed the view of those who wished to limit tenure of office when it said that sheriffs who retained the position for several years would be encouraged to commit many oppressions and serve the King and his people badly.[13] But the county communities may not have been the only sufferers. A parliamentary petition of Richard II's reign, unfortunately not too specific in its wording, suggested that the sheriff himself could sometimes find himself out of pocket at the end of his term of office: because of the loss and hardship

[10] *Stat. Realm*, i, 174. [11] Ibid., i, 283.
[12] *Red Book of the Exchequer*, iii, ed. H. Hall (Rolls Series, 1896), 960–1.
[13] *Stat. Realm*, i, 283.

incurred in holding the shrievalty, a man should not be appointed more than once if someone else in the shire was suitably qualified.[14]

The turning point in the history of the shrievalty came with the parliament of February 1371. As so often before, the Commons submitted a petition on the shrievalty which on this occasion, however, was significant not only in its contents but also to the extent that its demands were met by the government.[15] For the first time the Commons combined in a single petition requests for reform of not only the shrievalty but also the escheatorship, and by this means they were able to extend to the former office concessions that had been secured in respect of the latter. Three years earlier, in 1368, the Commons had petitioned for re-affirmation of a statute of 1362 which regulated the conduct of the escheator but which had not mentioned qualifications for office.[16] What they requested, however, was not simply a reaffirmation, for they advanced their claims to demand that none should be made an escheator who did not hold lands worth at least £20 a year. The petition was granted; and for the first time the land holding obligation was quantified. Next, in 1371 the Commons successfully sought to extend the same principle to the shrievalty. Once £20 was accepted as the qualification required for the escheator it seemed reasonable to expect the same of the sheriff. The twin demands of annual replacement and an adequate landed income found concise expression in this short petition to which the King gave his assent, but because the statute roll for this year is incomplete there is no record of its enrolment. One thing, however, is reasonably clear: its terms were implemented. It is not always easy to tell if every sheriff held lands and rents worth £20, though it seems that the majority did; but there can be no doubt that henceforth sheriffs were changed annually. In Gloucestershire, for example, terms of office of two or three years which had been common still in the 1350s and 1360s came to an abrupt end.[17] The same was true of nearly every other county. The only exceptions were those counties like Cornwall and Worcester, the shrievalties of which were held in

[14] *Rot. Parl.*, iii, 96.
[15] *Rot. Parl.*, ii, 308.
[16] Ibid., ii, 296. For the statute of 1362 see *Stat. Realm*, i, 374-5.
[17] *List of Sheriffs*, pp. 49-50.

fee, and Westmorland, where perhaps there was a shortage of resident gentry to fill the office.[18]

In view of the government's long-standing reluctance to accede to the demands of the Commons this sudden volte-face demands some explanation. The initiative of the Commons in placing a value on the lands an official needed to hold probably stemmed from the belief that only by this means could the argument over the enforcement of this qualification be conducted in precise terms. In granting this the Crown was not making a great concession since the appointments suggest that most of the sheriffs, though not the escheators, were knights or rich esquires anyway.[19] More important was the decision to change the sheriffs annually which must be seen in the light of the political crisis of 1371. The clerical administration of Wykeham and Brantingham had been driven out in favour of a government which looked to the leadership of John of Gaunt.[20] It may not be unreasonable to suppose that the new administration aimed to recruit the support of the Commons by acceding to their long-standing demands over the shrievalty. The extent of the Commons' victory should not be underestimated. Although petitions continued to be submitted in parliament from time to time reminding the Crown of the commitment to annual rotation, there was little reason for complaint: after 1371 the sheriffs of almost every county were changed each year.[21]

It is in the light of these conflicting attitudes that we must look at the forty-seven men who held the office of sheriff of Gloucester in the fourteenth century. An examination of their careers will provide an ample commentary on the critique of current practice which is found in the parliamentary petitions.

The first observation that can be made is that in the fourteenth century the shrievalty was largely the preserve of local men, appointments to it being governed by local influences and rivalries. But the two periods when national politics intruded are sufficiently important to merit some consideration. Edward II's reign saw the most overtly political appointment made in the

[18] Ibid., pp. 21, 150, 157.
[19] See below, pp. 117–8, 137–9.
[20] M. McKisack, *The Fourteenth Century*, pp. 384–5.
[21] According to the statute of 1340 sheriffs were to be appointed annually on the Morrow of All Souls (3 November) at the Exchequer.

county in the fourteenth century: Sir Robert Darcy, appointed sheriff on 2 April 1313, was a Lincolnshire man with no lands at all in Gloucestershire.[22] Through the favour of Gaveston he became a household knight of Edward II, and it was presumably the curial connection that earned him the Gloucestershire appointment.[23] Five years later one Thomas de Berton was appointed for five months, perhaps on a temporary basis.[24] His successor in 1318 was John de Hampton, significantly, a retainer of the Despensers at a time when that family were strengthening their hold at court.[25] After a term of office of five years Hampton was finally replaced on 28 December 1323 by a local man, John Besemaunsel. He was not of great standing, but there is some evidence to suggest that he too may have been a Despenser dependant.[26] In these middle years of Edward II's reign the recurrent prominence of retainers of Gaveston or Despenser suggests that political factors were at work in choosing sheriffs.

It was not until the reign of Richard II that appointments were again made with national political considerations in mind. Article 36 of the appeal of the Merciless Parliament alleged that the King had ordered the appointment of sheriffs who would influence the election of shire knights, and the chroniclers made several statements to a similar effect.[27] Nevertheless the surviving evidence points to an attempt to manipulate local government in the 'tyranny' at the end of the reign rather than in 1387: the appointments to the shrievalty in Gloucestershire between 1385 and 1389 reveal no political flavour.[28] Ten years later, however,

---

[22] On 10 April 1311, however, the King had granted him the keeping of the castle and honour of Chepstow (*Cal. Pat. Rolls 1307–13*, p. 332).

[23] On 12 February 1310 the King confirmed a grant by Gaveston to Darcy and his wife of the manor of Patchesham (Surrey) (*Cal. Pat. Rolls 1307–13*, p. 209). Darcy was a knight of the King's household by 1313 (ibid., p. 555).

[24] The identity of this man is unclear. He may have been the vicar of Melksham (Wilts.) of that name, though it would have been strange for one of the clergy to be appointed to the office of sheriff (*Cal. Close Rolls 1313–18*, p. 623).

[25] S.C.8/66/3288.

[26] In 1327 he sat on a jury at Tewkesbury, a Despenser manor, though he did not reside there (K.B.27/271m. 105).

[27] *The Reign of Richard II*, ed. F. R. H. Du Boulay & C. M. Barron (London, 1971), pp. 141, 221.

[28] Thomas de Berkeley of Coberley (sheriff 1385, 1387) was retained by Gaunt (*John of Gaunt's Reg., 1379–83*, i, no. 35), and Bridges (sheriff 1385–6) by both Despenser and Gaunt (K.B.27/471 Rex m. 9d; *John of Gaunt's Reg., 1379–*

the position was very different. On 1 December 1396, Robert Pointz was appointed sheriff. It was fortunate for the King, from the point of view of the elections to the important parliament which opened at Westminster in the following September, that Pointz was a retainer of the courtier Thomas Despenser, later earl of Gloucester.[29] Pointz was succeeded on 3 November 1397 by Sir John Berkeley who had no obvious political affiliations. But with the appointment on 17 November 1398 of John Brouning political considerations once again become apparent, for he, like Pointz, was a retainer of Despenser.[30] In Gloucestershire, then, Richard II sought to secure the allegiance of the local administration by the appointment of local retainers of the magnate whose power he was seeking to build up.[31] The approach was more subtle than that of Edward II who simply placed a Lincolnshire courtier knight in the shrievalty in 1313. Nevertheless, where he could not use clients of sympathetic magnates Richard appointed knights or esquires of the household. At the end of the reign no fewer than six such men were holding shrievalties, some of them in the second or third year of their term of office, though in deference to convention they were generally resident in the counties to which they were appointed.[32]

It may be possible also to discern political significance in the appointment of Sir John Dalyngrygg in November 1401. Dalyngrygg, whose father, Sir Edward, built Bodiam Castle in Sussex, married Alice, widow of Sir Thomas Boteler of Sudeley.[33] Sir John Dalyngrygg did have some claim to be interested in

83, i, nos. 70, 644). Thomas de Bradewell, who succeeded Bridges was probably not retained. It would be unwise to overstress the succession of Gaunt retainers, as he was in Spain at the time; and of course he had an exceptionally large retinue.

[29] Cal. Close Rolls 1399–1402, p. 306.
[30] Ibid.; Cal. Pat. Rolls 1391–6, p. 510.
[31] For a comparative study revealing broadly similar conclusions see A. Steel, 'The Sheriffs of Cambridgeshire and Huntingdonshire in the Reign of Richard II', Procs. Cambs. Ant. Soc., xxxvi (1934–5), 1–34.
[32] John Worship (Beds. & Bucks.), Andrew Newport (Camb. & Hunts.), Thomas Clanvow (Heref.), John Golofre (Oxon. & Berks.), William Walsall (Staffs.) and Richard Mawardyn (Wilts.). For lists of Household knights and esquires see E.101/403/22 (16–17 Richard II) and E.101/403/10 (19–20 Richard II).
[33] G.E.C., xii, i, 419.

Gloucestershire affairs; but it is more significant in these early insecure years of the Lancastrian monarchy to find that he was a King's knight.[34] His power base insecure, Henry IV found it necessary, like his predecessor, to insert into the local administration men on whose loyalty he could count.[35]

In the hundred years before Dalyngrygg's appointment four other men found their way into Gloucestershire affairs, and eventually into the shrievalty, by marriage. John de Annesley (sheriff, 1310–11) from Nottinghamshire married Lucy, widow of Sir Robert de la Mare of Cherington; Sir Robert de Hildesley (sheriff, 1356–60) married Isabel, widow of Sir Richard de Haudlo; Sir Thomas Moigne (sheriff, 1360–3) married Margery, widow of John de Knovill; and in Richard II's reign Laurence Sebrok (sheriff, 1388–9) married Margaret, widow of Edmund Blount of Bitton.[36] All played a prominent part in the life of the county, although land by marriage was not invariably considered sufficient to make a man a local vavasour: in 1318 the people of Leicestershire petitioned for the removal of their sheriff since he held no land in the county except his wife's dower.[37] The demand of the Provisions of Oxford and subsequent petitions that sheriffs should hold sufficient lands in their shires seem to have articulated grievances which were felt locally. But a more powerful complaint lay at the root of that clause in the Provisions. In the second half of the thirteenth century the practice grew of switching sheriffs from one county to another in succession. In the reign of Edward I the Exchequer was still doing this. Robert Hereward, sheriff of Cambridgeshire 1300–1, then served as sheriff of Norfolk till 1306. Robert de Bayouse, sheriff of Cambridgeshire 1301–6, was immediately transferred to serve as sheriff of Warwick and Leicester in 1306–7.[38] Similar transfers were made between counties in the West Country. John de

---

[34] *Cal. Pat. Rolls 1399–1401*, p. 69; Sir John Dalyngrygg was buried at Robertsbridge Abbey, and his effigy, showing him wearing the Lancastrian collar of SS, is now in the museum at Bodiam Castle (C. Morton, *Bodiam Castle* (National Trust, 1975), p. 23).

[35] Cf. S. B. Chrimes, C. D. Ross and R. A. Griffiths, *Fifteenth-Century England* (Manchester, 1972), pp. 23–4.

[36] *Cal. Close Rolls 1313–18*, p. 526; *G.E.C.*, vi, 401; vii, 349; *Visitation of the County of Gloucester*, 232.

[37] S.C.8/58/2881.

[38] Cam, *Liberties and Communities*, p. 33.

Newborough was appointed sheriff of Gloucester on 16 October 1301 only six days after his replacement as sheriff of Wiltshire.[39] John de Acton of Iron Acton near Bristol served as sheriff of Hereford 1294–9, April to November 1303, 1305–6 and as sheriff of Gloucester, 1311–12.[40] Finally, William Tracy, a retainer of the Berkeleys, was sheriff of Worcester, 1318–21, and sheriff of Gloucester, 1324–7.[41] By the 1330s this practice had all but disappeared.[42] Sheriffs were rarely appointed in more than one county thereafter. Sir John Berkeley of Beverstone affords the one notable exception: in the course of a long career which spanned the reigns of Richard II and Henry IV he was twice sheriff of Gloucester (1392–3, 1397–8), twice sheriff of Somerset and Dorset (1390–1, 1394–5), twice sheriff of Hampshire (1402–3, 1406–7), and once sheriff of Wiltshire (1410–11), all counties in which he was a landowner.[43] By the end of the fourteenth century, the Crown and the Exchequer had long since conceded defeat. The practices of the later thirteenth century, designed to serve the fiscal needs of the King, were dropped during the reign of Edward III.

To argue thus is not to say that the sheriffs of this period became increasingly devoid of administrative experience. Knowledge of the workings of the shrievalty could be gained either by reappointment or by serving a term of office of several years. In the first half of the century several sheriffs must have become very experienced—Thomas de Gardinis and John de Hampton who served for five years, Richard de Foxcote for six and Sir Simon Basset whose term of office lasted for no less than nine years. Durations such as this certainly provided adequate

[39] *List of Sheriffs*, pp. 49, 152. Newborough held the manor of Minety on the borders of Gloucestershire and Wiltshire.

[40] Since four successive generations of the Acton family were named John and rarely was any attempt made to distinguish between father and son, it is possible that the sheriff of Gloucester was the son of the sheriff of Hereford. John de Acton, alive in 1303, married Margaret de Aller (*V.C.H. Somerset*, iii, 63), while John de Acton who is known to have died in 1312 married first Helena and then Sibyl (*Cal. Pat. Rolls 1301–7*, p. 131; *The Visitation of the County of Gloucester*, p. 131). But no inquisition *post mortem* survives to indicate that a John de Acton died between 1303 and 1312.

[41] *List of Sheriffs*, pp. 49, 157.

[42] *English Government at Work*, ii, 48–9 and n.

[43] *Feud. Aids*, ii, 294; v, 229; *V.C.H. Somerset*, iii, 233; *V.C.H. Hampshire*, iv, 580, 609, 639; v, 114.

grounds for complaint by the Commons. Reappointment was rarer in the first six decades than it was to become once annual rotation became the practice after 1371: only five sheriffs completed two or more terms of the shrievalty after that year. Annual appointments to the shrievalty posed a problem, however. Were the same few men to be chosen over and over again, or were the ranks of the office-holders to be widened? The first option seems to have been practised. Twenty-one men were appointed to the shrievalty in the last thirty years of the century, not so many more than the seventeen who held the same office in the first thirty years when terms of office were longer. Of these twenty-one four served three terms, and a fourth, Sir John Berkeley, served in the course of his long career no fewer than six terms of office in various counties. Five others held the shrievalty twice. Moreover, most of these men served in other positions, on the bench, for example, or as knights of the shire.[44] Sixteen of them served as knights of the shire before 1400. Even though experience was purchased by fairly frequent reappointment to office, the government did keep its promise not to reappoint sheriffs before three years. Between 1377, when a Commons petition to this effect was granted, and 1400 no Gloucestershire sheriff was chosen to serve again until more than three years had elapsed since the expiry of his last term of office.[45] If a sheriff could find himself out of pocket at the end of his term of office, as a parliamentary petition of 1380 claimed, there is no evidence to indicate unwillingness to hold the shrievalty several times.

These conclusions prompt reflection on the method of appointment to the shrievalty. The formal procedure is well known. After 1311 sheriffs were chosen by the Chancellor, Treasurer and others of the Council who might be present.[46] But it is more important to consider the backstage influence that would be brought to bear on the officers of state. A letter from the King requesting the appointment to a shrievalty of the retainer of a trusted magnate would surely not be ignored.[47] But notification of that kind was probably not the only way by which the Chancellor or Treasurer came to know the names of men who sought appointment. In the crisis of 1258–60 there is evidence

---

[44] See below, pp. 161–5.   [45] Rot. Parl., iii, 24.   [46] Stat. Realm, i, 160.
[47] For the influence of patronage on appointments see below, pp. 152–60.

that possible sheriffs were nominated by a local panel of knights;[48] it may be that in the fourteenth century the county court performed a similar role. Perhaps also the outgoing sheriff may have had a say in nominating his successor. At the very least, the localized nature of appointments to the shrievalty in the later fourteenth century suggests a deference by the Exchequer to the wishes of the community of the shire, however the Treasurer and Chancellor came to hear of their views. It might be supposed, then, that the concession to the shires of the right of electing the sheriff would be greatly valued. Yet it was not. When it was granted by Edward I in the *Articuli super Cartas* in 1300 it was taken up by only one county—Shropshire—and in 1338, when it was granted again, by just three pairs of counties.[49]

If the shires did not avail themselves of the opportunity given to them for once of choosing good and sufficient men, were they satisfied with the standing of the men to whom the office was given? The sheriffs of Gloucester do for the most part seem to have been men of substance. Of the forty-seven men who held the office in the fourteenth century, at least twenty-eight were knights. This must be regarded as no more than a minimum figure for the clerks rarely troubled regularly to record the status of the new appointee until the 1380s, and even then there were omissions.[50] Of those who were probably not knights, several may still have been well endowed. Thomas de Gardinis (1302–7) had lands in several counties,[51] and Ralph Walsh (1379–80, 1383–4) held manors in Gloucestershire and South Wales.[52] Undoubtedly, though, some of the sheriffs were not wealthy. In the reign of Edward II Thomas de Berton and John Besemaunsel

[48] Cam, *Liberties and Communities*, p. 32 and n.

[49] Morris, *The Medieval English Sheriff*, pp. 184–5; T. F. Tout, *Chapters in the Administrative History of Medieval England*, iii (Manchester, 1928), 94.

[50] For example, Henry de la Rivere was noted as a knight in 1391 but not on his reappointment in 1399.

[51] He held knights fees or manors at Exning (Suffolk), Elkstone (Gloucs.), Cogges and Fringford (Oxon.) (*Feud. Aids*, ii, 247; iv, 163, 169; v, 47). He also held demesne lands in the two Gloucestershire vills of Colesbourne and Duntisbourne Rous (*Cartulary of Eynsham Abbey*, ii, ed. H. E. Salter (Oxf. Hist. Soc., li, 1908), xxxix).

[52] The Walsh family held Woolstrop (Gloucs.) and Llanwaryn and Dynan in South Wales (*V.C.H. Gloucs.*, x, 218; *Gloucs. Inqs. post Mortem*, v, 226–7). Ralph Walsh was receiver of Thomas de Berkeley (Berkeley Castle, general series account rolls, account of William atte Nasche).

can be singled out.[53] In the reign of Edward III the four most humble sheriffs were Richard de Foxcote (1332–8, 1351–2), Philip Mareschal (1351), John de Weston (1352–4), and Thomas de Okle (1372–3). Foxcote held land in two manors, of neither of which was he the lord.[54] Mareschal and Weston were both appointed in the wake of the Black Death, and the former's term of office was particularly short.[55] It is possible that they owed their undue prominence to a shortage of suitable candidates for office, although the plague does not seem to have done much to thin the ranks of the county gentry. Okle, whose shrievalty came near the end of the reign, is a mysterious figure, almost certainly of sub-gentry standing.[56] All but two of the sheriffs of Richard II's reign were well-endowed men. One of the exceptions was William Barwell, who, though appointed twice, in November 1384 and January 1385, accounted for neither term of office.[57] The other, Thomas de Bradewell (1377–8, 1380–1, 1386–7), described as an *armiger* in the poll tax returns of 1380, held an estate in the Evesham Abbey manor of Broadwell near Stow-on-the-Wold.[58]

Although the majority of the sheriffs were knights, sufficient were of lesser standing to afford support for the complaints which the Commons made in parliament. The appearance of men of obviously inadequate means may have been an effect of the workings of magnate influence.[59] The objection of the Commons to sheriffs of insufficient means was probably rooted in the

[53] For Besemaunsel see *Gloucs. Inqs. post Mortem*, v, 96–7. For Thomas de Berton see p. 112n above.

[54] In the parliamentary subsidy of 1327 he was assessed at 3s. 3½d. at Duntisbourne Rous and 4s. 3¾d. at Turkdean (*Gloucs. Subsidy Roll*, pp. 9, 12). No inquisition was taken on his death.

[55] In 1344 Philip le Mareschal held a messuage, a carucate of land, 12 acres of wood and 40s. rents in Blaisdon for one quarter of a knight's fee. He also held the advowson of Blaisdon Church (C.P.25(1)/77/65/240; *Feud. Aids*, ii, 284). He held a messuage, a carucate of land and 8s. rents at Longhope nearby (C.P.25(1)/77/65/240). For John de Weston, who probably resided at Hinton, in the parish of Dyrham (*Feud. Aids*, ii, 281), see below, p. 228.

[56] The only man of that name in Gloucestershire in the 1370s was a rector of Winterbourne who exchanged benefices to become dean of South Malling in 1371 (*Cal. Pat. Rolls 1370–4*, p. 67). More plausible in his identification with Thomas de Okle who was a juror in 1363 (K.B.27/411 Rex m. 8).

[57] Barwell was escheator, 1385–6. See below, p. 201.

[58] E.179/113/31 m. 1.   [59] See below, pp. 152–9.

knowledge that these men were retainers who owed their position not to their standing in the shire but to their place in a magnate retinue. Moreover, there was the prospect that the lands of such a poor sheriff would not be of sufficient value to pay his outstanding debts if he defaulted.

If such were the case, why did the counties apparently treasure so little the right granted to them of electing their own sheriffs? Their main fear was probably liability for the sheriff's debts. As W. A. Morris has said, the principle that the sheriff's land was security for his acts and obligations held even after his death: thus, if he or his heir were no longer alive, the tenants of the lands which he held in fee could be distrained for payment of his outstanding debts to the Crown.[60] By the Walton Ordinances, however, the counties had to take financial responsibility for those they elected, and this almost certainly made them reluctant to elect.[61] Although the county communities showed little interest in the concession when it was granted in 1300 and 1338 they may well in practice have come by the end of the century to have had some say in the nomination of candidates for office. By such influence and by the exertion of pressure in parliament the development of the shrievalty was shaped in the fourteenth century in response to the wishes of the gentry whose demands were voiced by the Commons in parliament.

iii

Similar questions may be asked in respect of the county's parliamentary representation. Since the 1290s the writs for election had told each sheriff to cause to be chosen two knights from his shire and two citizens from each borough *de discretioribus et ad laborandum potentioribus* and to cause them to come to parliament provided with full and sufficient power to consent to whatever might be done there.[62] Despite this injunction, however, *valletti* were being elected as early as 1324.

The presence in parliament of 'knights of the shire' who had not been dubbed has, of course, long been recognized; but their

---

[60] *English Government at Work*, ii, 49.
[61] For the text of the ordinance see Tout, *Chapters*, iii, 146.
[62] *English Government at Work*, i, 101.

numbers cannot be computed on the evidence of the writs *de expensis* alone. The clerks of Chancery rarely bothered to record details of personal style. Only when they are supplemented by other sources is it possible to estimate how many of them had assumed knighthood. Of the 102 men who represented Gloucestershire in the fourteenth century at least fifty are known to have been knights. This is a minimum figure and as the date of dubbing is not often known some of the members may have been knighted only after they had served in parliament. Crude though the estimate may be, it does indicate how little regard was paid to the instruction in the writ to elect two knights. Thus a considerable alteration in the composition of the parliamentary Commons could be effected when the writ to the sheriff ordered the election in each shire of two belted knights. To the parliament of January 1340, to which the Commons in 1339 had requested the election only of belted knights, Sir John de Sudeley and Sir Philip Joce were returned, neither of whom had sat in parliament before and neither of whom was to sit again.[63]

Even though perhaps no more than half of the Gloucestershire 'knights of the shire' were actually knights, they may not necessarily have been all of humble means. Some may have been richer esquires who simply did not want to assume knighthood. As the information needed to determine the income of the members is rarely forthcoming, a simple counting of manors will have to prove adequate; it will give some idea of their relative economic standing even if it cannot take into account revenue from sources other than land. Of the 102 men who represented the county in the fourteenth century, however, twenty-seven were of such humble origin as to leave no trace on the records of holding any manors at all. Another two were burgesses. Eleven held of other lords than the King, with the result that it is nearly impossible to determine the extent of their lands. Of the remaining sixty-two knights of the shire, fifteen held a single manor, twelve two manors, sixteen three manors, seven four manors and eleven five manors or more. It would be quite wrong,

---

[63] The parliament opened on 20 January and Sir John de Sudeley died on or before 19 February (*G.E.C.*, xii, i, 417). He never held any local offices, but in 1338 he was nominated by the county to be a keeper of the peace (see below, p. 129). Sir Philip Joce had been summoned to the great council in 1324, and two years earlier he had acted as a commissioner of array (Moor, ii, 273).

then, to discern the dominance of any stratum of the gentry among the county's representatives in parliament: they were drawn from both the richly and the poorly endowed. What does perhaps call for comment is the presence of such a large number of very humble men who seem to have held no manorial rights at all. These men were preponderant in the 1330s. For example, there was William de Bradewell, whose parliamentary career began in 1322 when he sat for Worcestershire, and two years later was elected for Gloucestershire for the first time. During the next eight years he represented the county four times. Other obscure men who represented the county in these years were John de Cromhall (1330, 1335), William Westhall (1343, 1344), Walter de Okle (1324), William de Arches (1326), John de Sevenhampton (1328), William de Tytherington (1330, and for the borough of Gloucester in 1332 and 1336), Richard de la Hale (1334), John de Chadesle (1336), Walter de Combe (1336), Richard Fraunceys (1338) and Henry de Corsham (1339).

There is little to indicate the identity of these men. Richard Fraunceys may have been a burgess; two contemporaries of his, John Fraunceys, a coroner, and Eborard Fraunceys, were merchants of Bristol.[64] But evidence like this is too thin to provide an all-embracing explanation for the presence of these men as knights of the shire. The few clues that there are all point to quite humble origins. Richard de la Hale was a bailiff of the liberty of Cirencester and a constable of the peace.[65] William de Tytherington, who sat for both the borough and county of Gloucester, was the sheriff's itinerant bailiff between 1314 and 1318.[66] These men, it seems, held few lands. John de Cromhall resided at Mitcheldean, and held jointly some lands for life in the nearby village of Westbury-on-Severn.[67] Henry de Corsham, who was bailiff of the abbot of Fecamp's hundred of Slaughter in 1347, may have come from Corsham (Wilts);[68] but he held lands—how much is not known—at Fairford and Broughton

---

[64] Eborard de Fraunceys attended a great council at Northampton in August 1338 on behalf of Bristol (*Cal. Close Rolls 1337–9*, p. 526). In 1331 the sheriff of Gloucester was told to cause another coroner to be elected in place of John Fraunceys of Bristol who was a merchant (*Cal. Close Rolls 1330–3*, p. 185).

[65] Just. 3/122n. 3.   [66] Just. 1/296 m. 4.

[67] *Cal. Close Rolls 1327–30*, p. 188.

[68] K.B.27/349 m. 25d.

Mauduit (Oxon).[69] These examples hardly add up to very much. Such men could not reasonably claim to represent their county in parliament on the strength of their meagre landed interests, and how they came to be elected is a question to which further attention will have to be devoted.[70] However, it may not only have been Gloucestershire which elected a number of 'sub-gentry' to parliament in this period. Walter Poul, a member for Bedfordshire in 1336, was a clerk in the sheriff's office who appeared on five occasions at the Exchequer as deputy-sheriff.[71] In the same period some of the knights of the shire for Somerset were men about whom little or nothing is known other than their attendance in parliament.[72] Whatever questions may be prompted about the value placed upon representation in parliament in the 1330s, as the century progressed such men tend to disappear from the scene, and by the 1370s the knights of the shire are usually knights or wealthy esquires endowed with several manors. Berkeley of Coberley, Berkeley of Beverstone, Tracy and FitzNichol are the names encountered most frequently.

A practice that grew in the second half of the century was that of electing the current sheriff.[73] In January 1348, April 1357, January 1361, October 1362, May 1366, May 1368, May 1382, and February and October 1383 the sitting sheriff was returned. Even if this practice began as a result of a shortage of possible candidates after the Black Death, and the coincidence of timing is suggestive, such justification could not apply in 1382 and 1383 ten years after an ordinance had forbidden the election of sheriffs during their term of office.[74] Knights came forward for other offices; it is difficult to believe that the sheriff took on this task because there was no other suitable and willing candidate. Perhaps the connections enjoyed by these sheriffs counted for something. In January 1348 Sir Simon Basset was the first sheriff

[69] K.B.27/324 m. 85d; *Cal. Close Rolls 1346–9*, p. 405.

[70] See below, pp. 152–9.

[71] M. Bassett, *Knights of the Shire for Bedfordshire* (Beds. Hist. Rec. Soc., xxix, 1949), 79.

[72] e.g. John de Draycote, Robert de Paulseye, Robert de Raddeston and Walter de Putney; S. W. Bates Harbin, *Members of Parliament for the County of Somerset* (Somerset Arch. & Nat. Hist. Soc., 1939), pp. 30, 35, 38, 46.

[73] K. L. Wood-Legh, 'Sheriffs, Lawyers and Belted Knights in the Parliaments of Edward III', *Eng. Hist. Rev.*, xlvi (1931), 372–88.

[74] *Stat. Realm*, i, 394.

of Gloucester to return himself to parliament: a man high in Thomas de Berkeley's favour he had been a household knight of the King in the 1330s.[75] Sir Thomas Moigne, who returned himself twice, was a retainer of Lord Talbot.[76] John Thorp, elected in 1382, was a household knight of the King,[77] and Sir Thomas FitzNichol, the final sheriff in this group, was a neighbour of Thomas de Berkeley and retainer of Lord Stafford.[78] All the sheriffs, then, with the possible exception of Robert de Hildesley, were retainers of influential magnates. It would be quite unwarranted to argue that Berkeley or Talbot engineered the return of his men to parliament. But if the sheriff had wished to return himself, an understandable wish once parliament had assumed some importance, he was well placed to bend the rules successfully.

The political influences discernible in some of the appointments to the shrievalty in the reign of Edward II and Richard II can also be found operating in elections to parliament. To the first parliament of 1324, during the years of Edward II's personal rule, was returned John le Boteler of Llantwit, a local steward of the younger Despenser.[79] The reversal of fortunes three years later found reflection in the parliamentary representation of Gloucestershire. When a parliament was called in December 1326, after the downfall of the Despensers it is not surprising that one of the Gloucestershire knights was Sir Richard de la Rivere, a dependant of Henry of Lancaster whose family was now restored to favour.[80] While prominent magnates may have helped to secure the election of some of their clients, there is little evidence of attempts to pack these early parliaments.[81] The election of a prominent retainer may signify not so much manipulation as the desire of the county community to obtain the services of one who enjoyed access to the powerful. In a later reign, the attempts by Richard II to influence the election of knights of the shire by wooing the sheriffs was commented on by Walsingham and the Monk of Westminster, and although they were describing the

[75] E.36/203 m. 119d.
[76] E.159/145 Easter Recorda.   [77] Cal. Pat. Rolls 1377–81, p. 157.
[78] Stafford Rec. Office D.641/1/2/152.
[79] Rot. Parl., ii, 385.
[80] Phillips, Aymer de Valence, pp. 256–7.
[81] Maddicott, Thomas of Lancaster, pp. 51–2.

events of 1387 the evidence suggests that such interference was more widespread in 1397.[82] In Norfolk and Suffolk there was certainly some substance to these allegations.[83] What does the Gloucestershire evidence reveal? On 1 December 1396 Robert Pointz of Iron Acton was appointed sheriff. He was, as has been shown, almost certainly a retainer of the courtier, Thomas Despenser.[84] As his term of office did not expire until 3 November 1397 it was he who made the returns to the notorious parliament which opened at Westminster of 17 September 1397 and which was subsequently adjourned to Shrewsbury. Neither of the two men chosen had represented the county before. Hugh Mortimer had hitherto had no connection with Gloucestershire where he was not a landowner; he held half a knight's fee at King's Pyon in Herefordshire.[85] But in 1399 he was an esquire of Thomas Despenser, to whom he had transferred, probably as early as 1394, from the service of Roger Mortimer, earl of March.[86] His colleague in this parliament was John Brouning, also in Despenser's affinity, but who at least held land in Gloucestershire.[87] The network of magnate patronage, then, is clearly revealed: in Gloucestershire as elsewhere Richard II was working through his trusted courtiers to ensure that men sympathetic to his cause were placed in positions of influence locally, both to secure the co-operation of the shires and to return to parliament men who would ratify the revolution of 1397.

Whether in the 1320s or the 1390s, whether for political ends or for less discernible reasons, some unlikely people were elected from time to time to represent Gloucestershire in parliament.

[82] Also article 36 of the appeal of the Merciless Parliament alleged that the King had ordered the appointment of sheriffs who would influence the elections (*Stat. Realm*, ii, 4). See also above, p. 112.

[83] R. Virgoe, 'The Crown and Local Government: East Anglia under Richard II', in *The Reign of Richard II*, ed. Du Boulay & Barron, p. 231.

[84] See above p. 113.   [85] *Cal. Close Rolls 1396–9*, p. 459.

[86] *Cal. Pat. Rolls 1391–6*, pp. 481, 510; *1396–9*, pp. 431, 520.

[87] *Cal. Close Rolls 1399–1402*, p. 306; *Cal. Pat. Rolls 1391–6*, p. 510. Brouning came from Dorset (see his will, Prob. 11/2B (Reg. Marche)), but married Katherine, daughter and coheir of Sir Thomas FitzNichol (H. Jenner Fust, 'Hill, Gloucestershire', *Trans. Bristol & Gloucs. Arch. Soc.*, llii (1931), 145). His second marriage was to Alice, widow of Thomas de Bridges, in 1408 (*Cal. Pat. Rolls 1405–8*, p. 447). His son John inherited Nympsfield on the death of FitzNichol in 1418 (*Cal. Fine Rolls 1413–22*, pp. 269–70).

What influences were brought to bear to ensure their election—if election, rather than selection, it was—cannot be pinpointed because so little is known about the procedure of the shire court in this period.[88] A case that reached King's Bench in 1338 suggests that though the right of election was valued it was sometimes set aside. Contrary to ancient custom, it was alleged, the sheriffs of Cambridgeshire over the previous seven years had chosen a colleague of their choice outside the county court, without troubling to hold an election: William Muschet had simply chosen two knights *de sua covina*.[89] An open election in the county court, the procedure understood as early as 1338 to be implied by the writ, represented the ideal even if the reality often fell short of that.

Important though the exceptions are for the light which they cast upon possible practice in the shire court, they should not distract attention from the general picture that emerges. By the 1390s most of the shire knights were not only men of substance but also residents of the shires they represented. Just as sheriffs were switched to serve in different counties, so knights of the shire seem in the early decades of the century to have represented different counties far more than they were to do later on. John de Acton, whose estates extended across Somerset, Gloucestershire and Herefordshire, represented Herefordshire in parliament in 1300, and both that county and Gloucestershire in 1301. Sir William de Wauton, Sir John Bishop, John de Bradenstock, Sir John de Vivonia, Sir Walter de Gacelyn and Sir Henry de Preyers all represented Gloucestershire and Wiltshire separately in different parliaments between 1300 and 1320. Preyers, who represented Gloucestershire in October 1320, represented Wiltshire in 1311, 1318 and 1319; his father, another Henry, represented Bedfordshire in 1300 and 1301.[90] William de Bradewell represented Gloucestershire in 1324, 1331 and December 1332, Worcestershire in 1322 and 1324, and both Worcestershire and Gloucestershire in March 1332. The returns,

[88] The judicial aspect of its work has been illuminated by R. Palmer, 'County Year Book Reports: the professional lawyer in the medieval county court', *Eng. Hist. Rev.*, xci (1976), 776–801.

[89] M. M. Taylor, 'Parliamentary Elections in Cambridgeshire, 1332–8', *Bull. Inst. Hist. Res.*, xviii (1940–1), 26.

[90] M. Basset, 'Knights of the Shire for Bedfordshire', pp. 79–80 & n.

then do not suggest that the same knight sat for widely scattered counties; rather he represented any county in which his lands lay, and these were usually neighbouring counties. Sometimes, even, a man would represent two counties in the same parliament.[91]

As the bonds of loyalty to one county grew stronger in the fourteenth century, so it became more usual for a knight to represent only the county where he resided. Thus, of the knights of the shire for Gloucestershire in Richard II's reign only Sir John Berkeley of Beverstone and Maurice Wyther sat for another county. Maurice Wyther of Portbury represented his own county, Somerset, in parliament in 1377, 1378 and 1381.[92] Sir John Berkeley, who represented Somerset in November 1390 and who held the shrievalties of no fewer than four counties in the course of his long career, was decidedly the exception. Parliamentary representation, moreover, was falling into the hands of a smaller circle of men than before. In the last thirty years of the century this found expression in the more frequent occurrence of re-election to parliament. N. B. Lewis calculated that whereas between 1295 and January 1327 only 43 per cent were re-elected, between 1376 and 1397 52 per cent of the shire representatives were re-elected.[93] Some of those elected most frequently in Richard II's reign were admittedly courtiers: for example, Sir William Bagot was elected to ten consecutive parliaments for Warwickshire between February 1388 and September 1397. But Sir Thomas Sakevill who represented Buckinghamshire fourteen times between October 1377 and September 1388 seems not to have enjoyed such exalted favour. Nor did Sir Thomas FitzNichol who was returned for Gloucestershire fourteen times between October 1382 and 1414. Perhaps this may have reflected a desire on the part of the county community to be represented in parliament by men experienced in the arts of politics. This quality would go some way to compensate for the short duration of parliaments which rendered control of the King's actions impossible to achieve. It is probably in such terms that the appearance of burgesses as knights of the shire is also to be explained. For example, Andrew Pendock, who

[91] N. Denholm-Young, *History and Heraldry* (Oxford, 1965), p. 152.
[92] Bates Harbin, 'Members of Parliament for the County of Somerset', p. 60.
[93] N. B. Lewis, 'Re-election to Parliament in the Reign of Richard II', *Eng. Hist. Rev.*, xlviii (1933), 376.

had represented the town of Gloucester at least eight times between 1307 and 1326, represented the shire in 1327.[94] His career was far excelled, however, by that of William Heyberer half a century later. Heyberer, like Pendock, began by sitting for the borough of Gloucester which he represented eight times between 1361 and January 1380. He went on to represent the shire in five more parliaments.[95] Once again, re-election is seen to be more prevalent in the 1380s than 1320s.

A desire by the shire to have experienced representatives in parliament is certainly part of the explanation. But the desire of local knights and esquires to speak for their shire in parliament may well have been equally important. Re-election to parliament, even if by itself it cannot be taken to prove a positive willingness, certainly implies no reluctance on the part of that circle of the country gentry to accept a responsibility that could confer lustre and distinction.[96] As the century went on, sheriffs and knights of the shire came increasingly to be chosen in each shire from the same group of men. Between 1299 and 1340 twenty men held the shrievalty in Gloucestershire; of these eight were returned at some time to parliament. Of the twenty men who held the shrievalty in the last twenty-eight years of the century, when tenure of office was limited to just one year, no fewer than fourteen went to at least one parliament. There is an indication too that a *cursus honorum* was developing. Between 1300 and 1400 three sheriffs of Gloucester were chosen to represent their shire very soon after completing their term of office in the shrievalty: John Clifford, Sir Peter le Veel and Laurence Sebrok. But far more striking is the recurrence of the reverse sequence of events: no fewer than eleven men were appointed to the shrievalty

[94] For a discussion see M. McKisack, *The Parliamentary Representation of the English Boroughs during the Middle Ages* (Oxford, 1932), pp. 116–7.

[95] Equally, knights or esquires are occasionally returned by boroughs in this period. Although the invasion of the boroughs did not begin in earnest until the fifteenth century, John Sergeant of Stone, for example, secured election at Bristol in 1363.

[96] J. R. Maddicott, 'The County Community and the Making of Public Opinion in Fourteenth-Century England', *Trans. Roy. Hist. Soc.*, 5th series, xxviii (1978), 33, reaches the similar conclusion that 'election had become a privilege for the elected'. The declining importance attached to mainperning as early as 1327 suggests that attendance at parliament was no longer seen as a burden to be avoided.

almost immediately after sitting in parliament. The first was Sir Richard de la Rivere: having sat in the parliament of April 1314 he was appointed sheriff of Gloucester in the following November. After 1350 the practice gathers pace. For example, Sir John Pointz who sat in the parliament of May 1368 was appointed sheriff on the following 27 November; and Ralph Walsh who represented Gloucestershire in October 1383 was selected to fill the shrievalty on 1 December next. The practice seems too common in the later fourteenth century to be mere coincidence. Perhaps a session of parliament provided the Council and Exchequer with the opportunity to become acquainted with men from the shires who could be candidates for office. By 1380, a knight who had just distinguished himself by serving in parliament stood a good chance of becoming sheriff of his county in the following November or December when the sheriffs were changed.

iv

If the history of the shrievalty in the late middle ages is seen as one of decline, it is because some of the duties which once pertained to it were now performed by newer officials such as the escheator and the keepers of the peace.

The origins of the latter lay in the disturbed conditions of 1264–5 when rival sets of local captains were appointed throughout the shire by the King and his baronial opponents.[97] After 1265 the office came to be associated with law enforcement rather than defence, and by the reign of Edward II the keepers had become a regular part of the administrative machinery for the enforcement of the policing clauses of the Statute of Winchester. Their commissions empowered them to enquire by sworn inquest of felonies and trespasses, and to arrest and imprison the indicted until the cases could be brought before the justices of gaol delivery, of assize or even of King's Bench if it was itinerant.[98] But in the reign of Edward III the powers of the keepers were the subject of a heated debate between the Commons on the one hand and the King and magnates on the other. The view of the

[97] A. Harding, *The Law Courts of Medieval England* (London, 1973), p. 93.
[98] *English Government at Work*, iii, 187.

latter that effective law enforcement could best be achieved by the use of commissions with wide powers was challenged by the gentry who preferred that the keepers of the peace should be permitted not only to hear but also to determine indictments.[99] But the argument did not rest there. The Commons did not merely want a more comprehensive commission for the keepers; they also demanded a say in their appointment. If the old demand for a right to nominate the sheriff was all but extinct in the fourteenth century, it carried conviction still in respect of the keepers. The wishes of the Commons were met in the Walton Ordinances of July 1338. In addition to conceding the election of sheriffs Edward III allowed the shires to nominate 'touz les autres grantz ministres des countes', a phrase which was taken to include the keepers.[100] The evidence suggests that the power to nominate keepers of the peace was greatly valued. In April 1338 the government had summoned representatives from the shires to assemblies at York and Westminster to discuss the enforcement of law and order. From these meetings, Miss Putnam suggested, the representatives returned to their counties to draw up lists of nominees from which the King's council chose the members of the commissions of the peace of 6 July.[101] It is instructive to compare these lists of nominees, drawn up perhaps in the county court, with those who were eventually appointed. Gloucestershire submitted the names of Sir Thomas de Berkeley of Berkeley, Sir John de Bures, John Giffard of Leckhampton, Sir John de Sudeley and Sir Thomas de Berkeley of Coberley, but of these only the last appeared in the commission of 6 July.[102] Although the lord of Berkeley was omitted from this final commission it may well have been his influence that was responsible for the changes. Bures, Giffard and Sudeley were replaced by three men of whom at least two—Sir William Tracy and William de Cheltenham—were his retainers.[103] Thus the effect of this concession to gentry aspirations which the Walton Ordinances represented, was nullified by amendments made subsequently to the list of county nominees.

[99] B. H. Putnam, 'The Transformation of the Keepers of the Peace into the Justices of the Peace', *Trans. Roy. Hist. Soc.*, 4th series, xii (1929), 19–48.
[100] Ibid., 35–6.   [101] Ibid., 37.
[102] C.267/9 m. 5; *Cal. Pat. Rolls 1338–40*, p. 135.
[103] Smyth, i, 313, 342.

Nevertheless, the Commons continued to press their point of view. At first they wanted the keepers to be chosen locally by the kind of procedure for choosing sheriffs which was envisaged in the *Articuli super Cartas* and presumably too in the Walton Ordinances. In January 1348 the Commons petitioned for two lords, two knights and two men of law to be chosen by the people of each shire to keep the peace.[104] Lancashire had actually elected keepers and submitted lists of nominees to the government in 1345.[105] But in the second parliament of 1348, held in March, they changed their approach by demanding that keepers should be chosen and sworn during parliament;[106] and this was to be the line that they took for as long as the manner of appointment of the keepers was a subject of controversy in the fourteenth century. In 1363 the Commons successfully petitioned that the knights and burgesses then assembled in parliament should choose the justices of labourers and keepers of the peace who were not to be removed at the suggestion of evil-wishers to make way for men of lesser means.[107] Similar demands from the Commons, however, met with a polite refusal in 1365, 1376, 1379, and 1390.[108] But they must have had frequent opportunity to exert pressure on the King and his council as full lists of commissions of the peace were often issued just after a session of parliament, as in 1351, 1361, 1364, and 1380.[109]

It seems significant that the Commons claimed for themselves in parliament, and not for the county court, the power to nominate keepers. They were probably trying to avoid the pitfalls of 1338. Even if the King assented to a petition the Commons had no ability to enforce its will once parliament had dispersed; thus the way was clear for magnate influence to assert itself in the interval in the appointment of local officials. Only if the keepers of the peace were chosen and sworn while parliament was sitting could this danger be averted. But the concern which the Commons showed over the selection of keepers accords ill with their apparent disregard for the similar power to nominate sheriffs. The main difference of course was that the keepers of the

---

[104] *Rot. Parl.*, ii, 174.
[105] Putnam, 'The Transformation of the Keepers of the Peace', p. 43.
[106] *Rot. Parl.*, ii, 201.   [107] Ibid., ii, 277.
[108] Ibid., ii, 286, 333; iii, 65, 269.
[109] Putnam, 'The Transformation of the Keepers of the Peace', pp. 43–4.

peace, not being financial agents of the Crown, would never incur debts for which those who selected them would be held responsible. Moreover, in an age when the packed jury and the false indictment were the stock-in-trade of local politics, the power and influence which lay at the disposal of the keepers was enormous. The Commons were therefore not slow to appreciate how the grant in 1344 of the power to determine cases when lawyers were present enhanced the local standing of the justices, for it was soon afterwards, in the parliament of March 1348, that the demand for parliamentary nomination of the keepers was first made.[110]

Such an interpretation sees the keepers at the centre of local rivalries and influences rather than, as the sheriffs occasionally were, local actors in the drama of national politics. Until Richard II's reign there is little to suggest that this was not the case. In the 1320s the keepers were not yet of sufficient importance to attract the attention of the Despensers, and there is no evidence of the appointment in Gloucestershire of any of their dependants. Only with the appointment of Thomas de Berkeley, Mortimer's son-in-law, and his trusted retainer Sir William de Wauton in March. 1327 does political partisanship become apparent.[111] It is in the reign of Richard II that political influence might be expected to assert itself. In Gloucestershire, as in East Anglia, though, the political role of the J.P.s was not sufficiently important to lead the Appellants to issue a new commission.[112] The only commission of the reign to reveal political nominees was that of 14 November 1398 when the prominent courtier, Sir John Russell of Strensham (Worcs.) was appointed for the first time; he also made his first appearance on the commission of the peace for Suffolk where he held lands by right of his wife.[113] The commission of 14 November 1398 was the last to be appointed for Gloucestershire in the reign of Richard II. But there are clear signs in other

[110] It is worth recalling that once the J.P.s recovered the determining power in 1368 they never again lost it.

[111] Cal. Pat. Rolls 1327–30, p. 89.

[112] R. L. Storey, 'Liveries and Commissions of the Peace, 1388–1390', in The Reign of Richard II, ed. Du Boulay & Barron, p. 234.

[113] Cal. Pat. Rolls 1396–9, p. 435. For Russell's marriage to the widow of Sir John Wingfield see J. M. Wingfield, Some Records of the Wingfield Family (London, 1925), p. 3. For his career see A. Goodman, The Loyal Conspiracy, pp. 150–2.

counties of J.P.s being appointed for political reasons in these closing years when Richard II was also manipulating his men into the shrievalties. The commission of the peace for neighbouring Herefordshire issued on 27 July 1397, shortly after Richard had moved against the former Appellant lords, numbered two esquires of the household, Robert Witney and Thomas Clanvow, among its ten members.[114] Witney and Clanvow remained J.P.s until the accession of Henry IV when they were both removed. When a new commission for Warwickshire was issued on 26 April 1399 the opportunity was taken to appoint Sir John Russell a justice in a third county; Sir William Bagot, of course, had long been a J.P. in this, his home shire.[115] The indications are, then, that courtiers were being placed in the commissions of the peace just as surely as they were being appointed to the shrievalties and returned to parliament as knights of the shire. Even in these closing years of the reign, though, political nominees were in a tiny minority on the commissions of the peace. Of the eleven members of the Gloucestershire commission of 14 November 1398 three were magnates, three justices, one a courtier, and four local gentry whose connections, if any, are not known.

But how many of these J.P.s might be expected to be present at one of the quarterly sessions of the bench? Clearly, the magnates who were nominal members of the peace commission in several counties could hardly be expected to attend when most of their time was devoted to the great affairs of the realm. The surviving rolls of the Gloucestershire sessions of the peace show, not surprisingly, that the gentry were the most regular attenders: they were the advocates of the cause of the J.P.s, and it was they who would have had the most time to devote to local affairs. The records of ten sessions of the peace held at Gloucester between 1361 and 1398 give an idea of the attendance record of the J.P.s. On 10 March 1395, 4 August 1395, and 16 December 1395 three justices were present of whom one was a justice of the central courts and two were local gentlemen. At another four sessions four J.P.s attended; and at three sessions those present rose to five, on each occasion the justice whose attendance was required

[114] *Cal. Pat. Rolls 1396–9*, p. 227; cf. E.101/403/22 (Wardrobe Book, 16–17 Richard II).

[115] *Cal. Pat. Rolls 1396–9*, p. 437; Bagot was first appointed as J.P. on 10 November 1389 (*Cal. Pat. Rolls 1388–92*, p. 139).

being Sir John Cassy, an Exchequer baron who lived at Wightfield near Deerhurst. Of the local lords who might have put in an appearance Gilbert Talbot attended on 27 May 1361; Thomas de Berkeley was not present at any of these ten sessions.[116]

The question of attendance, of course, has to be seen within the context of the expansion in size of the commissions of the peace. The nominal size of the commissions far exceeded the attendance at the sessions held at Gloucester. In the 1390s the Gloucestershire J.P.s were usually nine or ten in number, of whom never more than four or five could be expected to attend. But the magnates hardly ever turned up, and never more than one or two of the King's justices were present. It therefore fell to the gentry to transact most of the business that came before the bench. Small wonder, then, that the Commons were so anxious for stronger powers to be granted to the keepers when the quarterly sessions were almost entirely the preserve of the local gentlemen.

During the reign of Edward II the keepers of the peace in Gloucestershire never numbered more than four, and in the reign of his son they never exceeded five until 1352.[117] Yet thereafter the pressure for expansion seemed inexorable. Once the determining power was securely theirs, the importance of the J.P.s in the local community was bound to increase, and correspondingly the pressure for a place on the bench must have increased too. In 1348 the Commons had said the commissions should be composed of six men—two lords, two gentry, and two men of law.[118] This notion seems to have survived into Richard II's reign when at Cambridge in 1388, the Commons requested that six gentlemen and two men of law should be appointed to each commission.[119] But in most respects it was the gentry who stood to benefit if more J.P.s were appointed and the later history of this demand is not known.[120] In the 1370s eight J.P.s were usually chosen in Gloucestershire, but with the commission of 8 March

116 *Rolls of the Gloucestershire Sessions of the Peace, 1362–98*, ed. E. G. Kimball (Trans. Bristol & Gloucs. Arch. Soc., 62, 1940), 54–7.

117 The commission of 3 December 1355 shrank from nine to seven, but that of 16 February 1359 reverted to nine (*Cal. Pat. Rolls 1354–8*, p. 227; *1358–61*, p. 219).

118 *Rot. Parl.*, ii, 174.

119 *The Reign of Richard II*, ed. Du Boulay and Barron, p. 139.

120 See also below, p. 155.

1382 the number rose to no fewer than twenty-one.[121] If this commission was probably exceptional because of its responsibility for dealing with the Peasants Revolt, that issued on 21 December 1382 was just as large, and when a reduction was finally effected, on 2 July 1383, the commission was still sizeable at fourteen J.P.s.[122] It remained at about this size until 1389 when it was brought down to eight, in accordance with the wishes that the Commons had expressed at Cambridge in the previous year.[123]

It was the addition of men from the locality that was responsible for this explosion in members in the 1380s; but few of them were knights or even wealthy esquires. Of the twenty-one members of the commission of 8 March 1382 six were knights, two men of law, four richer esquires, one or possibly two burgesses, and as many as five whose origins are shrouded in almost impenetrable obscurity.[124] Many of these newcomers, of course, lost their places on the bench later in the 1380s. But a few of them—John de Staunton, John atte Yate, Thomas Catewy and John Derhurst—survived to sit alongside the knights in the 1390s. The identity of these men can only be guessed at. They came from outside the ranks of the knightly families, and they were not lords of manors. Perhaps they were local lawyers. Or perhaps they were just the nominees of competing magnates who tried to gain control of this novel institution. However, there is no evidence to suggest that these considerable numbers of men were retainers. The social standing in the community of a few of these newcomers can be discerned. Thomas de Bradewell, of Broadwell, who was appointed to the commissions of the peace on 8 March 1382 and 21 December 1382, served as sheriff for three terms of office.[125] Described as an *armiger* in the poll tax returns, he perhaps belonged to that class of men whose fortunes improved in the post-Black Death world.[126] One of his colleagues on the bench in these years was John Chese, a resident of Thornbury where he took a lease on part of the demesne.

---

[121] *Cal. Pat. Rolls 1381–5*, p. 138.
[122] Ibid., p. 346.
[123] *Cal. Pat. Rolls 1388–92*, p. 135.
[124] These five are Thomas Catewy, John Gayner, John Stanshawe, John Cosyn, William Grenefield.
[125] See above pp. 19, 112n.   [126] E.179/113/31 m. 1.

Although Chese could not have supported knighthood, prosperity probably did not elude him: from 1371 to 1386 he was the earl of Stafford's receiver at Thornbury and in 1385–6 he was the earl's steward in the counties of Hereford and Gloucester.[127] If these two men are typical of those who were serving on the bench for the first time in Richard II's reign, then both magnate patronage and the ambitions of the newly prosperous must be numbered among the factors that led to the expansion in the numbers of the J.P.s.

v

The history of the office of escheator in the later fourteenth century echoes that of the sheriff. Similar demands made by the Commons evoke a similar response from the Crown. In the earlier decades, though, when it underwent many changes, the office was the subject of a tussle between the Crown and the nobility.

In the reign of Edward I the river Trent formed the boundary which divided England into two escheatries. This arrangement lasted until the accession of Edward III when there was a reversion to the earlier system. After further changes in the 1330s, in November 1341 the escheatries were regrouped to coincide with the shrievalties.[128] Lasting until 1357 this proved more durable than earlier arrangements; but from 1357 to 1360 an escheator was appointed to account for Gloucestershire, Herefordshire, Shropshire and the Welsh March. His successor, appointed in 1360, accounted for only Gloucestershire, Herefordshire and the March. This escheatry lasted until 1395 when Gloucestershire and Herefordshire were finally separated, each now having its own escheator. In the evolution of the office in the fourteenth century 1341 is probably the most important date: thereafter, no serious attempt was ever made to revive the huge escheatries which had characterized the reign of Edward I. The changes which were made between 1323 and 1341 have been explained in terms of the interplay of court and baronial ideas.

[127] Stafford Record Office, D.641/1/2/143–150.
[128] S. T. Gibson, 'The Escheatries, 1327–41', *Eng. Hist. Rev.*, xxxvi (1921), 218–25.

The barons who reacted against the innovations of the Despenser era by favouring two great escheatorships in 1327 had come by 1340 to clamour for local escheatries. But the history of the escheator's office has not been worked out as thoroughly as the sheriff's, and much of the reasoning that lay behind the various stages in its evolution remains obscure. Other questions were at stake in addition to the size of the escheatries.

The evidence suggests that corruption on the part of escheators was attracting more criticism. In 1362 for the first time the Commons submitted a comprehensive petition which was enacted as a statute.[129] It listed a number of ills and imposed two years imprisonment if its terms were infringed. Like most medieval legislation this may well have gone unheeded: in the following year another petition made a more specific complaint: that escheators and other ministers of the King were seizing the lands of those whom they incorrectly assumed to be outlaws.[130] Such malpractice was still going on in 1387 when William Barwell, a Gloucestershire escheator, took five marks from John Ball of Lemington, who had been declared an outlaw, not to seize his lands and chattels.[131] Barwell was indicted before King's Bench in 1388 and eventually paid a fine of two marks.[132] Thus he still made a profit, just out of this single piece of corruption. To the complaints about the escheator's conduct was added another petition in 1368 on eligibility for office. It recalled that an escheator should hold sufficient land to answer to the King and his people; but it was more important for the successful introduction of the £20 income qualification.[133] The significance of this was considerable, for it was by coupling the shrievalty to a demand for its confirmation in 1371 that the Commons secured the £20 landed qualification for that office as well as the escheatorship.[134] By the 1370s it looked as if the Commons had secured the enforcement of their two time-honoured demands for annual replacement and a land-holding obligation, now defined at £20, which had been nominally conceded by the King so long before. Suspicion of the government's sincerity, of course,

[129] Rot. Parl., ii, 272; Stat. Realm, i, 374–5.
[130] Rot. Parl., ii, 277.
[131] K.B.27/507 Rex m. 30d.
[132] K.B.27/512 Fines.   [133] Rot. Parl., ii, 296.
[134] See above, p. 110.

remained, and in respect of the escheatorship these fears were justified.

The call for annual replacement, as required by the 1340 statute, came up again in 1372, 1377, and 1378.[135] On the last occasion the Crown made its position clearer than it had before. It agreed to limit the term of office of sheriffs and sub-sheriffs to twelve months; but because it would not be advantageous to change them annually, escheators and sub-escheators could remain in office for up to three years. This was a correct description of current policy. Sheriffs were now being changed annually. Escheators, however, were not. They often enjoyed a two years' term of office. Between 1360 when the escheatorship of Gloucestershire and Herefordshire was created and 1400 twenty-four men held this bailiwick.[136] Of these, just one, Philip de Lutteley, served for five years (1361–5). One, William Auncell, served for three years (1368–71). As many as seven served for terms of office of two years. The remainder held the post for one year each. Despite further petitions calling for annual rotation of both offices, royal policy remained consistent until 1397 in enforcing the 1340 statutes only in respect of the shrievalty.

If annual replacement remained as elusive as ever, did the Commons fare any better with their demand that the escheator hold lands or rents worth at least £20 a year? A study of the escheators for Gloucestershire and Herefordshire may cast some light on the standing of men who held the office after it was separated from that of sheriff. The twenty-four men appointed are a varied group. One came from Staffordshire, one from Warwickshire, two from Worcestershire, seven from Herefordshire and eight from Gloucestershire. For the remaining six there is no surviving evidence to indicate a place of residence. Philip de Lutteley, whose term of office was the longest of these escheators, held land in Staffordshire and Shropshire when he died in 1369.[137] John Lucy (1377–8) was probably a member of the family from Charlecote (Warwick.) whose local prominence may have been due to his position as steward to Edmund, earl of March.[138] Of the two escheators from Worcestershire Thomas

[135] Rot. Parl., ii, 313; iii, 24, 44.
[136] List of Escheators, pp. 52–3.
[137] Cal. Fine Rolls 1369–77, p. 58.
[138] K.B.27/471 Rex m. 9.

Saunders of Newbold (1360–1) is otherwise unknown, but Edmund Bridges (1375–6) held land in both Gloucestershire and Worcestershire.[139] Between 1363 and 1369 he was under-sheriff of Worcester, and he served as sheriff of Hereford 1374–5. Some men of similar standing can be numbered among those from Herefordshire who held the escheatorship. Two were knights— John ap Rees (1372–4), and Thomas Oldcastle (1388–9)—and two more—Thomas Walwyn (1386–7, 1391–2) and John Scudamore (1389–90)—could have supported knighthood.[140] William Jouet (1394–5) was probably a burgess of Hereford.[141] Little is known about the remaining two Herefordshire escheators, John Hortesley of Letton (1371–2) and William Hampton (1387–8), but they were probably not men of great means.[142]

The escheators who came from Gloucestershire also included some well-known names, some obscure. John Sergeant (1374–5) and John Couley (1384–5) were both stewards of Thomas de Berkeley.[143] Hugh de Bisley (1380–1, 1382–4) held just one manor, in the village from which he took his name, but was prominent in the minor offices of local administration.[144] Robert Whittington[145] (1392–4), Ralph Walsh[146] (1376–77), and Robert Pointz[147] (1395–97, 1399–1400) were all members of

[139] Gloucs. Inqs. post Mortem, vi, 251; V. C. H. Worcs., iii, 40.

[140] In 1316 the Walwyn family held manors in Byford, Yarkhill and Weston and Stoke Edith (Feud. Aids, ii, 386, 389) and they later inherited the estates of the Helyons. John Scudamore was an esquire of the King's household in 1396–7 (E.101/403/10) and was knighted by 1409. He received a fee from the Talbots, confirmed during the minority of Gilbert Talbot in 1397 (Cal. Pat. Rolls 1396–9, p. 145).

[141] He represented the City of Hereford in the parliaments of 1381 and February and September, 1388.

[142] In 1316 one John de Hortesley held the manor of Letton, but its absence from later feudal surveys makes the descent of the manor difficult to trace (Feud. Aids, ii, 387).

[143] Just. 3/60/4 m. 21d; Just. 3/180 m. 24d.

[144] He was appointed to the commission of the peace once, on 2 July 1383 (Cal. Pat. Rolls 1381–5, p. 346). Otherwise his activities were confined mainly to assessing and collecting taxes (Cal. Fine Rolls 1377–83, p. 339).

[145] He held the manors of Pauntley (Gloucs.), Sollers Hope (Heref.), Upton-by-Haselor (Warwicks.) and by 1391 Staunton (Worcs.).

[146] See above pp. 72, 117.

[147] He held Iron Acton and Elkstone (Gloucs.) and several manors in Somerset.

respectable knightly families in Gloucestershire. Of all these men something is known, but Thomas de Monnington (1361), John Benet of Cirencester (1367–8) and Thomas Laurence of Compton (1378–80) remain shadowy figures. Thomas de Monnington, though said to be of Gloucestershire, may be a kinsman of Hugh de Monnington, sheriff of Hereford 1390–1. John Benet was presumably a burgess. Nor were these the only obscure men to find their way into the escheatorship. Robert de Hadham (1365–7), perhaps to be identified with the escheator for Middlesex in 1355 of the same name, William Auncell, Henry Moton, William Barwell, John Gomond, and David Vaghan were almost certainly ineligible under the terms of the statute of 1368.[148] The very silence of the records points to this conclusion. If the importance of an office is to be measured by the standing of the men who occupied it, then the escheatorship must be counted inferior to the shrievalty.

Though it was not the most prestigious office in the shire in the eyes of the local gentry the escheatorship could still be vital to the King. It was the task of the escheator to take into the King's keeping the lands of the former Appellant lords whom Richard II arrested in July 1397. Thus it was in Richard's interest to have in this job men just as reliable as those who were appointed sheriff or elected to parliament. The men chosen for Gloucestershire in the closing years of the reign reflect this thinking, and the presence of at least one puzzling figure is explained. Robert Pointz of Iron Acton, the retainer of Thomas Despenser, held the escheatorship for two years from 1395 to 1397. Contrary to what had become accepted practice his tenure of the shrievalty (1396–7) ran concurrently with the last year of his escheatorship. Pointz was succeeded as escheator in February 1397 by one David Vaghan who was a King's esquire and Marshal of the Hall in 1393 when he received an annuity of £16 at the Exchequer.[149] Vaghan held office for two years. His replacement on 28 November 1399 by Robert Pointz is rather curious in view of Richard's fall a few months earlier. Perhaps there was no political significance behind this second term of office of his. Nevertheless, the

[148] For Hadham see *List of Escheators*, p. 43. William Auncell was escheator of Wiltshire, 1371–2 (ibid., p. 147), where his lands probably lay (*Cal. Close Rolls 1349–54*, p. 201).
[149] *Cal. Pat. Rolls 1391–6*, p. 246.

appointments to the escheatorship in the closing years of the reign do seem to be consistent with Richard II's general policy towards other local offices.

This discussion has concentrated on the second half of the century: until 1341 there were either two large or eight smaller escheatries, and under both forms of organization sub-escheators would have been appointed for each county. Unfortunately it is rarely possible to identify these sub-escheators as their names were not recorded on the extents which they took: thus any discussion of their economic standing is bound to be speculative. The enquiries conducted in each shire in 1324 to unearth the corrupt and oppressive practices of sheriffs and other ministers of the Crown provide the names of two sub-escheators in Gloucestershire:[150] Nicholas Pulesdon is otherwise unknown to history, but John de Sloghtre held lands, the extent of which is difficult to guess, in Gloucestershire and Worcestershire.[151] A third sub-escheator known to have held office in the country at this time was Richard de Foxcote. Although he went on to become sheriff in 1332 there is no reason to believe that he was very much wealthier than Pulesdon or Sloghtre.[152] None of the three came from a family capable of supporting knighthood.

E. R. Stevenson, who published a valuable list of fifteen sub-escheators from 1327–30, suggested, however, that they were 'definitely among the substantial landowners, or, failing that, as having influential friends in the counties in which they acted'.[153] Perhaps the stress should be placed on the latter half of his statement, for if Richard de Haresfield, the sub-escheator he names for Gloucestershire, is typical of his colleagues, they were definitely not substantial landowners.[154] Stevenson pointed to the recognisances for £100 which each made to Simon de Bereford, escheator south of Trent. But the common form adopted when enrolling the bond to the effect that the debt

---

[150] Just. 1/296 mm. 1d, 2.

[151] The Sloghtre family held an estate at Upper Slaughter (V.C.H. Gloucs., vi, 136) where John de Sloghtre paid 4s. in the parliamentary subsidy of 1327. He also had an estate at South Cerney where he was assessed at 3s. 1½d. (Gloucs. Subsidy Roll, pp. 8, 18). In Worcestershire he held a chief messuage at Eckington (V.C.H. Worcs., iv, 70n).

[152] See above, p. 118.

[153] English Government at Work, ii, 165.

[154] Ibid., 164.

would be levied in default on the contractor's lands does not mean that he necessarily held lands to the precise value of his debt.[155] Richard de Haresfield held no manors in Gloucestershire, and only one transaction which he made is known to us.[156] Nor does he appear to have held any other office of importance. It would, of course, be unwise to generalise from these four cases. Gilbert de Berewick, sub-escheator in Somerset and Dorset, went on to become sheriff of Wiltshire in 1334.[157] Suffice it to argue simply that Stevenson's suggestion was not soundly based, and that other sub-escheators seem to have had more in common with Richard de Haresfield than Gilbert de Berewick.

vi

It is unnecessary to trace in such detail the history of the coroner who has already been the subject of a detailed monograph.[158] Coroners were first appointed in 1194 to 'keep the pleas of the crown'; and their duties included holding inquests upon dead bodies, receiving abjurations of the realm made by felons in sanctuary, hearing appeals and attending and sometimes organizing exactions and outlawries promulgated in the county court.

Not only their conduct but their qualifications for office formed the subject of petitions of the Commons in parliament. However, the Commons complained about the coroner less often than they did about the sheriff and escheator. One demand was common to all three officials; in 1351 they asked for sheriffs, escheators and coroners to be changed annually, alleging incorrectly in the case of coroners that a statute required this. The King's answer, that the existing statute be enforced, could only apply to the second part of the petition which called for coroners

---

[155] For example, John de Elkstone acted as a mainpernor for a man who had defaulted. In 1358–9 the King took possession of the lands at Leckhampton which John had held at the time of his death. Described as *frisca et inculta*, these were worth only 15s. 6d. in the first year of accounting and 13s. in the following two years (S.C.6/856/12).

[156] *Cal. Pat. Rolls 1327–30*, p. 553.

[157] *English Government at Work*, ii, 165.

[158] R. F. Hunnisett, *The Medieval Coroner* (Cambridge, 1961).

to be chosen from those who had sufficient possessions in the county to answer the King and his people.[159] Earlier legislation had not in fact limited the coroner's term of office: the statute of 1340 applied only to sheriffs and escheators. Of coroners it required only that they hold sufficient lands in fee in their county.[160]

The standing in the community both of the coroner and of those that elected him formed the subject of a petition three years later in 1354.[161] Whereas the coroner used to be elected by the most substantial people in the counties, it said, his office was now secured only for the profit it brought. The King agreed to their remedy that coroners should be elected in the full county court by the men of most substance.

But the amount of land which a coroner was expected to hold was never defined in money terms. The first Statute of Westminster (1275) had ordered that coroners should be chosen from 'the most wise and discreet knights' and in 1300 some knights are still found taking up office: in Gloucestershire, Sir Nicholas Gamage and Sir John Bishop.[162] For most of the century, though, there is an almost complete absence of knights. They only reappear in this office as a result of the writ sent to all sheriffs in 1392 which required knights to be elected as coroners in accordance with the all but dormant clause in the Statute of Westminster.[163] In the last six years of Richard II's reign the election or appointment of at least three knights in Gloucestershire—Sir Alan Boteler, Sir Thomas FitzNichol, and Sir Maurice Russel—testifies to the enforcement of this writ.[164]

Most of the county coroners were men of lesser means. Unfortunately, it is not possible to compile a complete list of the holders of this office as it is of the shrievalty. The main sources are the few coroners' rolls that survive and the writs *de coronatore eligendo* enrolled on the Close Rolls. For Gloucestershire these combine to give the names of at least forty-two coroners, enough perhaps to offer some idea of the kind of men who held the office. Most noteworthy is the almost total non-representation of the

[159] *Rot. Parl.*, ii, 229.   [160] *Stat. Realm*, i, 283.
[161] *Rot. Parl.*, ii, 260.
[162] *Cal. Close Rolls 1296–1302*, p. 269; *1302–7*, p. 261.
[163] *Cal. Close Rolls 1389–92*, pp. 449–50.
[164] Ibid., *1392–6*, p. 333; *1396–9*, p. 35; *1397–9*, p. 359.

knightly families, except in the opening and closing years of the century. In the long period that lay between only William de Rodborough (1371-4) came from a family which could have supported knighthood.[165] The others were not lords of manors: they are absent alike from the inquisitions *post mortem* and the surveys occasioned by the levying of feudal aids. The indications are, then, that the office of coroner in the fourteenth century had fallen to men of little substance. Some, at least, were of notoriously little means: the reason given in the writs for their replacement was that they were insufficiently qualified. Once again, though, the evidence is too sparse to give a clear idea of what constituted insufficiency. In Edward I's reign one coroner was replaced who held land and rents worth 10 marks yearly and another who held only 50s. yearly.[166] Perhaps no one figure commanded acceptance; if it had, it might have received a statutory recognition, as the £20 level did for the other two offices. At least six Gloucestershire coroners were removed for insufficiency: Ralph Hathewy, Thomas Herland, George Bellamy, Richard de Compton, John Champeneys and John Butte 'corvesor'.[167] Another, Walter de Combe, who was a Gloucestershire coroner in 1333, was removed from office as a coroner in Wiltshire in 1356 for the same reason.[168]

How much landed income men such as these enjoyed is impossible to say. Ten marks would probably be a generous estimate. If their income remains elusive, an idea of their standing in the local community can also be obtained by considering how many of them held other offices in the shire. Three of the five knights who served as coroners in Gloucestershire sat in parliament; but so did three of the less well endowed coroners: William de Tytherington, Walter de Combe and Elias de Filton.[169] Among the knights of the shire these men were among the most obscure. Five held the shrievalty. Of these,

[165] R. F. Hunnisett, 'Medieval Coroners Rolls', *American Jnl. of Legal Hist.*, iii (1959). William held the manors of Leigh and Hedon (C. E. Watson, 'The Minchinhampton Custumal', *Trans. Bristol & Gloucs. Arch. Soc.*, 54 (1932), opp. p. 355; *Gloucs. Inqs. post Mortem*, vi, 127, 133-4, 183).

[166] Hunnisett, *The Medieval Coroner*, p. 176.

[167] *Cal. Close Rolls 1313-18*, p. 249; *1318-23*, p. 169; *1360-4*, p. 20; *1381-5*, p. 375; *1385-9*, p. 43.

[168] *Cal. Close Rolls 1354-60*, p. 260.

[169] On these men see also below, pp. 156-9.

Robert Whittington, Sir Maurice Russel, Sir Thomas FitzNichol and Robert Somerville came from the group of wealthy coroners elected after the 1392 writ, and only Philip Mareschal, coroner in 1348 and sheriff in 1351, came from a humbler background. As his tenure of the shrievalty lasted only six months, his may have been no more than a temporary appointment at a time when the Black Death may have reduced the number of potential office-holders. One coroner was an under-sheriff of Gloucester. This was Thomas Cole, about whom a little more is known. He was also clerk to the J.P.s in Gloucestershire, and in this office he collaborated with Richard Ruyhall to produce a false record of a hearing before the bench.[170] By this time, in 1392, he was elderly: three years before he had been replaced as a coroner on grounds of infirmity.[171] In 1379 he and William Henley, a King's clerk, had been appointed farmers of the alien priory of Beckford, not far from the vill of Northway where Cole probably resided.[172] Though Thomas Cole was not from a well-established gentry family, the evidence suggests that he was entering the ranks of the lower gentry in the highly mobile society of the later fourteenth century.

A number of coroners served at various times as assessors and collectors of taxes. Elias de Filton, William de Rodborough, Richard Monmouth, Thomas Tresham and John Champeneys all served in this office on one or more occasions.[173] Of these only Filton moved higher in the *cursus honorum* of local office holding: he was a knight of the shire for Gloucestershire in 1346. While Hunnisett is quite correct to observe that coroners did undertake other tasks of local administration, these tasks must have been among those least esteemed as they were usually performed by men from lesser gentry families.[174]

It was the practice to appoint separate coroners for county and borough, but many writs did not distinguish between the two.[175] The caveat must be entered, then, that some at least of these

[170] *Cal. Pat. Rolls 1391–6*, p. 155.
[171] *Cal. Close Rolls 1389–92*, p. 44.
[172] *Cal. Pat. Rolls 1377–81*, p. 341.
[173] *Cal. Fine Rolls 1347–56*, p. 335; *1369–77*, p. 269; *1383–91*, pp. 19, 116–7; *1391–99*, p. 26.
[174] Hunnisett, *The Medieval Coroner*, p. 170.
[175] Ibid., p. 156.

coroners whose background is hidden from us may have been not county but borough coroners or burgesses who were elected to serve in the county. John Fraunceys of Bristol was removed from office as a county coroner in 1331 because as a merchant of Bristol he could not attend to his duties.[176] Richard Monmouth, a coroner at the end of the 1380s, was a contemporary and perhaps a relative of John Monmouth, a burgess of Gloucester who farmed the abbot of Westminster's demesnes at Elmstone Hardwick.[177] Richard witnessed a charter of John Adynet, a merchant of the Cotswold wool town of Northleach.[178] But if he began life in trade, he did not neglect to seek a stake in the land: in 1384 he is holding a moiety of a knight's fee in Shipton Solers (Gloucs.).[179] The estimate of 50s no doubt undervalued this estate, but it was hardly sufficient to place him alongside the old gentry families in wealth.

vii

The remaining offices can be dismissed summarily. They were mostly less important, and filled, it seems, by men below the gentry in rank.

The taxers have already been mentioned: a number of those who served as coroner also appear as collectors and assessors of the taxes on moveables granted by parliament. But the picture does not remain static. When parliament granted a subsidy at the beginning of the century the chief taxers in each county were usually two in number, underneath whom collectors would be appointed in the hundreds and, beneath them again, in the vills.[180] During the last thirty years of the fourteenth century, however, the tax commissions shared the tendency of the commissions of the peace to increase in size. The two chief taxers of 1320 or 1330 had become a large commission of ten or twelve

---

[176] *Cal. Close Rolls 1330–3*, p. 185.

[177] B. F. Harvey, 'The Leasing of the Abbot of Westminster's Demesnes in the Later Middle Ages', *Econ. Hist. Rev.*, 2nd series, xxii, i (1969), 21.

[178] *Cal. Close Rolls 1389–92*, pp. 357–8.

[179] *Cal. Close Rolls 1381–5*, p. 513.

[180] *A Lincolnshire Assize Roll for 1298*, ed. W. S. Thomson (Lincoln Rec. Soc., 36, 1944), xliv–xlv.

by the 1380s. The men appointed on 16 December 1384 typified those who assessed and collected the taxes in the reign of Richard II: Robert Whittington, Sir John Giffard, William Heyberer, Richard Busshell, Hugh Sencler, Thomas atte Yate, Thomas Weston the younger, John atte Yate, Philip de Aune, and Richard Brain.[181] Whittington and Giffard were the wealthiest of the taxers, each endowed with three manors, and with Heyberer, the Gloucester burgess, they had shared the honour of representing their county in parliament.[182] None of the other collectors named went on to hold other offices, but two came from families which were on the rise: Richard Busshell of Broad Marston and Richard Brain of the Forest of Dean.[183] If there were sufficient evidence to illuminate the careers of their colleagues it might be possible to show that the expansion in the size of these commissions was the result of pressure from newly prosperous men among the lesser gentry who sought to gain admission to the ranks of the office-holders.[184]

Of the sub-sheriffs and the officials in the hundreds little can be said. The 1324 enquiries into the misconduct of the King's ministers provide the names of two sub-escheators—Nicholas Pulesdon and John de Sloghtre[185]—and some bailiffs.[186] As the one complete subsidy roll for Gloucestershire to survive dates from only three years later it should be possible to gain some idea, however imprecise, of the economic status of these men. Yet, unfortunately, only one of them, Richard de Blebury, a bailiff of Kiftsgate hundred and of the liberty of Temple Guiting, can be traced in the subsidy roll. He paid the tiny sum of 8d. in Winchcombe.[187] Laurence de Abenhall was the bailiff of Botteslow hundred. Did he simply come from Abenhall or was he a member of the gentry family of that name? About him as about the other hundred bailiffs whose malpractices were uncovered the records are silent. Thomas Cole, who lived at the end of the

[181] Cal. Fine Rolls 1383–91, p. 69.

[182] For Heyberer see above, p. 127.

[183] The Brain family was armigerous by the sixteenth century. For a pedigree see Trans. Bristol & Gloucs. Arch. Soc., vi (1881–2), 296–7. For the Busshell family see The Visitation of the County of Gloucester, pp. 239–41.

[184] See also above, pp. 133–5.   [185] See above, p. 140.

[186] Just. 1/296 mm. 1–4.

[187] Gloucs. Subsidy Roll, p. 4.

century, is the only sub-sheriff of Gloucester whose name has survived. His career as a coroner and clerk to the J.P.s had already been noticed.[188] It is probably safe to assume that these minor office holders came from the shadowy area where the lesser gentry merged with the richer freeholders. Nevertheless, the occasional appearance of such men in offices usually filled by knights or wealthy esquires far above them in station prompts further reflection about the nature of office holding in the fourteenth century. How, for example, did Richard de la Hale, bailiff of the liberty of Cirencester and constable of the peace, come to sit in the parliament of February 1334 as one of the knights of the shire for Gloucestershire?[189] If he felt out of place there so too must Walter Poul, the clerk from the sheriff's office at Bedford, in the parliament of September 1336. It is time now to draw the various threads together.

viii

Historians have generally assumed that the burdens of local administration were willingly shouldered by the gentry; without the tacit consent of the knights and esquires who undertook these tasks medieval government, which lacked a paid bureaucracy in the shire, could not have been carried on. If they received no remuneration from the Exchequer, the local gentry may nevertheless have received unofficial rewards which made office holdings prestigious and perhaps even lucrative. Their willingness to accept the burdens would be the more understandable the less that it could be shown to spring from motives of pure altruism.

Of the offices to which the gentry aspired only that of knight of the shire in parliament was paid; the representatives of the shire received 4s. a day for the duration of the parliament and for the time they spent in travelling to and from Westminster. With the purely local offices it was different, for though they were unpaid there was opportunity for corruption. A knight or esquire appointed sheriff, keeper of the peace or escheator would be in a position directly to influence the lives of his neighbours and to

[188] See above, p. 144.   [189] See above, p. 122.

profit from those who sought to curry his favour or engage his support. The opportunities for such men to line their own pockets, it was realized by contemporaries, were considerable. As McKisack wrote, 'officials from the highest to the lowest were corruptible and the people knew it'.[190] The main check upon corruption was provided by the Exchequer. The obligation on the sheriff to present his accounts there twice each year, either personally or by attorney, prevented him from profiting at the King's expense, though not necessarily at that of his neighbours. For some sheriffs the responsibilities of office were undoubtedly a burden. In 1295 the Exchequer was still trying to collect the debts bequeathed by a sheriff of Surrey who had left office in 1257.[191] A negligent sheriff could incur debts which would afflict his family for generations.[192] His indebtedness on leaving the Gloucestershire shrievalty on 12 December 1372 led to John Clifford's removal from a commission to assess and collect a tax. Within a month of being appointed on 24 December 1372 Clifford was replaced because he still owed money to the King.[193] The fines which were imposed for neglect of duty, though seldom large, were yet another of those irritants which could combine to make the office of sheriff a source of intense worry for its holder.[194] Because it involved the heaviest responsibilities the shrievalty carried the greatest risks in its wake. It was such considerations, no doubt, that found expression in a Commons petition of 1380: because of *la grande grevance* borne by those who have served repeated or lengthy terms in the shrievalty, a man should not be appointed again if there was someone of sufficient standing in the county who has not held the office. In the view of the King's

---

[190] McKisack, *The Fourteenth Century*, p. 205.

[191] M. Mills, *Surrey Pipe Roll for 1295* (Surrey Rec. Soc., xxi, 1924), xxxi.

[192] Not only sheriffs but other ministers of the Crown faced this threat. Thomas, son of Sir Thomas Boteler of Badminton, was being pursued by the Exchequer in 1330–1 to account for the scutage for Edward II's army in Scotland, levied in 1319 when his father was a collector (*Cal. Fine Rolls 1319–27*, pp. 9–10; E.368/103 m. 32).

[193] *Cal. Fine Rolls 1369–77*, pp. 192, 199.

[194] For example, Sir Thomas Moigne (sheriff, 1360–3) was fined half a mark for an inadequate return to a writ and one mark for failing to make a return at all (K.B.27/412 Fines), and Sir John Tracy (sheriff, 1363–8, 1369–71) £5 for allowing a prisoner to escape (K.B.27/429 Fines).

council, however, the existing statutes provided adequate remedy.[195]

There were of course compensating advantages. The sheriff benefited financially from the desire of the rich and powerful in the neighbourhood to bend the law to their advantage. Sometimes he could collect quite substantial fees. The Hospitallers were paying an annuity of £30 to Richard de Foxcote, the sheriff of Gloucestershire in 1338:[196] an appreciable increase in the income of esquire like Foxcote who probably lacked the means to support knighthood. On a more modest scale was the fee of 40s. which Worcester Cathedral Priory was paying in 1369 to the earl of Warwick's deputy as sheriff of Worcester.[197] Those who held the major offices of the shire, moreover, were more likely than less influential country gentry to be invited by magnates, lay or ecclesiastical, to take stewardships. Such positions in seignorial administration could follow as well as precede prominence in local office-holding.

The opportunities for corruption open to the sheriff, too numerous to detail, may go a long way towards explaining his unpopularity in the fourteenth century. Some sheriffs, respectful of the oath which they swore at the beginning of their term of office, may have been honest and even-handed.[198] But such men were probably in the minority. The chance to pursue personal vendettas or to make an easy profit was also open to the escheator and coroner. The former might accept from relatives of the deceased tenant-in-chief a bribe to return a low valuation of an estate that was passing temporarily into the King's keeping; the latter expected a payment before viewing a dead body. Such corruption was endemic and if it was uncovered, it seems, to judge from the fines imposed in King's Bench, rarely to have incurred severe penalties.[199] The escheator's illicit income, to a

[195] *Rot. Parl.*, iii, 96.

[196] *The Knights Hospitaller in England*, ed. L. B. Larkin, 208.

[197] Worcester Cathedral Library, C.66 (account of Robert Wenlock, cellarer, 1369–70).

[198] One such was the sheriff of Norfolk and Suffolk who, when faced with demands for horses and carts for Berwick between 1312 and 1316, told the King that he had purveyed all that he could. Rather than resort to corruption or exploitation he begged to be excused (J. R. Maddicott, 'The English Peasantry and the Demands of the Crown' (*Past and Present* Supplement 1, 1975), p. 29).

[199] For the punishment of a corrupt escheator see above, p. 136.

greater extent than that of the sheriff perhaps, would have come from lay tenants; an undying ecclesiastical corporation would have no need to influence him except possibly to secure a sympathetic outcome to an enquiry into a possible alienation in mortmain. Still, Worcester Cathedral Priory made payments when the need arose. In 1344 the monks paid 40s. to the escheator and 6s. 8d. to the sub-escheator in connection with an inquisition the details of which are unspecified.[200] In 1345 they paid 20s. to the escheator of Shropshire and one mark each to the escheator and sub-escheator of Worcester.[201] Not only these officials but the taxers too intercepted income that should have passed to the Crown. Here the initiative lay with those who were closest to the taxpayer, but in 1324 various juries in Gloucestershire complained of both taxers and sub-taxers who kept money to line their own pockets and who had not made fair assessments of moveables.[202]

Office-holding might be a risk. But it is easy to see how it could be profitable; and if we are correct to surmise that pressure for expansion in the size of the bench came from below, then it may also have offered prestige. Nevertheless, the enrolment in considerable numbers in Chancery of exemptions from holding local office suggests that to some at least the prospect was too irksome to contemplate. In the fourteenth century nine Gloucestershire gentlemen were granted such exemptions. Their reasons for seeking them can only be the subject of enlightened guesswork, but circumstantial evidence may provide some pointers. Of the nine, at least two were prominent retainers.[203] For such men who were already busy or who spent time abroad on military or diplomatic expeditions, the purchase of an exemption would avoid much inconvenience. Two more of them were past their prime. Sir Richard de Croupes, whose military career had opened in the 1280s was granted an exemption on 19 July 1333, only three years before his death.[204] If he were twenty-

---

[200] Worcester Cathedral Library, C.59 (account of Robert de Weston, cellarer, 1344–5).

[201] Worcester Cathedral Library, C.60 (account of Robert de Weston, 1345–6).

[202] Just. 1/296 m. 3.

[203] Sir Peter and Sir Robert de la Mare, for whom see Fowler, *Henry of Grosmont*, p. 284 n. 40. Also see above p. 46.

[204] *Cal. Pat. Rolls 1330–4*, p. 459.

one when he was granted livery of his lands in 1278 Richard would have been seventy-nine when he died.[205] Another knight for whom considerations of ill health or old age may have been uppermost was Sir Thomas Boteler of Sudeley. If the inquisitions *post mortem* can be trusted he was aged twelve when he succeeded to the estates of Sir John de Sudeley in 1367.[206] Thus he was not elderly when he died in 1398.[207] But only seven months before his death on 21 September he obtained an exemption from holding office.[208] Pressing ill health may have influenced him. There are no extenuating circumstances to suggest why the other five men sought exemptions. They may have seen it as a useful precaution, or perhaps they took action on finding themselves suddenly pressed to take up local office. This would explain why Peter Corbet of Syston petitioned the Chancellor in 1350 to confirm an exemption he had been granted in 1337.[209] Such suggestions find some support in a parliamentary petition of 1377. The Commons requested that bachelors, esquires and other subjects of the King who were fighting, or were going to fight, in his wars, or were more than sixty years old, should not be appointed sheriff, escheator, coroner or tax collector or be put on juries. The King agreed to excuse such persons.[210]

Once obtained, these exemptions were not always used. Sir Thomas de Berkeley of Coberley, one of the busiest knights in the county, obtained an exemption on 7 October 1342.[211] Yet, in the next fifteen years he still served on many commissions, and held the shrievalty for the third time in 1355–6.[212] The precautionary nature of these exemptions is surely emphasized by the right which they conferred on the grantee to refuse to hold office *against his will*. They were granted, for example, to fighting knights or to stewards or busy retainers to be used if need be; they do not necessarily imply the unpopularity of office-holding. Some of the exemptions were granted to men who had never held office and apparently never wanted to hold office. One such in Gloucester-

[205] *Cal. Fine Rolls 1272*, p. 96.
[206] *C.I.P.M.*, xii, no. 166.   [207] *Gloucs. Inqs. post Mortem*, vi, 211–12.
[208] *Cal. Pat. Rolls 1396–9*, p. 316.
[209] S.C.8/246/12269; *Cal. Pat. Rolls 1334–8*, p. 388.
[210] *Rot. Parl.*, iii, 22.   [211] *Cal. Pat. Rolls 1350–3*, p. 534.
[212] For a summary of his career see Sir H. Barkley, 'The Berkeleys of Coberley', *Trans. Bristol & Gloucs. Arch. Soc.*, xvii (1892–3), 109–21.

shire was Geoffrey Archer of Stoke Archer.[213] To others local office was worth seeking, even if it was not always an unmixed blessing. A tenure of the shrievalty in particular carried great risks; but if the sheriff was unscrupulous and enjoyed powerful connections the gamble might pay off handsomely.

Influential connections certainly counted for something in medieval England. Patronage was a constituent of power both locally and at court. One of the ways by which a magnate who enjoyed royal favour could reward a retainer was to obtain for him a lucrative office in the shires. If a magnate had patronage to bestow, he also had support to seek. So far from being divorced from the drama of national politics, the complex network of local power was connected to it not only by the increasing burden of duties which the government required of the shire knights but also by the thread of influences and reciprocal interests which bound King, magnate and knight. Historians of local government in the sixteenth and seventeenth centuries, aided by collections of family correspondence, have been able to analyse in some detail the influences on the appointment of officials. All too often, in contrast, the medievalist can only point to the effects of patronage while being powerless to discern its inner workings. These difficulties nevertheless should not deter the historian from making the most of the material at his disposal. One important petition, to begin with, illuminates the workings of Gloucestershire politics in about 1330. John de Berkeley of Dursley complained to the King that he could not obtain justice in his own county because Thomas de Berkeley of Berkeley who was, moreover, Mortimer's son-in-law, held the King's ministers in the county at his fees and robes.[214] The survival of a number of account rolls of this date in the Muniment Room at Berkeley enables us to identify a fair number, though perhaps not all, of the local gentry on Thomas' payroll and thus to test the truth of John de Berkeley's assertion.

For a period of six years, even during the Despenser dominance, the shrievalty was taken by retainers of Maurice de Berkeley and his son Thomas: Sir William Tracy (1324–7), Sir Thomas de Rodborough (1327–30) and William Gamage

[213] Cal. Pat. Rolls 1334–8, p. 167.
[214] S.C.8/157/7832, reproduced in Appendix I, no. 2.

(April–December 1330) are known to have been in the family's service.[215] More diverse connections are to be found among the knights of the shire returned in this period. In February and April 1328 Gloucestershire sent to parliament Robert de Aston, a retainer of Henry of Lancaster,[216] and in July 1328 even John de Berkeley himself. But, of course, Berkeley's men were noticeable too. In April 1328, 1331, September and December 1332, February and September 1334, 1335, September 1336, and July 1338 William de Cheltenham, Berkeley's ubiquitous steward, was chosen. In November 1330 the two men elected, neither of them a knight, were Henry de Brocworth and Robert Dabetot. The latter, at least, was a retainer of Thomas de Berkeley.[217] However, it was of more use to Berkeley to have his men in the shrievalty than in the Chapter House at Westminster, and in this period the baronage showed little interest in packing parliament. Cheltenham may have been chosen by the county court simply because he was competent and not out of deference to the expressed wish to Thomas de Berkeley.

It is clear, then, that considerable truth attached to John de Berkeley's complaint in 1330. Nevertheless, this was a time when political conditions peculiarly favoured the advancement of Berkeley's men: their lord was Mortimer's son-in-law. At other times his dominance may not have been so pervasive.

In December 1330, after Edward III's coup at Nottingham, all the sheriffs were changed, and Thomas de Berkeley's power was eclipsed, temporarily at least. William Gamage was replaced by Thomas de Berkeley of Coberley, who seems to have been independent of any affiliations. Before the end of his long career this knight was to hold the shrievalty for two further terms of office. Once their lord was restored to favour, Thomas de Berkeley's men reappeared in the office of sheriff—Sir Simon Basset (1331–40) and Sir John Tracy (1363–8, 1369–71, 1378–9), for example—but other lords' retainers were appointed too: Sir Thomas Moigne, a dependant of the Talbots, enjoyed several years of office (1360–3).[218] Two more Berkeley men are among the numerous retainers found in the shrievalty in the 1370s and

[215] Smyth, i, 313; Berkeley Castle S.R. 39, 61, 63.
[216] R. Somerville, *History of the Duchy of Lancaster*, i (London, 1953), 354.
[217] Berkeley Castle S.R. 39; Bod. Lib. microfilms, bk. 10, fo. xxxii.
[218] E.159/143 Easter Recorda.

1380s: Ralph Walsh of Woolstrop and Sir Nicholas de Berkeley of Dursley.[219] John Joce, who served two terms of office (1373–4, 1376–7), and Sir John Thorp, who served one (1381–2), received robes from the King.[220] Sir Peter le Veel, sheriff in 1375, was a dependant of the Black Prince,[221] and Sir Thomas FitzNichol, a Gloucestershire steward of the earl of Stafford.[222] Of the forty-seven men who held the office of sheriff in the fourteenth century at least twenty-two are known to have been retainers. Incomplete though they may be, these figures illustrate the prominence of magnate retainers among the holders of the shrievalty.

It is worth glancing also at the keepers of the peace. The commissions of the peace of Edward II's reign were small, and presumably therefore easy to pack. In fact, however, there is no more sign that lordly nominees were placed on them than there is that parliaments of this reign were packed. The keepers appointed in 1307, 1308, 1310, 1314, and 1320 were substantial county gentry. The only retainer found on these early commissions was Sir Nicholas de Kingston, who a few years after his appointment in 1314 was to sue his lord, Alan Plokenet of Kilpeck, for non-payment of his fee.[223] In 1327 the position changed. The two keepers appointed on 8 March were Thomas de Berkeley and his man, Sir William de Wauton.[224] After the fall of Mortimer in 1330, Berkeley was in eclipse, but he returned as a keeper in 1336 and was appointed to every commission after 1344; even during the 1330s there were always some of his men on the bench. By the middle years of the reign Berkeley and his dependants made up half of the keepers and sometimes, as in 1336, 1344, 1355, and 1359, they formed a majority.[225] Once the commissions grew in size, other lords and their retainers found a place on the bench. For example, on 8 March 1362 Robert Palet, steward of Edward Despenser, was associated with the commission of the peace; his reappointment on 7 June 1364 should occasion no surprise bearing in mind that the commission was headed not for once by

[219] Berkeley Castle, general series account rolls, account of William atte Nasche; Smyth, ii, 3.
[220] Cal. Pat. Rolls 1370–4, p. 27; 1377–81, p. 157.
[221] Black Prince's Register, iv, 74, 384, 403.
[222] Just. 3/180 m. 16.   [223] K.B.27/246 m. 136d.
[224] Cal. Pat. Rolls 1327–30, p. 89.
[225] Cal. Pat. Rolls 1334–8, p. 367; 1343–5, p. 394; 1354–8, p. 227; 1358–61, p. 219.

an ill and ageing lord of Berkeley but by Edward Despenser.[226] A typical commission of the peace of the closing years of Edward III's reign was that issued on 15 November 1374 to Thomas de Berkeley, Walter Perle, David Hanmere, Sir Nicholas de Berkeley, Sir John Bromwich, John Sergeant, John Clifford the elder and John Lucy.[227] Of the five local men Sir Nicholas de Berkeley was a retainer of the senior branch of the family, Bromwich and Lucy were retained by the Earl of March and John Sergeant by both Thomas de Berkeley and John of Gaunt.[228] There is no evidence to show what connections John Clifford enjoyed, but this is not to say he did not have any. Retainers, then, were well in evidence on the commissions of the peace. The expansion in their size in the 1380s caused by the appointment of members of the lesser gentry must have made it more difficult for any one magnate to exercise a dominating influence. It is possible that there was a divergence of interest here: if magnate interests were served by a small commission, easily susceptible to influence and favour, the interests of the Commons would be favoured by larger commissions, composed of more local knights, which would be less likely to fall under the influence of one or two dominant lords. In practice, though, the division was by no means so clear cut. The Commons felt that the price of enlargement was the appearance on the bench of too many insubstantial figures instead of the 'most sufficient' knights and esquires, and in the Statute of Cambridge, probably in response to a Commons petition, the size of the commission was again fixed at six with two justices of assize.[229]

Whether the lesser gentry who found their way onto the commissions of the peace in the 1380s were liveried retainers or not is difficult to say. The evidence is purely negative: there is little to suggest that they were, and it is hard to believe that they all owed their elevation to the exercise of magnate influence at a time when economic conditions anyway may well have been

[226] *Cal. Pat. Rolls 1361–4*, pp. 208, 531. Palet was reappointed on 16 May 1366 when the commission was headed by Sir Edward Despenser (*Cal. Pat. Rolls 1364–7*, p. 283).

[227] *Cal. Pat. Rolls 1370–4*, p. 478.

[228] Smyth, ii 3; *Cal. Close Rolls 1381–5*, p. 59; K.B.27/471 Rex m. 9; *John of Gaunt's Reg*, i, 209; Just. 3/60/4 m. 21d.

[229] *The Reign of Richard II*, ed. Du Boulay and Barron, p. 139.

favouring the improvement of lesser landowners such as themselves.[230] But the presence alongside the knights of apparently obscure or humble men is noticeable on commissions of the peace much earlier in the century: Robert Dabetot, appointed on 16 October 1336, Hugh de Aston, appointed on 3 August 1353, 3 December 1355 and 16 February 1359, Robert Palet appointed on 8 March 1364, 16 May 1366 and 10 July 1368, John de la Lee, appointed on 8 March 1364 and John de Sloghtre appointed in 1366, 1368, 1369, and 1371 did not come from knightly families. Occasionally, the appointment is made to the shrievalty of someone like Thomas de Okle in 1372 or Philip le Mareshal whose landed income alone would hardly have entitled him to hold office. More often men of limited means are found as knights of the shire: William de Arches in 1326, Robert Dabetot in 1330, Richard de la Hale in 1334, John de Cromhall in 1330 and 1335, William de Tytherington in 1330, Henry de Corsham in 1339, William de Westhall in 1343 and 1344 and Robert Palet in 1351 and 1371. None of these possessed a landed estate of £40 or more which might be expected of a knight who played a part in county affairs; yet, as we have seen they were the men with whom the knights of the shire shared their power.

The participation of such men is probably to be explained by their connections. William de Tytherington, a knight of the shire in the 1330s, was Lord Stafford's steward at Thornbury.[231] John de Weston, a sheriff of obscure origin shortly after the Black Death, was also a steward of Lord Stafford.[232] Robert Palet, known to have been Despenser's steward in 1375, may already have been employed by him when he was chosen a keeper of the peace with Despenser in 1366.[233] Palet was also steward of St. Peter's Abbey, Gloucester, and the two connections together would have been enough to ensure his reappointment to subsequent commissions.[234] The appointment to the commission of the peace in 1364 of the otherwise unknown John de la Lee may be explicable in terms of his former position, attested in a Llanthony register, as steward of Elizabeth de Burgh, lady of

[230] For the connections enjoyed by one J. P. in these years, see above, pp. 134–5.
[231] Stafford Rec. Office, D.641/1/2/124–7.
[232] Stafford Rec. Office, D.641/1/2/132–9.
[233] For references see below, Appendix III.
[234] See above, Table IV (p. 88).

Clare.[235] But in Gloucestershire, of course, it was the influence of the lord of Berkeley which was most pervasive. Robert Dabetot, who was a keeper of the peace and justice of oyer and terminer in the 1330s and 1340s appears in the steward of Berkeley's account for 1327, and again as a charter witness at Berkeley.[236] William Westhall, a freeholder of the hundred of Berkeley, probably owed his election as a knight of the shire in 1343 and 1344 to Berkeley's influence: a connection with the family is established by the appointment of William de Cheltenham and William de West-hall as guardians of Thomas, son of Maurice de Berkeley of Uley on 8 November 1351.[237] There is plenty of evidence to illustrate the connections with both Thomas de Berkeley and Thomas de Bradeston of Henry de Corsham who was a shire knight and justice of oyer and terminer several times in the 1340s.[238] Later in the century John de Couley, who held a modest estate in the hundred of Berkeley, came to sit on the bench and to serve as escheator in 1384.[239] These appointments he may have owed to the favour of Thomas de Berkeley whose steward he was.[240]

But perhaps the most remarkable and active man in four-teenth-century Gloucestershire was William de Cheltenham. His prominence in county affairs was due to the position of favour he held with his lord, the third Thomas de Berkeley, whom he served as steward. Knight of the shire, keeper of the peace, justice of labourers, justice of oyer and terminer, he held almost every office in the shire except that of sheriff, perhaps out of token deference to the Statute of Lincoln which forbade stewards to hold the shrievalty.[241] He did not come from a gentry family, but he probably founded one.[242] Once his lord began to heap rewards upon him William began to acquire landed estates which allowed him to become a respected and respectable member of the county community.[243] William's brother, John, another

[235] C.115/L.1/6688 f. 33d.

[236] Berkeley Castle S.R. 39; Bod. Lib. microfilms, bk. 10, fo. xxxii.

[237] Cal. Pat. Rolls 1350–4, p. 171; Cal. Pat. Rolls 1361–4, p. 335.

[238] Cal. Close Rolls 1343–6, p. 640; for Bradeston and Corsham see C.76/15 m. 21, C.76/17 m. 27, C.76/18 m. 13.

[239] For the Couley estate see below, p. 247.

[240] Just. 3/180 m. 24d.   [241] Stat. Realm, i, 174.

[242] Maurice de Cheltenham, his son, represented Gloucestershire in parliament in 1360.

[243] See above p. 90.

steward of the same Thomas de Berkeley, represented Gloucestershire in parliament in January 1339 when his colleague was Henry de Corsham.[244]

William de Cheltenham was exceptional only in terms of the success of his career, for he, just like the other men we have been considering, owed his prominence not to any landed stake in the county but to the position of favour which he held with his lord. These lords were usually secular magnates; but the retainers of the great ecclesiastical lords, too, sometimes worked their way into the world of local politics. For example, it must have been his office as steward of the abbot of Winchcombe that recommended the otherwise obscure William de Bradewell to the county courts of Worcester and Gloucester which returned him to parliament six times in the 1320s and 1330s.[245] Viewed from a distance the pattern is clear. The nature of government in medieval society made possible the appointment of men who were ill qualified in landed terms to hold office. No doubt a magnate would wish his interests in the shire to be served by knights or rich esquires who could cut a figure in the neighbourhood; but if retainers of such standing were not always available, or were serving abroad, he was prepared to nominate a trusted menial servant for local office. Perhaps the presence of so many lesser figures in the local administration in the 1330s and 1340s may be connected with the near-continuous warfare of those decades, first in Scotland and then in the Low Countries and France, which drew knights away from the shires.[246] Richard de Foxcote, who was not a knight, enjoyed the shrievalty for six years between 1332 and 1338, a tenure prolonged, perhaps, because few knights remaining in the county were willing to accept office. In 1346 the sheriff, Sir Simon

[244] S.C.1/39/90.

[245] William de Bradewell, described as the abbot's steward, was granted a corrody at Winchcombe on 16 November 1319 (*Landboc . . . de Winchelcumba*, i, ed. D. Royce (Exeter, 1892), 289–90).

[246] Local duties usually fell to the lot of knights who had settled down after an early career in active service (see above, p. 56). But between 1338 and 1347 Edward III's wars did succeed in attracting larger numbers of knights than any campaigns since the time of Edward I. From Gloucestershire could be numbered Sir Simon Basset, Sir Peter de la Mare, Sir Walter Daston, Sir John de Acton and Sir Robert de Hildesley, all knights who held office locally at one time or another.

Basset, abandoned his duties to join the Crecy expedition.[247] Of the two Gloucestershire members in the parliament held in September 1346, while Edward III's army was besieging Calais, Elias de Filton was certainly not, and John de Clopton possibly not, a knight. But not in every case need the initiative have necessarily come from a great magnate. For an elected honour, such as that of representing the shire in parliament, the county court may have chosen a man precisely because he was known to enjoy the favour of a lord close to the King.

In the light of these conditions it is easy to understand the insistence of the Commons on the land-holding qualification. Of course until 1368 for the escheator and 1372 for the sheriff this obligation was defined vaguely as the obligation to hold sufficient land wherewith to answer King and people, but it seems clear that in Gloucestershire in this period a substantial minority of office-holders simply could not have satisfied even that requirement. Thus in 1346 the Commons petitioned that both sheriffs and keepers of the peace should be chosen from the most substantial men of the shire.[248] Three years earlier when the justices of oyer and terminer were the subject of a parliamentary petition it was their ill-repute that was criticized.[249] That men like William and John de Cheltenham were being attacked in this petition is strongly suggested by the demand that no sheriff or steward of a magnate who held franchises would be appointed to commissions of oyer and terminer.[250] A curious practice, of which there is no local evidence from Gloucestershire, was the subject of a successful petition in 1378. Lords who were unable to attend sessions of the peace in person appointed men of low standing to attend in their place; these men then refused to hand the indictments over to the sheriffs.[251] The King agreed to replace these people with the most substantial men of the counties. It is not difficult to imagine that the nominees so criticized were of similar standing to the retainers who managed to secure permanent inclusion in the commissions of the peace. Thus the

[247] G. Wrottesley, *Crecy and Calais* (London, 1898), p. 109.
[248] *Rot. Parl.*, ii, 161.
[249] Ibid., 141.
[250] The King's reply was evasive. He agreed that sheriffs should not be appointed justices, but made no mention of stewards.
[251] *Rot. Parl.*, iii, 44.

demand for enforcement of an adequate land-holding obligation was linked to criticism of the prominence of magnate dependants.

Where the historian of the sixteenth and seventeenth centuries can illuminate his study of local government from collections of correspondence, the medievalist can usually only point to the results of patronage. But a little can be said about its workings. Access to the King's ear was clearly a help. It benefited Sir Robert Fitzpayn, a Dorset knight who was steward of the household in the time of Edward II. In January 1311 John Sandale, the Treasurer, was ordered to perform whatever Fitzpayn should inform him on the royal behalf. Following the writ of privy seal he appeared in the Exchequer and on the King's behalf required that the sheriff of Gloucester be removed and that Sir Nicholas de Kingston be appointed in his place.[252] Nevertheless, presence at court was not essential. A letter could achieve the desired effect. In 1352 John Talbot of Richard's Castle wrote to suggest that William atte Mersh should take the place of his retainer William Maunsel on a commission of array.[253] On the commission as enrolled it is Mersh's name that appears.[254] In a society where petitioning was a widespread and legitimate means of securing favours the King or Chancellor were quite prepared to pass onto the Exchequer for sympathetic consideration a request from a magnate for the appointment to an office or commission of one of his clients.

Such, then, were the influences brought to bear on the Chancellor, Treasurer and barons of the Exchequer. There was a flow of information about possible candidates for office coming in from many quarters—from the King, from influential magnates, from the knights of the shire if parliament was sitting, from existing holders of office. It is unlikely therefore that there was any shortage of names of eligible men. But it would be quite wrong to assume that the office-holding class of the shire can be identified with the gentry as a whole. At any one time the group among whom most of the local offices were distributed never exceeded more than about a dozen and a half men. These were

[252] J. Conway Davis, *The Baronial Opposition to Edward II* (Cambridge, 1918), p. 522.
[253] S.C.1/41/105.
[254] *Cal. Close Rolls 1349–54, p.429*

not always drawn from the same families for the duration of the entire century. The high rate of extinction of families saw to that. But even within families that continued in the male line there was little continuity of service from one generation to the next. In Gloucestershire only members of the families of Tracy and Berkeley of Coberley are found holding the main offices of the shire generation after generation.

Thus the hierarchy of office-holders in the county was constantly changing in composition as one family replaced another. But was it changing also in either size or structure in this period? It is probably significant that it is less easy to identify the group of office-holders or *buzones* in 1300 than in 1400. At the beginning of the century it was common to find men serving for any number of counties where they happened to hold lands. The county hierarchies faded into each other; they overlapped. In 1300 not more than about seven men, all but one of them knights, bore the brunt of county administration in Gloucestershire: Sir John de Langley,[255] Sir John de Acton,[256] Sir Nicholas de Kingston,[257] Sir William Maunsel,[258] Sir William de Wauton,[259] Sir Richard de Croupes,[260] and John de Annesley.[261] But in addition to these men there were others such as Thomas de Gardinis,[262] and John de Newborough[263] who served as administrators in other counties than Gloucestershire alone. By 1350 the active county elite is still small: Sir Thomas de Berkeley of

[255] P. R. Coss, *The Langley Family and its Cartulary* (Dugdale Soc. Occasional Papers, 22, 1974), pp. 6–8.

[256] Sheriff of Hereford, 1294–9, April–November 1303; sheriff of Salop and Staffs., 1304–5; knight of the shire, Hereford, 1300, 1301 and for Gloucestershire too, 1301.

[257] For a biography see McFarlane, 'An Indenture of Agreement', p. 209.

[258] Ibid.

[259] Knight of the shire, Gloucestershire, 1302 and Wiltshire, 1321; keeper of the peace, 1327, 1332; commissioner of array, 1321, 1322; justice of oyer and terminer.

[260] Knight of the shire for Gloucestershire, 1301.

[261] Sheriff, 1310–11; Keeper of the peace, 1335; commissioner of array, 1324, 1325; justice of oyer and terminer.

[262] Sheriff, 1293–8, 1302–7; sheriff of Cambridge and Huntingdon, 1298–1300; commissioner of array in Oxfordshire, 1316; justice of oyer and terminer in Oxfordshire, 1317.

[263] Sheriff, 1301–2; knight of the shire, Dorset, 1307.

Coberley,[264] Sir Walter Daston,[265] Sir William Tracy[266] and his son, Sir John,[267] Richard de Foxcote,[268] William de Cheltenham,[269] John Clifford,[270] and John de Weston.[271] But in character it was beginning to change. These men all resided in Gloucestershire, the county to which their interests were confined. No longer did the Exchequer appoint knights to shrievalties or other offices in counties where they would be regarded as 'foreigners'. Yet the well-established knights were sharing power with men of lesser means who owed their prominence to a magnate's favour. By the 1390s the *buzones* were a larger group numbering a dozen or more knights and richer esquires: Sir John Cheyne,[272] Sir John Cassy,[273] Sir Maurice Russell,[274] Sir Henry de la Rivere,[275] Sir Thomas FitzNichol[276]

[264] Sheriff, 1330–2, 1338–40, 1355–6; commissioner of array, 1333, 1352; surveyor of ships 1332; keeper of the peace, 1335, 1338, 1344, 1351, 1353; knight of the shire, 1358.

[265] Sheriff, 1340–1, 1350–1; commissioner of array, 1338; justice of oyer and terminer, 1345.

[266] Sheriff, 1324–7; sheriff of Worcester, 1318–21; knight of the shire, 1313, 1322; commissioner of array, 1322, 1324; keeper of the peace, 1331, 1338, 1344; justice of oyer and terminer.

[267] Sheriff, 1363–8, 1369–71, 1378–9; knight of the shire, 1358, 1363, 1366, 1368, 1369; keeper of the peace, 1361, 1362, 1364, 1369; commissioner of array, 1371; commissioner to investigate chantries, 1364; justice of oyer and terminer.

[268] Sub-escheator of Gloucestershire, 1320–1; escheator, 1351–2; sheriff, 1332–8, 1351–2; keeper of confiscated manors, 1322; commissioner to collect taxes, 1350.

[269] Knight of the shire, 1325, 1331–5, 1336, 1338; commissioner of array, 1338; keeper of the peace, 1336–59; justice of labourers, 1351–9; surveyor of weights and measures, 1343, 1358.

[270] Sheriff, 1371–2; knight of the shire, 1372; keeper of the peace, 1369, 1371, 1374.

[271] Sheriff, 1352–4; knight of the shire, 1348, 1352; tax collector, 1344; coroner in Herefordshire until 1350.

[272] See J. S. Roskell, 'Sir John Cheyne of Beckford', *Trans. Bristol & Gloucs. Arch Soc.*, 75 (1956), 43–72.

[273] J. P. in Gloucestershire and other counties; justice of oyer and terminer; appointed Chief Baron of the Exchequer, 1389.

[274] Sheriff, 1390–1, 1395–6, 1400–1, 1406–7; knight of the shire, 1402; J. P., 1394 onwards; coroner, 1392–7.

[275] Sheriff, 1391–2, 1399–1400; knight of the shire, 1394; J.P., 1389, 1390, 1394; justice of oyer and terminer.

[276] Sheriff, 1382–3; knight of the shire fourteen times, 1382–1414; J. P., 1382; coroner, 1392–5.

Sir John de Berkeley,[277] Sir Gilbert Denys,[278] Robert Whittington,[279] John Derhurst,[280] Robert Poinz[281] and Laurence Sebrok.[282]

The reason for this expansion is not hard to find. The King needed the help of the gentry in administration more and more as the century progressed. While the number of offices and the number and size of commissions grew, so did the desire of the gentry to secure these jobs for the prestige in local society which they conferred and the perquisites they might bring. But if, on the one hand, the county elite became wider, in another sense it became a more closed community. By 1400 each county community had clearly assumed an identity of its own: the days had long passed when a knight could hold office in any shire where he held land or even in one where he did not. Only Sir John Berkeley of Beverstone resembled the roving sheriff of earlier days: but he is unlikely to have been the agent of an Exchequer searching for every way to extract money from the shires. Moreover, the major offices of the shire were held not just by local gentry but by very much the richer sort of gentry. Interlopers of little means who rose through magnate favour had almost disappeared by 1400. Retainers there were in all the major offices in the 1390s just as in any other decade, but they were clients of the standing of knight or rich esquire, not menial servants. A hierarchy too was now established between the various offices. The coroner carried little esteem; he was on a par with the assessors and collectors of parliamentary subsidies. The escheator was a little higher. But most sought after of all were a place on the bench, a term of the shrievalty and the chance of representing the shire in parliament. A knight who had represented his county stood a good chance of becoming sheriff soon

[277] Sheriff of Gloucester and other neighbouring counties. See above, pp. 115, 126.

[278] Sheriff, 1393–4; knight of the shire, 1390, 1395; commissioner to enquire into trespasses on Kingswood and Fulwood Chases, 1391.

[279] Sheriff, 1402–3; 1407–8; escheator, 1392–4, 1401–2, 1409–10; knight of the shire, 1391; commissioner of array, 1377, 1380, 1392, 1399; J. P., 1382 onwards.

[280] J. P., 1389 onwards; escheator, 1410; justice of gaol delivery, 1407.

[281] Sheriff, 1396–7; escheator, 1395–7, 1399–1400; knight of the shire, 1417.

[282] Sheriff, 1388–9; knight of the shire, 1388, 1390; J.P., 1389, 1390; commissioner of array, 1385; justice of oyer and terminer, 1390.

afterwards. Such was the *cursus honorum* of local politics.

The extent to which this evolution in the community of the shire represents a victory for the parliamentary Commons should not be underestimated. Their demands had found concise expression in a petition of 1333, when they said that escheators, sheriffs, hundredors and errant bailiffs should be resident in the counties they served; and that they should hold sufficient lands there according to the Statutes of Lincoln and Westminster.[283] It took some time to secure the enforcement of these demands even when they had been nominally conceded. In 1368 it was granted that the escheator should hold lands to the value of £20, a requirement demanded of the sheriff too after 1372. Imperfectly enforced though the statute was in respect of the escheatorship, sheriffs of adequate means were appointed henceforth.[284] Another concession that the Commons gained, although enforced only long after it was nominally granted, was annual rotation of the same two offices. Equally significant in the Commons' framework of thought was the demand that the minister's land should lie within the county, or bailiwick if it was a pair of shires, where he held office. This was conceded in a number of statutes in the second and third decades of the century, and although it may have been breached in a few later appointments by the second half of the fourteenth century it commanded complete acceptance. The most intractable problem was that of the liveried retainer. Stewards were prevented by the Statute of Lincoln, 1316, from holding the shrievalty and a subsequent enactment extended the prohibition to keepers.[285] Not only were these statutes honoured as much in the breach as in the observance, but they tackled only a part of the problem. It was the proliferation of liveried retainers, not just stewards, and their prominence in local government that was the subject in Richard II's reign of a heated debate in which the Commons gained few substantial concessions from the magnates.[286] With this exception, however, the Commons could count themselves well

[283] *Rotuli Parliamentorum Anglie Hactenus Inediti*, ed. H. G. Richardson and G. O. Sayles (Camden third series, li, 1935), 225.

[284] See above, pp. 110, 117.

[285] *Stat. Realm*, i, 174; *The Reign of Richard II*, ed. Du Boulay and Barron, p. 139.

[286] *The Reign of Richard II*, ed. Du Boulay and Barron, pp. 131–52.

satisfied by 1400. The community of the shire in the form which it had assumed by the end of the fourteenth century was a reflection of the view which the gentry held of the pattern of office-holding and its relationship with the King's government.

Could their views on the administration of the shires be dignified by the name of a policy? The petitions to parliament, if it be accepted that they represent the attitudes and grievances of the gentry in the shires, do express, sometimes with tedious repetitiveness, a coherent set of ideas. If criticism is to be made it must be that the rigid adherence by the Commons to their demands over so long a period as a century or more indicates lack of originality and inflexibility of approach. Long after the Crown had met their wishes the Commons were still calling for annual replacement of sheriffs. The 1390s differed from earlier decades largely to the extent that the granting of liveries had become a subject of debate between King, Lords and Commons. Although in the 1380s and 1390s its implications for lawlessness may have been uppermost in the minds of those who complained, the proliferation of liveries also affected the conduct of administration. If large scale lawlessness was stirred up by a magnate, order could not be restored by a sheriff and J.P.s who themselves were wearing his livery. The Commons who placed their faith in the J.P.s—provided, best of all, that the bench was purged of magnates' stewards—likewise placed their faith in sheriffs whose substantial landed stake in the county would permit them to take an independent line. In 1389–90 the policy came as close to fruition as at any time in the late middle ages with the removal of the magnates and their stewards from the commissions of the peace; but as Storey has observed, the experiment could only be a failure because 'those shire knights who were justices had found from experience that it was an impossible task to carry out their duties without the moral and practical support of the most influential men in their shires, of those "who had the power" to have the law enforced'.[287] Most of the Gloucestershire sheriffs of Richard II's reign held estates worth not the statutory £20, but £40 or £60 or more. Yet possession of a 'sufficient' estate was hardly a potent weapon in the sheriff's armoury when he was confronted with the scale of

[287] Ibid., p. 150.

defiance described in a petition from Thomas Cone, prebendary of Woodford in the collegiate church of Westbury-on-Trym near Bristol. On 16 February 1389 a gang numbering 300 beseiged Thomas Cone at Woodford. When told to disperse by the sheriff's bailiffs these men said that they would not be arrested and that they were responsible only to John Poleyn, their master.[288] The services of Poleyn, an esquire of Thomas de Berkeley, were secured by John Trevisa who was disputing a prebend with Cone. The Commons understood the helplessness of the sheriff in the face of such violence; for well placed though he was to prey on the weak, he lacked the means to confront the powerful. It was therefore in an attempt to raise the stature of the shrievalty that they asked for substantial men to be appointed. But the remedy hardly rose to the gravity of the occasion. Nor did the J.P.s offer the prospect of a solution since they relied for executive action on the assistance of the sheriff.

That the gentry were putting forward such ideas does at least dispel any lingering illusion that they were mere clay in the hands of the lords in the fourteenth century. As has been shown, there was no shortage among the parliamentary Commons of magnate nominees. But on the issue of law enforcement at least, the majority of the shire representatives were prepared to take a line that differed from that of the lords. Their independence of mind and speech would be the more understandable too if it was accompanied by an independence of magnate connections. Although such a suggestion can only be speculative it is quite possible. It would be rather difficult for a magnate to manipulate an election in the county court, most of all once the local communities had come to cherish their right to elect two knights to this important honour independently of magnate influences. That in the second half of the century the Commons had to petition for free election of shire knights in the county court only once, in 1376, suggests not so much that 'fixed' elections were frequent as that they were now rare enough to incur condemnation when they were uncovered.[289]

If the gentry who ran the shires were distrustful of magnate dominance, they were distrustful too of competition from those

[288] S.C.8/84/4193.
[289] Rot. Parl., ii, 355.

below them in the social hierarchy. The demand for the appointment of men of substance to offices and commissions can easily be caricatured as a denial of opportunity to those outside the charmed circle; the gentry, in short, were bent on keeping the perquisites to themselves. To an extent, of course, they were. But their views did not spring entirely from selfishness. As they met more often locally in the county courts and nationally in parliament they became more conscious of their own political role. They came to apply their ideas not only to local but also to the King's government. The unpopularity in parliament of the knights, esquires and clerks, apprenticed in the service of the Duchy of Lancaster, who filled important offices of state in the early years of Henry IV's reign sprang from a critique of government no different from that which had been applied at the local level in the previous century. Men of little means would be tempted by magnate fees, prone to corruption and incapable of resisting the powerful or the lawless. Such was the outlook of the country gentry; ironically, what might seem to suggest selfishness may well have sprung from a desire to root out corruption and maladministration.

V

LAWLESSNESS AND LANDED SOCIETY

By the fourteenth century the county had become more than a unit of local government created for the convenience of the administrative and fiscal needs of the King. Indeed, it was the increasing force of the burdens imposed by the King and the response they evoked which helped to make the shire something more: it became a community, with an identity of its own, to which the local gentry felt tied by the bonds of a local patriotism. If it was upon the county that royal sanctions fell, it was also through the county that they could be resisted. The corporate voice of the county community was heard in the shire court; but the fourteenth century saw the establishment alongside that court of an institution by which it was eventually to be supplanted in the Tudor period as the meeting place, social and political, of the county gentry. The victory of the Commons in winning the determining power for the J.P.s, which they were never again to lose after 1368, gained for the quarterly sessions of the Bench a permanent place both in the world of local politics and the administration of local justice. In the fourteenth century, nevertheless, the Crown was able to prevent power from prematurely slipping back to the shires by the control which it exercised through the assize justices, the oyer and terminer commissions and occasional visitations of the Court of King's Bench.

Even so, the eyre, which had brought all local courts and communities under royal surveillance in the thirteenth century, virtually ceased to exist after 1294. It is doubtful whether there is any more than a merely chronological connection between the demise of the eyre and the apparent upsurge of lawlessness which characterized the closing years of Edward I's reign;[1] for the articles of the eyre had functioned as much to raise money as to suppress crime, and once the sharp rise in direct taxation in the

[1] See for example the comments in *Chronicle of Peter de Langtoft*, ed. T. Wright (Rolls Series, 1866–8), ii, 361.

1290s assured the Crown of an income, judicial profits were no longer so important. The lawlessness of the time was more likely to have been a consequence of the Scottish Wars. In Edward III's reign too complaints about disorder increased in time of hostilities. In 1332 the keeping of the peace was given as one of the reasons for the summons of parliament; and in 1360 the return of demobilized soldiers from France after the Treaty of Brétigny signalled the outbreak of more lawlessness.[2]

But whether such complaints can tell us very much about the level of lawlessness is questionable. One part of the country may have been in disorder when another was comparatively peaceful. Conditions in Gloucestershire, for example, called for special measures in 1385. In February of that year two commissions were issued, one to enquire into insurrections and felonies in the county, the other to arrest burgesses at Cirencester who had attacked the abbey there, and two months later, on 25 April 1385, the sheriff of Gloucester, John Joce and John Greyndour were appointed to proclaim the peace at Westbury-on-Severn.[3] In tracing the chronology of crime in this period the record sources are as difficult to interpret as the narrative. During the first forty years of the fourteenth century the King's Bench plea rolls became bigger and bigger. But this could indicate less an increase in lawlessness than a growth in the number of adjournments or merely a rise in the number of cases coming to court. Similarly the reduction in size of the plea rolls in the second half of the century cannot be taken to signify a fall in the crime rate; coming after the Black Death it is more likely to reflect a sharp reduction in the size of the population.

Evidence of a general nature, then, cannot reliably be used to trace the rise and fall of crime in the middle ages. The roots of lawlessness lay in the localities, and it is to what was happening there that the historian's gaze must be directed. Petty crime at the village level was probably endemic in all medieval societies. What contemporaries looked to the King to suppress was the large scale disorder in which the gentry seem often to have been implicated. As R. H. Hilton has written, 'members of the gentry families appear with such considerable frequency, in proportion

---

[2] *Rot. Parl.*, ii, 64; *Cal. Pat. Rolls 1361–4*, p. 282; *Chron. Henrici Knighton*, ed. J. R. Lumby (Rolls Series, 1889–95), ii, 120.

[3] *Cal. Pat. Rolls 1381–5*, pp. 587, 593, 596.

to their total numbers, that disorder appears to be almost a by-occupation of the class'.[4] The sources are not sensitive enough to permit a convincing statistical analysis of medieval crime, but they may reveal characteristics unique to fourteenth-century landed society which could account for the willingness of those who enforced the law in the shires so flagrantly to break it.

The sources are, for the most part, the records of the courts. The crime which these court rolls recorded was only a proportion of the total volume of crime, but just how large a proportion is impossible to say. The suppression of crime, it has been observed, was a responsibility placed squarely upon local administration.[5] So too was the detection of crime. Since the reign of Henry II it had been the responsibility of twelve men from each hundred and four from each township within it to present the names of people suspected of murder and theft. Such juries presented indictments before the sheriff in the county court, before the justices in eyre, and in the fourteenth century before the assize justices, the justices of King's Bench and the J.P.s. If there was a failure to report crime, then, the omission lay with the jurors. What looks like rather selective reporting of crime is noticeable in the rolls of the J.P.s. In the four Gloucestershire peace rolls which survive between 1361 and 1398 only one member of the gentry was indicted: Aymer le Boteler of Park, described as a common malefactor and maintainer, was accused of three offences in 1378.[6] Felonies known from other sources to have been committed by knights simply went unreported. The status of these hundred jurors is hard to assess. They were certainly not all humble men; their names are toponymic rather than occupational. But nor are they drawn from the ruling elite of the shire. Rarely did a jury contain more than a single member from a 'gentry' family. At a session of the peace on 22 September 1389, however, it was a jury which included four knights and another four very substantial esquires that made the initial presentment in a protracted case involving Thomas de Berkeley.[7] Again, the twenty-four jurors whom the sheriff of Gloucester was ordered to summon for the sitting of the Bench on 3 June 1398 included one

[4] Hilton, *A Medieval Society*, p. 254.
[5] *Select Cases in the Court of King's Bench, Edward II*, p. xxxv.
[6] *Rolls of the Gloucestershire Sessions of the Peace, 1361–98*, pp. 83, 93, 94.
[7] K.B.27/533 Rex m. 15.

knight, three or four rich esquires and a former J.P.[8] But these two juries were definitely exceptional. Intriguing possibilities are opened up by the appearance as hundred jurors in 1378 of John Magot and in 1398 of John Chaunterell, both of whom joined Ralph Greyndour in a life of crime in the Forest of Dean in the 1380s.[9] They would hardly have made presentments against a gang leader whose family held several manors in the Forest of Dean. If the jurors refrained from making presentments against 'gentry' at the sessions of the peace, it was not because they would have been accusing themselves; for the most part jurors were substantial tenants rather than knights. But they may still have had little inclination to indict members of the gentry. Some like Magot and Chaunterell were accomplices in crime, perhaps the tenants of a criminous knight; others, who may have wished to be forthright, thought it safer to keep quiet. Nevertheless, disorderly behaviour by those who escaped indictment at the sessions of the peace was usually uncovered when the Court of King's Bench visited the county. There is not enough evidence to show if the presentment juries then were any different in composition. All too often, unfortunately, the roll records simply that a presentment was made by jurors of diverse hundreds. But in 1363 it was before a sitting of King's Bench at Gloucester that a jury which included three or four gentry, a coroner and a future sheriff gave details of an affray at Walton Cardiff manor house.[10] The explanation for its relative success is, surely, that King's Bench commanded greater respect and carried greater authority than the local hearings. Although the King's justices did not stand as high in popular estimation in the fourteenth century as they once had, a visitation by the King's Bench provided the opportunity for jurors to indict evil-doers whom they would normally fear to name. The very presence of the court in a shire may have been enough to produce at least some order, even when the penalties it imposed were trifling.

Petty crime was dealt with at the local level. Important suits would come before the central courts at Westminster, where it had become the practice by the end of the fourteenth century for Common Pleas to hear civil pleas and King's Bench criminal

<hr />

[8] *Rolls of the Gloucestershire Sessions of the Peace*, p. 160.
[9] Ibid., pp. 82, 155. See also below, pp. 179–80.
[10] K.B.27/411 Rex m. 8.

pleas. Before the latter court would be called all the most serious breaches of the King's peace. Its periodic visitations of the shires have led to its being called a kind of 'superior eyre'.[11] In the earlier part of the century the movements of King's Bench followed those of the government. Thus it spent much of the 1330s in the north, and as late as Richard II's reign when parliament met away from Westminster, as it did for example at Gloucester in 1378 and at Cambridge in 1388, King's Bench accompanied it. After remaining sedentary during Edward III's later years the Court undertook perambulations more often in the reign of his successor. Unfortunately there is nothing to show why Gloucestershire in particular was chosen in 1363, 1368, 1387, and 1398, although the visit in 1378 was no doubt occasioned by the holding of a parliament at Gloucester.[12] At each of these sessions so many more Gloucestershire offences were presented as to suggest that many felonies and trespasses never came to the notice of the Court when it was at Westminster. But the rolls for the perambulations are no larger than usual because cases from the south-eastern counties, which would have been heard at Westminster, were taken in fewer number; and if a visit to Gloucester was considered necessary in 1363 or 1387, when there is no other evidence of greater disorder in the county, it is difficult to see why one was not undertaken in 1385, when there is such evidence.[13]

About the causes of crime, as J. G. Bellamy has observed, medieval men showed little curiosity, and society's lack of concern with motivation was reflected in the vagueness of the law itself.[14] For example, it was not until the end of the fourteenth century that the idea of secret killing was given special treatment by the law. Most crimes came within the two great categories of felony and trespass. The former embraced homicide, rape,

---

[11] B. H. Putnam, *Proceedings before the Justices of the Peace in the Fourteenth and Fifteenth Centuries, Edward III to Richard III* (Ames Foundation, 1938), p. lxii.

[12] In 1363, however, Bristol, Newport and Worcester were visited as well as Gloucester, in 1387 Reading, and in 1398 the visit to Gloucester only lasted for a part of the term (*Select Cases in the Court of King's Bench, Edward III* (Selden Soc., 82, 1965), p. xlix; *Select Cases in the Court of King's Bench, Richard II, Henry IV, Henry V* (Selden Soc., 88, 1971), pp. liii–lvii).

[13] See above, p. 169.

[14] J. G. Bellamy, *Crime and Public Order in England in the Later Middle Ages* (London, 1973), p. 31.

larceny and burglary, the latter, assault, abduction and conspiracy. Of the felonies of which the gentry were accused homicide was the least frequent. The only member of the land-owning class in Gloucestershire to be indicted for murder in this period was James Clifford of Frampton, in 1386;[15] several decades earlier, however, Hawisia, widow of Sir John de Bitton, and Henry de Furneaux, vicar of Slimbridge, were named as accessories to the murder of John le Hunt at Bitton.[16]

Most of the offences of which the gentry were indicted were pleas of trespass. Assault was probably the commonest category. At home or on the highway members of the gentry were the frequent victims of attacks by their peers or by their social inferiors. For example, Matilda, wife of John de Cromhall, who had twice sat as a knight of the shire, was assaulted by two men near Newnham-on-Severn.[17] Retainers suffered too. In 1347 Sir Ralph de Wilington accused Sir Richard Talbot of attacking Adam de Crossley, a servant of his whose services he lost as a result.[18] There is plenty of similar evidence to show that life was hazardous for the dependants of unpopular lords; they no less than their masters could easily fall victim to robbers and local ruffians who felt themselves to be wronged or oppressed. On other occasions the description of the trespass suggests that the intention was to inflict damage on both person and property. Thus, when Sir Nicholas de Berkeley's men visited Walter Broun's manor of Lasborough they not only broke down the close and houses but also captured Walter and carried him off to their lord's castle at Dursley.[19] Less serious were park break-ins, the purpose of which may have been no more than the enjoyment of an afternoon's hunting on the property of an absentee neighbour. In 1333, for example, Sir William de Whittington and three accomplices were indicted for taking game on the chases of William la Zouche at Corse, Hartpury and Hasfield.[20] The nobility were no less guilty: on 9 October 1387 Thomas lord Berkeley and others were pardoned for hunting without licence in the Forest of Dean.[21] Perhaps it was in the same spirit that Thomas' grandfather led a following of local gentry into the

[15] Just. 3/172 m. 6.   [16] K.B.27/318 Rex m. 19d.
[17] K.B.27/288 m. 144d.   [18] K.B.27/349 m. 68d.
[19] K.B.27/471 Rex m. 22d.   [20] K.B.27/290 Rex m. 37.
[21] Cal. Pat. Rolls 1385–9, p. 358.

King's park at Brimpsfield in about 1328.[22] If there was any purpose behind the more prolonged gentry feuds, the evidence would seem to suggest that it was to combine personal intimidation with attacks on property and only very rarely to settle scores by resort to homicide. Just how many knights and esquires in each generation violated the law is difficult to estimate, but the sources suggest that under Edward II at least twenty-five knights and esquires of the forty or more in Gloucestershire, and under Richard II at least twenty knights and esquires, committed at least one felony or trespass. These must be minimum figures only, and it would be unwise to conclude that there was necessarily any improvement in public order by 1400. The absence of recorded crime may imply not that a man observed the law but rather that he was never brought to book.

Who, then, were the criminals? The petitions of the Commons in parliament identify some of the groups responsible. They complained of illicit confederacies and leagues in 1320.[23] Robbers and bandits, they said in 1348, were riding up and down the land.[24] They pleaded then, as on many other occasions, that such men should not be maintained by magnates. In 1327, though, they had drawn the net wider: none of the King's councillors and ministers and none of his household should maintain a dispute or quarrel.[25] The appalling abuses practised by Edward II's favourites must have inspired this petition. But at no time did the knights and esquires who spoke for the parliamentary Commons point the finger of guilt at themselves. Maintenance was practised by 'les grantz'; those who broke the peace were described in vague terms as 'mesfesours et destourbers de la pees'. Beyond these broad phrases the petitions give no indication of the identity of the criminals they condemned. Perhaps this anonymity sprang from self-interest, since some of the knights who sat in parliament were themselves proven malefactors. Sir Roger de Nowers, who sat for Oxfordshire in 1320, 1327, February and July 1328, and 1330, was accused in 1325 of assaulting one Nicholas de Fulbrook at Churchill (Oxon.); twelve years later he was imprisoned for the murder of an Oxfordshire coroner. During the years when he sat in parliament, moreover, he was engaged in a bitter feud with Thomas de Berkeley of Coberley

[22] K.B.27/274 Rex m. 18.
[23] *Rot. Parl.*, i, 371.   [24] Ibid., ii, 201.   [25] Ibid., ii, 10.

and John Giffard of Leckhampton.[26] Thomas de Gurney of
Harptree, who sat as a knight of the shire for Somerset in 1334
and 1336, was a notorious criminal. A long list of indictments
against him was presented to the King's justices at Wells on 12
February 1341.[27] If the careers of Gurney and Nowers were not
unusual, the reluctance of both Crown and Commons to identify
the criminals becomes understandable. On the other hand,
petitions in the name of 'the Commons' may represent only the
interest of that particular group who were most aggrieved at the
activities of the criminous.

Certainly, enough is known about the misdeeds of some of the
well-born evil-doers for their careers to be reconstructed in some
detail. Professor Hilton has already drawn attention to one such
malefactor whose life resembled that of the outlaw in the ballads:
Malcolm Musard, whose field of operations lay in north
Gloucestershire and south Worcestershire.[28] Men like Musard
were usually surrounded by their brothers and close relatives who
formed the nucleus of a gang. However, Aymer le Boteler, lord of
Park (Gloucs.) and grandson of the younger Despenser's steward
in the western counties, was a cleric whose only following came
from his tenantry. His criminal career opens in 1363 when he was
alleged to have assaulted Agnes Keynes whom he then imprisoned until she was freed by John Caudener and Walter
Sampson.[29] Five years later a commission of oyer and terminer
was issued on receipt of a complaint by Sir John de Burley that
Aymer and others had broken into his park at Haresfield where
they had hunted without licence.[30] A career in lawlessness
covering the next ten years was revealed, and then probably only
in part, when King's Bench visited Gloucester in Michaelmas
Term 1378. The presentments made before the keepers of the
peace were called into the court, and eleven charges were made
against Aymer who was described as a common disturber of the
peace and maintainer of quarrels.[31]

[26] *Return of Members of Parliament*, pp. 60–90 *passim*; *Cal. Pat. Rolls 1324–7*,
p. 233; *1333–7*, p. 574. Nowers is a commissioner of array and keeper of the
peace (*Cal. Pat. Rolls 1324–7*, pp. 29, 55, 286). For the feud see K.B.27/283 mm.
6d, 108d; K.B.27/282 m. 66.
[27] Just. 1/770 m. 8.   [28] Hilton, *A Medieval Society*, pp. 255–8.
[29] K.B.27/411 Rex m. 17.   [30] *Cal. Pat. Rolls 1367–70*, p. 196.
[31] *Rolls of the Gloucestershire Sessions of the Peace*, pp. 84, 93, 94; K.B.27/471 Rex
m. 5.

In the reign of Richard II two well-born criminals were active. The services of John Poleyn esquire of Kingsweston, near Bristol, were secured by John Trevisa, the Berkeleys' chaplain, who was disputing the prebend of Woodford in the collegiate church of Westbury-on-Trym with Thomas Cone; and when the sheriff's ministers called upon Poleyn's followers to leave the prebend they were occupying, they shouted back that they would surrender to no one but John Poleyn, their master.[32] The career of his contemporary, James Clifford esquire of Frampton, is without parallel in the annals of crime in fourteenth-century Gloucestershire. He first appears, surprisingly as the innocent party for once, in 1363 when he complained that a collusive deal between Richard Yanworth and Adam Shareshull had deprived him of his claim to the manor of Stowell.[33] But James must have enforced his right to the manor, for the Cliffords subsequently appear in possession of it.[34] The recorded criminal career of this ruffian opens in 1385 when he murdered one John Tailor at Saul, near Frampton. Tailor's son prosecuted an appeal, but a few months later Clifford produced a royal pardon and was acquitted by the justices of gaol delivery. In the following year he began a vendetta against William Fairoak in an effort to oust him from the church of Fretherne; for most of that time Clifford took the petty tithes and profits pertaining to the church.[35] In 1396 a group of Clifford's neighbours offered surety that he would threaten no more harm to one John Wotton;[36] and in 1399 he was accused of illegally occupying lands and rents in Frampton that had been taken into the King's keeping by the escheator.[37] In his later exploits James collaborated with a neighbour, Anselm Guise of Elmore, who married his daughter Catherine. Together they conspired to secure a false inquest to indict John atte Wode of felony. Atte Wode was imprisoned for three and a half years, and in the meantime Clifford and Guise occupied his lands which they were still holding seven years later.[38] Atte Wode's attempts

[32] K.B.27/512 Rex m. 17; S.C.8/148/7355; S.C.8/84/4193. See also above, p. 240, for the connection between Poleyn and the Berkeleys.

[33] K.B.9/29 m. 46; K.B.27/411 Rex m. 17.

[34] See below, pp. 185–6.

[35] Rot. Parl., iii, 514; Cal. Close Rolls 1392–6, p. 261.

[36] Cal. Pat. Rolls 1392–6, p. 516.   [37] Cal. Pat. Rolls 1396–9, p. 585.

[38] Select Cases before the King's Council, 1243–1482, ed. I. S. Leadam and J. F. Baldwin (Selden Soc., xxxv, 1918), 86–92; Rot. Parl., iii, 513.

to get justice by petitioning parliament in 1402 availed him little. By 1406 he had been murdered. In King's Bench Clifford was convicted of having abetted and procured one Bartholomew Hunte *alias* Wyther to murder John atte Wode at *Gyldenacre* in the parish of St. Martin by le Mewes, Middlesex.[39] There is evidence to suggest that Clifford protected his interests by the employment of corrupt practices in the courts: in 1397 he was done for embracery.[40] It is worth noting too that, while he held none of the main offices in the county, James Clifford was elected once as a knight of the shire, representing Gloucestershire in the parliament which met at Coventry in October 1404.[41] Whether he had an influential local patron is not known. If he did, it was certainly not Thomas de Berkeley who had to be prevented from doing physical violence to him.[42] But he was retained by both Richard II and Henry IV—from the latter he received a handsome fee of £40, which suggests that he was not exactly without friends.[43]

More often than not such malefactors did not act alone. In the 1390s Clifford came to operate in league with Guise. Aymer le Boteler and John Poleyn could rely on a band of followers and well-wishers. The indictments on the plea rolls and the enrolments of commissions of oyer and terminer often reveal knights at the head of innumerable hangers-on when they commit acts of aggression.[44] It seems that at the very least a lord could expect his tenants and menial servants to assist him in an attack or assault; peasant obligations may not have been confined exclusively to labour services.

Aymer le Boteler appears to have organized his crimes virtually on his own; the role of his accomplices was simply to assist him in their execution. But when collaboration became more formal, based usually on the family unit, a gang or confederacy emerged. The brothers Robert and Thomas de Gloucester operated in this way. In 1324 the jury of Kiftsgate hundred presented that these two sons of Sir Walter de

[39] S.C.8/190/9473; *Cal. Pat. Rolls 1405–8*, p. 280.
[40] K.B.27/546 m. 37.
[41] *Return of Members of Parliament*, p. 267; he had also been a commissioner of array in 1385, 1392 and 1402 (*Cal. Pat. Rolls 1381–5*, p. 589; *1401–5*, p. 138).
[42] *Cal. Close Rolls 1385–9*, p. 672.
[43] *Cal. Pat. Rolls 1399–1401*, p. 191.
[44] See below, p. 184.

Gloucester, the King's escheator south of Trent who had died in 1311, had taken eight sheep belonging to the Prior of St. Oswald's, Gloucester, at Eylesworth, where they had also burned down houses. Associated with them on this occasion were William de Cotes, a former rector of Saintbury, and ten other men.[45] The de Gloucesters themselves claimed benefit of clergy. In the following year the two brothers were indicted for the robbery of Roger atte Broke at Sodbury and for other robberies, felonies and homicides, unspecified, at Oldbury and Rodmarton.[46] Such men were not without their allies in the community; indeed, it was through such assistance that they were able to remain immune for so long from the processes of law. In Hilary Term 1330 John le Walsh of Paganhill was indicted in King's Bench for sheltering the 'notorious robber' Thomas, brother of Robert de Gloucester, who had been outlawed for the robbery at Chipping Sodbury. When a jury was finally empanelled in July 1331 John le Walsh, it is not surprising to find, was acquitted.[47] The robbery had probably taken place in 1324; thus it was six years before the fruitless action against le Walsh reached King's Bench.[48]

The exploits of the gang led by William de Kingscot of Kingscote in the 1330s and 1340s are of more interest. A presentment made by the jurors of Berkeley hundred in about 1336 illuminates the activities of a gang organized around three brothers, William, Walter and John de Kingscot.[49] In the same way, Eustace Folville, leader of the famous Leicestershire gang, had relied on his four brothers.[50] The Kingscots were said to have threatened and wounded John Coriot of Hampton at Aston and Henry Saunter of Hampton at Tetbury. They disseised men of their tenements, of which William de Kingscot was himself then enfeoffed—presumably to make their recovery more difficult at law.[51] Described as common malefactors and disturbers of the

---

[45] K.B.27/255 Rex m. 24d.

[46] K.B.27/259 Rex m. 11.   [47] K.B.27/279 Rex m. 9.

[48] For the delays in the courts see below, pp. 197–9.

[49] Just. 1/1421 m. 10.

[50] E. L. G. Stones, 'The Folvilles of Ashby Folville, Leicestershire, and their Associates in Crime, 1326–1341', *Trans. Roy. Hist. Soc.*, 5th series, vii (1957), 117–36.

[51] The same tactic appears to have been employed by James Clifford once he had secured possession of the manor of Stowell (C.P.25(1)78/77/526; and see below, p. 186.

peace, the Kingscots broke the houses of Robert de Nailsworth at Lodgemore, and carried off trees from the close of Elizabeth de Burgh at Nailsworth. The Kingscots were said also to have made a nuisance at fairs and markets, and details of one such incident were given in King's Bench in Hilary Term 1346. Three years before, on 22 July 1343, Walter and John de Kingscot and others attacked the servants of Sir Thomas de Breouse at Tetbury fair where they collected the tolls and profits which should have gone to Thomas as lord of the manor.[52] The Kingscots' career in crime lasted at least ten years. How were they able to remain at large for so long when notorious gangs like those of James Coterel and Eustace Folville operated for periods of only three or four years?[53] It is probable that there was a link with the lords of Berkeley. William de Kingscot's father, Nigel, had been Master of the Horse to Thomas de Berkeley, and if the Kingscot family were still enjoying Thomas' favour in the 1340s another exploit of theirs would become comprehensible.[54] In Trinity Term 1345 John de Berkeley of Dursley began an action of trespass against William, John and Walter de Kingscot and Thomas, described as son of Nigel de Kingscot; unfortunately, no further details are given.[55] But John de Berkeley had long been an adversary of the baronial house, and it is at least possible that the Kingscots had attacked John's property at Dursley at the initiative of Thomas de Berkeley. To make money for themselves Malcolm Musard and the Coterels both offered their services to men engaged in feuds; in the case of the Kingscots such work may have been done as the price of continued immunity from the processes of law.[56]

In the closing decades of the century the bandit country west of the Severn was dominated by the Greyndour clan; the wide expanses of the Forest of Dean afforded secure cover for gangs of outlaws. Although most members of the family were implicated to some extent in crime, the man at the centre of the gang for at least ten years was Ralph Greyndour whose kinsman, John, was lord of manors in Mitcheldean, Littledean and Abenhall.[57]

[52] K.B.27/343 m. 68.　　[53] Bellamy, op. cit., p. 83.
[54] Smyth, Lives, i, 301.　　[55] K.B.27/341 m. 120.
[56] Bellamy, op. cit., pp. 73–4.
[57] In 1387 he was described as Ralph Greyndour junior, lately bailiff of Westbury (K.B.27/506 Rex m. 9d). In 1396 the indictment named Ralph Greyndour senior (K.B.27/544 Rex m. 22d); but there is no reason to believe

According to an indictment it was at conventicles held at Earlswood in the lordship of Lydney and in other places that Ralph Greyndour the younger, John Magot and John Chaunterell plotted to kill Sir Gilbert Denys and John Poleyn. The same three also held conventicles in the same places on 1 July 1387 to plot the killing of Henry Warner and Nicholas More and of Thomas de Berkeley of Berkeley when he came hunting in the Forest with the King's licence. Of these charges all three were acquitted.[58] Like other outlaws Greyndour relied on sympathizers who helped him to escape from the clutches of the law: John Magot and William Wyther were said to have harboured Greyndour himself, John Chaunterell and William Roberd so that the poor men of the Forest dared not to prosecute these malefactors in any of the King's courts.[59] Another indictment suggests that the confederacy was very loosely organized and that all of these men were involved together. William Wyther, who had harboured the criminals, was accused of the murder of John Wyther and William Malmesbury at Hewelsfield on 19 August 1387; subsequently he was himself sheltered by John Greyndour at St. Briavels. The jury acquitted both men.[60] Ralph Greyndour's exploits continued into the 1390s. Assembling about sixty supporters together in illegal conventicles at Mitcheldean, in 1396 he forcibly prevented Robert Whittington, a J.P., from carrying out his duties. Later his gang seized Richard Ailberton, one of the men in Whittington's custody, and detained him until he agreed to pay £100 to John Dene, an accomplice of Greyndour's.[61]

Of these three gangs probably the most closely-knit was that led by William de Kingscot. For ten years or more he and his three brothers operated together. Their associates, to judge from the indictments, were mainly local men: Peter Gilbert of

---

that this is not the same man. On 5 March 1377 the King retained one Ralph Greyndour junior as an archer for the safeguarding of the King's vert and venison in Dean (*Cal. Pat. Rolls 1374–7*, p. 429). He is apparently to be distinguished from one Ralph Greyndour senior who resided at Ruardean (*Cal. Pat. Rolls 1374–7*, p. 221). It is not clear how Ralph the outlaw would fit into the pedigree of the family given above, p. 80.

[58] K.B.27/507 Rex m. 31.

[59] K.B.9/32 m. 28; K.B.27/507 Rex m. 31d. John Magot, *labrator* of Littledean, paid 6d. in the poll tax of 1379 (E.179/113/35A).

[60] K.B.27/506 Rex m. 13d.   [61] K.B.27/544 Rex m. 22d.

Nailsworth, Richard de Nailsworth and John Milbury of Horsley
were of local provenance.[62] The gang of outlaws in the Forest of
Dean was dependent on the leadership of just one man, Ralph
Greyndour. Clearly he enjoyed the support, given freely or
otherwise, of a number of sympathizers, notably his kinsfolk, but
his accomplices in crime were a shifting group. By the 1390s the
places of such hardened criminals as Magot and Chaunterell had
been taken by John Dene and other new men. Like William de
Kingscot, Ralph had a long and successful criminal career,
although in his case there is no suggestion of immunity gained by
magnate patronage; there is probably no need to look further
than the forest cover which sheltered many an outlaw in the
middle ages. Those who made a living out of lawlessness like the
Gloucesters, Kingscots and Ralph Greyndour, or the Coterels
and the Folvilles in the north Midlands, may have been relatively
few; but they caused a commotion out of all proportion to their
numbers. William de Kingscot was said to have servants who
were not men of good condition, but outlaws and common
malefactors.[63] There is a suggestion that Greyndour was not
afraid to use coercion.[64] There may well be some justification for
the view that such outlaws were regarded 'not altogether
unsympathetically' by the population, and without support from
outside their own circle they could not have survived for as long
as they did.[65] But equally it would be idle to deny the nuisance
value to a neighbourhood of the presence of a bandits' lair in its
midst.

In the parts of the country where outlaw bands held sway the
King's writ ran not. In the north of England their power was such
that they could ape the diplomatic forms of the King's
administration.[66] Such mimicry probably struck a sympathetic
chord with those who had suffered at the hands of ministers of the
Crown well versed in the ways of corruption. If outlaws were
tolerated, and even glorified in ballads, it was the gentry who
were at least partly to blame, for their own criminal behaviour

[62] Just. 1/1421 m. 10.   [63] Ibid.
[64] The poor people of the Forest of Dean were said to be afraid to speak out
against him (K.B.27/507 Rex m. 31d).
[65] Stones, 'The Folvilles of Ashby Folville', pp. 135–6.
[66] Select Cases in the Court of King's Bench, Edward III, ed. G. O. Sayles (Selden
Soc., 76, 1957) p. 93.

and abuse of the authority of office left the reputation of the law in tatters. The presence of habitual criminals like Sir Roger de Nowers in parliament has already been noticed. But so long as magnate power was influential in the distribution of local offices such malefactors would turn up not only in parliament but in the shrievalty and elsewhere. Through the power of magnates to secure the appointment of their retainers to offices in the shires, men with criminal records worked their way into positions of local dominance. In 1376 the Commons submitted a petition which reiterated the twin demands of old that sheriffs should serve for no more than one year, and that knights of the shire should be freely elected by the best people of the shire; sheriffs, they said, should not be appointed at court through the influence of maintainers to further their false quarrels.[67] Some of the men whose appointment inspired petitions like this can be identified: Sir Robert Darcy, for example, a Lincolnshire knight who was appointed to the shrievalty of Gloucester in 1313. He was a knight of the King's household and stood high in the favour of Gaveston;[68] back in his home county he had been indicted before the justices of trailbaston in 1305.[69] In the same way it occasions no surprise to find John le Boteler of Llantwit, the overbearing retainer of the younger Despenser, returned to parliament for Gloucestershire in 1324.

That some of those whom they appointed to the shrievalty were already notorious malefactors must surely have been known to the Chancellor and Treasurer. The careers of the two sheriffs who held office in succession in the 1330s provide some support for this suggestion. Less than three years before his appointment in December 1330 Thomas de Berkeley of Coberley had been locked in a violent feud with Roger de Nowers which led to affrays at Leckhampton, Witney and Dunstable and which was dragging on in the Court of King's Bench until 1331.[70] On 30 September 1332 Berkeley was succeeded by Richard de Foxcote whose conduct had been equally disorderly. In 1327 Foxcote and Robert de Aston, later a keeper of the peace, had raided the property of Sir John de Wilington at Yate, Frampton and

[67] *Rot. Parl.*, ii, 355.
[68] *Cal. Pat. Rolls 1307–13*, p. 555; Maddicott, *Thomas of Lancaster*, p. 78 & n.
[69] Just. 1/509 mm. 7d, 9d.
[70] K.B.27/283 mm. 6d, 108d.

Tormarton, stealing livestock to the value of £300.[71] In 1328 they were raiding the property of Sir John de Acton at Iron Acton and Elkstone.[72] Also in 1327 Richard and Thomas de Foxcote were engaged in a feud with the parson of Duntisbourne whom they had imprisoned at Gloucester until he had paid to Richard a fine of £20.[73] These incidents came to the notice of the Crown as the complainants each obtained a commission of oyer and terminer. In May 1338 Foxcote was succeeded by Thomas de Berkeley of Coberley once again. It could be argued that the Crown made such appointments in an attempt to curb the misbehaviour of two lawless men and that success is indicated by the absence of subsequent complaints. But if this was a deliberate policy, confidence in the King's administration was hardly likely to be served by the nomination of such men of ill-repute. Nor need the absence of further indictments be taken to indicate reformed character, for it was always dangerous to speak out against a powerful sheriff.

To their past criminal misdeeds must be added the malpractices to which the local ministers of the Crown were drawn during their terms of office, and which were occasionally brought to light in proceedings instigated by the Crown. In 1324, for example, the jury of Westbury Hundred presented that Sir Robert Darcy, who had been sheriff no less than ten years before, had imprisoned Hugh, vicar of Lydney, and six other men until they paid him £7. But disreputable as Darcy was, his conduct in office may not necessarily have been very much worse than that of others who held the office of sheriff. The same jury presented that Sir Nicholas de Kingston, sheriff 1308–10, had imprisoned Henry Casey by a false return of writ of trespass until he extorted 40s. from him.[74] In the reign of Richard II two coroners, John Joye and Robert Southorle, and an escheator, William Barwell, were indicted for their excesses. These officials were just the unlucky ones who were caught.[75]

It is perhaps not surprising that official corruption should run rampant in an age when the government lacked the means to effect a close control over its ministers in the shires. But the prolonged and bitter feuding among the gentry cannot so easily

---

[71] *Cal. Pat. Rolls 1327–30*, p. 75.   [72] Ibid., p. 285.
[73] Ibid., pp. 80–1.   [74] Just. 1/295 m. 9.
[75] K.B.9/32 m. 1; K.B.27/471 Rex m. 21; K.B.27/507 Rex m. 30d.

be explained. Before this problem is considered in detail, some of the difficulties raised by the evidence need to be examined. Much of it comes from the indictments made by juries of presentment and recorded by the clerks of the court. Contemporaries felt that these did not always spring from pure motives. In 1354 the Commons complained that when King's Bench was migrating people delivered to its justices false indictments to the detriment of good men.[76] A petition in a similar vein was presented in the following year when this evil was connected with that of biased juries.[77] The matter was raised once again in 1379. At the Gloucester parliament in the previous year it had been ordained that J.P.s should have the power to imprison those whom they heard to be disturbing the peace until the justices of gaol delivery came round again. Rather late in the day the Commons pointed out how innocent people could thus become the victims of maintainers and false informers.[78] These fears were well founded in contemporary practice. In his petition of 1402 John atte Wode told how James Clifford and Anselm Guise had procured a false inquest to indict him for a felony. He languished in prison for three-and-a-half years before he was acquitted. It has to be remembered, then, that the indictment is an *ex parte* submission by the plaintiff; his motives may not have been disinterested.

Our suspicion is aroused also by the long lists of offenders which are given by plaintiffs when, for example, they request a commission of oyer and terminer. Adam Shareshull named twenty-seven assailants who robbed him at Northleach on 5 July 1358.[79] In King's Bench thirty-nine followers of Thomas de Berkeley were called to answer for their trespass in the King's park at Brimpsfield.[80] But no fewer than fifty-one were named by Aymer de Valence as intruders at Painswick in 1319.[81] How could such large numbers possibly be identified with certainty? Perhaps Aymer de Valence or his attorneys, knowing that Thomas de Berkeley was responsible for the attack, simply listed those whom they thought might accompany him on such an occasion. Valence's servants at Painswick may after all never have seen Berkeley or his retainers before. These lists of offenders

[76] *Rot. Parl.*, ii, 259.   [77] Ibid., 266.
[78] Ibid., iii, 65.   [79] K.B.27/394 m. 26d.
[80] K.B.27/274 Rex m. 18.
[81] *Cal. Pat. Rolls 1317–21*, pp. 307, 364.

are unlikely to be trustworthy: they do no more than indicate
who might have taken part in any misdeed.

Such reservations compel a cautious approach to the use of
indictments; but they do not make it impossible to understand
the reasons for the chronic disorder of the late middle ages. For
the details that they give, the cases recorded on the Rex
membranes of the King's Bench rolls repay close examination.
When King's Bench visited Gloucester in 1363 a complaint
from James Clifford was made the basis of an indictment
presented by the juries of several hundreds.[82] Clifford had
procured a writ of *scire facias* against Sir Adam Shareshull in
relation to the manor of Stowell.[83] But while the plea was
pending, Richard Yanworth, *menour* of the abbot of Cirencester,
conspired with Shareshull to purchase the manor from him for
£50, a price that may have been rather below the market value.[84]
At the same time, Richard Yanworth sent letters to the vicar of
Northleach and to other local vicars ordering them to pronounce
in their churches on pain of excommunication that no one should
attend the inquest to be held at Gloucester unless to speak on
Adam's behalf. Yanworth was said to be a maintainer of quarrels
in the abbot's consistory. If the dominance which he exercised
locally can be connected, as seems possible, with the abbot's
lordship of the five hundreds around Cirencester, the power
which private hundredal jurisdiction could bestow was evidently
still considerable in the fourteenth century.[85] In 1362 James
Clifford clearly had a claim to Stowell which he was prevented
from pursuing by the collusion between Yanworth and
Shareshull. But why Shareshull should wish to sell the manor at
such a low price is puzzling. Four years before, on 5 July 1358

[82] K.B.9/29 m. 46; K.B.27/411 Rex m. 17.
[83] The manor of Stowell had long been the residence of the Martel family
(K.B.27/191 m. 27). When it passed to Shareshull is not clear.
[84] In the fifteenth century it was widely held that the market price of a manor
was twenty times its annual net revenue (McFarlane, *The Nobility of Later
Medieval England*, pp. 56–7), but this rule was not rigorously observed. For the
fourteenth century there is insufficient evidence for any generalization to be
made with safety.
[85] For the hundredal jurisdiction of the abbot of Cirencester see *The Cartulary
of Cirencester Abbey*, ed. C. D. Ross, i (Oxford, 1964), xxxiii–xxxiv. John de
Berkeley of Dursley complained of the hundredal jurisdiction of Thomas de
Berkeley of Berkeley: S.C.8/157/7832.

Yanworth and twenty-six followers had attacked Shareshull at Northleach where they stole from him 63 florins said to be worth £21.[86] They imprisoned their victim for a day and attacked his servants so that he lost their service. The collusive sale of Stowell, then, may not have been an amicable agreement to exclude Clifford. To judge from his aggressive behaviour in the past, Yanworth may have compelled Adam Shareshull to part with the manor against his will at less than market value. To achieve this end Yanworth employed methods of chicanery and intimidation. The attack on Shareshull at Northleach was not an isolated act of aggression; more likely it was part of a wider feud in which possession of a manor proved to be the ultimate goal. The outcome of the proceedings in King's Bench in 1363 is not known. But James Clifford seems to have won possession, for in 1374 he and his wife Margaret enfeoffed John Clifford, probably his father, of the manor of Stowell. Twenty years later James made a fresh enfeoffment before crossing to Ireland with Richard II.[87] If the owner's title to a manor was likely to be challenged, an enfeoffment to use would make any action at law redundant.

Another interesting case presented in 1363 involved the Cardiff family. On 11 April 1363 Robert Knight, Thomas Hardhed and others ejected Edward Cardiff from his house at Walton Cardiff near Tewkesbury in the presence of the assize justices, and took possessions of his to the value of £100.[88] Hardhed and Knight, it is surprising to find, actually came to defend themselves in court where they pleaded not guilty. In their defence they drew upon the complicated history of the descent of the manor. The house *que vocatur domus Edwardi de Kerdif* was held at her death in 1349 by Joan, daughter and heiress of William Cardiff.[89] Joan left as her three daughters, Elizabeth, who also died in 1349, Margaret, later known as Elizabeth, who married John Baudrip, and Juetta, who married Robert Underhill. Then, said the defendants, Robert and Juetta, John and Elizabeth remitted the reversion of the manor, as they

---

[86] K.B.27/394 m. 26d.

[87] C.P.25(1)78/77/526; *Sede Vacante Register*, iv, ed. J. W. Willis Bund (Worc. Hist. Soc., 1897), 358–9.

[88] K.B.27/411 Rex m. 8.

[89] Some of the confusions and errors in the account of the Cardiff family in *V.C.H. Worcs.*, iii, 488–9, are corrected in *V.C.H. Gloucs.*, viii, 238.

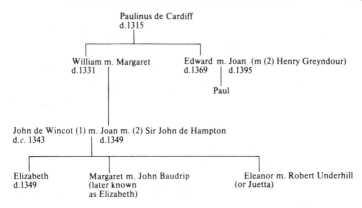

Cardiff of Walton Cardiff

were permitted to do.[90] The narrative is vague; but Hardhed and Knight seem to be referring to a fine made in 1363 by which Robert and Juetta Underhill and John and Elizabeth Baudrip settled the Cardiff manors of Queenhill (Worcs.) and Walton Cardiff (Gloucs.) on Edward Cardiff and his wife Joan.[91] Edward was the uncle of the heiress Joan who had died in 1349. It was this settlement, in which on the surviving evidence all the parties seem to have acquiesced at the time, that provoked the attack on Edward Cardiff who was in residence at Walton in 1363.

Although the account is far from clear on a number of points, it seems that Hardhed and Knight were acting on behalf of the daughters, Elizabeth and Juetta. Apparently they did not acknowledge Edward's right to the manor of Walton; yet it was precisely that which was surrendered to him by the fine of 1363. In attempting to explain this puzzling state of affairs we enter the realm of speculation; but some suggestions can be made. A settlement of some of the Cardiff lands had been made earlier by Joan. In 1334, three years after the death of her father, Joan de Cardiff settled the manor of Queenhill on the heirs of her body.[92]

[90] Confusion surrounds the names of the daughters. When the eldest daughter, Elizabeth, died in 1349, her heirs were said to be her sisters Margaret and Eleanor (*C.I.P.M.*, ix, no. 440). Eleanor is to be identified with Juetta, and Margaret subsequently seems to have assumed the name of her elder sister Elizabeth (*V.C.H. Gloucs.*, viii, 238).

[91] *V.C.H. Gloucs.*, viii, 238.   [92] *V.C.H. Worcs.*, iii, 488.

Thus the estate should have passed to her daughters; but in 1350 Joan's uncle, Edward, is found to be in seisin of Queenhill. Since the Cardiff lands were theirs by right the daughters Elizabeth and Juetta would hardly want to surrender them to Edward. But Edward, already in possession of Queenhill, may well have wanted to acquire Walton too; had the fine of 1363 been made under coercion, the daughters' readiness to repudiate it and the attempt to disseise Edward would at least become explicable. When he died in 1369 Edward Cardiff still held both manors.[93] Some support for this interpretation is given by an earlier indictment in King's Bench. In Hilary Term 1358 Edward Cardiff began an action of trespass against John and Elizabeth Baudrip, John's brother Simon and seven others; no further details were given, and the action was adjourned.[94] But the plea does suggest that the attack on 11 April 1363 was not the first incident in this feud between the daughters and their great-uncle.

What is incontrovertible in this tangled affair is the connection between the affray in April 1363 and the disputed ownership of the manor of Walton. Hardhed and Knight appear to have acted not on their own initiative but on behalf of the daughters to whom the manor of Queenhill, and possibly also that of Walton, passed by the settlement of 1343. The daughters may have employed force to recover the right to Walton which they had just surrendered by fine to Edward. Further resort to the courts was hardly open to the daughters and their husbands when the fine to which Edward owed his claim was registered in the Court of Common Pleas.[95] Their disregard for it suggests that the daughter never accepted the terms of the settlement: the laconic wording of a fine may itself conceal a story of violence and intimidation. The possibility is, therefore, that Edward had succeeded by adept use of the legal process in depriving the daughters of their inheritance; and that they were employing force to recover it because no other means was open. The law could be used, as it had been in the 1320s by the Despensers, to

[93] *Gloucs. Inqs. Post Mortem*, iv, 56–7.   [94] K.B.27/390 m. 3.

[95] Had the two daughters taken an action of novel disseisin against Edward Cardiff, he could have employed the normal defence offered by a defendant in such circumstances: that the lands had been given to him by the plaintiff, as he could prove by the evidence of the final concord (D. M. Sutherland, *The Assize of Novel Disseisin* (Oxford, 1973), p. 71).

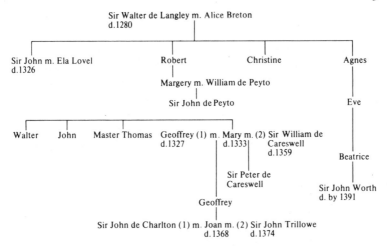

Langley of Siddington

legitimize settlements achieved by illicit means. Deprived of the natural process of redress, a plaintiff could then resort only to violence.

The illuminating story of the break-up of the Langley inheritance is worth recounting next, for the picture it reveals of lawlessness provoked by a dispute over an inheritance is not dissimilar to the other cases.[96] When Geoffrey de Langley died in 1327 leaving a minor, his widow Mary married Sir William de Careswell. Geoffrey's clerical brother Thomas, in contravention of his father's entail, enfeoffed William and Mary jointly of the Langley estates for their lives with successive remainders to Geoffrey, the young son of Geoffrey de Langley, and his heirs and to the heirs of William de Careswell. Mary died in 1333, but Careswell survived not only Thomas but also the younger Geoffrey. He strove to secure his position by purchasing the marriage of young Geoffrey's daughter and heir, Joan, whom he betrothed to Sir John de Charlton. Two years after Careswell's death in 1359 these careful plans were upset: in 1361 Sir John Trillowe, John de Langley and others abducted Joan, who two

[96] P. R. Coss, *The Langley Family and its Cartulary* (Dugdale Soc. Occasional Papers, no. 22, 1974).

years later is found to be married not to Charlton but to Trillowe. Apart from a rental in the manor of Milcote (Warwicks.) Trillowe acquired Joan's entire inheritance, of which he enfeoffed Sir Baldwin de Frevill, lord of Tamworth, presumably as a measure of self-protection. As a result Frevill held the Langley properties around Coventry, and Trillowe those in south Warwickshire and Gloucestershire. When Joan died in 1368 Trillowe claimed to hold these properties still, but there were no fewer than five other claimants: Sir John de Peyto, grandson of Robert de Langley of Wolfhamcote, Sir John Worth, great-grandson of Christine, sister of Sir John de Langley, John de Langley of Atherstone-on-Stour (Warwicks.), Elizabeth de Barnsley, great-granddaughter of Sir Edmund de Langley and Peter, son of Sir William de Careswell. One of those who staked a claim, Sir John de Peyto, tried to resolve the matter by use of force; he seized the manor of Milcote, possession of which he secured by making an enfeoffment to use. Nevertheless, he was ousted by Trillowe, who held both Milcote and Siddington until his death in 1374. Elizabeth de Barnsley was named as heir. In the meantime, however, John de Langley entered Siddington 'but for fear of his life dared not continue his estate'. Sir John Worth, it seems, had entered Siddington, and until his death fifteen years later he enjoyed possession of those parts of the Langley inheritance which had not by now passed permanently into the hands of Baldwin de Frevill. As Dr Coss has pointed out, lawlessness was an important factor in the break-up of the Langley inheritance, for after Joan's death in 1368 the issue was decided by force rather than by due process of law.[97] *De facto* possession of a manor constituted a title that was as strong in practice as a title in law. Problems like those which John Paston the elder experienced in fifteenth century Norfolk are already recognizable in fourteenth-century Gloucestershire.

An equally complicated dispute centred on the inheritance of Sir Simon Basset. In 1362 Simon's son John died in the life time of his father holding the manor of Lasborough near Dursley.[98] In the inquest no heir was named; but on 20 February 1363 Simon Basset was granted the wardship of all the lands which John had held in chief in Gloucestershire along with the marriage of John's

[97] Ibid., p. 18.   [98] *Gloucs. Inqs. Post Mortem*, vi, 20–1.

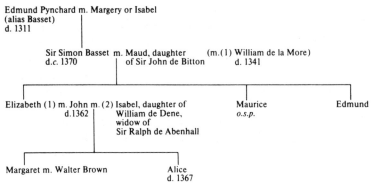

Basset of Uley

heir.[99] Twenty years later, however, the Crown decided to claim
the custody of these lands. Probably the grant was for benefit of
Simon only, and not for his widow. Thus on 17 June 1383 the
King sent a writ to the sheriff of Somerset explaining that an
inquest before the escheator of Gloucestershire had found that
the manor and advowson of Lasborough, held in chief by knight
service, had come into the hands of Edward III after the death of
John Basset because of the minority of his daughters Alice, who
had since died, and Margaret. Meanwhile, an inquest in
Somerset had found that the profit of lands in that county had
been taken since John's death by his father, Simon, till his death
and since then by his widow and executrix, Maud. The Crown
now claimed custody of all these lands.[100] Maud was summoned
to appear in Chancery. She was represented there by her
attorneys who argued that in 1341 Simon had settled his
Somerset property on John and John's first wife Elizabeth in tail
but that he had afterwards demised the lands to John as a tenant-
at-will. Maud's attorneys showed also a second deed, dated 1363,
by which Sir Simon Basset enfeoffed John Clavile and Richard
Goldney, chaplains, of all his lands in Gloucestershire and the
Welsh Marches. The feoffees regranted the lands to Simon and
Maud for their lives with successive remainders to their sons
Maurice and Edmund in tail.[101] According to an inquest before
the escheator of Somerset on 7 October 1389 Simon made an

[99] Cal. Pat. Rolls 1361–4, p. 317.
[100] Gloucs. Inqs. Post Mortem, vi, 140.   [101] Ibid., 140–1.

identical enfeoffment of his Somerset lands.[102] Within a year of the death of his eldest son John, who had died without issue by his first wife Elizabeth, Simon had therefore made a new settlement of his lands. In 1363 all the estates in Gloucestershire and Somerset, apparently with the exception of Lasborough which was not mentioned, were settled on Maurice and in the event of his death on Edmund. It seems that it was not until 1383 that the Crown decided to challenge the right of Simon's widow to take the profits of wardship. Maud claimed that as John had died without heir by his first wife, his Somerset lands reverted to the grantor. This seems to have happened; if not, Simon could hardly have settled them again in 1363. On the other hand, the argument of John's daughter and heir Margaret and her husband Walter Broun was to be that the grant had been at will.

Walter and Margaret Broun were apparently residing at Lasborough in 1377; on 16 February that year Maud Basset, her sons Maurice and Edmund, Nicholas Cook, John Stoutshill junior and William Tracy, tailor, raided Lasborough, where they raped Margaret Broun and stole many of Walter's possessions including linen, cloth, rings and jewellery. This case first makes its appearance in King's Bench in Trinity Term 1384, seven years after the affray took place, and it was dragging on at least until 1386.[103] Meanwhile the Bassets for their part were resorting to litigation too.[104] Maud clearly believed that John's daughter had no right either to Lasborough or to the Somerset estates; and as the lands had not reverted to the grantor or his widow, her sons were being deprived of part of their inheritance. Their willingness to take part in the assault on Lasborough is understandable.

On 30 April 1384 King's Bench was ordered by writ of *nisi prius* to inquire whether John Basset had held at will or for term of the grantor's life.[105] But three months later, on 20 July, a writ of *supersedeas* was issued on the grounds that a speedy inquisition would place the King and Maud Basset at a disadvantage.[106] In

---

[102] *Cal. Inqs. Post Mortem*, xvi, no. 798.

[103] K.B.27/493m. 17; K.B.27/495m. 43d; K.B.27/498m. 49d; K.B.27/500m. 21.

[104] K.B.27/514 Rex m. 33.

[105] *Cal. Close Rolls 1381–5*, p. 377.

[106] Ibid., p. 569.

Michaelmas 1389 the case reappeared in King's Bench only to
suffer successive adjournments. After it had been adjourned to
Michaelmas 1390 *nisi prius* the case was remitted to the assize
justices in Somerset.[107] In Eastern Term 1391 the King then sent
a writ to the Chief Justice, Sir Walter Clopton, requesting that
the record and process be sent into Chancery.[108] Eight months
earlier the King had ordered the escheator of Somerset to take a
fresh inquest concerning the lands of which John had died seised.
The findings were the same as before: that he had died on 13
January 1362 leaving his daughter Margaret as his heir.[109] Still a
solution was no nearer. On 25 September 1392 a commission of
local gentry was appointed to enquire into the tenure of the lands
of which John Basset was seised at his death.[110] By this date
Walter and Margaret were holding the manor of Lasborough but
not the Somerset lands. They had taken up residence at
Lasborough as early as 1377, and in 1384 the escheator was
ordered to grant to Walter his estate in Gloucestershire now that
he had proved his age.[111] Both parties to the dispute, however,
were petitioning to recover the lands in Somerset. An undated
petition in the name of Walter and Margaret Broun was
probably submitted at the time that Edmund Basset placed his
own bill before the parliament of November 1391.[112] He
requested tenure of his inheritance which a writ of *scire facias* had
caused to be taken into the King's hands. The reply was that the
status quo should prevail until consideration was given to the
petition in the following parliament;[113] but it may well have been
in response to these two petitions that the commission was
appointed on 25 September 1392. There matters rested at the
end of the century. Yet the affair dragged on into the reign of
Henry V when Edmund Basset, probably a son of Edmund, was
exonerated from accounting for the issues of the manor of
Lasborough.[114]

In each of these cases what might otherwise appear to be an

[107] K.B.27/514 Rex m. 33.
[108] Ibid. [109] *Cal. Inqs. Post Mortem*, xvi, no. 798.
[110] *Cal. Pat. Rolls 1391–6*, p. 231.
[111] *Cal. Close Rolls 1381–5*, p. 466.
[112] S.C.8/232/11600; S.C.8/22/1072.
[113] *Rot. Parl.*, iii, 461.
[114] T. D. Fosbrooke, *Abstracts . . . concerning the County of Gloucester*, i
(Gloucester, 1807), 409 & n.

isolated affray takes its place in a longer sequence of events. The possibility can be suggested, but no more than suggested, that behind other violent episodes a similar background lies concealed: for it is the interminaable litigation surrounding a disputed title which emerges as the dominant theme.

In a society where land was the principal source of wealth and measure of social standing it is natural that lawsuits between lords should have centred on its ownership and descent. For many who resided on their estates and whose energies were not channelled into foreign warfare or county administration such litigation may have been a constant pastime. It has been suggested that a knowledge of legal technicalities and of the workings of the processes of law was more widely diffused in the middle ages than it is today.[115] Any landowner who had property to protect needed to be well-versed in the forms of law. As P. S. Lewis has observed, a landowner's estates were a permanent temptation to his neighbours.[116] If a suitable opportunity arose for a rival to disposses him, litigation and violence were the weapons that would be employed alongside each other. But it was not only against other families that a lord had to guard his property. The histories of the Cardiff, Basset and Langley families show how some of the bitterest feuds were occasioned when rival heirs fought over a disputed inheritance. The evidence of the plea rolls shows once again how disastrous inheritance by a female could turn out to be. The Cardiff daughters lost out to an uncle: Edward, who had already somehow gained seisin of Queenhill, seems to have compelled the heiresses to sign over to him their rights in Walton Cardiff, and despite attacks on his manors he died in possession of both in 1369. The premature deaths of Sir John de Langley's sons and grandson left as heir a young girl who became the object of the competing ambitions of those with claims to the inheritance; and after her death the issue was resolved by the use of force. The dispute over the Cardiff inheritance had a sequel similar to the abduction of the Langley heiress, Joan, by John de Trillowe. In Michaelmas 1378 the juries of various hundreds presented that on 12 September that year Henry Greyndour had seized Joan

---

[115] *The Paston Letters, 1422–1509*, i, ed. J. Gairdner (London, 1904), 117–18.
[116] P. S. Lewis, 'Sir John Fastolf's Lawsuit over Titchwell, 1448–55', *Historical Jnl.*, i (1958), 1–2.

Cardiff against her will at Walton. Joan must have escaped, for
the juries went on to say that Henry seized her again on 19 and 20
September.[117] He carried her off to the Forest of Dean, and later
she appears as his wife.[118]

These extraordinary happenings raise other questions. If
vulnerable heiresses were an unsettling influence, as they were,
landless younger sons were equally so. Henry Greyndour was
probably a younger son in search of an inheritance, and his
kinsman Ralph, the outlaw, may have resorted to a career in
crime because he too lacked a landed estate.[119] Edward Cardiff
who acquired the inheritance of the two heiresses was a younger
son who inherited no lands. There is some evidence that he found
a living in the service of Sir Guy Brien;[120] but by 1363 he had
established himself as a country gentleman at the expense of the
two daughters, albeit daughters who were married. Even those
who refrained from a life of professional crime did not hesitate to
combine force with dexterous legal manipulation to dispossess a
vulnerable daughter of her rightful inheritance.

Among the nobility the plight of younger sons was eased in the
late middle ages by the employment of the use, which enabled
lands to be devised for their benefit. However, this legal device
brought little relief to younger sons of knights and esquires whose
estates were not wide enough to permit substantial permanent
alienations. If the likes of Ralph Greyndour and Edward Cardiff,
the latter certainly a younger son, were impelled towards crime,
it may well have been because they were landless men, whose
position was unaffected by the development of the use.[121]
Changes in land law certainly influenced the level of lawlessness,
but in quite another way. In the fourteenth century many landowners were settling their lands by final concords recorded in the
Court of Common Pleas. A lord granted his fief to a group of

[117] K.B.27/471 Rex m. 23d.
[118] Cal. Pat. Rolls 1391–6, p. 554.
[119] For the descent of the Greyndours see above, p. 80. Unfortunately the
relationship of Henry Greyndour to other members of the family cannot be
determined.
[120] Cal. Pat. Rolls 1350–4, p. 491.
[121] See, however, J. M. W. Bean, The Decline of English Feudalism, 1215–1540
(Manchester, 1968), pp. 104–48, who argues that employment of the use spread
from the smaller landowners to the higher nobility. Evidence from the
fourteenth century to support that hypothesis is certainly not abundant.

feoffees from whom he would receive it back on terms different from those which normally governed descent in fee simple.[122] By thus entailing his lands a lord could regulate the descent of his property; but the complications, and even the violence, to which such settlements could lead, are amply illustrated by the disputes over the Basset and Langley estates. The law became not so much an instrument by which differences could be reconciled as a means by which uncertainties could be exploited and title challenged. Legal expertise was vital to landowners who effected settlements, if they were not to store up problems for the future as Sir Simon Basset did. The legislation of the twelfth century had clarified land law; but by the fourteenth century the increased employment of the use, entail and jointure had created confusions and entanglements which became a nightmare. All the cases which have been examined in detail come from the second half of the century when King's Bench visited Gloucestershire more often than before. If such bitter and protracted disputes appear to be on the increase, then it may simply be because King's Bench visited the county only twice in the first sixty years of the century and five times in the last forty.[123] But on the other hand, if it was the increasing complexity of land settlements which was in large measure responsible for the disorder, it is possible that feuds became more common as litigation grew more tangled.[124]

To suggest that disputed titles lay at the problem of gentry lawlessness is only part of the answer, for the quick resort to the use of force needs to be explained. That litigation should be accompanied by violence suggests that the courts of common law were no longer able to cope. Their failings were many and obvious. The judges were notoriously corruptible; they could not be relied on to show impartiality because so many of them were in receipt of fees from secular and ecclesiastical magnates.[125] The

[122] McFarlane, *The Nobility of Later Medieval England*, p. 270.

[123] See above, p. 172.

[124] For an early fifteenth-century feud which arose when the terms of an entail regulating the descent of the manor of Dodford (Northants.) were overridden, see Nigel Saul, 'Two Fifteenth-Century Brasses at Dodford, Northants.', *Trans. Monumental Brass Soc.* xii, pt. iii (1977), 210–14.

[125] J. R. Maddicott, 'Law and Lordship: Royal Justices as Retainers in Thirteenth and Fourteenth Century England' (*Past and Present* Supplement 4, 1978).

execution of Sir John Cavendish by the rebels in 1381 indicated the deep unpopularity of the judiciary. Judicial processes were held in lower regard than ever before. In 1347 Sir William de Beauchamp and Sir William Shareshull were assaulted at Tredington (Warwicks) while they were hearing a plea of trespass against Sir John de Beauchamp under a commission of oyer and terminer.[126] Moreover it was in the presence of the justices of assize that Edward Cardiff was attacked in his own home in 1363.[127]

The machinery of the courts was evidently ceasing to operate effectively. The central courts were incapable any longer of handling the burden of work thrust upon them. In the thirteenth century the growth in the number of writs brought more business to the courts; in the fourteenth century this was remitted to the assize justices and later to the J.P.s, but the burden on the central courts was still heavy. Delays were incessant. A plea of trespass in King's Bench between Sir Thomas Blaunkfront and John Besemaunsel that suffered adjournment for eight successive terms or more was not unusual.[128] Sir Thomas de Breouse's suit against the Kingscots for the affray at Tetbury market dragged on for more than thirteen terms.[129] In Michaelmas 1365 the Prior of Bath, Matthew de Bitton and Sir Simon Basset were summoned to appear in King's Bench to answer articles that had been presented against them.[130] At the time of his death four years later Simon Basset had still not bothered to appear in court; nor did the others.[131] There was no adequate machinery to compel attendance in court; and under common law a man could not usually be tried on a criminal charge in his absence. On only one occasion so far discovered did the King's attorney prosecute a man in his absence.[132] Normally if men were found guilty in their absence it was by outlawry not trial. On other occasions the jury would fail to turn up. In Trinity Term 1363 the sheriff of Gloucester was ordered to distrain on the lands of Laurence

[126] *Cal. Pat. Rolls 1345–8*, p. 386. For Sir Robert Darcy's attacks on the justices in Lincolnshire see *Cal. Pat. Rolls 1358–61*, p. 463.
[127] K.B.27/411 Rex m. 8.   [128] K.B.27/318–K.B.27/325.
[129] K.B.27/333–K.B.27/346.   [130] K.B.27/421 Rex m. 16.
[131] K.B.27/425 Rex m. 6d.
[132] The one exception was the prosecution in 1282 in his absence of John de Clifford at the King's suit of the rape of Rose le Savage (Bellamy, op. cit., p. 104).

Sebrok, keeper of Gloucester Castle. Ten years later Sebrok had still not appeared in court, and in 1373 and 1374 the case was adjourned for lack of a jury.[133]

A case which spent four years or more in King's Bench could have taken as long to reach the court in the first place. On 30 September 1384 Richard Byl and others were reported to have seized John Bray at Aure, whence they took him to be imprisoned at Berkeley Castle. The case was brought initially before the keepers of the peace. Not until Easter 1395 did it reach King's Bench where it suffered the normal fate of adjournment for term after term.[134] The power of the lord of Berkeley no doubt prevented this plea from proceeding more speedily, but the effectiveness of the courts was reduced in another way. Defendants and appellants could secure acquittal on mere technicalities and points of detail. In Hilary Term 1368 in King's Bench John son of Ralph Trye accused Sir Thomas Apadam, John his son and many others of disseising him of his half of the manor of Redwick and Northwick. Apadam and the others, of course, did not bother to attend in person, but their attorney answered on their behalf to the effect that Northwick was not a vill but only a hamlet of Redwick; and that two acres of land and 20s. of rents named in the view were in Usulport, which was not named in the writ. Such arguments proved adequate to secure an acquittal.[135]

Contemporaries were well aware of the failings of the central courts. As early as 1334, for example, Richard de Grey of Codnor, petitioning parliament for recovery of his manor of Oveston, complained of great delays in the Court of King's Bench.[136] Because of the futility of proceedings in the courts of common law litigants came to look elsewhere for redress. Thus in Michaelmas Term 1397 Lewis Cardigan, Alice his wife and William Hathewik, who were claiming the manor of Ladbroke (Warwicks) submitted a petition to the King's Council. This was reffered to a sub-committee of the dukes of Exeter and Surrey who were not technically competent to advise and who therefore appointed a committee of four sergeants.[137] The point of this

[133] K.B.27/411 Rex m. 27d; K.B.27/451 Rex m. 10; K.B.27/454 m. 9d.
[134] K.B.27/536 Rex m. 21.
[135] K.B.27/429 m. 30d.   [136] *Rot. Parl.*, ii, 88.
[137] *Select Cases in the Court of King's Bench, Richard II, Henry IV, Henry V*, pp. lxv–lxvi.

procedure seems to have been to avoid the delays of formal proceedings at common law. The plaintiffs alleged that they could not afford the cost of a long action, and to deny them justice because they were poor was *encountre la ley et concience*. Because poverty prevented them from seeking remedy at common law they considered themselves entitled to a remedy according to equity. Faced by such interminable delays, which they could afford neither in time nor in money, other litigants by-passed the courts to settle their differences by extra-legal means. In many cases it is clear that this was synonymous with force. Forty years after the death of John Basset the fate of his lands was still undecided; in addition to the delays in the courts two inquisitions *post mortem* had been ordered and the dispute had been referred to a commission of local gentry. It is hardly surprising that the Bassets took matters into their own hands by attacking Walter and Margaret Broun. Violence could be used as a substitute for litigation: thus John de Trillowe abducted Joan, the Langley heiress, in order to present his opponents with a *fait accompli*. But violence can be seen too as an extension of litigation by other means: a way of putting pressure on the other party. So few actions in the central courts ever reached a conclusion that many litigants must have come to a settlement out of court. The use of violence and intimidation may have served to achieve this end. It is only partly true that in fourteenth-century England recourse was made first to arms and secondly to litigation;[138] the two also went hand-in-hand. Violence grew out of litigation.

It would be wrong to suggest that no attempt was made to rectify the failings of the common law. The extension of conciliar jurisdiction was one reaction.[139] The Statutes of Forcible Entry were another. These sought to limit the means by which an entry could be effected, even by one who claimed a title. The first such statute, dating from 1391, prescribed fines or imprisonment for those who resorted to unlawful violence to seize land which they took to be their lawful property. This was a civil action; but out of the statute and the others which followed it developed the criminal proceeding of indictment for forcible entry which could be heard before the J.P.s. In this the defendant could not claim in

<hr/>

[138] Coss, *The Langley Family and its Cartulary*, p. 14.
[139] See above, p. 198.

extenuation as he could in the civil proceedings that he had a lawful right of entry; he was guilty simply if he had used illegal violence. The enactment of this legislation not only shows that the King's justices attempted to strengthen the sanctions of the common law but also points directly to the connection between violence and claims to land.[140]

The fines prescribed by the statute were intended to deter would-be assailants. But, at least until the 1390s, most of the common law penalties for lawlessness were manifestly ineffective. If a fine was imposed on a sheriff for a misdemeanor it was unlikely to be collected since responsibility for the collection of fines rested with the sheriff and bailiffs. Such fines, anyway, were small. One of the largest was a fine of 100s. imposed on Sir John Tracy (sheriff, 1363-8) for allowing a felon to escape from his custody.[141] The penalty for failure to return a writ was often just half a mark.[142] The imposition of heavy fines by King's Bench in the 1350s when Shareshull was Chief Justice was not a policy that was followed at other times during the century.[143] For a large scale raid on Lasborough in April 1378 Sir Nicholas de Berkeley was fined 20s. and his followers 40d. each.[144] The coroner John Joye could count himself distinctly unlucky on being fined as much as 40s. in 1387 for his trespasses and extortions.[145] But those actions which resulted in a judgment against the defendant and the imposition of a fine were themselves in a minority. Many actions resulted in an acquittal; many others were probably settled out of court. Thus a malefactor knew that if he were unlucky enough to be brought to trial he would stand a good chance of ultimate acquittal even if the plaintiff were to press ahead with the plea. In Michaelmas Term 1378, for example, when King's Bench visited Gloucester the juries of several hundreds presented that Thomas Catewy, constable of Glouces-ter Castle, conspired with John Billing of Bosley and others to arrest Thomas Billing, John Billing senior, and Philip de Aune and to detain them until they swore in John Billing's favour in an

---

[140] Sutherland, *The Assize of Novel Disseisin*, pp. 173-4.
[141] K.B.27/429, Fines.
[142] K.B.27/412, Fines.
[143] For Shareshull's policy see B. H. Putnam, *The Place in Legal History of Sir William Shareshull* (Cambridge, 1950), pp. 72, 78.
[144] K.B.27/471, Fines.   [145] K.B.27/506, Fines.

inquest.[146] Yet Catewy was found not guilty. Bribery and intimidation of juries go some way towards explaining the low rate of convictions. Juries must also have become wary by the knowledge that some indictments were malicious and devoid of any foundation of truth. Equally, jurors must have hesitated before finding a man guilty when they remembered how many convicted felons secured pardons from the King. Once free, such felons would be quick to wreak vengeance on the jurors who convicted them. In 1360, when a Linconshire knight, Sir Robert Darcy, secured a pardon from the King for a lengthy catalogue of crimes, local jurors had good reason to fear, since once before he had come back to besiege a man who had dared to indict him.[147]

In most cases, however, the defendant simply failed to appear in court: hence the interminable adjournments. In a society which lacked a proper police force, the difficulty of securing the attendance of the parties at court was one which crippled the effective administration of law and justice. If he feared arrest, a man could flee to a neighbouring county to escape the penalties of life as an outlaw in his own shire, as James Coterel did. But it is doubtful if members of the gentry were often forced to resort to such extremities. Ralph Greyndour and his followers lived in the Forest of Dean which afforded ample cover. The continued immunity of the Kingscots was furthered by the support which they received from Thomas de Berkeley. Such men were bandits; but in the case of knights who resorted to violence only occasionally and who deferred appearance in court, it is difficult to believe that they were ever seriously threatened with arrest or harassment by the King's ministers in the shire. Admittedly the evidence is largely negative: there is simply nothing to suggest that members of the gentry were put to serious inconvenience as a result of failure to attend court. A knight who was the social equal of the sheriff, the social superior of the bailiffs, and perhaps the retainer of a powerful lord, was not one easily to be intimidated; and if he found himself in the unpleasant surroundings of one of the King's prisons, he could easily rely on his friends and neighbours to offer mainprise on his behalf. Even a notorious

[146] K.B.27/471 Rex m. 5.
[147] Cal. Pat. Rolls 1358–61, p. 463–4.

malefactor like John Poleyn—admittedly an esquire of Thomas de Berkeley—was released as soon as he had found four guarantors to vouch for his peaceable behaviour in future.[148] That so many men with criminal records held office and sat in parliament is a tribute to the ineffectiveness of the sanctions of the common law. Those who by-passed the courts in resorting to violence did so safe in the knowledge that the law was unlikely ever to catch up with them.

By the fourteenth century, then, the machinery of the common law was breaking down. The central courts were ceasing to function effectively and the authority of the King's judges counted for less and less. The known corruptibility of the judges and the ponderous weight of the system over which they presided encouraged litigants to settle their differences outside the courts. At a local level too the workings of justice were far from perfect. As John de Berkeley of Dursley pointed out in his petition in 1330, the local office holders would be the feed servants of a powerful magnate.[149] One of the counts of a Commons petition of 1376 was that maintainers procured the appointment to the office of sheriff of men who would advance their false quarrels.[150] This, of course, they needed to do because it was his responsibility to empanel a jury. The power which a sheriff wielded was well described in a case heard in King's Bench in Hilary Term 1395. It related to events that had taken place ten years earlier. Richard Byl and others were accused of wrongfully imprisoning John Bray at the behest of Thomas de Berkeley. When the case finally came to trial, the King's attorney pointed out that William Tracy, the sheriff, was a tenant of both Thomas de Berkeley and the earl of Warwick whose son had married Berkeley's daughter Elizabeth, and that he had arrayed a jury favourable to Berkeley's side of the case at the nomination of Richard Ruyhall and others of that party.[151] It was instances such as this that lay behind the Commons' petition. The power of the sheriff both in empanelling a jury and in executing the judgments of courts made him an invaluable, indeed an indispensable, ally to have in a suit.

Partiality in the local courts of the shire, as in the central

---

[148] *Cal. Close Rolls 1389–92*, p. 25.
[149] S.C.8/157/7832.   [150] *Rot. Parl.*, ii, 355.
[151] K.B.27/536 Rex mm. 21–21d.

courts, had the effect of driving those who feared they would never secure justice to settle their scores by other means. Most of these suitors were humble folk, but their social superiors suffered too. John de Berkeley may have been the loudest in his denunciations of seignorial heavy-handedness, but his plight was probably fairly common among those who lacked a powerful patron. John alleged that Thomas de Berkeley, who was one of the keepers of the peace, had distrained on his beasts by force of his office; moreover, with Mortimer's aid he had procured the franchise of return of writs within the hundred of Berkeley. The case came before King's Bench in Hilary 1330 when the sheriff of Gloucester was called to explain why he had failed to deliver to John de Berkeley the cattle which Thomas de Berkeley and Henry Rockhill, his steward, had seized and still held.[152] Since the sheriff of the day was William Gamage, a retainer of Berkeley, it is hardly surprising that nothing was done. But the lord of Berkeley was not the only man with whom John was at odds. In Michaelmas 1325 he, his brother and others from Dursley were indicted for attacking the servants of Robert Swinborne, lord of nearby Woodmancote.[153] In 1336 he led an assault on Sir John de la Rivere's park at Tormarton.[154] It is difficult to think that such behaviour over a period of more than ten years can entirely be explained by an inability to obtain redress within the shire by legal means. Sir Henry Barkley described John as 'hot-tempered', and he certainly seems to have had a bent for lawlessness.[155] The desire to seek an outlet for aggressive instincts may have motivated the behaviour not only of John de Berkeley but also of men like James Clifford who led the lives of bandits. In seeking explanations of a general nature for the prevalent disorder of the late middle ages it would be foolish of the historian to lose sight of individual personalities, difficult to perceive though they may be.

Whatever calculations may have entered the mind of a knight or esquire, his ready resort to violence in this period may not entirely have been without reason. Land was the most precious asset a man could hold: it lay at the heart of the inheritance and

[152] K.B.27/279 m. 108d; B.B.27/280 m. 21.
[153] K.B.27/262 m. 6d.   [154] *Cal. Pat. Rolls 1334–8*, p. 283.
[155] Sir H. Barkley, 'The Berkeleys of Dursley', *Trans. Bristol & Gloucs. Arch. Soc.*, ix (1884–5), 262.

its descent was regulated by rules which grew ever more complicated as the century progressed. Medieval society had developed a highly sophisticated code of land law which left the holder of a doubtful title at the mercy of the lawyer and the litigant. The mountain of business which arose from disputes over property was more than could be borne by courts that were already falling in the public estimation; it was but a small step from litigation to the use of force. Whether delays in the courts were becoming more protracted is hard to say; it is at least possible that as settlements became more complex so they gave rise to more disputes which eventually came before the courts. In the Lancastrian period, according to K. B. McFarlane, 'inheritances disputed between heirs male and heirs general were becoming commoner'.[156] When such litigation spilled over into violence feuds were allowed to run almost unchecked, for the King had not the technical means to curb the gentry who wielded in the shires the powers of law enforcement delegated by him. However high its intentions may periodically have been, the Westminster-based government was almost powerless to enforce internal peace. Justice was not dispensed, and the law not enforced. Medieval society's ability to control the descent of land had outrun its ability to resolve the disputes to which it gave rise.

[156] K B. McFarlane, 'The Wars of the Roses', *Procs. Brit. Academy*, 50 (1964), 105.

VI

THE INCOME OF THE GENTRY

Overshadowed by the debate over the 'declining' gentry of the thirteenth century and the 'rising' gentry of the sixteenth, the economic history of the knights and esquires of the late middle ages has been passed over almost unnoticed. If it was the suspicion that they were in difficulty that has attracted historians to study the knights of the thirteenth century, it was the need to explain the dramatic confrontation between King and parliament three centuries later that led historians to associate the growing wealth of the gentry with the expansion in the land market created by the dissolution of the monastries. For the period of the later middle ages, however, the baronial struggles known as the Wars of the Roses have failed to provide the kind of stimulus to historical studies that the Civil War has.

But the problem is also one of evidence. The barons and ecclesiastical corporations have left account rolls, cartularies and livery rolls from which the historian can build up his picture.[1] Ironically, at the other end of society, even the peasantry, provided that they held land, are better documented than the gentry. Sufficient information has been gleaned from manorial records to fuel many an argument about their standard of living in the middle ages. Of the landowners who drew up accounts and compiled cartularies the gentry are the most anonymous for being the least bureaucratic in their methods of administration. For these reasons the conventional sources of the economic historian are not always of great help. There are no account rolls

[1] The only two cartularies relating to gentry families in Gloucestershire are those of the Langleys (Brit. Lib. MS Harley 7) and the Spilmans of Rodborough (Glos. R.O. D/149, published in *Trans. Bristol & Gloucs. Arch. Soc.*, lxi (1939), 50–94). All but two of the charters in the Spilman cartulary are thirteenth century. For a discussion of the cartulary of the Langley family see P. R. Coss, *The Langley Family and its Cartulary* (Dugdale Soc. Occasional Papers, 22, 1974). G. R. C. Davis, *Medieval Cartularies of Great Britain* (London, 1958) lists more than a thousand cartularies of English monastic houses and 158 secular cartularies; many of the latter were compiled by or for magnate families.

of any knight's estate in Gloucestershire, and rentals are preserved of just two manors in the county—from Tibberton in 1358, and from Oldland in 1344 and 1363.[2]

Perhaps it may be worth glancing at some of the other sources which can be used. Extents of manors can be found in the inquisitions *post mortem* drawn up by the escheator on information given by a local jury when the death of a tenant-in-chief brought his lands into the temporary keeping of the King. After 1322 similar extents were made of the lands of the defeated Contrariants which passed into royal custody for five years.[3] Both sources need to be used with care. The escheator had an interest in returning as low a valuation as possible since he had to account for the issues to the Exchequer which would check his figures against those given in the inquisition. Juries, moreover, could not hope to make an accurate estimate of demesne profits. Thus, the usual method of estimating average net revenue of the demesne was simply to reckon what annual rent could be realized by leasing out. As Kosminsky has written, estimates of this sort, made by rule of thumb, often give a figure which is quite unreal.[4] Difficulties also arise in regard to the revenue from pasture land. In many cases it seems that the valuation included only the enclosed pasture belonging to the lord, ignoring his share of the common pasture.[5] In a county like Gloucester, where sheep breeding was widespread, this could constitute a serious omission of income; indeed, the almost total absence of sheep from the inquisitions as a source of income is a mark of their unreality. The rental income of the manor is usually under-estimated too, though by not so much as might be feared.[6]

That their use should be subject to so many qualifications is regrettable when only inquisitions *post mortem* give estimates of landed revenue over the period of the whole century. But the danger of placing too much reliance on the figures they yield can be illustrated by the startling variations in the value of the manor of Oldland over the last fifteen years of the century. In 1385 it was valued at £4 13s. 4d., in 1393 at £5—both very low figures

[2] D.L.3/35; Brit. Lib. Add. Ch. 26434, 26441.
[3] S.C.12/36/11; E.142/24, 25.
[4] E. A. Kosminsky, *Studies in the Agrarian History of England in the Thirteenth Century* (Oxford, 1956), p. 48.
[5] Ibid., p. 52.   [6] Ibid., p. 58.

compared with the total valuation of £12 12s. 3d. in the rental of
1363—but then in 1396 at no less than £26.[7] On the other hand,
when inquisitions taken within the space of a few years of each
other produce very similar results the suspicion arises that the
later inquisition is simply a duplicate of the earlier. The
inquisition taken on the death of John le Boteler of Park in 1352 is
almost identical to that taken on the death of his mother three
years earlier, even down to the amount and value of arable land
in each manor.[8] It is rare indeed to find reality creeping into these
fossilized returns.

Documents compiled for fiscal purposes constitute another line
of enquiry. Assessments of moveable wealth are provided by the
roll of the taxers in Gloucestershire of the twentieth granted in
1327, an invaluable document because it is the only roll for the
county to survive from the period when individual assessments
were made in each vill.[9] As a measure of personal wealth, though,
it is of limited assistance; only moveable property, not rental
income, was taxed. Moreover, the list of exempted goods was
large. The gentry paid no tax on their military accoutrements,
jewels or clothing; nor were they assessed on their demesne
equipment, ploughs or carts, which were considered to be as
necessary for their upkeep as was their armour for the performance of their military duties.[10] To draw estimates of knightly
wealth from these assessments would be to use them for purposes
for which they were never intended. Even for making com-
parisons between the moveable wealth of lords of manors the
figures need to be treated with care: as always where the
collection of money was concerned in the middle ages corruption
was inescapable.

Much has been written about the defects of another set of
documents occasioned by the King's need for money—the poll
tax returns. They are certainly a tribute to the extent to which
payment of taxation was avoided. Although the only Gloucestershire returns to survive are those of 1380–1—and even they are

[7] *Gloucs. Inqs. post Mortem*, vi, 147, 185; *Cal. Inqs. Misc.*, 1392–9, no. 144; Brit.
Lib. Add. Ch. 26441.
[8] *Gloucs. Inqs. post Mortem*, vi, 1–2, 21–2.　　　　[9] *Gloucs. Subsidy Roll.*
[10] *Early Taxation Returns*, ed. A. C. Chibnall (Buckinghamshire Record Soc.,
xiv, 1966), xii.

very patchy[11]—the returns for other counties of the graduated poll tax of 1379 can be used for comparative purposes.

Such are the main classes of evidence at the disposal of the historian. Because of the unreliability of the most prolific source—the inquisitions *post mortem*—it is rarely possible to compare manorial values over a period of fifty or a hundred years. For the second half of the century, however, the sources may be used to trace some of the social and economic changes that were coming across England. It is these later decades of the century that present the most interesting problems of interpretation. But before these can be considered it is necessary first to consider the fortunes of the gentry on the eve of the Black Death.

The period between 1300 and 1348 can be seen as a postscript to the debate about the lesser landowners in the thirteenth century. In the two centuries after the Norman Conquest the position of the knight had been transformed. The vavassor of Domesday Book, whose landed basis was rarely greater than $1\frac{1}{2}$ hides, had been replaced by the knight of local importance and military distinction.[12] The indications are that the use of scutage and the employment of mercenaries had allowed the vavassor class to drop out. But the inflation which began in the 1180s forced up still more the cost of equipping a knight, and the reduction of commitment which had eliminated the early professional now spread up the tenurial hierarchy. The thirteenth century saw a sweeping reduction of the *servitia debita* of the greater tenants-in-chief who were called upon to provide a mere fraction of their normal contingent.[13] This further reduction in the ranks of the knights is recorded in the deeds which fill monastic cartularies in the thirteenth century, but scepticism has been expressed because the evidence for the apparent knightly indebtedness comes from the purchasers of land.[14] Since

[11] E.179/113/31, 31A. They are discussed by R. H. Hilton, *The English Peasantry in the Later Middle Ages*, pp. 31–4.

[12] S. Harvey, 'The Knight and the Knight's Fee in England'. R. H. Hilton, *A Medieval Society*, p. 50.

[13] H. M. Chew, *The English Ecclesiastical Tenants-in-Chief and Knight Service* (Oxford, 1932), p. 47.

[14] Hilton, *A Medieval Society*, p. 51, shows how the estates of some 'declining' knights were bought up by Worcester Cathedral Priory. J. Z. Titow, *English Rural Society, 1200–1350* (London, 1969), p. 47, offers criticisms.

it was the buyer of land who received a charter we see the larger institutions acquiring the land of lesser men, whereas the latter, with no muniment rooms in which to preserve their charters, appear almost exclusively as sellers of land. However, Professor Hilton's suggestion of a 'crisis of the gentry' has been supported by Dr P. R. Coss who has shown how Henry III's marshal of the household, Sir Geoffrey de Langley, was acquiring encumbered estates from men who dealt in Jewish bonds. Dr Coss stresses the connection between the monasteries and the Jews.[15] Jewish debtors came from the whole range of knightly families, both well and less well endowed. In most cases the major sale came after either a period of leasing or after a string of minor alienations: better endowed families, it is suggested, were able to survive longer because they enjoyed the scope to dispose of property without immediate consequences.

Some historians associate this crisis with the inflation which erupted at the end of Henry II's reign. The upward movement of prices, of which the rise in the cost of war was but one manifestation, was bound to benefit agricultural entrepreneurs, among whom could be numbered the gentry. But, according to the argument of Professor Postan, some benefited more than others. 'The smaller monastic houses and smaller lay landowners themselves consumed the greater part of their demesnes' output, and were therefore unable to reap the full benefits of the buoyant market for agricultural produce. The economic situation should therefore have favoured the magnates rather than the small owners.'[16] Sale of demesne produce was of course but one constituent in the income of a manorial lord. Another was rents. Rents of unfree tenants, known as rents of assize, fixed as they were according to immemorial custom, could not be adjusted upwards easily in an age of inflation. The only alternative was to increase entry fines and extract the incidents of villein tenure to the full. A lord heavily reliant on rents was more likely to be in difficulties in a period of inflation than one who drew a larger proportion of his income from production for the market.

However attractive may be the logic of the argument, the

[15] P. R. Coss, 'Sir Geoffrey de Langley and the Crisis of the Knightly Class', *Past & Present*, 68 (1975), 3–37.

[16] *Cambridge Economic History of Europe*, i, ed. M. M. Postan (Cambridge, 1966), 593.

evidence adduced in its support has so far been rather patchy. But the debate is bound to colour any discussion of the fortunes of the gentry in the half century before the outbreak of the Black Death. If the prosperity of the gentry is found to be insecurely based when the fourteenth century opens, some support will be lent to those who argue that the lesser land-owners were in difficulties in the time of Henry III.

A knight's estate often combined the characteristics of a home farm with those of a cash manor. One such small economy was Lionel de Bradenham's manor of Langenhoe (Essex) which is known to us in more detail than most other estates of corresponding size thanks to the survival of five account rolls from the years 1325–48.[17] Wheat was the principal cash crop, and the manorial sergeant used 21.4 per cent of his total wheat receipts for seed, paid 18.9 per cent in wages to workers on the demesne, sent 22.8 per cent to the lord's household, and sold 29.9 per cent. In the period covered by the accounts income from sales of grain, wool and leases of livestock brought the lord of the manor the considerable sum of £37 *per annum*. Unfortunately, Gloucestershire offers no series of accounts to set alongside those from a manor in Essex. The extents in the inquisitions *post mortem* do not yield comparable figures because they give only the lease value of the demesne lands. If in the absence of such accounts it is difficult to estimate the regular income which knights were receiving, less direct means can still be employed; it is best to begin by looking at the size of demesnes.

Langenhoe in Essex was a well-endowed manor with a demesne of 250 acres of arable. The evidence from Gloucestershire suggests that this was still small by the standards of some of the magnate demesnes. At Childswickham, a manor of the earl of Warwick, in 1316 there were 360 acres of arable, sixteen acres of meadow and three acres of pasture.[18] The inquisitions taken in 1327 on the estates held at his death five years earlier by the last of the Giffards of Brimpsfield, known appropriately as John the Rich, suggest that the profits of cultivation may have contributed in large part to his wealth. At Winterbourne there were 300 acres of arable and fifteen acres of meadow, and at Brimpsfield itself

---

[17] R. H. Britnell, 'Production for the Market on a Small Fourteenth-Century Estate', *Econ. Hist. Rev.*, 2nd series, xix (1966), 380–7.

[18] *Gloucs. Inqs. post Mortem*, v, 157.

600 acres of arable, four acres of meadow and twenty-four acres of pasture; while at Badgeworth, significantly a manor of which the Giffards had been enfeoffed by the earl of Gloucester, the demesne extended to no fewer than 710 acres of arable and 12 acres of meadow.[19] According to the inquisition *post mortem* taken in 1331, after the execution of Edmund, earl of Kent, the late earl's manor of Lechlade had 468 acres of arable, 800 acres of meadow and 200 acres of pasture.[20] It is not just the sheer acreage here that is exceptional; Lechlade must have been one of the few manors in the county where meadowland, in notoriously short supply before the Black Death, actually exceeded the area of arable. Edmund of Kent's three remaining manors in the county did not have such extensive demesnes. But those attached to other Gloucestershire manors held by secular magnates— Fairford, Thornbury, Tewkesbury, Chipping Sodbury, and Tidenham—were also of impressive size.[21]

On the estates of the lesser landowners there is no shortage of evidence to suggest a totally different picture, as a few examples will show. Walton Cardiff had 200 acres of arable, twenty-seven acres of meadow and forty acres of wood in 1315.[22] Two years later at Abenhall there were 140 acres of arable and six acres of wood.[23] At Lypiatt in 1324 there were 192 acres of arable, six acres of meadow and six acres of pasture.[24] Rarely did a knight's demesne extend much beyond 200 acres. One exception was the Russel manor of Dyrham where in 1311 there were 420 acres of arable and sixty acres of meadow.[25] Professor Hilton has, however, pointed to some large demesnes of lords who held few manors, or perhaps only one: in Leicestershire in the early fourteenth century there were three manors held by men of knightly rank with demesnes of more than 300 acres, and, as has been shown, Dyrham affords a similar instance in Gloucestershire.[26] But more attention perhaps should be paid to the general picture than to these exceptions, for here the bent of

---

[19] Ibid., 208–11.   [20] Ibid., 231.
[21] Ibid., 143–50. For the demesne at Tewkesbury see also *V.C.H. Gloucs.*,viii, 137, and below, p. 218.
[22] *Gloucs. Inqs. post Mortem*, v, 154.
[23] Ibid., 163.   [24] Ibid., 190.   [25] Ibid., 120.
[26] R. H. Hilton, *The Economic Development of some Leicestershire Estates in the Fourteenth and Fifteenth Centuries* (Oxford, 1947), p. 4n.

the evidence is clear. Perhaps this is best expressed by giving average figures. The average size of the seventeen demesnes on magnate manors extended between 1300 and 1347 was 338 acres, while the average size of twenty-four demesnes on 'gentry' manors over the same period was only 200 acres. If in absolute terms these figures underestimate demesne acreage, relatively they may not be too inaccurate. As the larger landowners, secular and probably ecclesiastical too, had the most extensive demesnes, it is understandable that they would have been in a better position to benefit during the era of rising prices in the thirteenth century.

The manorial demesne was the product of centuries of development: the nature of the original settlement and the presence of the established ecclesiastical estates from the Saxon period had their influence on the extent and nature of demesne agriculture in the fourteenth century.[27] Geography was also important. The earl of Warwick's manor of Chedworth had a demesne of only 200 acres, by contrast with that on the earl's other manor in Gloucestershire at Childswickham, for the land there was hilly; such a manor, high on the Cotswold plateau, was better suited to pastoral than arable cultivation. Finally, and perhaps most important of all to this argument, the process of sub-infeudation ensured that the richest manors were retained in hand by the tenants-in-chief. At the time of his death at Bannockburn in 1314, Gilbert de Clare, earl of Gloucester, held Fairford with its demesne of 510 acres of arable, Thornbury with 300 acres and Tewkesbury with 460 acres and a park.[28] Two hundred years earlier, when his ancestors decided to meet their *servitium debitum* by creating knights' fees on their estates, they took care to retain their most valuable manors. In Gloucestershire this meant that the manors where urban characteristics were developing, mainly as a result of the wool trade, were held by magnates or, as in the cases of Northleach and Cirencester, by monasteries. Thus, the manors which were subinfeudated were those which were usually smaller and less wealthy. If the figures in the inquisitions can be trusted, then, it would have been surprising if the greater landowners had not been in a stronger

---

[27] Ibid., p. 69.
[28] *Gloucs. Inqs. post Mortem*, v, 143–50.

position than the gentry to take advantage of the thirteenth century boom. On the classic manor of the thirteenth century the lord's demesne was cultivated by a work force of permanent labourers or *famuli* and villein tenants who owed labour services as part of their rent. The manors in which the demands for estate labour were met by heavy reliance on labour services were mainly those of the great monasteries.[29] Such services were demanded to provide a labour force for the demesnes; and although their ultimate demise was associated with the abandonment of demesne cultivation in the late fourteenth and fifteenth centuries, the process of commutation had been initiated long before. The chronology of labour services, as it is at present understood, rests of course largely on evidence drawn from large estates. To see whether the smaller landowners were still relying on the use of labour services on the eve of the Black Death we have little alternative but to turn to the inquisitions *post mortem*.

For our purposes, among the most useful extents which they contain are those of the manor of Tockington made in 1308, 1311 and 1345. In 1308 the sixteen half-virgaters who held in villeinage each owed between Michaelmas and 24 June seventy manual works worth 2s. 11d. and seventeen ploughs worth 2s. 1½d. In other words, they were required to do seventeen days ploughing, not an intolerable burden over a period of nine months. Between 24 June and 1 August each of these tenants owed twenty manual works, worth 1s. 8d., and from then until Michaelmas thirty-two works, worth 4s. In sum these works were valued at £8 11s. 4d. *per annum*. There were also twelve quarter-virgaters each of whom owed from Michaelmas to 24 June seventy works worth 2s. 11d., from 24 June till 1 August ten works worth 10d., and from 1 August to Michaelmas eighteen works worth 2s. 3d. The works and services of these quarter-virgaters were worth £3 12s. 0d. *per annum*. Such works and services would probably only have proved adequate for the demesne at Tockington, said to be 160 acres in extent, if supplemented by the hire of wage labour.[30] Three years later, when another inquisition was taken, on the death of Nicholas Pointz, the labour

[29] Hilton, *A Medieval Society*, p. 127.
[30] *Gloucs. Inqs. post Mortem*, v, 98–100. Demesne acreage may have been underestimated. In 1273 the jurors testified that the demesne at Tockington

services remained the same.[31] As this extent is suspiciously similar to that of 1308 it is tempting to think that there was no attempt to make a fresh valuation of the manor. But by 1345 the position was quite different. The element of labour rent had entirely disappeared, and all the tenants, both free and unfree, discharged their obligations in money rents which totalled £58 11s. 9d.[32] At some time, then, between 1311 and 1345, all labour services had been commuted, apparently for good. The inquisitions *post mortem* allow us to trace the gradual disappearance of villein labour on at least two other manors. At Magor, near Chepstow, held by the Rodboroughs of Senkley, in 1327 eighteen villein tenants paid part money and part labour rent, though the labour services are unfortunately not described in great detail.[33] As it turned out, this inquisition was not only inadequate but inaccurate. In 1333 on the death of Thomas de Rodborough it was found that there were not eighteen but twenty-seven tenants in villeinage; and in the intervening six years the labour works had been commuted in favour of money rents. The rents of the unfree tenants totalling £6 11s. 3d. were paid at the usual four terms of the year.[34] The extent, now partly mutilated, of the manor of Shipton Moyne, made in 1315 on the death of Sir Henry le Moyne, records that at this relatively early date the four customers were paying money rent for their works.[35] An inquisition taken on the death of Sir Henry's widow twenty-five years later makes it clear that the unfree tenants of Shipton Moyne, virgaters and half-virgaters, were discharging all their dues in money. Commuted labour works had become fully assimilated into the money rents.[36]

On these three manors, then, and no doubt on the manors of other smaller landowners too, the labour element in rent disappeared entirely between 1300 and 1348.[37] It is quite impossible however to say, simply on the evidence of the inquisitions, that most or all of the knights abandoned the use of

comprised 215 acres of arable land and 40 acres of meadow (*Gloucs. Inqs. post Mortem*, iv, 73).

[31] *Gloucs. Inqs. post Mortem*, v, 123–4.

[32] Ibid., 308–9.   [33] Ibid., 207.   [34] Ibid., 249–50.

[35] Ibid., 140–1.   [36] Ibid., 280–1.

[37] See below, pp. 216–7, for a discussion of how soon works were sold on a regular basis on the manors of the smaller landowners.

labour services in this period. On the contrary, there was a wide variety of practice. At Abenhall, for example, it seems that as early as 1317 the villein tenants owed services only at harvest time, from 1 August till Michaelmas, and no mention is made of labour services in the remainder of the year.[38] In 1347 the Abenhall villeins were still paying their rent partly in money and partly in labour: each was required to work two days in autumn.[39] Labour services on this manor were probably never very onerous because the hilly terrain rendered demesne arable cultivation impracticable. The position was similar on the nearby manors of Mitcheldean and Littledean, held by William de Dene at his death in 1319. On the former manor the eighteen villein tenants paid 29s. in rents; each owed three days' work in autumn. At Littledean also each of the two *nativi*, like their neighbours at Mitcheldean, paid a money rent and owed three days' work in autumn.[40]

The extent of labour services was determined ultimately by the laws of supply and demand on the manors of the gentry just as much as on the estates of the Benedictine abbeys. Where the demesne was small and there was little need for supply of villein labour, so the services demanded of the unfree tenants were light. It is not so clear if the reverse were true. On the estates of the knightly landowners were large demesnes, admittedly quite few in number, necessarily accompanied by heavy labour dues? Sir William Russel had one of the largest arable demesnes in the county on his manor of Dyrham, and it is fortunate that when he died in 1311 fairly detailed extents were made of the lands which he held in Gloucestershire.[41] Despite the presence at Dyrham of a massive demesne of 420 acres of arable land and sixty acres of meadow, the villein tenants paid money rents and no mention was made in the extent of labour services. It is possible, of course, that the jurors simply included the money value of the labour obligations in the estimate of rental income. But the same jurors were present when Russel's other manor of Aust was extended. Here the vill was divided into two manors, and the demesne in Russel's half, covering only sixty acres of arable and ten acres of meadow, was not so extensive as at Dyrham. But there were nine half-virgaters who paid 6*s*. in money rent and owed specified labour services which were still available even if they were not taken up. Since the jurors were evidently not oblivious to the existence of labour services, it seems unlikely that they were demanded of the villeins at Dyrham in 1311. In the absence of any earlier extent of the manor it is idle to speculate if labour services had been exacted in the thirteenth century; but had they ever been heavy it is difficult to believe that they would have been completely relaxed as early as 1311.

On a few manors, however, the evidence suggests that labour services played an important part in demesne cultivation—at Westbury-on-Severn, for example, where they were detailed in an extent of 1303.[42] At Cold Aston, one of the eight manors in southern England which Ralph Pipard held at his death in 1309, there were nine customary tenants whose works were worth £3 *per annum* and who, it was said, paid nothing in money rent.[43] But these two instances are exceptional. Heavy labour services were not common on the estates of the smaller landowners; and we cannot be sure either just how many of the works which were theoretically available would actually be taken up. Lords may well have opted to enforce the works in some years, and to take a money equivalent in others. The extents in the inquisitions do their best to conceal such nuances. In most of the examples so far discussed the evidence is fairly unambiguous. At Tockington and Magor, for example, the final abandonment of labour services can be seen to have taken place between two terminal dates. But on other manors, where both the services and their money valuations are given, it is not clear how far the sale of works had proceeded. The extents of Westbury in 1303, Kingsholm in 1304, Tockington in 1308 and 1311, Stoke Archer and Syston in 1309, Godrington in 1310, Alveston, Brockworth and Uley in 1311, and Hill and Nympsfield in 1313 specify the labour works in some detail.[44] The implication is that the works were still theoretically available, even if the lord was not averse to their sale on an annual basis. In years when a good harvest was in prospect, no doubt lords made full use of the works of their villein tenants. By the late 1320s and 1330s, however, detailed valuations of works

<hr/>

[42] Ibid., 11.   [43] Ibid., 113.
[44] Ibid., 11, 20–22, 98, 123, 103, 109–11, 119, 125–31, 133.

became increasingly rare. In the extents of Elmore in 1326, Bitton and Olveston in 1327, Sapperton in 1332, Tortworth and Charfield in 1343 and Kingsholm in 1345 only the money value of the labour services was recorded.[45] In 1333 at Southrop, a manor of the St. Philibert family, there were still six customary tenants owing summer and autumn works from Whitsun until 10 November which were worth 30s.[46] Here, as·perhaps on some other manors, limited labour services, such as the autumn 'bedripes', were still claimed periodically. But the extent of the manor of Magor, in an inquisition of 1327, seems to be the last to record on the estates of a knightly family in Gloucestershire, even though not in great detail, annual labour works which were not of a purely seasonal nature.[47] On manors like Elmore and the others where works and services, no longer spelled out, were given simply a collective money value, it can tentatively be suggested that commutation had become permanent. During the third and fourth decades of the century the labour element in the rents of the villein tenants largely disappeared on these small estates. Commutation, however, may not necessarily have effected a radical transformation in the economy of the smaller landowners. If the inquisitions *post mortem* can be trusted, labour services could never have been imposed so fully on their manors as on the estates of the great Benedictine monasteries. Kosminsky reached such a conclusion using the evidence of the Hundred Rolls of 1279.[48] Demesne work, moreover, was almost certainly unpopular with the villein tenants obliged to perform it, and the coercion that would have been necessary to ensure its performance was less likely to be provided by a knight's manorial court than by the heavier hand of magnate lordship.

It was on manors where demesne husbandry was geared to production for the market that the labour element in rent survived for longest.[49] If we share the assumption that a majority of such manors was likely to be found on the larger estates, are we also justified in concluding that it was on those estates that labour services persisted for longest in the

[45] Ibid., 195, 199, 201, 221, 240, 300, 306.   [46] Ibid., 248.
[47] Ibid., 207.   [48] Kominsky, op. cit., pp. 271, 275–6.
[49] Production for the local market was, as we have seen (above, p. 210) undertaken on Lionel de Bradenham's manor of Langenhoe, but the account rolls afford no indication of the labour force he employed.

first half of the fourteenth century? In the West Midlands, as no doubt elsewhere, the proportion of labour works exacted seems to have varied, not surprisingly in a period when economic indicators were difficult to interpret. Lords sought flexibility in their arrangements, and this might better be served by partial commutation and the temporary hire of wage labour than by making full use of the available works. A pessimistic interpretation of his prospects was taken by the Bishop of Worcester when in February 1311 he authorized his steward, Robert de Clyderhowe, to remit the day works of the *nativi*: both men and animals were fatigued, it was said, and marginal land, located on the fringes of manors, was becoming exhausted.[50] On the other hand, the evidence of the inquisitions *post mortem* suggests that the example of the Bishop of Worcester may not have been followed by the secular magnates in Gloucestershire. At the time of the death of Hugh Despenser in 1349 the customary tenants on his manors of Tewkesbury, Fairford and Stoke Archer owed week works and autumn bedripes.[51] Few of these services could have been exacted in the chaotic conditions of 1349, but in an extent of Tewkesbury made ten years later in 1359 the detailed valuation of the labour services once again suggests a continued interest in making use of them if need be.[52] The last inquisition to contain extents of the Despenser lands in Gloucestershire, dating from 1375, is not so detailed; it suggests rather that, if not for certain at Tewkesbury, then at Fairford and Chipping Sodbury labour services had been commuted for good. On these two manors the labour rent was now incorporated in the rents of assize. At Tewkesbury the works of the bond tenants from Michaelmas to March 25 were valued at £5 0s. 8d., and thence to Michaelmas at £10 2s. 7d.[53] As the works are no longer specified it seems likely that they were in practice commuted for money at Tewkesbury as well as on the other manors. The evidence suggests therefore that on the Despenser estates in Gloucestershire the works of the unfree tenants were regarded as available for use for the first half

[50] *Register of Walter de Reynolds, Bishop of Worcester, 1308–13*, ed. R. A. Wilson (Worcestershire Hist. Soc., 1927), p. 34.

[51] *Gloucs. Inqs. post Mortem*, v, 331–6.

[52] Ibid., vi, 3–4. For the assumption that these works were actually taken up, and not just preserved to be taken up when need be, see below, pp. 232–3.

[53] *Gloucs. Inqs. post Mortem*, vi, 95–6.

of the century at least. However, we need not rely only on the uncertain testimony of the inquisitions. The account rolls of Lord Stafford's manor of Thornbury in the Severn Vale indicate that a large number of the manual services for which his customary tenants were liable were exacted right up to the 1340s. Thornbury was a valuable manor, worth over £400, and thoroughly characteristic of the Severn Vale in that much of its wealth was derived from money rents.[54] Nevertheless, the demesne was well equipped with labour services, some of which were regularly sold in the early fourteenth century. In 1339–40, for example, income under the heading 'vendicio operum' reached £23 15s. 5d., of which £15 5s. 5d. came from the sale of ploughing services.[55] But if seignorial policy favoured the remission of the ploughings, equally it favoured the retention of the manual works: in general fewer than a quarter of these were sold (table V).[56] The evidence from other estates in southern England points in a similar

TABLE V
Sale of works on Lord Stafford's Manor of Thornbury, 1339–40

	Total Number of Works	Number of Works Sold	Value of Works Sold
Commuted Ploughings*	225	175	£2 3s. 9d.
Boon Ploughings	41	38	15s. 10d.
Customary Ploughings	1,429	952	£9 18s. 4¾d.
Manual Works	7,001	1,473½	£3 1s. 4¾d.
Summer Works	989	327	£1 7s. 3d.
Autumn Ploughings	300	229¾	£2 17s. 5d.
Autumn Works	1,566¾	362¾	£2 5s. 4¾d.
Autumn Boon Works	41	36	13s. 6d.

Source: Stafford Co. Rec. Office, D.641/1/2/132.
* Gabul 'Arur'

[54] In 1327–8 at Thornbury total receipts (including arrears) came to £418 1s. 8¾d., of which £109 14s. 7½d. was derived from rents of assize and other rents, £27 1s. 7d. from sales of grain and stock, and the surprisingly large sum of £73 4s. 10d. from fines and the profits of jurisdiction (Stafford County Rec. Office, D.641/1/2/116).

[55] Stafford Co. Rec. Office, D.641/1/2/126.

[56] Ploughing services, so often the cause of disagreements, may have been the most difficult form of villein obligation to enforce (see the comments of B. Harvey, *Westminster Abbey and its Estates in the Middle Ages* (Oxford, 1977), p. 258).

direction. On eight of the manors of Crowland Abbey for which we have account rolls most of the labour works were exacted between 1319 and 1322, and if the manor of Oakington (Cambs.) can be taken to stand for the rest of the estate, these works were still being exacted in 1339. On the estates of Canterbury Cathedral Priory labour services which were intensified after the 1314–16 famine and the drought of 1325–6 were exacted in full between 1340 and 1390.[57] Thus when he authorized his steward to remit the day works of his *nativi*, the Bishop of Worcester may have intended not to commute them for good but rather to ease the demands on his tenants in a time of particular hardship. These examples certainly lend support to the view that labour services survived for longest in the arable counties of the Midlands and south-east where demesne husbandry on the great estates was geared to production for the market. Permanent commutation probably came more slowly than on the estates of the knightly proprietors.

Lords had begun to make use of labour services in the thirteenth century when rising prices favoured an expansion in demesne production. In the middle decades of that century sales of crops and produce formed as high a proportion of a lord's income as they were ever to do in the middle ages. It may therefore be suggested that in view of the advantages they enjoyed the greater lords drew a higher proportion of their income from demesne production than did their less well endowed neighbours. This hypothesis is more easily stated than proved. The larger estates are far more amply-documented than those of the gentry; yet strangely it is still difficult to formulate any general conclusions about the relative proportions of income which they derived from rents and from demesne profits. The importance of demesne production in the agrarian economy varied from estate to estate and from decade to decade. On the estates of the Bishop of Ely demesne profits accounted for about 50 per cent of gross revenue in 1255–6 in the period of 'high farming' and 40 per cent in 1298–9.[58] Of the income received by

[57] F. M. Page, *The Estates of Crowland Abbey* (Cambridge, 1934), pp. 99–105, 126; R. H. Hilton, *The Decline of Serfdom in Medieval England* (Economic History Society, 1969), pp. 40–1.
[58] E. Miller, *The Abbey and Bishopric of Ely* (Cambridge, 1951, reprinted, 1969), p. 82.

the treasurer of Leicester Abbey in 1297–8, one-third came from rents and two-thirds from the sale of grain and wool.[59] Perhaps the most important figures for our purposes are those for the Cathedral Priory of Worcester which held lands in the West Midlands. In 1293–4 50 per cent of the income of the bursar-cellarer of Worcester came from rent and aid and 49 per cent from sales of demesne produce. In the following year the respective proportions were 52 per cent and 47 per cent. But suddenly in 1313–14 sales accounted for 75 per cent of the total and rent and aid only 25 per cent.[60] The accounts for this year were probably exceptional. Recent research on the estates of the greater landlords has tended to suggest that, even in the height of the thirteenth century boom, demesne profits rarely accounted for more than half of total income.

A sceptical approach seems to be justified too by a survey of the evidence for production for the market on the smaller estates. Lionel de Bradenham's manor of Langenhoe (Essex) is of course unusually well documented. Lionel's income from rents, leases of fishing privileges and court dues averaged about £14 between 1325 and 1348. By contrast, however, he realized about £37 *per annum* over the same period from sales of grain and wool and leases of livestock.[61] Here was a landowner whose economy displayed the characteristics associated, for example, with the great monasteries. Nevertheless, Lionel de Bradenham enjoyed advantages for demesne production which were not always shared by landlords of similar standing. His demesne of 250 acres of arable with attached pasture land was a little larger than a typical knight in Gloucestershire would have held. Essex, moreover, was a county where both arable cultivation and the grazing of sheep could be practised alongside, and not far from Langenhoe was the borough of Colchester where Bradenham found a ready market for his produce.

What the Gloucestershire evidence needs to show is whether the economy of the manor of Langenhoe was typical. Certain differences can only be expected. The terrain of Gloucestershire was different. The Cotswold plateau was better suited to pastoral than arable farming; and in the Vale, which was imperfectly

---

[59] Hilton, *A Medieval Society*, p. 78. [60] Ibid.
[61] R. H. Britnell, 'Production for the Market', 381.

manorialized, the rents of free peasants predominated in the income even of lords, as the Berkeley accounts show. There, rents are likely to have formed the larger part of the income of all lords, lay or ecclesiastical, large or small. Precise figures of the demesne profits of smaller landowners are, as always, elusive, and resort must be made again to the extents of the manors of Tockington, which we have looked at already, and of Elmore, which were both occasioned by writs of distraint for debt. These extents value the crops under cultivation on the demesne. On his manor of Elmore in 1326 Sir John de Guise had only thirty-six acres sown with wheat, worth £7 6s. 0d., at 4s. an acre; seven acres of barley and beans, worth 18s. 9d., and thirty-four acres of oats worth £3 3s. 4d. The hay was said to be worth £5 2s. 0d.[62] The total value of these crops was £16 12s. 4d., or less than half the income which Lionel de Bradenham enjoyed from sales of demesne produce in an average year. John de Guise also had 215 acres of arable land for which a rental value of £5 6s. 6d. was given; if, as seems likely, this land belonged to the demesne, then more than half the available acreage was lying fallow at the time. The rents of his free and unfree tenants brought him £10 7s. 6d., and the works of the villeins were worth £2 17s. 6d. Other sources of income were a windmill worth 12s. and the perquisites of the manorial court, worth 10s. Assuming that labour services were commuted and that the extent does not underestimate rent, in 1326 demesne profits nevertheless accounted for just over half of the income which Sir John derived from his manor of Elmore.

At Sir Nicholas Pointz's manor of Tockington in 1345 the picture was very different. Lying at the southern edge of the Vale of Berkeley, this was a very valuable manor, worth £111 6s. 7d. On the demesne thirty-four acres were sown with corn said to be worth £11 6s. 8d. at 6s. 8d. an acre; fourteen and a half acres were sown with beans, worth £3 10s. 0d. at 5s. an acre, and five acres with pulse, worth 16s. 8d. at 3s. 4d. an acre. Finally, nineteen acres were sown with oats which, valued at 3s. an acre, were said to be worth £2 17s. 0d. The stock was also listed: there were two mares worth 8s., one colt worth 2s., two heifers worth £1, two wethers worth, after shearing, 3s., 104 hoggasters worth, after shearing, £5 4s. 0d., four ewes worth 4s., six lambs also worth 4s.,

---

[62] *Gloucs. Inqs. post Mortem*, v, 195–6.

twenty-five pigs worth 17s. 6d. and eighteen sucking pigs worth 2s. 6d. Thus, if we exclude livestock, the total income realized from sale of demesne produce would have been £18 10s. 4d. What occasions surprise once again is the low acreage under cultivation on this manor as at Elmore. The inquest jury returned only a rental value for 126 acres of arable land lying fallow which in the absence of suggestions to the contrary can be taken to belong to the demesne. This extent, like that at Elmore, was made in the summer before the harvest was taken in, and when the maximum acreage would be under crop. It was the rents rather than the demesne that made Tockington such a valuable manor. The tenants, free and unfree, paid rents totalling £58 11s. 9d., which made up just over a half of the income which Sir Nicholas Pointz enjoyed from the manor. The gardens, meadow land, dovecot, watermill, windmill and court contributed another £21 17s. 6d. Thus the profits of demesne cultivation accounted for less than one quarter of the total worth of the manor.[63]

Only on these two manors in Gloucestershire is it possible to examine the relative proportions of income derived from demesne and rents. The contrasting conclusions emphasize the danger of generalizing from the example of just one estate. Extents of other manors abound of course in the inquisitions *post mortem*, but they record only the lease value of the demesnes, and for the purpose of estimating income from the sale of demesne produce they are of little help.

But if the evidence prevents us from saying for certain whether the gentry were getting richer or poorer in the half century before the Black Death, it is easier to identify some of the limitations on the prosperity of these landowners. Little doubt can be entertained that their demesnes were smaller than those found on the manors of the greater lords, secular or ecclesiastical. It seems possible, too, that the knights and esquires were dependent for their income more on rents than on demesne profits, although it has to be admitted that some of the monasteries were in a similar position. There may have been no clear division between the income structure of the smaller landlords on the one hand and the greater lords on the other. Some knights, like Lionel de Bradenham, were never heavily reliant on rents; but others were,

---

[63] Ibid., 309.

and it is possible to understand how men of this standing could have found themselves in difficulty in the era of rising prices in the thirteenth century. Rents were difficult to adjust. A knight moreover would probably dispose of his crops locally, while a monastery governed by a centralized administration could sell in the most profitable market.[64] Bigger landowners had other advantages. They could employ more capital; they used text-books like Walter of Henley's.[65] Finally, the knights were probably remitting labour services on their manors more speedily than the greater lords. Again, it would be naive to posit a crude division between the practice of the gentry and the greater lords, as the example of the Bishop of Worcester shows. But the evidence suggests that while commutation on the larger estates was a gradual process lasting much of the century, the gentry were substantially dependent by the 1340s on wage labour for the cultivation of their demesnes. This left them vulnerable once the price of labour began to rise after the demographic catastrophe of 1348–9.

Professor Hilton has argued that the 'crisis' of the gentry in the thirteenth century was accompanied by a rise in the social standing of those who survived.[66] Social standing in the middle ages was intimately connected with the possession of landed wealth. Yet Hilton's analysis of the Worcestershire tax return of 1275 led him to the apparently paradoxical conclusion that 'the class of gentry . . . must have been as individually meagre in resources as they were collectively important politically and socially'.[67] Few, he argues, had establishments in more than two villages. A similar analysis can be made for Gloucestershire half a century later with the aid of the returns known as the *Nomina Villarum*. This survey was occasioned by the grant at the Lincoln parliament of 1316 of a foot soldier from every vill in the kingdom to raise an army for the war against Scotland.[68] Returns exist for

[64] Hilton, *A Medieval Society*, pp. 79–81. But knights who sold wool were no doubt brought into contact with an international market.

[65] The surviving evidence suggests that such textbooks were used mainly by the great landowners, but an edition of Walter of Henley with a legal textbook was owned by Henry de Solers and then by his nephew or grandson, John, who held the manor of Postlip, near Winchcombe (*Walter of Henley and other Treatises on Estate Management and Accounting*, ed. D. Oschinsky (Oxford, 1971), pp. 25–7).

[66] Hilton, *A Medieval Society*, pp. 50–1. [67] Ibid., p. 57.

[68] For a discussion of this source see Hilton, *A Medieval Society*, p. 125.

nearly every county in England, but within each shire the list of manors is not exhaustive. Fewer than half the vills in the hundred of Berkeley were included;[69] of the two manors in the county held by Sir William Tracy, Doynton was included and Toddington omitted. Nevertheless, when supplemented by other sources the *Nomina Villarum* can be used for the limited exercise of counting manors with some accuracy. Counting manors, though, is not the same thing as estimating income. Manors varied greatly in size and value. A manor like Iron Acton which was coincident with the vill would be worth £30 or more. At the vill of Up Ampney, which was divided between four lords, a single manor could not have been worth more than about £10. While in Gloucestershire vill and manor coincided far more than in the eastern counties of England, it would be unwise to jump straight from counting manors to estimating income. Table VI supplements the *Nomina Villarum* from other sources where necessary to show the number of manors the knights and esquires of Gloucestershire held in 1316.

It is clear that a description of the gentry as 'individually meagre in resources' oversimplifies the picture. Certainly a fair minority held only one manor—no fewer than a quarter. But there were wide disparities of wealth within the ranks of the gentry, and John de Acton, who was distrained for knighthood and never received a summons to parliament, held no fewer than ten manors in four counties. If the poorer gentry who held a single manor comprised a quarter of the forty-eight families about whom we have sufficient information to tabulate, it is equally true that 66 per cent of them held three or more manors, and 20 per cent more than five. There was wider diversity than Hilton allows.

By the time the inflationary pressures of the thirteenth century had eased, a fair number of poorly-endowed gentry were surviving still. But the majority of the gentry were men of substance in the shires who had the resources to cope with periods of temporary indebtedness. Indeed, there are indications that they approached the management of their estates in a business-like way. In 1303 John de Acton, who resided at Iron Acton,

---

[69] *Feudal Aids, 1284–1431*, ii, 266. Hinton, Nympsfield, Filton, Slimbridge and Alkington were omitted.

TABLE VI
Manors held by Gloucestershire Knights and Esquires in 1316.

	Gloucs.	Wilts.	Somerset	Heref.	Others	Total
John de Abenhall[1]	3					3
John de Acton	3	3	2		2	10
Thomas Apadam	3	3				6
Geoffrey Archer	1					1
Sir Nicholas de Bathonia	1					1
Sir John Berkeley of Arlingham	1		2			3
John Berkeley of Dursley	4					4
Thomas de Berkeley of Coberley[2]	1				2	3
Hugh Bisley	1					1
David le Blount	2					2
Ralph Bluet	1			1		2
John le Boteler of Llantwit	2				1	3
Sir Thomas Boteler of Badminton	1					1
Peter Corbet of Syston	1				2	3
Sir Roger Corbet	2				6	8
Sir John de Bures	5		4		1	10
Roger Crok	2					2
Sir Richard de Croupes	1					1
William de Dene[1]	3					3
John FitzNichol	2					2
William Gamage	1					1
Sir John Giffard of Leckhampton	1					1
Sir John Giffard of Weston	2				1	3
Sir Walter de Gloucester	2				4	6
Sir John de Guise	1				1	2
William Hathewy	1					1
Sir Philip Joce[1]	1					1
Sir Nicholas de Kingston	1					1
Sir John de Langley	1				4	5
Peter de la Mare of Cherington	1	1			3	5
Sir William Maunsel	2				2	4
Sir Stephen de la More	1					1
John le Moyne	1	1			2	4
Sir Aymer Pauncefot	1			1	3	5
John de la Rivere[2]	2	1			1	4
John de Rodborough of Rodborough	3					3

Table VI continued

	Gloucs.	Wilts.	Somerset	Heref.	Others	Total
Thomas de Rodborough of Senkley	1	1			1	3
Theobald Russel[2]	2	1	1		4	8
Sir John le Rous	2			4		6
Sir John de Sudeley	1				4	5
Sir William Tracy	2				1	3
Sir Peter le Veel	2		1		3	6
Sir Nicholas de Valers	1					1
William le Walsh	1				2	3
Sir William de Wauton	2					2
William de Whittington	1			1	1	3
Sir John de Wilington	5				8	13
Sir John de Wysham[1,3]	1			1	13	15

Notes: This table lists 'gentry' who were resident in the county. If place of residence is not known for certain, a knight or esquire is included if he held most of his lands in the county. The families of Daston and Basset, which did not hold in chief, are omitted because of the difficulty of identifying their manors.

[1] Since the Forest of Dean was imperfectly manorialised it is virtually impossible to estimate accurately the number of manors held by gentry in that part of the county.

[2] A minor in 1316.

[3] Based on *Cal. Charter Rolls 1327–41* p. 84 (grant of free warren).

granted two of his more distant manors at Elkstone and Winstone to John le Brun for life with remainder to his son John and his wife Elena.[70] By 1329, evidently, the manors had reverted to the Actons: for in that year Richard Belers was pardoned for acquiring the manor of Elkstone from John de Acton without licence. He was permitted to retain it.[71] Once again, apparently, the Actons had decided to lease it to a tenant. Administration of ten widely scattered manors must have been difficult. Perhaps John de Acton found it easier to farm some of his more distant manors—first Elkstone and Winstone, and then Elkstone alone—than to keep them in hand.

Few of the knights were sufficiently well-endowed to alienate permanently much of their patrimony to endow a younger son. But on the rare occasions when this was done it was the poorer

[70] *Cal. Pat. Rolls 1301–7*, p. 131.

[71] *Gloucs. Inqs. post Mortem*, v, 227–8; *Cal. Pat. Rolls 1327–30*, p. 385.

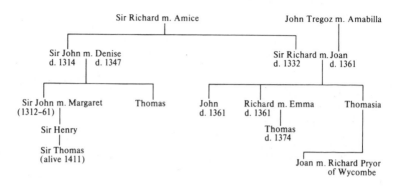

De la Rivere of Tormarton

and more far-flung manors which went, as the history of the de la
Rivere family showed. In October 1303 Amice de la Rivere
received a pardon for granting to her younger son Richard the
manor of Hampton, near Cricklade in Wiltshire.[72] Richard's
elder brother, Sir John, held Tormarton, Littleton and a manor
in Acton Turville, all within a few miles of each other in south
Gloucestershire, Worminghall in Buckinghamshire and Wootton
Rivers in Wiltshire; their mother, Amice, held Hampton in
dower. When Richard died in about 1332 the manor of Hampton
reverted to Sir John's son, another Sir John, who resided at the
family seat of Tormarton. The future of the manor was far from
settled, however: Richard left a widow, two sons and a daughter
who had to be catered for. Accordingly, in 1339 Sir John granted
the manors of Hampton and Westrop to Richard's widow, Joan,
for life with remainders in tail successively to John, Richard and
Thomasia, her children, and reversion in fee to John himself.[73]
The lapse of seven years after Richard's death suggests that John
was reluctant to confirm the alienation of the two manors to
Richard's family. Richard's two sons died within a few weeks of
each other in 1361, perhaps from the plague, and after the death
of the younger Richard's child in 1374 the manors passed to

[72] *Cal. Pat. Rolls 1301–7*, p. 165.
[73] *Gloucs. Inqs. post Mortem*, v, 277; *Cal. Pat. Rolls 1338–40*, p. 242.

Thomasia's daughter who was married to Richard Pryor of High Wycombe.[74] They then descended with the properties of the Pryor family, and despite the entail passed permanently out of the hands of the de la Riveres. Another possession of the family was the manor of Worminghall (Bucks.) which in 1336 Sir John de la Rivere sold to John de Hegham of Northampton.[75] It is possible that John was in debt; that he needed money quickly. But seen in the light of his attitude to Westrop and Hampton it is equally plausible that Sir John, like his neighbour, John de Acton, wanted to dispose of his more distant manors. This explanation would reconcile his sale of Worminghall with his apparent reluctance to part with Hampton and Westrop, which were not more than 25 miles from Tormarton by a direct road.

In 1348–9 the economic situation was, of course, transformed by the demographic crisis of the Black Death. This was not the only catastrophe to afflict the fourteenth century; it was followed by other visitations of the plague, though not on the same scale, and it was preceded in 1315–17 by a major famine. Severe blow that it was, most of all for the peasantry, the famine was probably not the turning point in the economic fortunes of the lesser landowners that the Black Death was to be. If soil productivity was declining, the famines failed to relieve population pressure because, as pressure fell, the capacity of the land to support the population fell too. Our sources are neither ample enough nor sufficiently sensitive to register the precise effects of the famine on the lesser landowners. No doubt it was very difficult to collect rents when peasant tenants were starving; but the pattern of supply and demand was not permanently altered.

After the Black Death had cut population by a third or more the position was very different. The changing scene was reflected in the activity of the land market. The price of land is a reflection of the level of demand for the produce that can be grown on it. In the thirteenth century rising land values reflected the steadily rising price of agricultural produce; when demand fell in the later fourteenth century there was a drop in the price of land. Paradoxically, however, estates seem to have changed hands with much greater frequency after the Black Death than before.

[74] *Gloucs. Inqs. post Mortem*, vi, 81.
[75] *Cal. Close Rolls 1333–7*, p. 674.

In the earlier decades magnate retainers like John le Boteler of Llantwit and William de Cheltenham had been eager buyers of small estates;[76] but it was usually through inheritance not purchase that a manor passed from one family to another. Towards the end of the century, on the other hand, the land market seems to have become brisker. Dating the change of ownership of a manor is sometimes difficult when the transaction was effected not by fine but by a private agreement. Thus it is only from the inquisition *post mortem* taken after his death in 1407 that we learn of Anselm Guise's acquisition of the manor of Daglingworth which had previously belonged to the Bluet family.[77] The feet of fines record other notable purchases in these years. In 1387 Richard Ruyhall acquired Sir Roger Northwood's manor in Dymock and by the time of his death he had added to this the remaining manor in the vill, that of Richard de Montagu.[78] Before he inherited Coberley in right of his wife, Thomas de Bridges had purchased a manor in Tirley, near Deerhurst, and a manor in Haresfield which had belonged to the Fitzherbert family.[79] In 1405 he bought from Walter and Joan Toky a manor in the vill of Pendock (Worcs.)[80]

For the most part these were exchanges within the landowning class of the shire. But Sir John Cassy, who established himself at Deerhurst, was a Worcestershire man, probably from Droitwich, appointed Chief Baron of the Exchequer in May, 1389.[81] In 1386 he began by purchasing the Wightfield estate in Deerhurst; later he bought the reversion of part of the manors of Little Taynton and Kilcot, in the west of the county, and finally in 1394 he purchased from William Hampton the reversion of the manor and advowson of Stratton-by-Cirencester.[82] Cassy was the one professional lawyer to found a gentry dynasty in fourteenth-century Gloucestershire; but he was not the only newcomer to invest in land in these decades. Nicholas Pointer of Cirencester,

---

[76] For William de Cheltenham see C.P.25(1)/77/62/171, C.P.25(1)/77/63/ 200A, C.P.25(1)/77/64/219. For John le Boteler see C.P.25(1)/76/54/314 and 317, C.P.25(1)/76/55/331.

[77] *Gloucs. Inqs. post Mortem*, vi, 263.

[78] C.P.25(1)/78/81/78; *Gloucs. Inqs. post Mortem*, vi, 249.

[79] *V.C.H. Gloucs.*, viii, 99; x, 193; *Cal. Pat. Rolls 1399–1401*, p. 534.

[80] *V.C.H. Worcs.*, iii, 480.   [81] *Cal. Pat. Rolls 1388–92*, p. 29.

[82] *Cal. Close Rolls 1381–5*, p. 205; C.P.25(1)/78/82/112; C.P.25(1)/79/83/131.

presumably a merchant, purchased land in Siddington in 1373; in 1387 he bought a messuage and four virgates of land in North Cerney and Woodmancote.[83] Another Cirencester merchant was John Cosyn who was rewarded with a 100 mark annuity for his part in capturing the earls of Kent and Salisbury in 1400.[84] In his will Cosyn referred to his lands and tenements not just in Cirencester but also in the villages of Elkstone and Winstone with the manor of Northcote.[85] In 1389 Thomas Adynet of Northleach, again presumably a merchant, enfeoffed three feoffees of lands and rents in Temple Dowdeswell, 'Pekelsworth', Notgrove and Great Upthorp in Northleach which he had bought in 1377 and 1382.[86] The best known wool merchant is of course William Grevel of Chipping Campden from whose sons two gentry families descended in the fifteenth century. His two earliest acquisitions were probably the manors of Charlton Kings, which he purchased from the Roos family in 1387, and Milcote, which Sir William Beauchamp sold to him sometime in the reign of Richard II.[87] These two manors, with Charingworth, were granted to John, probably William's second son.[88] The purchase of lands in Sezincote in 1386 reflects Grevel's early interest in that manor which he was later to acquire completely.[89]

Although the undoubted difficulties of landowners are amply illustrated by the petitions to parliament, land was still regarded by many as a desirable investment. For those who sought land cheaply the times were favourable. Here, then, was one way in which the economic changes wrought by the Black Death affected the composition of the gentry. To a greater extent than ever before merchants and burgesses like Pointer, Cosyn, Adynet and Grevel were taking advantage of the fall in the value of land to assume the status of landed proprietors. They may not have

[83] C.P.25(1)/78/81/76; C.P.25(1)/78/76/521.

[84] Cal. Pat. Rolls 1399–1401, pp. 182, 183.

[85] Prob. 11/2A (Reg. Marche f. 4).

[86] Cal. Close Rolls 1389–92, pp. 357–8.

[87] V.C.H. Warwicks., v, 200; Cal. Pat. Rolls 1399–1401, p. 440.

[88] Sir W. Dugdale, The Antiquities of Warwickshire, p. 530; T. D. Fosbroke, Abstracts respecting . . . the County of Gloucester, ii, p. 323.

[89] C.P.25(1)/78/80/73; Sir R. Atkyns, The Ancient and Present State of Gloucestershire, p. 336.

seen land as primarily an economic asset; rather it was the symbol of a status to which they aspired. When Cosyn, Pointer and Adynet were appointed to the minor tasks of local government, and Cosyn even to the commission of the peace, they were entering the fold of the country gentry.[90]

For the knights and esquires land was a measure of social status because it was an economic asset; and its profitability was gravely affected by the sudden fall in population. The Black Death carried away between a third and a half of the population. Thus in absolute terms a lord's rental was likely to be reduced unless the vacant holdings were taken by tenants previously landless who were prepared to pay a rent. But a lord was also likely to experience difficulty in collecting rents from the tenants who remained. Before the Black Death there was an excess of tenants over holdings; now that the reverse was true the lord was in no position to demand rents at the old levels. Some lords adjusted readily to the changed climate. On the estates of Worcester Cathedral Priory, for example, tenants were being tempted to take up vacant holdings in the immediate post-Plague years by a reduction of entry fines and a relaxation of heriots.[91] Other lords were more reluctant: they tried to compel peasants to accept the customary terms of tenure or to take up vacant holdings. But if the level of rents were to be held at the pre-Black Death level a measure of coercion would be needed that a magnate was more likely to provide than a simple knight. Lesser lords who could not exercise such pressure on their tenants may have been hit by falling rents earlier than their mighty neighbours.

If it is true that the knights derived the greater part of their income from rents, they may have been concerned more in the immediate post-Black Death decades with tenants who defaulted than with the continuing profitability of demesne cultivation. Indeed, the buoyant prices which characterized the 1350s and 1360s enabled landowners to make higher returns than perhaps they had ever known before. But the ability to match such prices with correspondingly high profits depended on the curtailment of wage bills. The lords most likely to be successful in this respect were those who had regularly exacted a high proportion of available works in the years before 1348: by continuing to enforce

[90] See below, p. 245.   [91] Hilton, *The Decline of Serfdom*, p. 43.

villein labour obligations after the Black Death they could escape the employment of expensive wage labour. Such thinking certainly seems to have been applied rigorously on some estates. The account rolls of Canterbury Cathedral Priory 'show that between 1340 and 1390 full labour services were performed';[92] and on the Ramsey Abbey lands an intensification of labour services accompanied a renewal of demesne husbandry in the 1380s and 1390s.[93] On the estates of Westminster Abbey in the 1350s and 1360s 'only where the demesne was small or on lease could the villeins hope to be safe from demands for labour services'.[94] For as long as the cost of hiring labourers to till the land exceeded the sum that could be realized from the sale of those works which had been adequate for the task in the past, so it would be to the lord's advantage to continue enforcing work obligations. Even so, not all lords with such labour services at their disposal made use of them. At Thornbury, to take a local example, the income realized from sale of works jumped from an annual average of about £23 before the Black Death to £43 in 1349–50. It rose to £49 13s. 11d. in 1353–4, but fell back to £48 13s. 0d. in 1357–8 and £46 in 1365–6. Thereafter it stabilized at about £49 a year.[95] The response of the earl of Stafford, contrasting as it does with what other large landowners were doing, reminds us that though it may have served the interests of lords to enforce the labour services still available to them, they acted variably, according to time and local circumstance; and the contrast between the policies of the greater and lesser lords may not perhaps have been so clear-cut in the 1350s and 1360s as it appears to have been before the Black Death.

However many of the lords chose to intensify the demands which they made for villein labour services, the indications are that they were taking a course which was not open to most of the knightly class. If we are right in supposing that the latter had for the most part commuted the works of their customary tenants, they must have been dependent for the cultivation of their demesnes on hired labour. Thus it would have been the knights and esquires who suffered most from the wage explosion that

[92] R. A. L. Smith, *Canterbury Cathedral Priory* (Cambridge, 1943), p. 127.
[93] J. A. Raftis, *The Estates of Ramsey Abbey* (Toronto, 1957), p. 261.
[94] B. Harvey, *Westminster Abbey and its Estates in the Middle Ages*, p. 260.
[95] Stafford Co. Rec. Office, D. 641/1/2/132–52.

followed the Black Death, and it would have been their voices which clamoured loudest for the rigorous enforcement of the labour legislation. *A priori* it seems unlikely therefore that the gentry were able to share in the 'Indian summer of demesne farming' that is said to have occurred in the 1360s.[96] If their dependence on wage labour prevented them from taking full advantage of the buoyant prices of the two decades after the Black Death, it might be supposed that they would fairly speedily abandon demesne cultivation altogether.

Unfortunately the evidence is too slender to indicate whether the chronology of demesne leasing in Gloucestershire had any characteristics of its own. So far as the great monasteries like Cirencester and Winchcombe are concerned, their estate records have disappeared as totally as their buildings.[97] The abbot of Westminster is the only monastic lord holding manors in the county whose policies we can discern. From about 1370 he opted increasingly to lease his demesnes, but on one manor, Bourton-on-the-Hill, the demesne was kept in hand until as late as the early fifteenth century.[98] Evidence for the secular lords in Gloucestershire is hardly more plentiful than for their ecclesiastical peers. On the earl of Stafford's manor of Thornbury the decline of demesne cultivation began rather earlier, but proceeded at an equally slow pace. Rents from lessees of parcels of the demesne appear for the first time in the accounts in 1357-8 when they realized the modest sum of £5 14s. 9d.[99] Ten years later, when they brought in £6 15s. 0d., little if any more of the demesne had been put on lease, but in 1375 the virtual abandonment of direct cultivation is indicated by a sharp rise to £21 9s. 6d.[100] On the estates of the Berkeley family the few surviving accounts show that the demesnes, which were still in hand in 1368, were put on lease by 1386.[101]

The evidence, exiguous as it is, suggests that in Gloucestershire

[96] A. R. Bridbury, 'The Black Death', *Econ. Hist. Rev.*, 2nd series, xxvi (1973), 584.

[97] Their splendid cartularies have survived, but, alas, no account rolls.

[98] B. F. Harvey, 'The Leasing of the Abbot of Westminister's Demesnes in the Later Middle Ages', *Econ. Hist. Rev.*, 2nd series, xxii (1969), 19.

[99] Stafford Co. Rec. Office, D.641/1/2/134.

[100] D.641/1/2/140; D.641/1/2/143.

[101] Berkeley Castle, S.R. 47, 48.

as elsewhere lords were hesitant to make any sudden and far-reaching changes in their method of agrarian organization. They may well have experimented with piecemeal leasing before deciding eventually to abandon the demesnes once and for all. On most of the great English estates this decision had been taken before the end of the fourteenth century—at Christ Church, Canterbury, for example, between 1391 and 1396 by a more dramatic reversal of previous policy than perhaps occurred elsewhere—but on just a few estates demesne husbandry was practised into the first decade of the fifteenth century.[102]

To enable us to see whether, or how far, the response of the gentry differed from that of the greater lords in Gloucestershire in the 1360s and 1370s we have only a few rentals for our guidance. The earliest is probably the rental of Tibberton, a village on the edge of the Forest of Dean. Its date is uncertain, but its preservation among the records of the Duchy of Lancaster suggests that it may have been made shortly after the death of John Blount in 1358, when the manor reverted to the duke of Lancaster of whom it was held.[103] It is not surprising to find that there is no mention of labour services: rents were by now discharged entirely in money. But for its date the rental presents a remarkably static picture. The land in Tibberton was distributed fairly evenly between the tenants, most of whom were semi-virgaters and none noticeably better off than the others. There is no sign of vacant holdings and no indication of decayed rents. None of the tenants was farming the demesne either wholly or in part. It seems likely on the available evidence that the demesne was not leased by 1358, although it is just conceivable that it was farmed by a lessee or lessees from outside the manor. A contemporary inquisition *post mortem* adds very little. However, its estimate of rental income proves to be unusually accurate:

[102] Around 1380 there began a renewed interest in demesne production on the Huntingdonshire manors of Ramsey Abbey; this came to an end in the early years of the fifteenth century (Raftis, *The Estates of Ramsey Abbey*, pp. 261, 290).

[103] D.L.3/35. The manor passed into the hands of the Duchy of Lancaster in 1358 (*Cal. Close Rolls 1354–60*, p. 475). The rental does not correspond sufficiently closely with the list of taxpayers in 1327 to suggest a date as early as that (*Gloucs. Subsidy Roll*, p. 35, lists the taxpayers at Tibberton). For the possibility that rentals were not kept up to date, see below, p. 237.

according to the panel of jurors rents of assize totalled £22, and according to the rental £23 10s. 7½d.[104]

Far more informative are the two rentals of Sir Simon Basset's manor of Oldland near Bristol which show clearly how the organization of the manor was changed to take account of the new economic conditions. The first, dated 1344, lists all the tenants and the rents which they paid at the customary four terms of the year. These totalled £8 13s. 8d. On the dorse is a rental of the hamlet of Inst, within the manor of Oldland.[105] This document is not an extent. The demesne is not mentioned, but it seems certain that lands held in demesne were nevertheless cultivated at this time. According to the inquisition taken in 1328 on the death of Sir Stephen de la More the total value of the manor was £10 0s. 3½d, of which rents paid by free tenants and *nativi* came to £5 12s. 10½d.[106] The demesne was said to include a capital messuage, 163 acres of arable and twenty-eight acres of meadow, the rental value being £3 4s. 1d. Rental income seems to have been underassessed in the inquisition by £2 or £3, but it would be unwise to press this point since sixteen years had elapsed between the compilation of the two documents.

By 1363, the date of the second rental, a third of Oldland seems to have been held in dower and the division of the manor was reflected in the rental. The first part lists the rents from the tenants, both free and unfree, from the cottagers and from the *novi redditus*. These total £6 10s. 11d. The tenants of the remaining third of the manor are divided into two categories, the first unspecified, the second described as tenants of the demesne. In the absence of any such tenants elsewhere in the rental, the dower third may be taken to include the whole of the former demesne. The value of this part of the manor was £6 2s. 4d.[107]

As early as 1363 the lord of Oldland had opted to lease his demesne. These years, however, have often been portrayed as ones of prosperity for landowners. Dr Bridbury, for example, has argued that 'the evidence of wages and prices bears out the impression of buoyancy rather than stability of income which

[104] *Gloucs. Inqs. post Mortem*, v, 366.

[105] Brit. Lib. Add. Ch. 26434.

[106] *Gloucs. Inqs. post Mortem*, v, 221–2. Simon Basset was holding the manor in right of his wife, Maud, widow of William de la More.

[107] Brit. Lib. Add. Ch. 26441.

several scholars have brought away from their investigations of big landed estates at this period'.[108] It is worthwhile to stress the qualification that the evidence upon which such a conclusion is based is drawn exclusively from the 'big landed estates'. So long as prices remained high, production for the market may well have been a viable proposition for some time, provided that costs could be contained. This the greater lords could achieve, if they so wished, by exacting labour services still available to them. But on the smaller estates commutation had proceeded apace before 1348. To the gentry, dependent as they had now become on labourers who were demanding higher wages, the advantage of buoyant prices would have been largely lost. Even if Dr Bridbury's 'age of equipoise' was not over for the nobility until after 1375, it was over some years earlier for lords who were vulnerable to the demands of labour.

The gentry, it is suggested, drew a larger proportion of their income from rents than from demesne cultivation, and rents may now have been seen as the more reliable source of profit. If a lord could collect his rents regularly at the appointed term, he would be assured of an income that was steady, if not buoyant. But just as the fall in population brought a rise in wages, so also it reduced the demand for land. No longer were peasants searching desperately for a strip of land on which to eke out a living; rather, the lord was looking for tenants for his holdings. On some estates tenants were leaving in search of better conditions elsewhere and arrears were allowed to develop. But at Oldland, at least, this seems not to have been happening. The 1363 rental notes that only three tenancies out of more than sixty were *in manu domini*. At Tibberton in 1358 there was no sign at all that an economic catastrophe had happened nine years earlier. Such evidence as there is tends to suggest, then, that the gentry were able to collect their rents; but its reliability is open to question. Rentals were not always kept up to date; they may indicate how much the bailiff was expected to collect rather than how much he really did collect. The unreality of the Tibberton rental may be explicable in these terms. The knights no doubt did all within their power to maintain their rental income at the old level; but it would be wrong to assume that they were always successful.

[108] Bridbury, 'The Black Death', 583–4.

The difficulties of the smaller landowners are further illuminated by some contemporary petitions submitted by the Commons in parliament. Because of the pestilences, they complained
in 1363, such tenants in bondage as there were could no longer be
found; to cut their losses lords were leasing their lands either
wholly or in part for the term of the lessee's life. But the problem
was that lands held in chief could not be so leased without the
King's permission.[109] On this occasion, and again in 1371 when
an almost identical petition was presented, the King gave an
evasive reply.[110] If, as seems the case, the petition was referring to
leases of demesne land, then Sir Simon Basset was not alone in
opting to lease his demesnes in the 1360s; and the Commons
clearly connected the contraction of demesne cultivation with
the absence of tenants in bondage. It is probably the attitude of
the gentry that finds expression too in a petition of 1368.
According to the Commons those who lived *par geynerie de lour
Terres ou Marchandise* and who did not have lordships or
seigneuries to support them were suffering from the outrageous
prises and salaries of servants and labourers; these people should
be made to pay back twice the excess wages they had extorted.[111]
The petition could be voicing the grievances of working farmers
who employed labour on a small scale. But its prime movers are
more likely to have been the gentry: those· who had neither
lordships nor villeins. Here is some fairly definite evidence that
such landowners did not expect their demesnes any longer to be
cultivated by customary tenants. Moreover, they could not
match the greater magnates in the use of coercion to make
unwilling labourers work on demesnes at below the market rate.
The reluctance to continue direct cultivation of demesnes is
understandable.

Even if they chose to abandon their own demesnes, the
possibilty remains that the gentry may have taken leases on
demesnes which were being demised by the magnates and
ecclesiastical corporations. Miss Harvey's examination of the
evidence for Westminster Abbey has shown that some of the
gentry were certainly attracted by favourable demesne leases,
such as two members of the Vampage family, father and son, who

---

[109] *Rot. Parl.*, ii, 279.
[110] Ibid., 304–5.   [111] Ibid., 296–7.

leased the demesne at Pershore in the fifteenth century.[112] But, as she admits, these men were exceptional: the ministerial type lessee predominated. At Deerhurst the Abbey's demesne was farmed in 1385–6 by the Prior of Deerhurst and in 1397–8 by one John atte Hall.[113] It is noteworthy that the Exchequer baron, Sir John Cassy, who bought the neighbouring estate at Wightfield, seems not to have been interested in taking a lease which a man of his position could pressumably have secured on favourable terms. The other Gloucestershire evidence confirms the impression that most of the lessees were drawn from the richer peasantry, with gentry lessees very much the exception. In the 1390s the manor, as opposed to just the demesne, at Wheatenhurst, was demised at far by Thomas of Woodstock, duke of Gloucester, to one John Wychestre, alias Walker.[114] In the following century the leases of the Gloucestershire demesnes of Pershore Abbey were being taken by officials, such as John Lane, the bailiff, who farmed the demesne at Cowley in 1426–7.[115] At Thornbury the lessees of the earl of Stafford's demesne included his ministers and local tenants, but not local gentry.[116] In 1365 Llanthony Abbey began to lease some of its rents and tithes. The lessees seem to have been practising farmers, with the important exception of John Derhurst, a J.P. and a man of growing importance in the county, who took a forty year lease on the vicarage at Prestbury in 1399.[117] Just two lessees from older gentry families can be identified. The first was Philip Rodborough, who with John Craft paid Thomas of Woodstock £106 13s. 4d. for a lease of the manor of Minchinhampton in 1391.[118] Craft was probably a ministerial type lessee, but Rodborough was a junior member of a. local gentry family.[119] The other was Laurence Sebrok, sheriff in

[112] B. F. Harvey, 'The Leasing of the Abbot of Westminster's Demesnes', 21.
[113] Westminster Abbey Muniments, 8452, 8453.
[114] *Cal. Inqs. Misc. 1392–9*, no. 224.
[115] R. A. L. Smith, 'The Estates of Pershore Abbey' (London University, M.A. thesis, 1938), p. 232.
[116] Stafford Co. Rec. Office, D.641/1/2/134–54. The demesne was leased in small parcels.
[117] C.115/L.1/6688 (Reg. of Prior Simon de Brocworth, 1362–76), fos. 14ᵛ–15, 17, 25–25ᵛ; C.115/K.2/6684 (Reg. of Prior William Cheryton, 1376–1401), fos. 63, 208ᵛ.
[118] *Cal. Pat. Rolls 1396–9*, p. 464.
[119] C. E. Watson, 'The Minchinhampton Custumal', *Trans. Bristol & Gloucs.*

1388–9, who farmed the manor of Stonehouse in 1389 on demise from Sir John Arundell.[120]

In the absence of any evidence from the Berkeley estates or from the abbeys of Gloucester, Tewkesbury, Cirencester and Winchcombe, our knowledge is hardly such as to allow us to make any generalization with confidence.[121] The instances of lessees drawn from the gentry are not so numerous as to suggest that many such men were attracted by demesne leases; but the possibility must be left open still that, even if they did not want to undertake cultivation themselves, knights may have taken demesnes which they perhaps then sublet: in other words, that they acted as middle-men. What lessees did with the demesnes they leased is a question to which no definite answer can be given. Nearly all of the Westminster Abbey indentures said that the lessee was not to sublet without the Abbey's permission; the fragmentation of two demesnes which were leased in lots was effected by the abbot himself and not by a middle-man.[122] Unfortunately there is no evidence from Gloucestershire to confirm or deny this suggestion that demesnes were exploited principally by the tenants named in the leases. When gentry lessees do occur, however, the lease usually comprises not just the demesne but the entire manor as at Stonehouse in 1389 and Minchinhampton in 1391. Perhaps the policy of the lay magnates differed from that of the monasteries, which if Westminster Abbey was typical, rarely leased manorial rights or the rents of tenants.[123]

But would conditions that were unfavourable for the lords have been beneficial for others? The big landowners, as we have seen, were doing well enough in the 1350s and 1360s until the fall in prices in the later 1370s that accelerated the process of demesne leasing. Once the era of booming prices had passed,

---

Arch. Soc., liv (1932), 357, gives a pedigree of the family of Rodborough of Rodborough.

[120] *Gloucs. Inqs. post Mortem*, vi, 158.

[121] Berkeley Castle S.R.48 shows that the demesne at Ham was leased by 1385, but in omitting to enter the names of the individual lessees on the manorial account roll, Thomas, Lord Berkeley showed greater trust than, for example, the earl of Stafford did at Thornbury in the honesty or ability of the reeve to keep an adequate record of those owing demesne rents.

[122] Harvey, 'The Leasing of the Abbot of Westminster's Demesnes', 26.

[123] Ibid., 25.

however, they must have found themselves in much the same position *vis-à-vis* their tenants as the knights did, dependent mainly on rental income and actively concerned to reduce arrears to a minimum.[124] The secular magnates, moreover, were encumbered with expenditure that did not burden the gentry. Because of the need both to cut a figure in society and to build up support among the knightly class for political purposes, they were committed to maintaining sizeable retinues, whereas their ecclesiastical peers had few inhibitions in reducing lists of annuitants once landed income began to decline. For this reason the higher nobility had a larger proportionate need for cash income than the knights and esquires who were the beneficiaries of magnate extravagance.

It is quite possible to argue that economic circumstances which were bad for the landowning class as a whole would have favoured their tenants. Once the landhunger of the thirteenth century had passed, those who had previously been landless could secure a holding for the first time; and the richer tenants and freeholders who had cash to spare could acquire more land by purchase or by taking demesne leases. As Professor Postan has written, in the post-Black Death world 'the whole village was given the opportunity for a general upgrading'.[125] The implication of this view is that conditions favoured the labourer and the tenant at the expense of the lord and the employer: that the peasantry, in other words, were prospering relatively more than the greater lords and knights. Cultivation of the land may well have passed from the lords of the big estates into the hands of such prosperous lesser proprietors. Dependent as they were for their livelihood on agricultural profits, for they derived little income from rents, they would have continued acquiring land until the cost of taking on more labour made further expansion unprofitable. Can we suppose, therefore, that the lower ranks of gentle society were being swollen by the entry for the first time of these aspiring lesser landowners? Can we even go so far as to suggest that the composition of landowning society was being transformed by the end of the fourteenth century?

[124] For the progress of demesne leasing in Gloucestershire see above, p. 234.
[125] Postan, *Essays on Medieval Agriculture and General Problems*, p. 211.

That the structure of land-holding became more intricate in the half-century after the Black Death is suggested by the complexity of the social order as revealed in the surviving returns for the 1379 poll tax; those for Gloucestershire being only fragmentary, it is helpful to look first at a county like the West Riding of Yorkshire for which the returns are complete. In the absence of any dukes or earls, society in the West Riding was headed by twenty-six knights and nine esquires whose wealth qualified them for knighthood. Next were thirty-six lesser esquires or *armati*, three of whom, Edmund Fitzwilliam, William de Aldborough and Thomas de Reresby, were the sons and heirs of knights. Eight men were described as sergeants, and twenty-nine as farmers of either manors or granges. But perhaps most striking is the preponderance of franklins, numbering sixty-six in all. Most vills had a franklin or *firmarius*, even when there was a resident lord of the manor too. The importance of the franklins, then, cannot be under-estimated: they were present in great numbers even in a county which was not amongst the richest in medieval England.[126] The Gloucestershire poll tax returns are too incomplete to show the distribution of franklins, but nearby, in south and east Warwickshire, there were over thirty.[127]

Unfortunately, no accounts survive to show the level of income enjoyed by the esquires, sergeants, *firmarii* or franklins who are so prominent in these returns. What evidence there is goes to confirm the impression given by the poll tax schedule that there was little distinction in economic, if not social, status between the richer franklins and the lesser esquires. Inquisitions *post mortem*, regrettably not an accurate source, are of some help. When John de Cawood, a franklin who was living in 1379 on the Archbishop of York's manor of Cawood, died in 1403 it was found that he held a capital messuage, $95\frac{1}{2}$ acres of arable land, $13\frac{1}{4}$ acres of meadow, $4\frac{1}{2}$ acres and $\frac{2}{3}$ of a rood of pasture. The income which he derived from rents totalled £1 8s. 2d. Twelve tofts were said to be lying waste, and one windmill ruinous.[128] If this inquisition *post mortem*, like most, undervalues the lands and rents of the deceased tenant, it still portrays an estate of a modest nature

[126] *Yorkshire Archaeological & Topographical Journal*, v, 5, 241; vi, 320.
[127] Hilton, *The English Peasantry in the Later Middle Ages*, p. 26.
[128] *Inquisitions post Mortem . . . Yorkshire*, ed. W. P. Baildon & J. W. Clay (Yorks. Arch. Soc. Record Series, lix, 1918), 40–1. See also below, p. 244.

carved out of the Archbishop's manor. Had he sold the grain produce of sixty acres at an average price of 3s. a quarter, John would have made about £9; with rents included, his gross income might have reached about £11 or £12, roughly the income of a gentleman in early Tudor England. The estate held at his death by Robert de Todenham, esquire, was of similar extent. He held in the vill of Elsternwick, near Hedon, twenty-three messuages and twenty oxgangs of land said to be worth £3 6s. 8d.: here was an esquire who was not the lord of a manor, and who hardly aspired to knighthood.[129]

The evidence of the Gloucestershire poll tax returns points in a similar direction. Of the four *armigeri* who appear in the surviving returns of 1380–1, two, Thomas Ludlow of Berrington and Robert Somerville, were lords of manors. The other two were not: Nicholas Cole lived at Littledean, but hardly any more is known about him. Finally, there was Thomas de Bradewell who paid 6s. at Broadwell near Stow-on-the-Wold and rose to be three times sheriff of Gloucester. Thomas seems to have been one of the newly-important esquires who were accused of aping the manners and dress of their superiors. His family had lived for generations on the manor of Broadwell, which belonged to Evesham Abbey, and it is possible, although there is no conclusive evidence, that Thomas was the lessee of the manorial demesne. If his lands were not so extensive as those of the knights alongside whom he worked, nevertheless he assembled an estate which later constituted the sub-manor of Nethercourt in Broadwell.[130]

The growing pretensions of these lesser landowners received recognition when they began to be appointed to offices and commissions in the shire. For example, more justices of the peace were appointed. In 1348 the size of the bench had been fixed at six, of whom two would be men of law, but in the Gloucestershire commission of 8 March 1382 no fewer than twenty-one J.P.s were appointed.[131] Of the two commissions of the peace issued later in the same year, that of 8 October numbered only ten; while that of 21 December returned to an unwieldy level with twenty-one

[129] Ibid., 47.
[130] E.179/113/31mm. 1, 3, 8d; E.179/113/35A m. 15. For the de Bradewell estate at Broadwell see *V.C.H. Gloucs.*, vi, 53. Cf. above, p. 19.
[131] *Cal. Pat. Rolls 1381–5*, p. 138.

members.[132] Commissions of about a dozen J.P.s were customary then in the 1380s until a determined effort to reduce their size was made on 15 July 1389.[133] For the remainder of the century between eight and eleven J.P.s were named in each commission.

The expansion in the size of the bench, common to most counties in the early 1380s, coincides with the aftermath of the Peasants Revolt.[134] It may be that they were afforced simply to deal with the crisis; but once the commission had been opened to newcomers, it proved difficult to return to a more manageable number again. The Crown could not have appointed J.P.s had there not been men in the shires of the standing of gentry who aspired to the ranks of the office-holders. The phenomenon was not peculiar to the commissions of the peace. Whereas earlier in the century two chief taxers had been appointed to collect the parliamentary subsidies on moveables, a commission of about a dozen was entrusted with the task in the reign of Richard II.[135] As taxation became more frequent it may have been felt necessary to spread the burden of collection among more taxers; but equally the pressure could have come from those who sought minor office—and, perhaps, the opportunity to line their pockets a little. In the West Riding, as in Gloucestershire, a commission of eight or nine was entrusted in the 1380s to collect the taxes previously collected by two chief taxers and their subordinates. The commission appointed on 2 November 1382 to collect a tenth and fifteenth was fairly typical.[136] It included three knights and one esquire; its five other members can be identified from the poll tax returns. Three, William de Gargrave, Thomas del Thwait of Marston and John de Cawood, were franklins.[137] A fourth, John de Scarborough, was described as a *firmarius* at

---

[132] Ibid., pp. 194, 246.

[133] *Cal. Pat. Rolls 1381–5*, p. 346 (2 July 1383), p. 347 (26 January and 28 February 1383); *Cal. Pat. Rolls 1388–92*, p. 135 (15 July 1389).

[134] Commissions were issued for most counties in March, 1382 (*Cal. Pat. Rolls 1381–5*, pp. 138–42).

[135] For example, two collectors were appointed for the twentieth of 1327 (*Cal. Pat. Rolls 1327–30*, p. 173); on 4 March 1377 two knights and eight others were appointed in Gloucestershire to collect the first poll tax (*Cal. Fine Rolls 1369–77*, p. 387).

[136] *Cal. Fine Rolls 1377–83*, p. 337.

[137] *Yorks. Arch. & Top. Jnl.*, vi, 139; vii, 165, 181. For John de Cawood see above, p. 242.

Grassington.[138] The final member, Richard Lewere of Doncaster, was described in 1379 as an *apprenticus*, perhaps an apprentice-at-law, as he paid the considerable sum of 20*s*. in tax.[139] It seems fairly clear, then, that the prosperous lesser gentry were well represented among the chief taxers of the West Riding. One franklin at least, John Malham of Calton, is known also to have held higher office: a tax collector in 1384, he had been appointed a J.P. on 20 December 1382.[140]

The shrievalty usually went to a knight or wealthy esquire. It was rather in the lower ranks of the office-holding hierarchy that men were to be found whose families had never before played a part in the work of the community of the shire. Who were these newcomers to local office? The Gloucestershire evidence is rather thin. Some of the taxers may be identified as burgesses or merchants, like Thomas Adynet and Nicholas Pointer who were acquiring estates in the country.[141] The poll tax returns, the obvious source for such an enquiry, are too fragmentary to be of much help. But a charter preserved in the British Library is suggestive. On 1 February 1387 John Cosyn, Nicholas Pointer, and William Quenington and John Rouel, chaplains, made a bond to re-infeoff John Campden of Ampney Crucis and Emma, his wife, of the lands in Ampney Crucis, Ablington and Arlington which John had granted to them.[142] Now John Campden was appointed a collector of subsidies on no fewer than seven occasions between 1373 and 1388. He might have been styled either an esquire or a franklin; and as a man who held land in four vills he was clearly of some consequence, although the extent and value of his property can only be a matter of conjecture. Of these vills three belonged to monasteries.[143] No more than the strong possibility can be urged that leases of monastic demesnes help to account for the rise to prosperity and local importance of men

---

[138] Ibid., vii, 149.   [139] Ibid., v, 50.

[140] *Cal. Pat. Rolls 1381–5*, p. 252; *Cal. Fine Rolls 1383–91*, p. 70.

[141] See above, p. 232. Thomas Adynet was appointed a collector of taxes on 4 March 1377 (*Cal. Fine Rolls 1369–77*, p. 387), 7 December 1380 (*Cal. Fine Rolls 1377–83*, p. 227). Nicholas Pointer was appointed to the same office on 4 March 1380 (ibid., p. 187).

[142] Brit. Lib. Egerton Ch. 754.

[143] Ampney Crucis belonged to Tewkesbury Abbey, Ampney St. Peter to Gloucester Abbey; Arlington was a hamlet in the Bishop of Worcester's manor of Bibury.

like John Campden and Thomas de Bradewell, the sheriff, who lived on the Evesham Abbey manor of Broadwell. The evidence becomes rather firmer when we consider the rising fortunes of the Greyndour family. They held a small estate at Hadnock near Monmouth, and service in the retinue of John of Gaunt put them in a good position to benefit in the scramble for leases when demesne agriculture came to an end. In 1363 Laurence Greyndour, who had married the daughter and heiress of Sir Ralph de Abenhall, became one of the co-lessees of 267 acres of Gaunt's demesne at Monmouth for twelve years. In the same year he also secured the farm of the manor at Baycourt near Abenhall for £3 6s. 8d. per annum.[144] No wonder therefore that it was Laurence who was responsible for lifting his family into the ranks of the county gentry.

The enhanced pretensions of the *nouveaux riches* can probably be explained in such terms. But whether the likes of Thomas de Bradewell, John Campden and Laurence Greyndour were arriving in such numbers as fundamentally to alter the shape of landowning society is a question to which no certain answer can be given. If they were not to encounter the very problems that had led the knights and the greater lords to abandon demesne cultivation, they would have had to limit their acquisition of land, to prevent the increased cost of hiring wage labour from exceeding the profits of extended cultivation. A small grange-type estate, composed of tenant and former demesne land in the same vill, might have had the advantage of containing administrative costs. But it is when we come to ask just how the smaller proprietors managed these estates that the evidence so signally fails us: even if the charters have sometimes survived to illuminate the transactions by which lands were acquired, the accounts which would tell us what was grown and how much was sold have not. However, we can certainly understand why the phrase *gentils et . . . autres* was employed in Henry V's reign to describe those who suffered from infringement of the Statutes of Labourers.[145] As they had now become the principal employers of agricultural

---

[144] R. R. Davies, 'The Bohun and Lancaster Lordships in Wales in the Fourteenth and Early Fifteenth Centuries' (Oxford D. Phil. thesis, 1965), pp. 206–8. I am grateful to Professor Davies for allowing me to use his thesis. For the Greyndour family see also above, p. 80.

[145] Harvey, 'The Leasing of the Abbot of Westminster's Demesnes', p. 27.

labour, it was in their interest to prevent richer lords from enticing workers by the prospect of higher reward elsewhere.

If the further accumulation of holdings was not always in the interest of smaller landowners, then we must begin to doubt whether such men really were entering the ranks of the gentry in the later fourteenth century in sufficient number as to tilt the balance of English landowning society. After all, substantial peasant proprietors had always existed even in the days of land hunger early in the century. The returns for the parliamentary subsidy of 1327 indicate no shortage of men in Gloucestershire who could contribute 5s. or 10s. or even more to the subsidy of one twentieth.[146] How did men of this standing in 1327 differ from their successors of half a century or more later? The question is posed at its simplest if we consider the fortunes of the Couley family. John de Couley, Thomas de Berkeley's steward in the 1390s, was described as an esquire in February 1401. Although there is regrettably no inquisition *post mortem* to record the lands which he held at his death, an inquisition taken on the death of his ancestor, another John de Couley, in 1325, shows that the Couley estate then included 180 acres of arable, eight acres of meadow, two acres of pasture and ten acres of wood.[147] At that time the Couleys' livelihood was derived entirely from cultivation since no rental income was mentioned, and the position was probably little different by the 1390s. If demesne leases figured at all, their contribution could hardly have been large, since the family's lands lay close to the Berkeley estates, where the demesnes were not very extensive. The rise of the esquire, John de Couley, to prominence in the 1390s is more likely to be explicable by his position in the favour of Thomas de Berkeley than by newly found landed wealth.

How then do we account for the apparent rise of esquires and franklins like Laurence Greyndour and John Campden whom we find swelling the ranks of the office-holders for the first time?

---

[146] At Up Ampney Geoffrey atte Style paid 11s. 9¼d. and Walter Chileyene 13s. 10d.; at Little Rissington John Appleheved paid 8s., and at Adlestrop and Oddington Reginald Passegaumbe and John de Wappenham respectively paid 10s. each (*Gloucs. Subsidy Roll*, pp. 8, 17, 19).

[147] John de Couley was described as an esquire in February, 1401 (*Cal. Pat. Rolls 1399–1401*, p. 493). For the inquisition *post mortem* of 1325 see *Gloucs. Inqs. post Mortem*, v, 191.

Undoubtedly the abandonment of demesne husbandry by the lords enabled some lesser proprietors, and no doubt the better placed of them like Laurence Greyndour, to obtain leases on sufficiently favourable terms that they could make the step upwards into landed society. But if at the same time it is true that the majority of the lessees were customary tenants, among whom demesnes were let severally in small parcels, the composition of landowning society could hardly have been radically upset. Undoubtedly new families were joining the gentry, as they had in the past and were to do in the future; yet purely economic factors alone surely cannot account for their rise in sufficient number as to constitute another rank of gentle society. For this is what happened in the late middle ages. Knight and esquire, the two ranks of the gentleborn in 1300, were transmuted into knight, esquire and gentleman by 1415. The terminology had changed; but was a gentleman in 1415 any different in economic standing from one of the *valletti* we meet in the Falkirk horse inventories in 1298?

In strictly economic standing probably not. But we can at least suggest that the gentleman had a recognized place in the hierarchy of noble and gentle society of which the *vallettus* was not yet assured in 1300. This enhancement of the status of those in approximately the £10 class was a product of the increasing social stratification which characterized the late middle ages.[148] In 1300 the lesser *valletti*, whose armigerous rank was not yet recognized, shaded off imperceptibly into the freeholders beneath. In the fifteenth century, however, the noble and gentle birth of the gentleman, and his entitlement to the use of a coat of arms, marked him out from those who could only be described as free. Indeed the interests of those who were advancing a claim to gentility coincided with the work of those who had recognition to bestow. Henry V, as we have seen, took measures which had the effect of bringing the conferment of arms under the control of the royal heralds, and at the same time Clarence's ordinances instructed the Kings of Arms to search for those of noble and gentle stock who ought to bear arms. We may imagine that if the heralds were seeking out men of gentle birth, those who considered themselves so qualified were no less eager in seeking

[148] See above, pp. 6–29.

out the heralds. An increasing consciousness of status, induced perhaps by the evidence of social mobility, brought more firmly within the ranks of the gentleborn those whose claims a century before to be noble and gentle would have been more questionable and more difficult to establish. Even so, in the fifteenth century definitions of nobility still concentrated on indefinable social rather than precise economic criteria; and it is not until 1530 that we learn that a man claiming gentle status was expected to hold lands to the value of £10 *per annum* or moveable goods worth £300.[149]

Significantly, it was to the late fourteenth or early fifteenth century that several gentry families whose pedigrees were compiled in the late sixteenth century traced their origin. The Derhurst family traced their rise from John Derhurst, a J.P. in the reigns of Richard II and Henry IV.[150] The Poleyns of Kingsweston traced their origin to John Poleyn, an esquire of Thomas de Berkeley in the reign of Richard II, who may have been an esquire in social rank as well as in official status.[151] The pedigrees of Cole of Northway and Brain of Littledean were traced back only to the fifteenth century, although it was in the closing decades of the fourteenth that each of these families like their counterparts, the Bradewells and the Campdens, came to be of some consequence.[152]

Having traced how changing economic fortunes affected the composition of the gentry in the fourteenth century, it is as well in conclusion to consider briefly what income the knights and esquires derived from sources other than arable cultivation. In Gloucestershire foremost among these would have been profits from the sale of wool. Professor Postan has said that sheep

[149] Wagner, *Heralds and Heraldry in the Middle Ages*, p. 79.

[150] *Visitation of the County of Gloucester*, p. 18. John Derhurst took a lease on the vicarage of Prestbury (above, p. 239). His son John, termed 'gentleman alias esquire' in a pardon of 1451 acquired the manor of Field Court in Hardwicke (*V.C.H. Gloucs.*, x, 184); for his biography see J. Wedgwood, *History of Parliament, 1439–1509* (London, 1936), pp. 270–1.

[151] *Visitation of the County of Gloucester*, p. 220; S.C.8/148/7355.

[152] For the Brain family see *Trans. Bristol & Gloucs. Arch. Soc.*, vi (1881–2), 296. William Brain of Newnham was acquiring land in 1382 (C.P.25(1)/78/79/47). Richard Brain was six times appointed a tax collector (*Cal. Fine Rolls 1369–77*, pp. 220, 269; *1377–83*, pp. 54, 339; *1383–91*, pp. 69, 156). For the Cole family see *Visitation of the County of Gloucester*, 43; *V.C.H. Gloucs.*, viii, 177.

farming was an attractive prospect in the late middle ages: 'Those of them (the gentry) who specialized in sheep and cattle must have suffered the least, since pastures were abundant and labour costs of sheep farming relatively low.'[153] But wool may not have been the panacea for hard-pressed landowners that it was once regarded. Following an immediate post-Black Death boom exports steadily dwindled after 1366; and if the increased affluence indicated by the sumptuary legislation brought a greater demand at home for fine clothing, wool prices were nevertheless depressed for most of the late middle ages.[154] If any producers were to make a profit out of wool, however, it would surely be the growers of the Cotswolds. Throughout those years of the middle ages for which we have figures, and admittedly they make a far from continuous series, the price of Cotswold wool was above the average mean price: by about 7*d*. a stone in 1365, 1*s*. 6*d*. in 1368, over 2*s*. in 1374–5, by 1*s*. 6*d*. again in 1398 and by over 2*s*. in 1404.[155] On the Cotswolds flocks must have been kept by the knights as well as by monasteries, but the evidence is disappointingly thin. In the thirteenth century 6,000 sheep were kept on the Gurneys' manor of Beverstone; and on 12 January 1344 Sir John de la Rivere of Tormarton sold a flock of 1,500 wethers to Sir Thomas de Berkeley of Berkeley.[156] By contrast, at Tockington in 1345 Nicholas Pointz had only two wethers, four ewes and 104 hoggasters.[157] Later in the century flocks of sheep were kept on Walter Broun's manor of Lasborough and James Clifford's of Frampton-on-Severn, but their size is not indicated.[158] These examples suggest that sheep were to be found on many manors, though the flocks may not always have been large; even if it was not perhaps a source of easy profit for hard-pressed landowners, wool must have been a boon for those

---

[153] *Cambridge Economic History*, i, ed. M. M. Postan, 596.
[154] T. H. Lloyd, 'The Movement of Wool Prices in Medieval England', *Econ. Hist. Rev. Supplement*, 6 (1973), 19–20.
[155] Ibid., Table I, 41–3.
[156] J. J. Simpson, 'Wool Trade and Woolmen of Gloucestershire', *Trans. Bristol & Gloucs. Arch. Soc.*, liii (1931), 86; Berkeley Castle, charter 3111. The manor of Beverstone passed from the Gurneys to the Apadams, and then to the Berkeleys of Berkeley who used it to endow a junior line of the family.
[157] *Gloucs. Inqs. post Mortem*, v, 309.
[158] K.B.27/471 Rex m. 22d; S.C.8/84/4192.

THE INCOME OF THE GENTRY 251

knights who owned extensive flocks in a highly favoured county like Gloucester. There were also non-landed sources of income. For some of the gentry, just how many it is difficult to say, incomes would be supplemented by retaining fees.[159] If as many fees were being distributed at the end of the century as before the Black Death, it would certainly be fair to argue that receipt of fees helped a fair number to maintain the level of their income. Fees were given by lords lay and eccelesiastical, of whom the latter, heavily dependent as they were on income from land, may well have been compelled to cut back on the number of annuitants.[160] Those most affected would have been gentry living in the neighbourhood of the monastery and office-holders like the sheriff feed by monasteries anxious to protect their own interests. The secular magnates, however, were not entirely dependent on income from land; moreover, their scope for economy was circumscribed by their need not only to recruit support among the gentry of the shires but also to maintain their standing in society. They are more likely than the monasteries to have kept up expenditure on fees throughout the century.

Perhaps, too, the profits of the Hundred Years War helped to compensate for the decline in income from other sources after about 1370. Professor Postan has offered general reasons for scepticism which merit consideration: 'however generous we may be in our estimates of net gains from offices, booty, estates and even ransoms, we should still find it very difficult to make them equal the five millions plus spent on national and private accounts'.[161] Over the whole period of the war there is certainly little reason to believe that the balance tilted in England's favour; but it is possible that the cost of the war fell largely on sections of society other than the knights who fought in France where the opportunities for enrichment were to be found. The English war effort was financed mainly by the wool subsidy and the taxes on moveables; the latter were paid predominantly by the peasantry. It is difficult to estimate how far the campaigns of Edward III's reign gathered enough booty to alter the fortunes of the knights and esquires as well as to enrich commanders like Knollys and

[159] For a discussion of this point see above, p. 89.
[160] See above, pp. 100–2.
[161] Postan, *Medieval Agriculture and General Problems*, p. 78.

Calverley. But the case of Sir Peter le Veel is suggestive. It may be possible to connect the large reserves of capital, which he had accumulated by the 1370s, with his almost continuous service in France and Gascony in the retinue of the Black Prince.[162] However, it seems that the numbers crossing the Channel regularly were too few for the profits of war greatly to alter the fortunes of the knightly class as a whole.[163] And the gains of one campaign could be wiped out by a ransom incurred in the next: in 1372 Robin d'Ougniez, a French esquire, acknowledged receipt of a ransom of 200 gold francs from Sir John Berkeley, who must have been captured in one of the English forces in France after the renewal of war.[164] By the 1370s the age of quick spoils had passed, and in the period of low prices during the last two decades of the century the gentry could hardly look to the profits of war to supplement their incomes from land. It was surely no coincidence that the Cheshire rising of 1393, simultaneous with Richard II's negotiations with France, was led by a knight, Sir Thomas Talbot.[165]

It would be wise to end on a cautionary note: the limitations of an enquiry such as this are many and obvious. Prevented by shortage of evidence from tracing the fortunes of individual knightly families over several generations in the way that is possible in the case of the estates of a magnate family, the historian is driven to make abstract generalizations about the lesser landowners or 'gentry' as a group. Yet never is it more difficult than when discussing economic history to define precisely what is meant by such elusive terms as 'esquire' and 'gentleman', for in application they were changing; and the forces which were moulding their evolution, we may suspect, were as much social as strictly economic. Allowance has to be made also for the diversity of wealth within the ranks of the

[162] Veel had lent Sir Robert Ashton £400 to the use of Edward III's mistress, Alice Perrers (G. A. Holmes, *The Good Parliament* (Oxford, 1975), p. 88). In the 1380s Veel was prosecuting Sir Richard de Stapledon to recover a debt of £2,000 (C.88/57 m. 58). Veel was in Gascony almost continuously from 1362 to 1367, and in France in 1370, 1372 and 1378 (see above, Table I (p. 53)).

[163] See above, pp. 48–59.

[164] I. Gray, 'A Berkeley Ransom', *Trans. Bristol & Gloucs. Arch. Soc.*, lxxxviii (1969), 213–15.

[165] J. G. Bellamy, 'The Northern Rebellions in the Later Years of Richard II', *Bull. John Rylands Lib.*, xlvii (1964–5), 261–74.

smaller landowners. Some lived on the resources of a single manor; others held manors scattered across four or five counties. Occasionally the evidence casts a disquieting shadow across the convenient generalizations made by the historian. What is to be made, for example, of John Giffard of Leckhampton, the lord of just one manor, who is commemorated with his wife on one of the most ornate tombs in the county?[166] Sir Peter le Veel was probably not the only knight to possess a treasure hidden from the historian's gaze. Such instances afford a much-needed reminder that income from land, though probably the most important component in a knight's income, may well have been supplemented sometimes by other, lucrative sources of profit. Unfortunately, these cannot be quantified. The profits of war and of office-holding were uncertain and unpredictable in their incidence. Rather than enrich the gentry as a whole, though, they may have served more to emphasize the uneven distribution of wealth within the gentry. Finally, personalities are largely hidden from us; little correspondence has survived to illuminate the characters of these men who ran their estates and administered the shires. Some were efficient; some may have neglected their lands. To guess the extent to which it was not the underlying trend but the competence of the individual that affected the fortunes of the gentry we are dependent on isolated shreds of information that are suggestive rather than conclusive.

---

[166] For a description of the tomb, which can be dated c.1330, see D. Verey, *Gloucestershire: The Vale and the Forest of Dean* (Harmondsworth, 1970), p. 284, where the assumption that the commemorated is one of the Giffards of Brimpsfield is probably misplaced.

CONCLUSION

It is all too easy for the historian to lose that sense of perspective so necessary if he is not to attach unwarranted significance to developments that he perceives within his own period. Think how often it is, for example, that the medievalist discovers within his own specialized field the origins of our modern state which the historians of the sixteenth century once claimed to be the creation of the Tudor monarchs. So far as the history of the gentry is concerned, we must be more than careful, for as Professor Holt has written, 'gentry are always rising; it is their habit'.[1] Once they were said to have risen in the sixteenth century, and any medievalist so rash as to assert that they rose not then, but in the fourteenth century would no doubt soon find himself outflanked by a colleague claiming that honour for the thirteenth. We must always remember that the gentry were to be indispensable to the Crown from the thirteenth century right through to the nineteenth as the class without whom English government, 'self government at the King's command' as it was once described,[2] could never have been carried on.

Notwithstanding these qualifications, we may still be justified in staking a claim for the importance in the evolution of the English gentry of the era that lasted from the reign of Edward I until the early fifteenth century. It is significant enough that the arguments of historians centre on what happened to the *knights* in the thirteenth century and what happened to the *gentry* in the sixteenth. That we should use the term 'gentry' with such facility by the time the Tudors came to the throne is a measure of the significance of what had happened in the meantime.

The emergence of the gentry in the late middle ages was, as K. B. McFarlane showed, a legacy of the process by which the nobility became identified solely with the parliamentary

---

[1] J. C. Holt, *The Northerners* (Oxford, 1961), p. 60.
[2] A. B. White, *Self-Government at the King's Command* (Minneapolis, 1933).

peerage. That is one part of the story, and certainly an important part: for although noble and gentle were to remain synonymous until the seventeenth century, the forces making for their eventual separation were strong enough for the origins of the process to be traced to this period. But what is equally important is the apparent enhancement in the status of the lesser ranks of the gentleborn during the fourteenth century consequent upon, or at least associated with, the increasing stratification of noble and gentle society. In 1300 we can identify just two ranks, those of knight and esquire, the latter rendered in Latin by *vallettus*, *armiger*, *scutifer* or *serviens ad arma*, all of them signifying a man-at-arms paid at half the rate of a knight. While capable of precise definition in a military context, *armiger*, *vallettus* and the other words however resist almost any attempts at definition according to economic criteria. They could describe esquires from the £10–£15 level up to those who qualified for knighthood. If the economic standing of the esquires was unclear in 1300, so too was their social status: though *vallettus* could be translated as *gentil homme* in 1319, the use by most esquires at the end of the thirteenth century of a signet rather than an heraldic seal of arms indicated both their inferiority to the knights and their rather unsure position at the foot of noble and gentle society.

In the course of the fourteenth century the position was clarified to the advantage of the esquires. Their right to use an heraldic seal was recognized well before 1350, and by 1370 their arms were being emblazoned on rolls of arms alongside those of the knights. The status of the esquires had risen greatly since the days in the thirteenth century when they were required to attend tournaments wearing blazons of the lords whom they served. Once it had started, however, the process of 'gentrification' proved difficult to halt. That the ranks of gentle society were proving too large to be embraced within the orders of knight and esquire is suggested by the emergence in 1415 of the word 'gentleman' to describe landowners in approximately the £10 class—those perhaps who were still being termed *vadlets* after that word had parted company with *armiger*.

If the hierarchy of society had come to be more clearly defined, it was a process of definition which had worked to the advantage of *les gentils*, whose superiority to the free was marked in the fifteenth century by their entitlement to the use of a coat of arms.

By the 1440s we are already in a world that would be familiar to Tudor historians, where those who aspired to a gentle manner of life sought out the heralds for the grant or confirmation of a coat of arms. The science of heraldry in fact was acquiring an existence quite independent from the military purpose which had called it into existence. In the fourteenth century, when coats of arms were still regularly serving their primary function of identification in battle, a knight who never saw active service might not have a coat of arms at all, or if he did would certainly understand how Otto de Maundell could be so careless as to lose the letters patent containing the grant of arms made by Edward III to his father.[3] In the fifteenth century, when heraldry conferred distinction, a gentleman obtained his arms and his patent of ennoblement, and made sure that neither was neglected or forgotten. Thus a connection between heraldry and gentility was being forged.

The process by which the knights came to share the distinctions conferred by noble and gentle birth first with the esquires and then with the gentlemen was of a complex nature, and influenced as much by social as by purely economic factors. After the Black Death rapid social mobility, evidenced by the rising pretensions of some of the lesser landed proprietors, led to a greater concern with status which removed the uncertainties of a century earlier and ended in the creation of a new rank within the fold of gentle society, that of the gentleman. Looking further back to the earlier decades of the fourteenth century, it seems quite impossible to associate the recognition of the armigerous standing of the esquires with any rise, or decline for that matter, in their economic fortunes. In hazarding a possible reason for the enhancement of their status we may point instead to the near-continuous warfare of the late thirteenth and fourteenth centuries. Arms in the heraldic sense were needed for identification not only by the knights but also by the esquires, who may well have assumed them without authorization. But in explaining how the esquires came to be accepted as the equals of the knights we may need to turn from the battlefield to the shires. The intensification of government, another consequence of the burdens of warfare, had led to the appointment of new royal

[3] *Cal. Pat. Rolls 1391–6*, p. 327.

ministers under the sheriffs. It was in the thirteenth century, certainly, that the escheator, keepers of the peace, arrayers and taxers first made their appearance, but it was in the fourteenth, when the demands made by the Crown became both heavier and more regular, that the commissions grew in size, drawing more of the gentry into local administration. Thus the political community, to which the knights had been admitted in the thirteenth century, was widened now to include the esquires and later the gentlemen too. It is in the fourteenth century that we can first speak of 'the gentry' in the sense of an elite in the shires comprising all the gentleborn rather than just the knights.[4]

If he was more amply endowed and figured more prominently in the political community than his ancestor of 1086, the fourteenth century knight or rich esquire still lived a life which, as some historians have pointed out, was bounded by remarkably narrow horizons.[5] The geographical interests of most knights hardly extended further than the range of their own estates. Such is the picture of local society which is suggested by the pattern of connections by marriage. Thus families whose lands were confined to Gloucestershire generally married into other families whose only lands were in Gloucestershire: it seems that the marriages contracted by the families of Abenhall, Archer, Kingston and de la More, whose manors were in Gloucestershire, were with families of the same shire.[6] This pattern was sometimes broken if there was an heiress to be married off. For example, Alice, sister and heiress of Edmund de Croupes, whose only manor was Whittington, near Cheltenham, married a Herefordshire man, Thomas Baskervill. Equally, families whose lands extended across a number of counties contracted marriages with a circle far wider, though still mainly within the shires where their holdings lay. The pedigrees of Acton, Bradeston, Corbet, Langley, Pauncefot, Russel, Sudeley and Veel indicate links by marriage with families in such neighbouring counties as Somerset, Dorset, Wiltshire, Herefordshire and Warwickshire.[7]

[4] See above, pp. 6–29.
[5] For example, by Hilton, *A Medieval Society*, p. 61.
[6] Sir J. Maclean, 'The History of the Manors of Dene Magna and Abenhall', pp. 182–3; *Cal. Close Rolls 1349–54*, p. 286; *Visitation of Gloucestershire*, pp. 231–3.
[7] *Visitation of Gloucestershire*, p. 131; R. Austin, 'Notes on the Family of Bradeston', *Trans. Bristol & Gloucs. Arch. Soc.*, lvii (1925), 279–86; Fosbrooke,

The network of personal connections known as bastard feudalism formed a not dissimilar geographical pattern in so far as most of those who were retained took the livery of a local magnate. In Gloucestershire and north Somerset those who sought the advantages of 'good lordship' looked to the Berkeleys of Berkeley Castle, the most important baronial family resident in the area, and to a lesser extent to such lords of the Marches as the Talbots, Mortimers and Despensers. Nevertheless, a magnate of national importance, a junior member of the royal family for example, could command the support of retainers in every county, many of them among the most substantial knights of that locality.[8] By taking such men into his pay a man like John of Gaunt could ensure that his interests received sympathetic consideration from those who carried the King's government into the shires.

Despite the predominantly local nature of such ties, retaining still posed a threat to the growing identity of gentry with shire that emerged in the fourteenth century. The Commons in parliament persistently sought to exclude from local office men who owed their prominence to magnate favour rather than to their standing in the county community; local offices, in the Commons' view, should be held by local men. That the parliamentary petitions which reiterate these demands were rooted in genuine local grievances can be demonstrated from the Gloucestershire evidence. In 1330 John de Berkeley of Dursley had complained that he could not obtain justice in his own shire because the sheriff and other ministers of the Crown were retainers of the lord of Berkeley.[9] Had the offending retainers or stewards always been men with a stake in the shire there would have been less reason to object. But too often they neither resided in the county nor had the financial resources to answer to King and people. By the end of Edward III's reign, however, the pattern of office-holding began to bear some resemblance to the

---

Abstracts . . . respecting the County of Gloucester, ii, 54; P. R. Coss, *The Langley Family and its Cartulary*; J. N. Langston, 'The Pauncefots', *Trans. Bristol & Gloucs. Arch. Soc.*, lxxi (1952), opp. p. 144; *Visitation of Gloucestershire*, p. 50; *Cal. Pat. Rolls 1413–19*, p. 399; G.E.C., xii, i, 416–17. The pedigree of the Veel family in *Visitation of Gloucestershire*, pp. 172–3, needs to be corrected from *Cal. Pat. Rolls 1292–1301*, p. 595 and C.I.P.M., viii, no. 466.

[8] See above, pp. 80–2.   [9] See above, pp. 152–3.

ideal for which the Commons had striven for so long. Stewards
and lesser retainers gradually disappeared from the more
important local offices, for example. Lengthy terms in the
shrievalty were rare after 1371, and men now lived in the shire
where they held office.[10] Whereas in 1300 a knight or esquire
would be appointed to any county where he held land and
sometimes to a county where he held none, in 1400 he held office
almost invariably in the shire where he resided. That was his shire,
his *patria*. Moreover, a hierarchy was established between the
various offices. The most substantial gentlemen became sheriffs
or secured election to parliament; their humbler colleagues had
to be content with the offices of coroner or escheator.

The petitions to which the Crown was at last persuaded to give
assent reflected the quite clear views which the gentry held about
the nature of provincial society. The knights and esquires
identified themselves with county communities within which
local loyalties and opinions were created and articulated. The
identity of gentry with shire was partly fostered by the changing
role of the county court which emerged as the institutional
expression of the community of the *comitatus*. While the purely
legal and judicial business which it handled was probably on the
decline, the court assumed far greater importance in the
fourteenth century as a political assembly where knights of the
shire were elected, royal proclamations read out, criticisms heard
and grievances aired. It was this strengthening of the ties between
gentry and shire, to which office-holding so powerfully
contributed, that Richard II challenged at the cost of his throne.

In parliament as in the shires, then, the evidence points to the
increasing political self-consciousness of the gentry. It would be
misleading to interpret this, any more than the 'rise of the
esquires', as the product of a crude economic determinism; if
there is little to suggest that the knights or the richer esquires were
forging ahead in prosperity in the fourteenth century, there is
little more to suggest that they were 'declining'. The inquisitions
post mortem imply that the smaller landowners had gone so far in
commuting labour services by 1348 that their vulnerability to
rising wage levels after the Black Death soon rendered direct

[10] See above, pp. 107–19. The closing years of Richard II's reign, however,
saw terms in the shrievalty extending to two or three years.

cultivation of demesnes unprofitable.[11] Thus it is probable that they became dependent on rental incomes sooner than the greater lords; and in the later decades of Edward III's reign it was their interest which lay behind the Commons' insistence on the enforcement of the Statutes of Labourers. The changed economic conditions of the time favoured the advancement of the substantial tenants. In the short term the expansion in the lower ranks of *les gentils*, so apparent by the early fifteenth century, produced a defensive reaction by the knights, but in the long run it may have contributed to the growing identity of the gentleborn as distinct from the parliamentary peerage.

It is as difficult in the fourteenth century as in the thirteenth to trace a definite link between the enhanced political role of the knights and their changing economic fortunes. Moreover, it may well be unnecessary. In part at least, the importance of the knights and esquires in the county communities was the handiwork not of themselves but of the Crown. On the stage of national politics they had played only a modest role in the early decades of the century. Except for the years of the baronial control of government in Edward II's reign the Commons had associated themselves with the magnate inspired critique of royal government. Once the magnates became allies of the King, however, after 1341, the Commons had to fight alone in resisting financial impositions and in critizing the Crown. But if the middle period of Edward III's reign saw the Commons attain greater freedom and independence, it also witnessed their absorption into the ranks of the ruling class.[12] After the Black Death the Commons 'began to adopt the proprietary attitude to public finance of the King and the Lords', an attitude that led in the following reign to the poll taxes.[13]

The common interests which linked nobility with gentry have, of course, become part of the standard currency of medieval history.[14] But it would be unwise to concentrate on the world of

---

[11] See above, pp. 213–7, 233–7.

[12] G. L. Harriss, *King, Parliament and Public Finance in Medieval England to 1369* (Oxford, 1975), pp. 514–16.

[13] Ibid., p. 517.

[14] The interdependence of magnates and gentry was emphasized by K. B. McFarlane, 'Parliament and Bastard Feudalism', *Trans. Roy. Hist. Soc.*, 4th series, xxvi (1944), 73.

the magnates and their retainers to the exclusion of those who lived outside the embrace of bastard feudalism. The latter may have numbered a considerable proportion of the gentry. Even supposing that the retainers were the most prominent men in the county community, simply because they enjoyed the patronage of the mighty, it would be unduly cynical to deny the independents any voice in the affairs of the shire. In parliament, moreover, it may well have been they who were most forceful in denunciation of the lawless abuses practised by magnate hangers-on in Richard II's reign.[15]

McFarlane was right to point to the complexity of the late medieval polity. Yet he may still have underestimated its subtleties.[16] In measuring their interests with the gentry, the magnates had to deal not only with their clients but also with the knights or esquires for whom there was no place on the livery roll. It would be wrong, too, to believe that the interests of the gentry, whether retainers or not, would always coincide with those of the lords. Shared sympathies may have been confined to taxation.

Commons and Lords, for example, had long had different ideas on the suppression of lawlessness. The former placed their faith in the keepers of the peace, the latter preferred commissions oyer and terminer or trailbaston. The Commons objected to the abuse of magnate power to which such heavy-handed weapons of peace keeping would surely lead—abuses which found expression not only in the practice of maintenance but also in the nomination of feed retainers as justices. In the reign of Richard II the disciplining of disorderly retainers led to further contention. The Lords' promises to discipline such hangers-on themselves failed to convince the Commons who continued to press for legislation to curb their excesses. After the Black Death magnates and gentry alike viewed with disapproval the demands of labourers who sought more pay. But the unity of the landlords may have been more apparent than real. The greater lords had the resources to pay higher wages, in the short term at least. Thus it was the smaller proprietors who were the real sufferers, not only from the demands of their own labourers but also indirectly from the drift of labour away to large landowners who were prepared, when necessary, to pay more.

[15] See above, p. 102.
[16] McFarlane, 'Parliament and Bastard Feudalism'.

If the Commons 'were more readily embraced by their political and social superiors' in the fourteenth century, nevertheless they neither abandoned their interests nor lost their identity.[17] Magnates and gentry had certain common interests: they were bound not just by indentures of retinue but by links of friendship. Nobility and gentility were shared by magnates, knights and esquires alike; yet in several important fields there was a divergence of interest between the greater and lesser lords which contributed to the growing identity and self-consciousness of the latter in parliament as well as in the shires. Were we to seek 'the rise of the gentry', we would do well to look to the fourteenth century as much as to the sixteenth.

[17] Harriss, *King, Parliament and Public Finance*, p. 517.

APPENDICES

APPENDIX I: DOCUMENTS

I

Assize of Novel Disseisin brought by Sir Nicholas de Kingston against Sir Alan Plokenet of Kilpeck (Herefordshire) in August, 1320. (K.B. 27/ 246 m. 136^d.)

Assisa capta apud Glouc' coram Henrico Spigurnel et Ade de Herwynton Justiciariis domini regis ad assisas in comitatu Glouc' capiendas assignatis die lune in crastino Sancti Laurencie anno regni regis nunc quartodecimo.

Assisa venit recognitura si Alanus Plokenet de Kilpek iniuste et sine judicio disseisivit Nicholaum de Kyngeston de libero tenemento suo in Syston etc. Et queritur quod disseisivit eum de quoddam annuo redditu duarum robarum cum pelura et linura de secta ipsius Alani et militum suorum et unius selle precium in toto centum tresdecim solidorum et quattuor denariorum per annum. Et Alanus non venit et fuit attachatus . . . Et Nicholaus pro titulo liberi tenementi sui in hac parte ostendendo dicit quod predictus Alanus concessit se teneri et obligatum esse eidem Nicholao pro servicio sibi impenso in duabus robis cum pellura et linura et una sella de secta ipsius Alani et aliorum militum suorum centum tresdecim solidorum et quattuor denariorum in omnibus valituris annuatim ad totam vitam ipsius Alani apud Syston iuxta Pokelchurch in comitatu isto ad duos terminos anni pro militibus usualibus percipiendis, ad quas quidem robas et sellas sic annuatim solvendas obligavit se heredes et assignatos suos ac manerium suum de Syston ad quorumcumque manus devenerit districtori predicti Nicholai et profert scriptum Alani etc. Et dicit quod ipse seisitus fuit de predictis robis et sella percipiendis in forma predicta quosque predictus Alanus districtionem quam idem Nicholaus fecerat in manerio de Syston pro arreragiis predictarum robarum et selle de septem annis a retro existentis rescussit etc. Et petit quod inquiratur per assisam. Ideo capiatur assisa—Iuratores dicunt quod Nicholaus seisitus fuit de predicto redditu robarum et selle etc. . . . . Ideo consideratum est quod Nicholaus recupererat inde seisinam suam versus predictum Alanum per visum recognicionis et dampna sua que taxantur per eosdem ad quaterviginti et novem marcas sex solidos et octo denarios etc. . . . . Preceptum fuit quod scire faceret predicto Alano . . . deinde continuato inde processu usque in octabis Sancti Martini proximo sequento etc. Et Alanus non venit. Ideo fiat execucio pro eius defaltis etc. Et super hoc predictus Nicholaus elegit sibi liberari omnia bona et catalla predicti Alani.

(Repetitions have not been transcribed).

2

Petition submitted by John de Berkeley of Dursley against Sir Thomas de Berkeley of Berkeley, c.1330–1.

P.R.O. Ancient Petitions, S.C.8/157/7832.

A nostre seignur le Roi a son conseil se plent Johan de Berkele de Derslee qe par ou il tient les maners de Durslee et de Neuton en la Counte de Gloucestr' de nostre dit seignur le Roi en chief par service de chivaler, Sir Thomas de Berkele qe est un des gardeins de la pees en le dit counte par sa seignurie et par force de son office destreint tortetousment le dit Johan par bestes de sa charue souvenfoitz et ne voet soeffrer nul deliveraunce estre fait par viscountz ne par bailiffs ne par nul autres ministres, kar il les tient a ses feez et a ses robes et de son menage et issint par sa seigneurie et par duresce et par colour de un novel purchacz qil ad fait ia de novel par eide et mantenaunce de Sir Roger de Mortimer nasgaires un des conseillers le Roi daver retourne du bref et de totes autres reales franchisez de deinz le hundred de Berkele, le quiel est cc li (?) enarere ad este geldable voleit acrocher a lui la tendaunce et la seignurie le dit Johan et desheritison et damage de nostre dit seignur le Roi, dount il prie remedie.

The petition is endorsed:
Soit veu le roule de Chancellerie.
Et soit ceste petition mande devant les prelatz, countes et barons qe sont assignez a surveer et examiner le dons faitz par le Roi.

3

Petition submitted by the people of the King's Barton near Gloucester against Sir Thomas de Bradeston, c.1330–40.

P.R.O. Ancient Petitions, S.C.8/97/4826.

A nostre seignur le Roi et a son bon consail monstrent ses poures lyges

gentz de la Bertoun de la fraunchise de Glouc' pur ceo qe sire Thomas
de Bradeston ad la garde de nostre seignur le Roi a tenir a sa volunte le
chastel de Glouc' ove les apurtenaunces. Le dit sire Thomas par le
consail qil ad fayt destreyndre les tenauntz ffraunkes et autres de les
mettre en autre servage qil ne deyvent fayre et les amerciez outrayuise-
mentz ereynt, issint qils sount reynt et destruyt et les uns veont geppyr
lour tenementz par dourece del gardein, kar ses gentz ne purront si mal
faire qils ne sount avowe et meyntenuz del dit sire Thom' et de sa
femme. Et auxi se fet il par Peres de Seynt Combe son vadlet, qe avoyt
ocys Will' de Melkesham les ditz sire Thomas et sa femme meynteyn-
drent tant le dit felon qil fyrent xii bons gentz estre periours, par qei il fut
aquite de la dit felonye a graunt deshonur de la corone et du Roi. Et
auxint le dit Peres devaunt Nowel cest an prist sa femme demeyne et la
lya en son lyt et fyt ardre son lyt et sa femme dedeynz le lyt tanqe a ses
genuz et quant ele fust morte et mourdry le dit Peres mist le corps en un
saak et enterra le corps en son herber et ensi demora le corps enterre vii
semaynes et plus tanqil fust consaille par ascuns de pays la deveryt
defower et la karyer a la ryvere. Set tanqe qil fust entour de karyer le
corps al ewe survendrent les parentz la dite femme et pristrent le felon et
le menerent en le chastel de Berkele. Et de illoqe fust maunde en le
chastel de Glouc' et la dame de Bradeston courteysement resceuyt le dit
Peres et ly fist seer pres de ly a maunger et le commaunda qil ne preyt ia
garde, car il serrayt auxi bien acquite de cele ffelonye come il fust de
lautre, issi qil vousit doner a ly le remenaunt de sa terre. En y tyeu
manere sount les malveytez, les malfesours, les felouns et les felonyes et
les malveys quereles meyntenuz en le dit counte, car il ne avera nulle
querele en le countee qe la dite femme et son seneschal naverount la une
partye. Issint qe les bons gentz sount rebukes et les malveys et les fous
tret avaunt et honure, par qey le countee va tut a hounte, dount ils
prient remedye si ly pleyse. Et vous plese saver qe les bons gentz qe
botent au Roi ceste bille ne osent avower les playntes, pur tant come sire
Thomas est si pres del Roi, mes apres le Roi avera mile billes sur ly et les
soens si de lour poer fuissent osteez. Car le dit Thomas ad pris deynz ces
v anz mil li des proffits au desheritaunce des bons gentz. Et fayt
pronuncyer par my le countee qil est chef consailler le Roi. Et qe nostre
seignur le Roi ne fra riens saunz son consail, par qei les gentz du countee
ne osent pleyndre od sils feissent lour playntes solom lour deserte le dit
sire Thomas et sa femme oveskes Hugh Arlos lour chief seneschal
perdreynt terres et chateux. Issi est nostre seignur desceu par tyeux kar
le dit sire Thomas se port en court come un seinturel et en son pays com
un lyon rampaunt dunt ils prient remedye.

The endorsement is indecipherable.

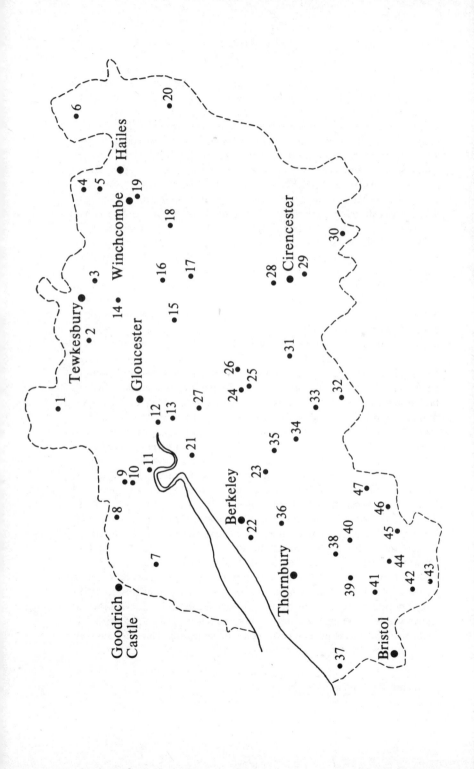

Goodrich
Castle

Tewkesbury

Gloucester

Winchcombe

Hailes

Cirencester

Berkeley

Thornbury

Bristol

•6

•20

•4
•5

•19

•18

•3

14•

•16
•17

•30

•28
•29

•2

•15

•1

•31

24 •26
•25

•12
•13

•27

•33

•32

•21

•34

•11

•35

•23

•9
•10

•47

•46

•8

•22

•36

•45

•38
•40

•44

•7

•39
•41

•42
•43

•37

APPENDIX II

Number	Manor	Resident family
1	Pauntley	Whittington
2	Hasfield	Pauncefot
3	Stoke Orchard	Archer
4	Dumbleton	Daston
5	Toddington	Tracy
6	Weston sub Edge	Giffard of Weston
7	Clearwell	Joce
8	Ruardean	Hathewy
9	Mitcheldean	de Dene/Greyndour
10	Abenhall	de Abenhall
11	Westbury	Bathonia/Gamage
12	Elmore	Guise
13	Hardwicke	Le Boteler of Llantwit
14	Boddington	de Bures
15	Brockworth	de Brocworth
16	Leckhampton	Giffard of Leckhampton
17	Coberley	Berkeley of Coberley
18	Whittington	de Croupes
19	Sudeley	de Sudeley
20	Broadwell	de Bradewell
21	Frampton-on-Severn	Clifford
22	Hill	FitzNichol
23	Dursley	Berkeley of Dursley
24	Rodborough	Rodborough of
		Rodborough

Number	Manor	Resident family
25	Senkley	Rodborough of Senkley
26	Bisley	de Bisley
27	Harescombe	de Rous
28	Daglingworth	Bluet
29	Siddington	Langley
30	Down Ampney	de Valers
31	Cherington	de la Mare
32	Shipton Moyne	de Moigne
33	Beverstone	Apadam/Berkeley of
		Beverstone
34	Lasborough	Broun
35	Uley	Berkeley of Uley
36	Cromhall	Basset
37	Kingsweston	Wauton
38	Iron Acton	Poleyn
39	Winterbourne	de Acton/Pointz
40	Yate	Bradeston
41	Mangotsfield	Wilington
42	Oldland	Blount
43	Bitton	de la More
44	Syston	de Bitton
45	Dyrham	Corbet/Denys
46	Tormarton	Russel
47	Badminton	de la Rivere
		Boteler of Badminton

APPENDIX III: THE GLOUCESTERSHIRE GENTRY: BARONIAL TIES, MILITARY SERVICE AND OFFENCES AGAINST THE LAW, 1300–1400

The five charts that follow summarize in tabular form details of baronial ties, military service and offences against the law of the Gloucestershire gentry at intervals of twenty-five years, in other words, approximately for each generation. Their purpose is simply to present for easy reference some of the evidence on which the arguments of the foregoing chapters have been based.

Column 2 names any lord by whom a knight or esquire seems likely to have been retained. An asterisk indicates that the evidence only suggests rather than confirms the relationship of lord and retainer.

Columns 3 and 4 give the years during which the knight or esquire is known to have been retained, and the sources from which the dates have been derived. For a discussion of the problems raised by the evidence see above, pp. 97–8.

Column 5 lists the dates of those military expeditions in which a Gloucestershire knight or esquire took part or expressed the intention of taking part by obtaining letters of protection from the King.

Column 6 lists the sources for military service. For a discussion of their value see above, p. 48. Full details of books cited by author or short title will be found in the bibliography.

Columns 7 and 8 list known criminal offences against the law and the sources from which the information has been extracted.

1300

Knight or Esquire	Lord	Date	Reference	Military Service	Reference	Offences	Reference
John de Abenhall	Ralph de Monthermer Gilbert de Clare, earl of Gloucester	1306–14	C.67/16 m.5 C.81/1727/15	1307	C.67/16 m.8		
Sir John de Acton							
Sir John Apadam							
Nicholas Archer							
John Basset	Thomas de Berkeley*	c.1300–10	Bod.Lib. microfilms Bk. 10, ff. 33^d, 43^d, 57^d	1298	Gough, p. 187		
Nicholas de Bathonia							
Thomas de Berkeley of Coberley (a minor)							
John de Berkeley of Arlingham	Thomas de Berkeley	1297–1309	Phillips, *Aymer de Valence*, p. 305	1298	Gough, p. 217		
David le Blount				1300	E.101/8/23		
Ralph Bluet				1298	Gough, p. 51		
Sir Thomas Boteler of Badminton							
John le Boteler of Llantwit	Thomas de Berkeley	c.1312	S.C.8/323/E563				
Sir Peter de Breouse							

Knight or Esquire	Lord	Date	Reference	Military Service	Reference	Offences	Reference
Sir John de Biton	Thomas de Berkeley	1313	Somerset Rec. Office, D/D/B Reg. 1, f. 69a				
Peter Crok							
Sir Richard de Croupes	Alan Plokenet*	1294–5	C.67/10 m. 1; C.67/11 mm. 1, 6	1303	Cal. Pat. Rolls 1301–7, p. 117		
William de Dene				1310–11	C.71/4 m. 11		
				1303	Reg. Ric. de Swinfield, Ed. W. W. Capes, p. 392		
Nicholas FitzRalph							
William Gamage	Thomas and Maurice de Berkeley	1298–1330	Phillips, Aymer de Valence, p. 305; Berkeley Castle S.R. 61	1298	Gough, p. 218		
				1306	C.67/16 m. 11		
Sir John Giffard of Leckhampton							
Sir John Giffard of Weston	Archbishop of York	1306	Reg. Greenfield, i, 168	1303	C.67/15 mm. 4, 8.	1306	Just. 1/286 m. 2
Sir Walter de Gloucester							
Sir John de Guise				1300	C.67/14 m. 10		
William Hathewy				1298	Gough, p. 192		
William Joce				1298	Gough, p. 192		

Name						
Sir Nicholas de Kingston	1298	*Bull. Inst. Hist. Res.,* xxxviii, 200–210	1298	Ibid.	1310	K.B.27/202 m.17
Sir William Maunsel						
Alan Plokenet	1313	K.B.27/246 m. 136[d]				
Sir John de Langley			1298 1300 1306	Gough, p. 34 C.67/14m. 5 *Cal. Pat. Rolls 1301–7,* p. 443		
Sir Robert de la Mare						
Sir William Maunsel Sir Nicholas de Kingston	1298	*Bull. Inst. Hist. Res.,* xxxviii, 200–210	1298	Ibid.		
Sir Henry le Moigne						
Sir Stephen de la More			1298 1300 1301 1307 1310 1300	Gough, p. 183 E.101/8/23 E.101/9/24 *Cal. Pat. Rolls 1301–7* p. 529 C.71/4 m. 10 C.67/14 m. 11		
Sir Grimbald Pauncefot			1301 1303	C.67/14 m. 7 C.67/15 m. 8		
Sir John de la Rivere	Aymer de Valence 1297–1314	Phillips, *Aymer de Valence,* pp. 256, 296	1298 1300 1301 1303	Gough, p. 216 C.67/14 m. 10 C.67/14 m. 2 C.67/15 m. 4		
Richard de la Rivere	Aymer de Valence 1297–1324	Phillips, *Aymer de Valence* pp. 256–7, 296	1298 1300	Gough, p. 216 C.67/14 m. 10	1310	K.B.27/198 m. 45
Henry of Lancaster 1308–29		"	1293 1307	C.67/15 m. 6 C.67/16 m. 5	1319	*Reg. Cobham,* ed. E. H. Pearce (W.H.S. 1930, 19).

Knight or Esquire	Lord	Date	Reference	Military Service	Reference	Offences	Reference
Sir Miles de Rodborough	Earl of Norfolk	c.1304	S.C.1/28/48			1311	Cal. Pat. Rolls 1307–13 p. 369
	King Edward II	1314	E.101/375/8 m. 33			c.1314	K.B.27/216 m. 84[d]
Thomas de Rodborough						1306	K.B.27/186 m. 23
Sir John le Rous				1300	E.101/8/23		
				1301	E.101/9/24		
				1307	C.67/16 m. 2		
				1310	C.71/4 m. 6		
Sir John de Sudeley	Chamberlain of King Edward I	1306	Cal. Pat. Rolls 1301–7, p. 460	1301	C.67/14 m. 5		
				1303	C.67/15 mm. 5, 13		
				1307	C.67/16 m. 6		
William Tracy (a minor)							
Sir Robert le Veel	Earl of Gloucester	1295	Cal. Pat. Rolls 1292–1301 p. 292				
Sir Nicholas de Valers				1298	Gough, p. 201	1313	Reg. Reynolds ed. R. A. Wilson (W.H.S., 1927), 180
				1301	E.101/9/23		
				1303	C.47/5/6		
				1307	C.67/16 m. 7		
				1310	C.71/4 m. 13		
Sir William de Wauton	Thomas & Maurice de Berkeley	1297–1330	Phillips, Aymer de Valence, p. 305	1298	Gough, p. 216		
				1300	C.67/14 m. 9		
				1301	E.101/9/23		
				1303	C.67/15 m. 10		
				1306	C.67/16 m. 11		
				1310	C.71/4 mm. 9, 10		
Sir John de Wilington				1310	C.71/4 m. 10		

Name		Date	Reference
Sir Reginald de Abenhall		1325	
Sir John de Acton		1298	Gough, p. 201
		1318	C.71/10 m. 4
		1334	Cal. Pat. Rolls 1334–8, p. 63
		1337	Cal. Pat. Rolls 1334–8, p. 514
		1339	Cal. Pat. Rolls 1338–40, p. 274
Thomas Apadam			
John Annesley		1300	C.67/14 m. 11
Richard de Apperley	Henry de Wilington	1322	Rot. Parl. ii, 410
		1322	K.B.27/247 m. 70d
Robert de Aston	Henry of Lancaster	1333	Somerville, Duchy of Lancaster, i, 354
		1316	Cal. Pat. Rolls 1313–17, p. 50
		1327	Cal. Pat. Rolls 1327–30, pp. 75, 81
		1328	Cal. Pat. Rolls 1327–30, p. 285
Geoffrey Archer		1336	E.101/19/36
Simon Basset	King Edward III	1330	
		1336	Cal. Mem. Rolls 1326–7, p. 379
Sir Nicholas de Bathonia		ante 1326	C.81/1733/109
John de Berkeley of Dursley		1333	Cal. Pat. Rolls 1330–41, p. 543
		1325	K.B.27/262 m. 6d
		1336	Cal. Pat. Rolls 1334–8, p. 283
		c.1330	C.81/193/5748

Knight or Esquire	Lord	Date	Reference	Military Service	Reference	Offences	Reference
Thomas de Berkeley of Coberley				1318	C.71/10 m. 4	1326–30	K.B.27/279 mm. 11, 21, K.B.27/280 m. 9, 100, 105, 116 K.B.27/281 mm. 28^d, 38, 51^d K.B.27/282 mm. 66, 66^d K.B.27/283 mm. 6^d, 108^d
Sir Maurice de Berkeley of Uley	King Edward III	1330–47	Cal. Pat. Rolls 1327–30, p. 530	1334 1336	C.71/13 m. 11 B.L. Nero C. VIII ff. 241^d, 242		
Hugh de Bisley	Thomas de Berkeley	1320	Jeayes, pp. 155–6				
Richard le Blount							
Sir Ralph Bluet	Gilbert and Richard Talbot	1333–47	E.159/112 m. 103^d C.76/25 m. 16	1347	E.159/112 m. 103^d		
Sir John de Bures	Earl of Lancaster	1317–22	G. Holmes, Estates of the Higher Nobility, p. 135	1314 1317 1318	E.159/101 mm. 156, 157 C.71/9 m. 8 C.71/10 m. 4		

Name		Date	Reference	Date	Reference
John de Bitton				1331	Cal. Pat. Rolls 1330-4, p. 217
Sir Thomas Boteler of Badminton					
John le Boteler of Llantwit	Hugh Despenser Younger	1322-6	Rot. Parl. ii, 385	c.1312; c.1322-6; c.1322-6; 1331	S.C.8/323/E563; Rot. Parl. ii, 385; S.C.8/72/3571; K.B.27/285 m. 148
Thomas de Brocworth		1322	S.C.8/112/5564		
Henry de Clifford		1330-5	Stafford Rec. Office D.641/1/2/119-23		
Peter Corbet					
Sir Richard de Croupes					
William de Dene		1313-19	Sir Christopher Hatton's Book of Seals, ed. Loyd. Stenton, no. 127		
Hugh Despenser elder			Cal. Close Rolls 1313-18, pp. 352-3		
Maurice de Berkeley		1316-46	Cal. Close Rolls 1313-18, pp. 352-3; Cal. Pat Rolls 1345-8, p. 12; Smyth, i, 227n., 228n., 342-3		
John FitzNichol		1320	Smyth, i, 228		
Richard de Foxcote				1327; 1327; 1328	Cal. Pat. Rolls 1327-30, p. 75; Cal. Pat. Rolls 1327-30, pp. 80-1; Cal. Pat. Rolls 1327-30, p. 285

Knight or Esquire	Lord	Date	Reference	Military Service	Reference	Reference	Reference
William Gamage	Thomas & Maurice de Berkeley	1297–1330	Phillips, *Aymer de Valence*, p. 305			1326–30	**K.B.**27/283 m. 108^d
Sir John Giffard of Leckhampton							
John Giffard of Weston				1327	C.71/11 m. 6		
Sir Walter de Gloucester				1318	C.71/10 mm. 4, 13	1315	*Cal. Pat. Rolls 1313–17,* p. 410
William Hathewy						1324–5	**K.B.**27/255 Rex m. 24^d
Sir Philip Joce							Moor, ii, 166–7
Sir John de Guise				1316–17	C.71/9 m. 7	1318	**K.B.**27/279 m. 41
						c.1330	
Sir John de Langley							
Peter de la Mare				1318	C.71/10 mm. 4, 12	1322	*Cal. Pat. Rolls 1321–4,* p. 162
				1322	*Cal. Pat. Rolls 1321–4,* p. 199	c.1328	**K.B.**27/274 Rex m. 18
				1333	*Cal. Pat. Rolls 1330–4,* p. 456		
John le Moigne							
Aymer Pauncefot	Roger Mortimer of Chirk	1318–21	C.71/9 m. 8; *Cal. Pat. Rolls 1321–4,* p. 19	1316–17	C.71/9 mm. 5, 8	1329	*Cal. Close Rolls 1327–30,* p. 471
				1318	C.71/10 m. 3		
				1325	E.101/16/39		

Sir Richard de la Rivere	Henry of Lancaster 1308–29	Phillips, *Aymer de Valence*, pp. 256–7	1318	C.71/10 mm. 2, 12	1322	*Cal. Pat. Rolls 1321–4*, pp. 153–4
			1325	C.61/36 m. 5	1326	K.B.27/286 m. 42
					1328	*Cal. Pat. Rolls 1327–30*, p. 285
Sir John de la Rivere			1333	C.71/13 m. 28		*Catalogue of Eng. Med. Rolls of Arms*, ed. Wagner, p. 55
			1335			
Sir Thomas de Rodborough	1327–9	Berkeley Castle, S.R. 39, 61, 63	1318	C.71/10 m. 12	1319	*Cal. Pat. Rolls 1317–21*, p. 307
Sir John le Rous						
Sir John de Sudeley			1318	C.71/10 m. 4		
Sir William Tracy	1326–52	Smyth i, 313			c.1328	K.B.27/274 Rex m. 18
Sir Peter le Veel						
Sir William de Wauton	1297–1327	Phillips, *Aymer de Valence*, p. 305	1320	*Cal. Pat. Rolls 1317–21*, p. 432	1324	Smyth, i, 239
Sir William de Whittington			1327	C.71/11 m. 6	1332	K.B.27/287 m. 20[d]
William le Walsh	Aymer de Valence 1315	*Rot. Parl.*, i, 311			1321	*Cal. Pat. Rolls 1317–21*, p. 544
Sir John de Wilington			1314	*Trans. B.G.A.S.*, xxi, 10–11		
			1315–16	*Parl. Writs* ii, ii, 458		
			1327	C.71/11 m. 6		

1350

Knight or Esquire	Lord	Date	Reference	Military Service	Reference	Offences	Reference
Sir Ralph de Abenhall	Richard Talbot*	1347	S.C.1/39/187 C.76/24 m. 20	1347 1340	Wrottesley, p. 280 C.76/15 m. 20		
Sir Robert de Apperley	Thomas de Bradeston	1345–7	C.81/1721/26, 31 C.76/20 m. 8				
				1344 1347 1347	C.76/19 m. 22 Wrottesley, p. 151 Wrottesley, p. 126	1351	Cal. Pat. Rolls 1350–4, pp. 166, 206
Sir John de Acton Thomas Apadam Geoffrey Archer							
Sir Simon Basset	King Edward III	1330	Cal. Mem. Rolls 1326–7, p. 379	1337 1338	E.101/388/5 m. 10 C.76/12 m. 4		
	Thomas de Berkeley	c.1330–60	Jeayes, pp. 154, 163	1340 1342 1346 1347 1360 1362	C.76/15 m. 21 C.76/17 m. 24 Wrottesley, p. 140 Wrottesley, p. 201 C.76/38 m. 18 C.61/75 m. 4		
Sir Thomas de Berkeley of Coberley				1355	C.61/67 m. 8		

Name	Lord / Period	Year	Reference	Additional reference	Additional reference
Sir Nicholas de Berkeley of Dursley		1360	C.76/38 m. 14		
Sir Maurice de Berkeley of Uley	King Edward III 1330–47	1338	C.76/12 m. 4	Cal. Pat. Rolls 1327–30, p. 530; Smyth, i, 248	
		1340	C.76/15 m. 21		
		1342	C.76/17 m. 27		
		1346	Wrottesley p. 136		
		1347	Wrottesley p. 136		
Edmund Blount					
Sir Ralph Bluet	Gilbert and Richard Talbot 1333–47	1347	Wrottesley p. 133	E.159/112 m. 103d; C.76/25 m. 16	K.B.27/349 m. 17d (1347)
John le Boteler of Park					
Sir Thomas le Boteler of Badminton		1340	C.76/15 m. 20		
Henry de Brocworth					
Sir John de Bures					
Matthew de Bitton					K.B.27/318 Rex m. 19d (1339)
Edward Cardiff	Sir Guy Brien* 1353			Cal. Pat. Rolls 1350–4, p. 491	
Sir William de Careswell		1336	C.71/16 mm. 5, 17		
		1340	C.76/15 m. 20		
		1342	C.76/17 m. 24		
		1346	Wrottesley, p. 136		
		1347	Wrottesley, p. 151		

Knight or Esquire	Lord	Date	Reference	Military Service	Reference	Offences	Reference
William de Cheltenham	Thomas de Berkeley	c.1330–60	Smyth, i, 342			1322	K.B.27/247 m. 76d
Sir Peter Corbet						1324	K.B.27/256 m. 21
Edmund Croupes				1347	Wrottesley, p. 147	1355	K.B.27/390 m. 36d
John de Clifford							
Sir Walter Daston	Earl of Warwick	1342–7	C.76/17 m. 39 Wrottesley, pp. 32, 238	1342 1346 1347	C.76/17 m. 39 Cal. Pat. Rolls 1345–8, p. 495 Wrottesley, pp. 32, 238	1345	Cal. Pat. Rolls 1345–8, p. 35
John FitzNichol	Maurice de Berkeley* junior	1346	Cal. Pat. Rolls 1345–8, p. 121				
John Giffard of Leckhampton							
John Giffard of Weston							
Sir Walter de Gloucester						1340	Cal. Pat. Rolls 1340–3, p. 100
Laurence Greyndour	John of Gaunt	1362	Cal. Close Rolls 1360–4, p. 418				
Sir John de Guise				1338 1342	C.76/12 m. 4 C.76/17 m. 27		
Sir Robert de Hildesley				1335 1338	C.71/15 m. 30 C.71/18 m. 23		

Name	Lord	Dates	Source	Year	Reference	Year	Reference
William Hathewy				1346	Wrottesley p. 91		
John Joce				1347	Wrottesley, p. 121		
Sir Peter de la Mare	Henry of Grosmont	1338–49	Fowler, *Henry of Grosmont*, p. 284 n. 40	1338	C.76/12 m. 8		
				1340	C.76/15 m. 18		
Sir Robert de la Mare	Henry of Grosmont	1338–61	Fowler, *Henry of Grosmont*, p. 284 n. 40	1342	C.76/17 m. 26		
				1347	Wrottesley, p. 140		
				1338	C.76/12 m. 8		
				1344	C.76/19 m. 19		
Sir Thomas Moigne	Richard Talbot	1356	E.159/143 Easter Recorda	1356	C.76/34 m. 14		
				1355	C.76/33 m. 7		
				1360	*Cal. Pat. Rolls 1358–61*, pp. 401, 520		
William Maunsel	John Talbot of Richard's Castle	1351	S.C.1/41/105	1346	Wrottesley, p. 117		
Sir Grimbald Pauncefot							
Hugh Pauncefot				1347	Wrottesley, p. 182		
Sir John de la Rivere				1338	C.71/18		
Thomas de Rodborough				1347	Wrottesley, p. 155	1352	K.B.27/366 m. 30[d]
Hugh de Rodborough				1346	Wrottesley, p. 91		
Thomas le Rous				1355	C.76/33 m. 11		

Knight or Esquire	Lord	Date	Reference	Military Service	Reference	Offences	Reference
Sir John de Sudeley				1362	C.61/75 m. 4		
				1363	C.61/76 m. 6		
				1365	C.61/78 m. 5		
				1366	C.61/79 m. 8		
Sir John Tracy	Thomas de Berkeley	1352–89	Smyth i, 313	1347	Shaw *The Knights of England*, ii, 6		
Sir Peter le Veel				1338	C.76/13 m. 13		
				1339	C.76/14 m. 13		
				1342	C.76/17 m. 18		
Sir Peter le Veel junior	Black Prince	1352–62	*Black Prince's Reg.*, iv, 74, 384, 403	1352	C.76/30 m. 7		
Andrew Walsh				1355	C.61/67 m. 8		
				1359	C.76/37 m. 3		
William Whittington	Hugh Despenser	1346–8	C.76/22 m. 7; S.C.1/39/194	1346	Wrottesley, pp. 84, 92		
				1347	Wrottesley, p. 141		
Sir Ralph Wilington				1341	C.71/21 m. 5		
				1347	Wrottesley, pp. 105, 155		

Sir Thomas Apadam					
Edmund Basset					
Thomas de Berkeley of Coberley	John of Gaunt	1381	*John of Gaunt's Reg.*, 1379–83, i, no. 35	1368 1377	K.B.27/429 m. 30^d K.B.27/493 m. 17
Sir Nicholas de Berkeley of Dursley	Maurice & Thomas Berkeley	1367	Smyth, ii, 3	1378	K.B.27/471 Rex m. 22^d
Sir Thomas de Berkeley of Uley		1355 1360	C.76/33 m. 8 C.76/38 m. 18		
Hugh Bisley					
Edmund Blount				1363	K.B.27/411 Rex m. 17
Aymer le Boteler of Park				1368 1377–8	*Cal. Pat. Rolls 1367–70*, p. 196 K.B.27/471 Rex m. 5
Sir Alan Boteler of Badminton					
Sir Thomas Boteler of Sudeley					
Sir Edmund Bradeston	The King	1368–95	*Cal. Pat. Rolls 1377–81*, p. 317	1360	C.76/38 m. 11
Thomas de Bridges	Elizabeth Despenser	1378	K.B.27/471 Rex m. 9^d;		
	John of Gaunt	1379–82	*John of Gaunt's Reg.*, 1379–83, i, nos. 70, 644		

1375

Knight or Esquire	Lord	Date	Reference	Military Service	Reference	Offences	Reference
Sir John Bromwich	Lionel of Clarence	1370	*Cal. Pat. Rolls 1370-4*, p. 87	1360	C.76/38 m. 14		
	Earl of March	1381	*Cal. Close Rolls 1381-5*, p. 59	1363	E.101/28/15		
				1374-5	C.76/57 m. 8		
	John of Gaunt	c.1380	*John of Gaunt's Reg., 1379-83*, i, 9				
John de Bitton				1372	E.101/32/26		
Henry de Clifford							
Thomas Daston				1369	C.61/82 m. 7		
Gilbert Denys				1378	C.76/62 m. 18		
				1383	C.76/67 m. 17; *Cal. Pat. Rolls 1381-5*, p. 111		
John FitzNichol							
John Foxcote							
Sir Gilbert Giffard	Earl of Hereford	1371-3	C.I.P.M., xiv, no. 29	1385-6	C.76/70 m. 32		
				1370	E.101/30/25		
				1371	E.101/31/15		
				1372	E.101/32/20		
John Giffard of Leckhampton	John of Gaunt	1381	*John of Gaunt's Reg., 1379-83*, i, no. 36	1373	C.76/56 mm. 18, 23		
John Giffard of Weston				1369	C.61/82 m. 7		

Name	Date	Reference
Ralph Greyndour	1374–5	C.76/57 m. 13
	1387	K.B.27/507 Rex m. 31
	1396	K.B.27/544 Rex m. 22ᵈ
Anselm Guise		
John Joce	1383	K.B.9/32 m. 6
Lionel of Clarence	1364	Cal. Pat. Rolls 1364–70, p. 56
King Edward III	1370	Cal. Pat. Rolls 1370–4, p. 27
	1371	E.101/31/11
	1378	B. L. MS Stowe 440 f.17ᵈ
Sir Peter de la Mare		
Philip Maunsel		
Robert Palet		
Hugh Pauncefot		
Sir John Pointz	1351	Cal. Pat. Rolls 1350–4, pp. 166, 206
Edward Despenser	1367	K.B.27/429 m. 21
Sir Henry de la Rivere		
William Rodborough		
Hugh Rodborough		
Maurice Russel		
Thomas de Berkeley 1384–95	1380	K.B.27/536 Rex m. 21ᵈ; Just. 3/180 m. 27
	c.1385	C.76/64 m. 19
Richard Ruyhall	c.1385	K.B.27/536 Rex m. 21ᵈ
Laurence Sebrok	1362	C.61/75 m. 4
	1368	K.B.27/429 Rex m.5
	1369	C.81/1712/31
	1374–5	E.101/33/15
	1377	C.76/61 m. 22

Knight or Esquire	Lord	Date	Reference	Military Service	Reference	Offences	Reference
John Sergeant	Earl of Stafford	1366–72	Stafford Rec. Office D. 641/1/2/135–42			1367	Cal. Pat. Rolls 1367–70, p. 69
	Thomas de Berkeley	1378	Just.3/60/4 m. 21^d				
	John of Gaunt	1379–82	John of Gaunt's Reg., 1379–83, i, nos. 75, 644				
Sir John Thorp	King Richard II	1365–86	Cal. Pat. Rolls 1377–81, p. 157	1372	E.101/32/26		
Sir John Tracy	Thomas de Berkeley	1352–89	Smyth, i, 313; ii, 3				
Sir Peter le Veel				1362–67	C.61/75–80	1368	K.B.27/429 m. 30^d
				1370	C.61/83 m. 7		
				1372	C.76/55 m. 17		
				1378	C.76/62 m. 21		
				1380–1	E.101/68/8/194		
Ralph Walsh	Thomas de Berkeley	1373	Berkeley Castle a/c of William atte Nash			1387	Cal. Pat. Rolls 1385–9, p. 358
William Whittington							
Sir John Wilington				1369	C.76/52 m. 3		

1400

Name							
Thomas Apadam							
Edmund Basset							
Sir Thomas de Berkeley of Coberley	John of Gaunt	1381	*John of Gaunt's Reg.*, *1379–83*, i, no. 35				
Sir John Berkeley of Beverstone		1380–1	C.76/65 m. 27				S.C.8/139/6916
Sir Maurice Berkeley of Uley	John of Gaunt	1391–99	*Camden Miscellany*, xxii, 103	1380	C.76/64 mm. 2, 25	n.d.	
				1383	C.76/67 mm. 9, 16		
				1385–6	C.76/70 m. 33		
	King Richard II	1399	*Cal. Pat. Rolls 1397–9*, p. 544	1393–5	C.61/104 m. 9		
William Blount							
Hugh Bisley							
Ralph Boteler of Badminton					1395		C.258/33 m. 3
Sir Thomas Boteler of Sudeley		1394	*Cal. Pat. Rolls 1391–6*, p. 472.				
Thomas Bradeston		1369	G.E.C., ii, 273				
		1373	C.76/56 m. 23				
Thomas de Bridges	Thomas Despenser 1378–99	Just.3/180 m. 26					
	Earl of Warwick 1391–5	Just. 3/180 mm. 21ᵈ, 26ᵈ				1396	K.B.27/544 m. 55
	Earl of Stafford 1397–8	Stafford Rec. Office D.641/1/2/154					
John Brouning	Thomas Despenser 1394–1400	*Cal. Pat. Rolls 1391–6*, p. 510	1394	*Cal. Pat. Rolls 1391–6*, p. 510			
		Cal. Close Rolls 1399–1402, p. 306					

Knight or Esquire	Lord	Date	Reference	Military Service	Reference	Offences	Reference
Sir John Cassy							
Sir John Cheyne	The King	1374–1410	J. S. Roskell, *Trans. B.G.-A.S.*, 75, 43–72	1394	*Cal. Pat. Rolls 1391–6*, p. 472		
James Clifford	Kings Richard II & Henry IV	1396–*c.*1413	E.101/403/10 m. 44^d, *Cal. Pat. Rolls 1399–1401*, p. 191	1394	*Cal. Pat. Rolls 1391–6*, p. 483	1385	Just. 3/172 m. 6
						1386–14	*Rot. Parl.* iii, 514
						1396	*Cal. Pat. Rolls 1392–6*, p. 516
						1399	*Cal. Pat. Rolls 1396–9*, p. 585
						1395–	*Rot. Parl.* iii, 513,
						1406	S.C.8/190/9473
						1393	K.B.27/530 m.41^d
John Clifford of Daneway							
John Couley	Thomas de Berkeley	1393	Just. 3/180 m. 24^d				
John Derhurst							
William Denys							
Sir Gilbert Denys	Thomas de Berkeley	1417	Jeayes, p. 182	1383	C.76/67 mm. 12, 17	1412	*Cal. Pat. Rolls 1408–13*, p. 433
	Earl of Stafford	1406	S.C.6/924/20				
Sir Thomas FitzNichol	Earl of Stafford	1388–9	Stafford Rec. Office D.641/1/2/152	1380	C.76/64 m. 2		

Name	Associate	Date	Reference	Date	Reference
John Giffard of Leckhampton					
John Giffard of Weston					
Sir John Greyndour	Gilbert Talbot	1397	Cal. Pat. Rolls 1396–9, p. 138		
	King Henry IV	1399	Cal. Pat. Rolls 1399–1401 p. 10		
	Thomas de Berkeley	1407	Smyth, ii, 23	1407	Smyth, i, 23
Anselm Guise				1395–1402	Rot. Parl. iii, 513
Sir Peter de la Mare					
Sir John Pauncefot	Earl of March	1394–8	Cal. Pat. Rolls 1391–6, p. 481	1394	Cal. Pat. Rolls 1391–6, p. 481
	King Henry IV	1401	Cal. Pat. Rolls 1399–1401, pp. 196, 426; Cal. Close Rolls 1402–6, p. 103	1400	Cal. Pat. Rolls 1399–1401, p. 426
Robert Pointz	Lady Despenser	1401	Cal. Close Rolls 1399–1402, p. 306	1383	C.76/67 mm. 15, 20
Earl of Stafford		1401–2	Stafford Rec. Office D.641/1/2/156 S.C.8/148/7355		
John Poleyn	Thomas de Berkeley	1388–90	S.C.8/148/7355	1388	S.C.8/148/7355
Sir Henry de la Rivere				1387–8	E.101/40/33
Edmund Rodborough					

Knight or Esquire	Lord	Date	Reference	Military Service	Reference	Offences	Reference
Sir Maurice Russel							
Richard Ruyhall	Thomas de Berkeley	1384–95	K.B.27/536 Rex m. 21^d, Just. 3/180 m. 27	1380	C.76/64 m. 19		
	Earl of Warwick	c.1390	C.115/K.2/6684 f. 166				
Lionel Sebrok	Thomas de Berkeley	1417	Jeayes, p. 183				
John Stanshawe							
William Tracy	Thomas de Berkeley	1384–6	K.B.27/536 Rex m. 21^d				
Henry le Veel							
Sir Peter le Veel						1391	K.B.27/521 Rex m. 30
Robert Whittington	King Henry IV	1400	Cal. Pat. Rolls 1399–1401, p. 183	1375	E.364/10 m. 4		

BIBLIOGRAPHY

I Manuscript Sources
II Printed Sources
III Secondary Sources

I MANUSCRIPT SOURCES

Public Record Office

C.47	Chancery Miscellanea
C.61	Gascon Rolls
C.67	Supplementary Patent Rolls
C.71	Scottish Rolls
C.76	French Rolls
C.81	Chancery Warrants
C.115/K.2/6684	Register of William de Cheryton, Prior of Llanthony
C.115/L.1/6688	Register of Simon de Brocworth, Prior of Llanthony
C.267/9	Certificates of election of keepers of the peace
C.P.25	Feet of Fines
D.L.3/35	Duchy of Lancaster, rental of the manor of Tibberton
E.36	Wardrobe Books
E.101	King's Remembrancer, Various Accounts
E.142/24	Extents of the Contrariants' lands
E.159	Exchequer Memoranda Rolls
E.179	Poll tax returns
Just. 1	Assize Rolls
Just. 3	Gaol Delivery Rolls
K.B.9	Ancient Indictments
K.B.27	King's Bench Rolls
Prob. 11/2A	Prerogative Court of Canterbury, Reg. Marche
S.C.1	Ancient Correspondence
S.C.6	Ministers' Accounts
S.C.8	Ancient Petitions
S.C.12/36/11	Extents of the Contrariants' lands

British Library
Additional Charters—   Rentals of the manor of Oldland
    26434, 26441
Egerton Charter 754   Ampney Crucis
Stowe Charter 622   Will of Sir Fulk de Pembridge

Berkeley Castle
    Select Rolls
    Series of Charters

Somerset County Record Office
    D/D/B Register 1 (Register of John de Drokensford, Bishop of Bath
    and Wells)

Stafford County Record Office
    D.641/1/2/117–156 (Accounts of the Receiver of Thornbury)

Worcester Cathedral Library
    Rolls of the Cellarer of the Cathedral Priory

Westminster Abbey
    24406, 24411 (Accounts of the Abbot's Receiver in Western Parts)

II PRINTED SOURCES

Abstracts of Inquisitions post Mortem for Gloucestershire, vol. iv, ed.
    S. J. Madge (Index Library, 1903); vol. v, ed. E. A. Fry (Index
    Library, 1910); vol. vi, ed. E. Stokes (Index Library, 1914).
Anglo-Norman Letters and Petitions, ed. M. D. Legge (Anglo-Norman
    Text Society, iii, 1941).
M. Basset, *Knights of the Shire for Bedfordshire* (Bedfordshire Historical
    Record Society, xxix, 1949).
S. W. Bates Harbin, *Members of Parliament for the County of Somerset*
    (Somerset Archaeological and Natural History Society, 1939).
Black Prince's Register (London: H.M.S.O., 4 vols., 1930–3).
Calendar of Close Rolls, 1296–1402 (London: H.M.S.O., 27 vols., 1906–
    27).
Calendar of Fine Rolls, 1272–1405 (London: H.M.S.O., 12 vols., 1911–
    31).
Calendar of Inquisitions Miscellaneous (London: H.M.S.O., 7 vols., 1916–
    68).
Calendar of Memoranda Rolls, 1326–7 (London: H.M.S.O., 1968).
Calendar of Patent Rolls, 1292–1401 (London: H.M.S.O., 30 vols., 1895–
    1903).

Calendar of Inquisitions post Mortem, Edward I–Richard II (London, H.M.S.O., 15 vols., 1906–74).

Cartulary of Cirencester Abbey, vols. i & ii, ed. C. D. Ross (Oxford, 1964).

Cartulary of Oseney Abbey, vol. v, ed. H. E. Salter (Oxford History Society, xcviii, 1935).

Chandos Herald, *Life of the Black Prince*, ed. M. K. Pope and E. C. Lodge (Oxford, 1910).

Chronicon Henrici Knighton, vol. ii, ed. J. R. Lumby (Rolls Series, 1890).

Chronicle of Pierre de Langtoft, vol. ii, ed. T. Wright (Rolls Series, 1868).

Collectanea Topographica et Genealogica.

Documents of the Baronial Movement of Reform and Rebellion, ed. R. F. Treharne and I. J. Sanders (Oxford, 1973).

English Historical Documents, 1189–1327, ed. H. R. Rothwell (London, 1975).

Engravings from Ancient Seals . . . in the Muniment Room of Stowe Bardolf, ed. G. H. Dashwood (Stowe Bardolf, 2 vols., 1847, 1862).

Feudal Aids, 1284–1431 (London: H.M.S.O., 6 vols., 1899–1920).

Glossarium ad Scriptores Mediae et Infimae Latinitatis, ed. D. du Cange (Paris, 6 vols., 1733–6).

Gloucestershire Subsidy Roll, 1 Edward III, 1327 (Middle Hill Press, n.d.).

H. Gough, *Scotland in 1298* (Paisley, 1888).

Herald and Genealogist, vol. iv, ed. J. G. Nichols (London, 1867).

Historia et Cartularium Monasterii Sancti Petri Gloucestriae, ed. W. H. Hart (Rolls Series, 3 vols., 1863–7).

I. H. Jeayes, *Catalogue of the Charters and Muniments . . . at Berkeley Castle* (Bristol, 1892).

John of Gaunt's Register, 1379–83, ed. E. Lodge and R. Somerville (Camden Society, 3rd series, lvi–lvii, 1937).

Knights Hospitaller in England, ed. L. B. Larkin (Camden Society, 1857).

Landboc . . . de Winchelcumba, ed. D. Royce (Exeter, 2 vols., 1892, 1903).

List of Escheators for England (P.R.O., Lists and Indexes, lxxii, 1932).

List of Sheriffs for England and Wales (P.R.O., List and Indexes, ix, 1898).

Parliamentary Writs, ed. F. Palgrave, 2 vols. in 4 (London, 1827–34).

Register of Godfrey Giffard, Bishop of Worcester, ed. J. W. Willis-Bund (Worcestershire Historical Society, 1902).

Registrum Ricardi de Swinfield, Bishop of Hereford, ed. W. W. Capes (Canterbury and York Society, 1909).

Register of Thomas de Cobham, Bishop of Worcester, 1317–27, ed. E. H. Pearce (Worcestershire Historical Society, 1930).

Register of William de Greenfield, Archbishop of York, 1306–15, vol. i, ed. A. H. Thompson (Surtees Society, cxlv, 1931).

Return of Members of Parliament, vol. i (House of Commons, 1878).

Rolls of the Gloucestershire Sessions of the Peace, 1361–98, ed. E. C. Kimball

(Transactions of the Bristol & Gloucestershire Archaeological Society, lxii, 1940).

Rotuli Parliamentorum, ed. J. Strachey (London, 6 vols., 1767–83).

Rotuli Parliamentorum Anglie Hactenus Inediti, ed. H. G. Richardson and G. O. Sayles (Camden Society, 3rd series, li, 1935).

Select Cases in the Court of King's Bench, Edward II, vol. iv (Selden Society, 74, 1955).

Select Cases in the Court of King's Bench, Edward III, vol. v (Selden Society, 76, 1957).

Select Cases in the Court of King's Bench, Edward III, vol. vi (Selden Society, 82, 1965).

Select Cases in the Court of King's Bench, Richard II, Henry IV, Henry V, vol. vii (Selden Society, 88, 1971).

Sede Vacante Register, vol. iv, ed. J. W. Willis-Bund (Worcestershire Historical Society, 1897).

J. Smyth, *The Berkeley MSS. I and II, The Lives of the Berkeleys; III, The Hundred of Berkeley*, ed. J. Maclean (Gloucester, 1883–5).

Statutes of the Realm.

Two Cartularies of Bath Abbey, ed. W. Hunt (Somerset Record Society, vii, 1893).

Visitation of the County of Gloucester, ed. J. Maclean and W. C. Heane (Harleian Society, xxi, 1885).

Walter of Henley and other Treatises on Estate Management and Accounting, ed. D. Oschinsky (Oxford, 1971).

G. Wrottesley, *Crecy and Calais* (London, 1898).

'Rolls of the Collectors in the West Riding of the Lay Subsidy (Poll Tax) 2 Richard II', *Yorkshire Archaeological and Topographical Journal*, v, 1–51, 241–66, 417–32; vi, 1–45, 129–71, 287–342; vii, 6–31, 145–86.

III SECONDARY SOURCES

Adam-Even, P., 'Les Sceaux d'Ecuyers au xiii[e] Siecle', *Archives heraldiques suisses*, lxv (1951), 19–29.

Atkyns, Sir R., *The Ancient and Present State of Gloucestershire* (2nd edn., London, 1768).

Austin, R., 'Notes on the Family of Bradeston', *Transactions of the Bristol and Gloucsestershire Archaeological Society*, xlvii (1925), 279–86.

Barkley, Sir H., 'The Berkeleys of Coberley', ibid., xvii (1892–3), 109–26.

——, 'The Berkeleys of Dursley', ibid., ix (1884–5), 227–76.

Batten, J., 'Stoke-sub-Hamden', *Transactions of the Somerset Archaeological and Natural History Society*, new series, xx (1894), 236–54.

Bean, J. M. W., *The Decline of English Feudalism, 1215–1540* (Manchester, 1968).
——, *The Estates of the Percy Family, 1416–1537* (Oxford, 1958).
Bellamy, J., *Crime and Public Order in England in the Later Middle Ages* (London, 1973).
Bridbury, A. R., 'The Black Death', *Economic History Review*, 2nd series, xxiv (1973), 577–92.
Britnell, R. H., 'Production for the Market on a Small Fourteenth Century Estate', ibid., 2nd series, xix (1966), 380–7.
Cam, H. M., *The Hundred and the Hundred Rolls* (London, 1930).
——, *Liberties and Communities in Medieval England* (Cambridge, 1944).
Cambridge Economic History of Europe, i, ed. M. M. Postan (Cambridge, 1966).
Campbell, M., *The English Yeoman* (London, 2nd edn., 1960).
Carpenter, D. A., 'The Decline of the Curial Sheriff in England 1194–1258', *English Historical Review*, xci (1976), 1–32.
Chaplais, P., *English Royal Documents* (Oxford, 1971).
Chew, H. M., *The English Ecclesiastical Tenants-in-Chief and Knight Service* (Oxford, 1932).
Child, F. J., *The English and Scottish Popular Ballads*, iii (New York, 1956).
Complete Peerage, The, ed. G.E.C., revised by Vicary Gibbs, H. A. Doubleday and Lord Howard de Walden, 12 vols. in 13 (London, 1910–57).
Cornwall, J., 'Early Tudor Gentry', *Economic History Review*, 2nd series, xvii (1964–5), 456–71.
Coss, P. R., *The Langley Family and its Cartulary* (Dugdale Society Occasional Papers, 22, 1974).
——, 'Sir Geoffrey de Langley and the Crisis of the Knightly Class in Thirteenth-Century England', *Past and Present*, 68 (1975), 3–37.
Darby, H. C., *Domesday England* (Cambridge, 1977).
Davies, J. C., *The Baronial Opposition to Edward II* (Cambridge, 1918).
Davies, R. R., 'The Bohun and Lancaster Lordships in Wales in the Fourteenth and Early Fifteenth Centuries' (Oxford D.Phil. thesis, 1965).
Davis, C. T., *The Monumental Brasses of Gloucestershire* (reprinted, Bath, 1969).
Denholm-Young, N., *Collected Papers* (Cardiff, 1969).
——, *The Country Gentry in the Fourteenth Century* (Oxford, 1969).
——, *History and Heraldry, 1254–1310* (Oxford, 1965).
——, *Seignorial Administration in England* (Oxford, 1937).
Du Boulay, F. R. H., and C. M. Barron (eds.), *The Reign of Richard II* (London, 1971).
Dugdale, Sir W., *The Antiquities of Warwickshire* (London, 1656).

Ellacombe, H. T., *History of the Parish of Bitton* (Exeter, 1881–3).

Emden, A. B., *A Biographical Register of the University of Oxford to A.D. 1500* (3 vols., Oxford, 1957–9).

Fosbrooke, T. D., *Abstracts . . . respecting the County of Gloucester* (Gloucester, 2 vols., 1807).

Fowler, K., *The King's Lieutenant: Henry of Grosmont* (London, 1969).

Gibson, S. T., 'The Escheatries, 1327–41', *English Historical Review*, xxxvi (1921), 218–25.

Glasscock, R. E., *The Lay Subsidy of 1334* (London, 1975).

Gloucestershire Studies, ed. H. P. R. Finberg (Leicester, 1957).

Goodman, A., *The Loyal Conspiracy* (London, 1971).

Gray, I., 'A Berkeley Ransom', *Transactions of the Bristol and Gloucestershire Archaeological Society*, lxxxviii (1969), 213–15.

Harding, A., *The Law Courts of Medieval England* (London, 1973).

Harriss, G. L., *King, Parliament and Public Finance in Medieval England to 1369* (Oxford, 1975).

Harvey, B. F., 'The Leasing of the Abbot of Westminster's Demesnes in the Later Middle Ages', *Economic History Review*, 2nd series, xxii (1969), 17–27.

——, *Westminster Abbey and its Estates in the Middle Ages* (Oxford, 1977).

Harvey, S., 'The Knight and the Knight's Fee in England', *Past and Present*, 49 (1970), 3–43.

Hewitt, H. J., *The Organisation of War under Edward III* (Manchester, 1966).

Hilton, R. H., *The Decline of Serfdom in Medieval England* (Economic History Society, 1969).

——, *The Economic Development of some Leicestershire Estates in the Fourteenth and Fifteenth Centuries* (Oxford, 1947).

——, *The English Peasantry in the Later Middle Ages* (Oxford, 1975).

——, *A Medieval Society: the West Midlands at the End of the Thirteenth Century* (London, 1966).

Holmes, G. A., *The Estates of the Higher Nobility in Fourteenth-Century England* (Cambridge, 1957).

Holt, J. C., 'The Origins and Audience of the Ballads of Robin Hood', *Past and Present*, 18 (1960), 89–110.

Hunnisett, R. F., 'Medieval Coroners Rolls', *American Journal of Legal History*, iii (1959), 95–124.

——, *The Medieval Coroner* (Cambridge, 1961).

Jenner-Fust, H., 'Hill, Gloucestershire', *Transactions of the Bristol and Gloucestershire Archaeological Society*, liii (1931), 145–90.

Jones, M., 'An Indenture between Robert, Lord Mohaut, and Sir John de Bracebridge for life service in peace and war, 1310', *Journal of the Society of Archivists*, iv (1972), 384–94.

Keen, M. H., *England in the Later Middle Ages* (London, 1973).

Knowles, D., *The Religious Orders in England* (Cambridge, 3 vols., 1947–59).

Lewis, N. B., 'A Contract Army, 1337', *Bulletin of the Institute of Historical Research*, xxxvii (1964), 1–19.

——, 'Indentures of Retinue with John of Gaunt, Duke of Lancaster, Enrolled in Chancery, 1367–1399', *Camden Miscellany*, xxii (Camden Soc., 4th series, i, 1964), 77–112.

——, 'The Organisation of Indentured Retinues in Fourteenth-Century England', *Transactions of the Royal Historical Society*, 4th series, xxvii (1945), 29–39.

——, 'Re-election to Parliament in the Reign of Richard II', *English Historical Review*, xlviii (1933), 364–94.

Lewis, P. S., 'Sir John Fastolf's Lawsuit over Titchwell, 1448–55', *Historical Journal*, i (1958), 1–20.

Lloyd, T. H., 'The Movement of Wool Prices in Medieval England', (*Economic History Review* Supplement 6, 1973).

Loyd, L. C. & D. M. Stenton, eds., *Sir Christopher Hatton's Book of Seals* (Oxford, 1950).

Maclean, J., 'The History of the Manors of Dene Magna and Abenhall', *Transactions of the Bristol and Gloucestershire Archaeological Society*, vi (1881–2), 123–209.

Maddicott, J. R., 'The County Community and the Making of Public Opinion in Fourteenth Century England', *Transactions of the Royal Historical Society*, 5th series, xxviii (1978), 27–43.

——, 'The English Peasantry and the Demands of the Crown, 1294–1341' (*Past and Present* Supplement i, 1975).

——, 'Law and Lordship: Royal Justices as Retainers in Thirteenth and Fourteenth Century England' (*Past and Present* Supplement 4, 1978).

——, *Thomas of Lancaster, 1307–22* (Oxford, 1970).

——, 'Thomas of Lancaster and Sir Robert Holand', *English Historical Review*, lxxxvi (1971), 449–72.

McFarlane, K. B., 'An Indenture of Agreement between two English Knights for Mutual Aid and Counsel in Peace and War', *Bulletin of the Institute of Historical Research*, xxxviii (1965), 200–10.

——, 'Bastard Feudalism', ibid., xx (1945), 161–81.

——, *The Nobility of Later Medieval England* (Oxford, 1973).

——, 'Parliament and Bastard Feudalism', *Transactions of the Royal Historical Society*, 4th series, xxvi (1944), 53–79.

——, 'The Wars of the Roses', *Proceedings of the British Academy*, l (1964), 87–119.

McKisack, M., *The Fourteenth Century* (Oxford, 1959).

Miller, E., *The Abbey and Bishopric of Ely* (Cambridge, 1951).

Moor, C., *Knights of Edward I* (Harleian Society, lxxx–lxxxiv, 1929–32).

Morris, J. E., *The Welsh Wars of Edward I* (Oxford, 1901).

Morris, R., 'Tewkesbury Abbey, the Despenser Mausoleum', *Transactions of the Bristol and Gloucestershire Archaeological Society*, xciii (1974), 142–55.
Morris, W. A., *The Medieval English Sheriff to 1300* (Manchester, 1927).
Nicolas, Sir N. H., *History of the Battle of Agincourt* (London, 1833).
Phillips, J. R. S., *Aymer de Valence, Earl of Pembroke, 1307–24* (Oxford, 1972).
Postan, M. M., *Essays on Medieval Agriculture and General Problems of the Medieval Economy* (Cambridge, 1973).
Powicke, F. M., *The Thirteenth Century* (Oxford, 2nd edn., 1962).
Powicke, M., *Military Obligation in Medieval England* (Oxford, 1962).
Prince, A. E., 'The Strength of English Armies in the Reign of Edward III', *English Historical Review*, xlvi (1931), 353–71.
Putnam, B. H., *Proceedings before the Justices of the Peace in the Fourteenth and Fifteenth Centuries, Edward III to Richard III* (Ames Foundation, 1938).
——, 'The Transformation of the Keepers of the Peace into the Justices of the Peace', *Transactions of the Royal Historical Society*, 4th series, xii (1929), 19–48.
——, *The Place in Legal History of Sir William Shareshull* (Cambridge, 1950).
Roskell, J. S., 'Sir John Cheyne of Beckford', *Transactions of the Bristol and Gloucestershire Archaeological Society*, lxxv (1956), 43–72.
——, *The Commons in the Parliament of 1422* (Manchester, 1954).
Saul, N. E., 'The Religious Sympathies of the Gentry in Gloucestershire, 1200–1500', *Transactions of the Bristol and Gloucestershire Archaeological Society*, 98, forthcoming.
——, 'Two Fifteenth Century Brasses at Dodford, Northants.', *Transactions of the Monumental Brass Society*, xii, pt. iii, (1977), 210–14.
Searle, E., *Battle Abbey and its Banlieu* (Toronto, 1974).
Sherborne, J. W., 'Indentured Retinues and English Expeditions to France, 1369–80', *English Historical Review*, lxxix (1964), 718–46.
Simpson, J. J., 'The Wool Trade and Woolmen of Gloucestershire', *Transactions of the Bristol and Gloucestershire Archaeological Society*, liii (1931), 65–97.
Sitwell, Sir G. O., 'The English Gentleman', *The Ancestor*, i (1902), 58–103.
Steel, A., 'The Sheriffs of Cambridgeshire and Huntingdonshire in the Reign of Richard II', *Proceedings of the Cambridgeshire Antiquarian Society*, xxxvi (1934–5), 1–34.
Stenton, F. M., *The First Century of English Feudalism* (Oxford, 2nd edn., 1961).
Stones, E. L. G., 'The Folvilles of Ashby Folville, Leicestershire, and

their Associates in Crime, 1326–41', *Transactions of the Royal Historical Society*, 5th series, vii (1957), 117–36.

Sudeley, Lord, 'The Tracys of Toddington', *Transactions of the Bristol and Gloucestershire Archaeological Society*, lxxxviii (1969).

Sutherland, D. M., *The Assize of Novel Disseisin* (Oxford, 1973).

Taylor, M. M., 'Parliamentary Elections in Cambridgeshire, 1332–8', *Bulletin of the Institute of Historical Research*, xviii (1940–1), 21–6.

Titow, J. Z., *English Rural Society, 1200–1350* (London, 1969).

Tout, T. F., *Chapters in the Administrative History of Medieval England* (6 vols., Manchester, 1920–33).

Verey, D., *Gloucestershire: the Vale and the Forest of Dean* (Harmondsworth, 1970).

Victoria History of the County of Gloucester (vols. 1, 2, 6, 8, 10, 11 and continuing).

Victoria History of the County of Worcester, i–iv (London, 1901–24).

'Uley Old Church', *Gloucestershire Notes and Queries*, v (1891–3), ed. W. P. W. Phillimore, 105.

Wagner, Sir A., *Heralds and Heraldry in the Middle Ages* (Oxford, 2nd edn., 1956).

Watson, C. E., 'The Minchinhampton Custumal', *Transactions of the Bristol and Gloucestershire Archaeological Society* lxvi (1932).

Willard, J. F., and W. A. Morris (eds.), *The English Government at Work 1327–36* (Cambridge, Mass., 3 vols., 1940–50).

Wingfield, J. M., *Some Records of the Wingfield Family* (London, 1925).

Winston, C. 'An Account of the Painted Glass in the East Window of Gloucester Cathedral', *Archaeological Journal*, xx (1863), 239–53, 319–30.

Wood-Legh, K. L., *Church Life under Edward III* (Cambridge, 1934).

——, 'Sheriffs, Lawyers and Belted Knights in the Parliaments of Edward III', *English Historical Review*, xlvi (1931), 372–88.

INDEX

Note: (1) Where it is possible to construct a reliable genealogy members of a family are listed generation by generation.

(2) Compound place-names are indexed under the principal element.

Barwell, William, 118, 136, 139, 183
Basset, John (*temp.* Edward I), 271
—, Sir Simon (d. *c.* 1370), 32, 53, 56,
　58, 74–5, 81, 90, 115, 122, 153,
　158–9, 190–2, 196, 197, 236, 280
—, —, Maud wife of, 190–3
—, —, John eldest son of, 190–3, 199
—, —, Edmund son of, 191–3, 285,
　289
—, —, Maurice son of, 191–3
Bath, Prior of, 86, 197
Bathonia, Sir Nicholas de, 30, 33, 226,
　271, 275
Battle Abbey, Sussex, 86
Batyn, Thomas, 87
Baudrip, John, 186–8
—, Elizabeth, alias Margaret, wife of,
　186–8
Baunton, Gloucs., 43
Bawdewyn, William, 100
Baycourt, Gloucs., 246
Bayouse, Robert de, 114
Beauchamp, Sir John, 197
—, Sir Roger, 8
—, Thomas, early of Warwick (d.
　1369), 98, 282
—, Thomas, earl of Warwick (d.
　1401), 65, 66, 87, 93, 94, 98, 202,
　289
—, Sir William, 197, 231
Beaumont, Henry de, 11
Beckford, Gloucs., 3, 144
Bedminster, Somerset, 62
Belers, Richard, 227
Bellamy, George, 143
Bellamy, J. G., 172
Benet, John, 139
Bereford, Simon de, 140
Berewick, Gilbert de, 141
Berkeley Castle, 198, 258
Berkeley, hundred of, 62, 73–4, 77,
　157, 203, 266
Berkeley, town of, 1
Berkeley, Vale of, 2, 62, 73
Berkeley, family of, 3–4, 49, 62–3, 69,
　78, 102; estates of, 62, 67–9
—, Thomas de, I, of Berkeley (d.
　1243), 74

Berkeley, Maurice de, II, of Berkeley
　(d. 1281), 63
—, Thomas de, II, of Berkeley, (d.
　1321), 15, 69, 84, 271, 272, 274,
　276, 278, 279
—, Maurice de, III, of Berkeley (d.
　1326), 14, 62, 64, 65, 69, 91, 152,
　272, 274, 278, 279
—, Thomas de, III, of Berkeley (d.
　1361), 15, 33, 62, 64, 65, 72, 84, 85,
　95, 129, 131, 152–3, 155, 157, 179,
　184, 266, 279, 280, 281, 284
—, —, Katherine second wife of, 75
—, Maurice de, IV, of Berkeley (d.
　1368), 72, 85, 285
—, Thomas de, IV, of Berkeley (d.
　1417), 51, 63, 65, 66, 72–3, 82, 97,
　123, 133, 138, 166, 170, 173, 177,
　180, 202, 247, 285, 287, 288, 290,
　291, 292
—, —, Margaret wife of, 63
—, James, lord (d. 1463), 63
—, William, lord, 63
—, John de, of Arlingham (*temp.*
　Edward II), 69, 90, 226, 271
—, Sir John, of Beverstone (d. 1428),
　115–16, 122, 126, 163, 289
—, Sir Giles de, of Coberley (d.
　1294), 49
—, Sir Thomas de, of Coberley (d.
　1365), 15, 16, 32, 34, 44, 45, 50, 92,
　129, 151, 153, 161–2, 174, 182–3,
　226, 271, 276, 280
—, Sir Thomas de, of Coberley (d.
　1405), 81, 92, 112n, 122, 285,
　289
—, Sir John de, of Dursley (d. 1349),
　43, 44, 45, 50, 74, 90, 152, 179, 202,
　203, 226, 258, 266, 275
—, Sir Nicholas de, of Dursley (d.
　1382), 72, 85, 154, 155, 173, 200,
　281, 285
—, William de, of Dursley (d. *ante*
　1300), 49
—, Sir Maurice de, of Uley (d. 1347),
　33, 51, 53, 55n, 75, 76–7, 157, 276,
　277, 281, 282
—, —, Sir Edward son of, 58